The Collector's Ultimate Encyclopedia of

HULL Pottery

IDENTIFICATION
AND
VALUES

Volume
One

Brenda Roberts

COLLECTOR BOOKS

A Division of Schroeder Publishing Co., Inc.

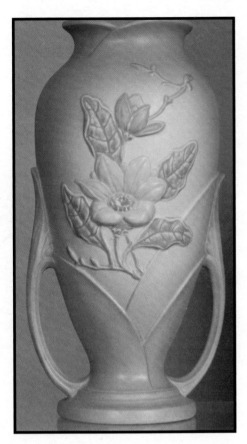

Plate 2. Magnolia Vase, "15-16"," $475.00 – 600.00.

Cover design by Beth Summers
Book design by Allan Ramsey

Preceding page, Plate 1:
Experimental Basket, 1950, unmarked, 13 x 15", $500.00 – 700.00.

On the front cover:
Clockwise:
Magnolia cornucopia, "19-8½"," $155.00 – 210.00.
Water Lily vase, "L-5-6½"," $90.00 – 125.00.
Water Lily cornucopia, "L-7-6½"," $115.00 – 160.00.
Bow-Knot ewer, "B-1-5½"," $210.00 – 270.00.
Crab Apple vase, unmarked, 5", $45.00 – 65.00.
Water Lily vase, "L-1-5½"," $55.00 – 80.00.
Iris vase, "405-4¾"," $125.00 – 145.00.
Magnolia vase, "12-6¼"," $75.00 – 100.00.

Vertical:
Calla Lily vase, "503-33-6"," $100.00 – 135.00.
Little Red Riding Hood shaker, 5¼", $95.00 – 140.00.
Head vase, "208-7"," $75.00 – 130.00.
Serenade bud vase, "S1-6½"," $50.00 – 70.00.

Bottom, left to right:
Swan, "70, 4"," $14.00 – 20.00.
Rabbit, "968-6"," $30.00 – 40.00.
Parchment and Pine vase, "S-1, 6"," $45.00 – 70.00.

On the back cover, clockwise:
Bow-Knot ewer, "B-15-13½"," $950.00 – 1,250.00.
Camellia mermaid planter, "104-10½"," $1,800.00 – 2,600.00.
Wheat yellow ware canister, 6½", $160.00 – 210.00.
Dancing Girl planter, "95, 7"," $60.00 – 85.00.
Flying Goose wall pocket, "67, 6"," $55.00 – 75.00.

Collector Books
P.O. Box 3009
Paducah, KY 42002-3009
www.collectorbooks.com

Copyright © 2006 Brenda Roberts

Searching For A Publisher?

We are always looking for people knowledgeable within their fields. If you feel that there is a real need for a book on your collectible subject and have a large comprehensive collection, contact Collector Books.

The current values in this book should be used only as a guide. They are not intended to set prices, which vary from one section of the country to another. Auction prices as well as dealer prices vary greatly and are affected by condition as well as demand. Neither the author nor the publisher assumes responsibility for any losses that might be incurred as a result of consulting this guide.

CONTENTS

When the blue clay glints through the rusty hillside,
It is not the eye of Man that it beckons,
Nor to his itching fingers;
But to his world-old instinct of obedience
That bids him carry on the trade and tradition of his Father,
Who wrought beauty
From the willing earth.

"The Potteries," by Jean Starr Untermeyer, inspired by
childhood memories of her native city, Zanesville, Ohio.

About the Author

Brenda Roberts

An avid American art pottery collector and dealer of general line antiques since 1974, Brenda Roberts has owned and operated an antiques and appraisal business as well as a mail order antiques business. Brenda was commisioned by Collector Books to write *The Collector's Encyclopedia of Hull Pottery* in 1980. Collector interest in Hull pottery has remained constant, enabling the volume to be reprinted a number of times, the most current edition being reprinted in 2005.

Since 1983, Brenda has been a member of the advisory board for, and a regular contributor to, *Schroeder's Antiques Price Guide* and *Garage Sale and Flea Market Annual*, both published annually by Collector Books. Roberts has also been a contributor to the *Wallace Homestead Flea Market/Collectibles Price Guide* and has written feature materials for publication in the *Antique Trader Weekly*, the *National Journal of Glass, Pottery & Collectables, Tri-State Trader, Antique Week, American Clay Exchange, The Collector, The Glaze, American Collector*, and *The Daze, Inc.*

Additional text publications include *Roberts' Ultimate Encyclopedia of Hull Pottery* and *The Companion Guide to Roberts' Ultimate Encyclopedia of Hull Pottery* in 1992.

This author's pioneering research of the Hull pottery has been a standard for collectors and dealers for 25 years, and Roberts's continuing interest in the Hull Pottery Company, her attention to detail, and the new spirit of collector interest in Hull has combined to bring about this all-new volume, which is devoted to the best of the best in Hull pottery.

While the reasons for collecting are many, Brenda Roberts fell in love with Hull's lovely pastels at age 12, when she was elected custodian of a Magnolia ewer purchased by her mother at an aunt's estate sale. What began as a single, cherished family momento escalated to the immense accumulation that allows her to share with you this historical account and pictoral essay of the rise and fall of the Hull Pottery Company. Since the introduction of her first Hull publication, the justification for continuing her Hull collection has been founded on the quest to bring together a full accounting of the history of the Hull firm.

It is hoped this volume will not only better acquaint the public of the superior excellence and predominant features of the products of the Hull Pottery Company, but also to coalesce the historical knowledge of this respected company in the manner it deserves.

Acknowledgments

Special tribute is extended to the Hull family, which made its pottery tradition monumental for over eighty years. Many members are now gone, but the memories remain.

I am most grateful for the remembrances of visits granted, personal correspondence, guided tours through the Hull plant, and more. I have always been made to feel welcome in the heart of Ohio's Pottery Valley. And not by the Hulls exclusively, but by the warm local people and the pottery craftsmen within Hull and the other potteries that I have had the pleasure to visit.

Thanks to Larry Taylor, who was always eager to offer his time and assistance in providing historical facts and information.

With deepest appreciation I wish to acknowledge the assistance of friends Gene Whitlatch, Bob Lloyd, Jean Kocmoud, Don and Kari Collett, Jerry Potmesil, Larry and Sharon Skillman, Jackie Bush, and Joe and Betty Yonis, who contributed by sharing items from their collections.

And, to Jerry Emke, a special note of thanks for encouragement and support, and more importantly, for challenging me each and every day.

Dedication

With love,
this book is dedicated to
my mother, Dora.

INTRODUCTION

The Hull Pottery journey took place in the small village of Crooksville, Ohio, where pottery was a way of life. The pottery industry in this area was so great that the region became known as the "pottery center of the world." Beginning in 1905, with a single plant, Hull soon advanced to a second factory in 1907, and both plants operated until 1930. The first years of pottery production were devoted to common stoneware and stoneware specialties. Soon afterward, semi-porcelain dinnerware lines appeared, as did artwares and decorative tile. By the 1940s, additional classic lines of pastel matte artware emerged. The 1950s were satiated by a multitude of high-quality art designs that were absolutely unequalled by others in style, content, and glaze treatments. Hull's final twenty-five years of pottery production centered on casual serving ware, suitable for the kitchen or patio, and on the vast Imperial floristware line.

Hull's days of reign over the wholesale and retail pottery markets have ended — or have they? After eighty extremely eventful and productive years, the Hull Pottery is at rest — or is it? While the tradition of operations has ended, the memories subsist, in lovely and serviceable wares that grace today's homes. During the company's near century of pottery production, Hull wares were known to the trade to be exceptional in quality and value. Hull's popularity then, as now, can only be termed monumental. The lines are quite diverse, and all are useful and decorative.

The disastrous 1950 flood and fire earned Hull a local audience that took notice of lines that were never again to be produced. There were those who contemplated market speculation; however, when the company was reconstructed, the wares basically remained uncollected even though the public was acutely aware that many designs and glaze formulas were lost to modern manufacturing processes.

Hull's popularity was apparent in the early 1970s, when a small group of collectors ventured from better-known potteries to build Hull collections. Although there were people in the know, Hull remained rather unobtrusive for nearly another decade while it remained on dealers' lowest shelves, taking a backseat to its formidable rivals. Early Hull harbingers guided, while others observed and eventually supervened, and by the late 1970s, collector interest was profound and observable throughout the United States and Canada. Since the final closing of the plant in 1985, Hull enthusiasts have become noticeably prominent in all segments of the collecting market.

There are Hull collectors that specialize in specific art designs, items such as wall pockets, ewers, baskets and cookie jars; specific time frames, such as pre- or post-1950; and specific clay bodies, such as stoneware, yellow ware, or tile; along with collectors of Hull's famous House 'n Garden dinnerwares and more. The diverse lines of Hull pottery offer limitless collecting potential. And, yes, there are collectors who collect all eras, bodies, styles, and glazes of Hull pottery, a phenomenon that has made this publication a reality.

History of the Hull Pottery Company

Ohio: The Pottery Center of the World

In the late 1800s, Ohio was noted for clay products ranging from brick and drain tile to excellent ornamental wares. The southern Muskingum and northern Perry counties of Ohio were booming in the stoneware industry at the turn of the century. Farming, clay digging, wood chopping, and potting were the primary livelihoods for men of this community. Ohio soon produced virtually every pottery style known, and in many cases, improved upon prior techniques used in the production of quality clays and glazes. Local clays, an abundance of wood, coal as well as natural gas to fire the kilns, and a multitude of skilled craftsmen in the area all led to Crooksville and the surrounding area becomming known as the "pottery center of the world."

Pioneers found superior local clay veins fourteen feet thick, and clay working, a fact of life in this region, grew out of the farmer's need for inexpensive containers and tableware. Practically every farm had a small pottery. The part-time early pottery operations, worked by farmers between fall and spring, were named "bluebirds," because their production resumed when the bluebirds returned from the South and the clay could be mined.

Farmers were soon selling the utility wares needed for canning and the like to others by way of door-to-door sales.

There was a development of the industry on a larger scale after flatboats began transporting cargoes from Zanesville to New Orleans. Country potters hauled their wares to the Putnam boat landing, where they unloaded them and stored them on the riverbank until the buyers could carry wares onto the flatboats and pack for the shipment south.

In 1888, the effort to expedite stoneware manufacture prompted some potters to produce wares at the foot of Zanesville's Pierce Street, right on the riverbank. The area potters were unable to produce adequate numbers when the demand for stoneware products rose to the thousands. However, the potters soon discovered they were able to increase their production by turning their wheels by steam power rather than foot power. Soon full production output was machine made.

When railroads began operating in Zanesville and surrounding communities, making the shipments of stoneware more practical, it guaranteed nationwide sales. The locals who had earlier sold wares by knocking on doors now billed the railroad car to some distant point with stopover privileges at intervening points. Here they sold wares and further accommodated merchants by delivering to shopkeepers' doors.

The Legacy Begins: Addis Emmet Hull

Born in Ireland in 1809, Henry M. Hull immigrated to the United States as a young man and made his home in Ohio. Hull, who lived his entire life in the Ohio Valley, was a farmer by trade, and he died in 1884. Hull and his wife, Vila, had eleven children, six being named in the United States Census of 1850: Jane, 10; Frances, 9; Mary, 7; Henrietta, 5; Robert, 2; and Elizabeth, 1.

One of the eleven, a son, Addis Emmet Hull, born in 1862 at Todd's Post Office in Morgan County, Ohio, was to create a family pottery tradition that not only would carry the Hull name through nearly a century of American manufacturing history, but also would leave the Hull name in the memories and in the hearts of countless historians, as well as stoneware and art pottery enthusiasts, years beyond the pottery's demise.

Hull Enters Manufacturing with Globe Pottery

The proven sales of stoneware, along with newfound marketing opportunities, could not be ignored by a determined businessmen by the name of Addis Hull. Hull had wide-gained experience in the pottery trade, which led to the future organization and management of the A. E. Hull Pottery Company in Crooksville, Ohio.

Crooksville was rapidly becoming the center of the stoneware industry in this section of Ohio, and Hull was acutely aware of the growing market for pottery. After finishing country schools, he attended Parsons Business College in Zanesville, Ohio. Addis Hull soon became a traveling salesman for his brother, J. J. Hull, who operated the Star Stonery Company. Hull's business training and personality traits made him a successful salesman, and during his travels for Star, he recognized the continually increasing demand for stoneware items.

Other potters' success had given Hull the confidence he needed to join the pottery movement. Promoting himself from sales, Hull entered the field of stoneware manufacturing in 1901, by his association with the initial organizers of the Globe Stoneware Company. Hull was awarded much success, for in Globe's first year of production, the company reportedly had a grade of stoneware that was far superior to any that was being produced in the valley. William A. Watts, Jeptha Darby Young, and Chester Tatman were Globe's initial organizers, and Globe's board of directors elected W. B. Cosgrave president, Addis E. Hull general manager, W. A. Watts secretary, S.H. Brown treasurer, and Jeptha Darby Young superintendent.

Workers of the Globe Stoneware Company are identified as Addis Hull, William Watts, J. D. Young, Ruben Dailey, Albert Aichele, John Wilson, Fred Young, George Aichele, Pat Spring, Frank Watts, Howard Spring, Walter Brown, George Watts, and Frank Wilson.

Hull Leaves Globe to Form A. E. Hull Pottery Company

Although the Globe Stoneware Company had been successful from its inception, conflicts between company officials were ever present. The differences of opinion concerned nearly every facet of the company's operation. Hull continued as manager of the Globe Pottery until 1904. At that time, major differences arose that could not be resolved, and Hull, Watts, and Young (Globe's manager, secretary, and superintendent) resigned. Hull sold his interest in Globe, and in July 1905 organized the A. E. Hull Pottery Company. William Watts and J. D. Young now served the A. E. Hull Pottery Company as secretary-treasurer and superintendent, respectively. G. E. McKeever, who had served as general salesman of the Star Stoneware Company, additionally pulled up stakes and accepted a sales position with Hull.

Addis Emmet Hull, company founder

Location Site: China Street, Crooksville, Ohio

The A. E. Hull Pottery Company, located at the north end of China Street in Crooksville, Ohio, was modern in every respect. Hull's newly constructed pottery plant had four updraft kilns, called "beehives," and two small kilns used for decorative firing. The four largest kilns, each twenty-two feet in diameter, were heated with natural gas produced nearby. The updraft kilns allowed the flames to pass through holes in the floor and up, through, and around the stacks of ware and then through apertures in the arched crown. The smoke was collected by a hovel, or cone-shaped chimney, which formed the roof. Records of an early engineer show the designated positions of trialed wares in muffle kilns. (This was no doubt shortly after Hull expanded to take in another facility.) In a muffle type of kiln, the chamber in which the ware was placed was closed to the flames by walls of fire clay, called a muffle. The flames passed under, around, and over the chamber, and the piece was fired by heat that radiated through the walls.

William Aurthur McClellan, an early ceramic engineer, included notations in his personal notebooks related to the company's additional firing by use of the tunnel kiln,

installed in 1923. The tunnel kiln operated 24 hours a day, firing continuously while cars moved very slowly through the tunnel.

Edward Watts was 29 when the Hull plant was erected. His varied pottery experience began when he started assisting bricklayers and kiln makers at the Hull. After the completion of the pottery, Watts gained employment with Hull and processed the first clay used by the pottery from a pug mill. Watts claimed to have had a hand in everything there was to do as a potter, and in 1966, he concluded his work record at age 90, retiring from the Hull Pottery.

As the current market dictated, the company's production centered on stoneware and stoneware specialties. There was no question as to the impending success of the new organization headed by Hull, a young man respected in the community for his known abilities and expertise in the field of sales. He soon established the same excellent reputation as a manufacturer. Through successful management and honest dealings, Hull merited and maintained the confidence of his entire community, and in years to come, merited this enviable stature from an entire nation.

Need for Expansion: Purchase of the Acme Pottery Company

Demand for kitchenware items was so great that only two years into production, Addis Hull found it necessary to expand operations. Keeping with current trends, Hull desired to continue all phases of stoneware manufacture, but also noted the acute interest in porcelain kitchenware items. Hull was anxious to make his move on a new market at the earliest possible date. In lieu of delaying production while current facilities were enlarged, and rather than building an entirely new plant, Hull secured control of Acme Pottery's building, equipment, and real estate. Hull suffered no delays in production, as Acme was readily equipped with the necessary machinery required for the manufacture of semiporcelain items. In 1907, while Hull's Plant No. 1 continued to produce stoneware and stoneware specialities, the conversion was made quickly to allow manufacture of Hull's porcelain kitchenware lines in Plant No. 2. Hull immediately discontinued manufacture of all Acme products.

The tiny village of Crooksville offered no opposition to Hull's plan, considering this allowed the almost 400 Acme craftsmen to retain employment. Hull's keen business sense had not only secured a readily equipped plant, needing only minor modifications, but also provided him with a predisposed, talented, and qualified workforce to man the operations. Hull was very fortunate indeed to enlist Acme's skilled dinnerware mechanics, imported from the West Liverpool pottery district, along with a select crew of hundreds of other highly experienced tradesmen for his new venture in porcelain production.

Constructing a new plant, installing the required machinery and equipment, and recruiting a skilled workforce would have taken months, perhaps years. However, with the purchase of The Acme Pottery, the entire operations and crew were immediately at Hull's disposal. Hull had previously completed carefully detailed studies of the lines needed in the kitchen, and the Acme Building, Hull's Plant No. 2, immediately converted production from Acme's semiporcelain dinnerware to Hull's own style of porcelain products, such as bowls, nappies, casseroles, butters, baking dishes, cereal sets, etc. Hull's Plant No. 1 on China Street continued to produce both common stoneware and a line of stoneware specialties. Hull heralded that it was "surpassed in quality and variety by no others."

A token accessory to the Acme building was Crooksville's first electric light plant. The Acme Electric Light Company was included as part of the package. One 75 kW two-phase generator had been installed in the pottery in 1905, and until 1908, the engine used for the pottery through the day was also the lighting generator at night.

In the earliest years that Hull occupied the old Acme building, there appeared to be a need for drinking water, and an enterprising eleven-year-old lad by the name of LeRoy "Sleepy" Moore found he could collect 50¢ a week from each employee to whom he served water daily. Sleepy made several trips a day, carrying heavy bottles, jugs, and chamber pots brimming with water, from Main Street, Crooksville, over the crest to Hull's Plant No. 2.

This postcard, illustrating Hull's Plant No. 2, was printed by Edmiston Book & Stationary Company. It is marked "Made in Germany, 1908."

With the additional plant, Hull was afforded unparalleled shipping facilities by now being located on both the Pennsylvania and the New York Central railroads. Carloads were shipped daily, and customers had the option of shipments being made by either railway. The two plants were responsible for shipping 900 carloads per year. Business was so great that Hull found it necessary to hire an expert traffic manager to take charge of all shipping arrangements.

Hull accepted all orders contingent upon a lack of strikes, legislation, fire, accidents, or other causes beyond the company's control. A. E. Hull Pottery was forced to advertise that due to variation in materials used in manufacture, it was impossible to produce earthenware (either porous or semivitreous) that would not craze eventually; therefore, its products could not be guaranteed against crazing after a long period of time. The guarantee to withstand crazing was for a reasonable period of time only, and the pottery reserved the right to refuse to adjust claims when, in its judgment, the merchandise had remained in stock too long.

Hull advertised that its products were fired with "stilts" and that stilt marks might be visible on any piece. For buyers who required pieces without these marks, special prices applied.

Although error was small, Hull could not guarantee sizes, capacities, and weights to be exactly as advertised. Shrinkage in the manufacture of pottery could not be precisely controlled due to varying materials and conditions, including the human element.

All goods were carefully packed, inspected, and delivered to transportation companies in good condition. Prices for bulk packing in trucks or railroad cars were based on packing with straw between the items ordered and did not include containers of any kind. Excelsior packing was used if specified by the customer, with an additional charge of five percent to regular prices. Containers supplied included crates, barrels, boxes, and kegs.

More costly were the L.C.L. (Less than Car Load) shipments that were provided by Hull's expert packers using handmade hardwood crates strapped with iron bands for strengthening. An additional 25% to the L.C.L. weight was the formula used to determine delivery cost, and while 24¢ delivered 100 pounds of stoneware in a L.C.L. shipment to Columbus, Ohio, the costs to western and southern customers was $2.96 per 100 pounds for the same delivery. Prices for packing in containers were based on the use of the cheapest containers that would suitably contain the items ordered and meet railroad company specifications for safe transportation to the items' destinations. Higher-priced containers carried extra charges.

Accidents, delays in delivery, and loss by transportation companies were beyond the pottery's control, and all claims were made against the transportation company. However, Hull offered assistance to the purchaser in claim adjustments against the transportation companies.

The A. E. Hull Pottery Co. No. 2, Crooksville, Ohio.

This postcard of 1912 illustrates the Hull plant shortly after the addition of a second kiln room and warehouse. Painted banners on the new addition advertise wares such as "pitchers, teapots, yellow ware, jardiniers, jugs, cuspidores, etc."

Hull Proclaims Itself Largest Manufacturer of Stoneware Specialties

With operations in full swing, Hull proclaimed it had unprecedented products and that its officers (all natives of Perry County, Ohio, with exception of one) had unprecedented numbers of years of experience. In 1910, Hull boasted that it was the largest manufacturer in the United States of blue banded kitchenware and Zane Grey stoneware, which was also referred to as "Bristol glazed." In this billing, Hull said of its two manufacturing plants:

We are now without question the largest manufacturers of Stoneware Specialties in the United States. We have grown from four kilns, to a capacity of ten kilns, and two decorating kilns. All the officers are natives of Perry County except Mr. Griswold, Vice President, whose home is in Boston, Mass., and all are men of practical worth in the business. Mr. Griswold, who employs from twenty to thirty traveling salesmen constantly, is one of the largest users of the company's products.

Almost all the staple articles in the Stoneware Specialty line have been originated by us, and we are at this time the exclusive makers of an entirely new line. We were the first to manufacture Decalcomania and Gold Decorated Stoneware, and have already placed these goods in all the principal markets of the United States.

While the company was only organized in 1905, all of its officers have been engaged in the manufacture of Stoneware and Stoneware Specialities for twenty years or more, and are giving their undivided attention to the development of an industry the perfection of the product of which is contingent upon a superior quality of clay for its base. It is conceded that the very best clay for this purpose is found in the hills of Perry County, Ohio.

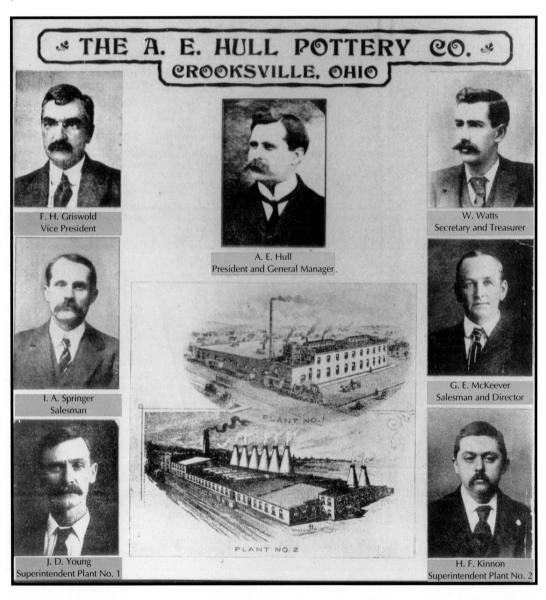

THE A. E. HULL POTTERY CO.
CROOKSVILLE, OHIO

F. H. Griswold
Vice President

A. E. Hull
President and General Manager

W. Watts
Secretary and Treasurer

I. A. Springer
Salesman

G. E. McKeever
Salesman and Director

J. D. Young
Superintendent Plant No. 1

H. F. Kinnon
Superintendent Plant No. 2

PLANT NO. 1

PLANT NO. 2

Diverse Lines Offered

The company was afforded the opportunity of two different railway companies that ran beside their two plant facilities where the company's initial manufacture was separated: stoneware production in Plant No. 1, and semiporcelain production in Plant No. 2.

Early Hull production centered on stoneware, stoneware specialties, and semiporcelain products. Many types of wares were introduced to the market, including a full line of quality blue and white stoneware, green-tinted stoneware, and brown stoneware with or without lined interiors and embossed with such motifs as plums, cherries, birds, and cattle. Other products included Zane Grey banded ware, yellow ware, and absolute white-bodied semiporcelain restaurant ware, hotel ware, toilet ware, and kitchenware, in plain and embossed shapes, that were decorated with bands, decalcomania, and stamps underglaze and overglaze, while others were airbrushed, blended, and hand decorated.

Early designs, including blue and white and green-tinted stoneware, were also manufactured by other area potteries and marketed through the combined effort of the American Clay Products Company.

Early black and white stoneware, used for food storage and preservation, included 15- to 30-gallon meat tubs, churns, shoulder jugs, preserve jars, bean pots, milk pans, French pots, and ½- to 6-gallon butters. Hull supplied many utilitarian wares, which included milk crocks, preserving jars, and refrigerator jars, to outside markets, as well as to farms and households within the Ohio area. Green glazed stew and bake pans with metal bails were used by nearly every area farm wife. Douglas Young, grandson of Jeptha Darby Young, began his work with the company around 1925, being paid 25¢ per hundred for attaching bails to those stew pans.

Hull was responsible for flooding the market with many banded semi-porcelain and stoneware utility items. These were decorated both underglaze and overglaze in nearly every color imaginable: blue, green, yellow, red, mauve, black, pink, ivory, brown, white, and peach, as well as others. Some of these color bandings were additionally teamed with gold lines, which varied in composition. Decorated items included, but were not limited to, range and refrigerator jars, bake dishes, jugs, nested bowls, casseroles with plates, handled individual casseroles, pie plates, and bean pots. Hull's sales campaigns advertised many of the bowls, jugs, and casseroles in sets as "bride's kitchen sets, pantry assortments and baking assortments." Bowl and nappy sets were advertised for baking as well as serving, for "salads, fruits or as mixing bowls."

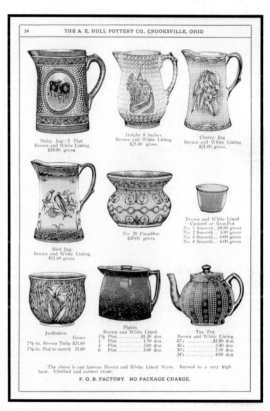

Plates 3 (top) and 4. Early Hull stoneware lines included the popular embossed designs illustrated above. These illustrations are reprinted from original company catalogues. These stoneware staples were offered in blue and green tints, mottled blue and white and brown ware lined with white.

The company was prolific in its manufacture of semi-porcelain cereal ware sets, which included cereal jars, spice jars, cruets, and salt boxes. Semiporcelain jars had Hull's high-fired absolute white bodies decorated with a variety of pleasing decalcomania. Stoneware cereal sets, plain and embossed, were offered in banded, decaled, or solid high-gloss colors.

Early art lines included vases, jardineres, flower pots, hanging baskets, and bulb bowls, which had either stoneware or semiporcelain bodies. Art lines were decorated in solid matte and high-gloss glazes, blended matte and high-gloss finishes, tinted glazes, and stark white matte glazes. Embossed art designs included tulips, hearts and arrows, basketweave, ropes and tassels, birds, trees, stylized fans, harps, ferns, and leaves. Plain and decorated florists' pots and saucers, and garden ware, were also produced during Hull's earliest years.

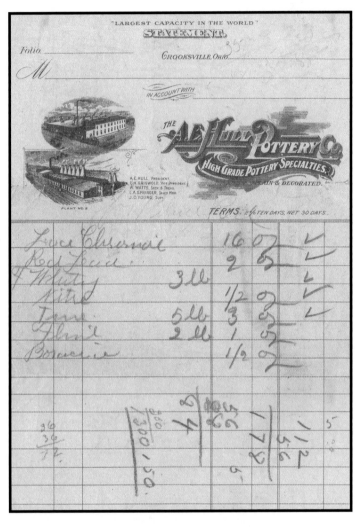

A. E. Hull's statement, dated 1908, illustrating both Plants No. 1 and No. 2, boasts the "Largest Capacity in the World," and further advertises production of "High Grade Pottery Specialties, Plain and decorated." The statement listed company officers: A. E. Hull, President; F. H. Griswold, Vice President; W. Watts, Secretary and Treasurer; L. A. Springer, Sales Manager; and J. D. Young, Superintendent. William Arthur McClellan, Hull's head ceramic engineer of the day, apparently jotted necessary ingredients and formulas on whatever was handy — in this case, the firm's statement.

Production of Zane Grey Ware

Kitchenware items such as salt boxes, jugs, nested bowls, nappies, custards, butters, and 1- to 6-gallon food containers were staple products in stoneware and were referred to as Hull's Zane Grey ware. Hull best described the evolution of Zane Grey in this early account:

The Zane Grey line is being introduced to the trade to meet the growing demand for a lower priced kitchen ware. The A. E. Hull Pottery Co. ceramists, after a year of research and experiments, have devised a body made of refined clays and a glaze of extra soft, glossy texture free from excessive pinholes and crazing, to suit this body. The

shapes of the bowls, nappies, jugs and butters are the same as the white and blue band ware with the above body practically vitreous and the blue band decoration under the glaze. Besides these kitchen specialties a line of food containers from one-half gallon capacity, including all sizes, to six gallons capacity are made, using the Zane Grey body, decoration and glazes. The quality of the whole line is on a par with the white ware and the price is substantially lower. With these qualifications we are recommending this line to the trade where cheapness, quality, design and texture, together with usual Hull service is desired.

An A. E. Hull Pottery Company letterhead of about 1910 advertised several of the company's distinctive lines: yellow ware, blended ware, stoneware, and white sanitary cooking ware. Add to this Blue Band, Zane Grey, porcelain toilet ware, cereal ware, and decorated kitchen ware, and you can readily see why Hull was thought to offer the most complete kitchen lines in the United States.

Plate 5. Stoneware art and utility.

Plates 6 and 7. Zane Grey stoneware jugs and bowls.

Plate 8. Blue and white toilet ware.

Blue and White Stoneware and Yellow Ware Production

Collectors and dealers alike will be amazed to learn that Hull manufactured most every popular design of blue and white stoneware that can be found in today's market. Add to this green-tinted wares and brown ware lined with white, in tankards, dairy jugs, butters, salt boxes, ewers and basins, and others, including a sanitary water keg embossed with deer decor, produced in 3-, 4-, 5-, and 6- gallon sizes. Designs included, but were not limited to, embossed roses, birds, plums, daisies, cherries, and cattle.

Yellow ware production composed a large portion of the company's output. Early advertising tells the story of the gradual unfolding of Hull's yellow ware production:

Yellow bowls have come to be almost a household necessity. For the kitchen they find a multitude of uses such as bread mixing, as food containers, and for hand receptacles for anything the housewife uses in her kitchen. The yellow bowl is first of all a more inexpensive bowl than most any other. The A. E. Hull Pottery Co. are manufacturing yellow bowls in large quantity at a remarkably low figure and combined with several other notable features. The Hull yellow bowl is made with a round spherical bottom which offers no hindrance to the housewife in stirring or cleaning the bowl. There are no sharp creases in the bottom. This yellow bowl is also made of a body that is fired until practically vitreous, thereby insuring a highly bonded and durable bowl with a bright glossy glaze and brown bands for decoration.

This early photo illustrates production of *H* in circle Alpine tankards and steins. Shown are finishers Iona Lauderbach and Zetta Wilson, caster Ray Conoaway, and workers Richard Rosser, Ralph Sherlock, and Ken Haymen.

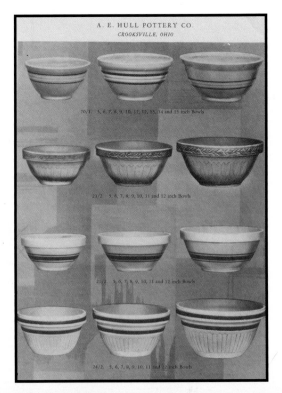

Plate 9. Yellowware utility bowls.

16

Production of White Sanitary Ware

Tremendous volumes of plain white hotel and toilet ware, along with enormous numbers of cooking ware and "American White Body" kitchenware items, were manufactured in Hull's early years.

Shapes were practical, and items were advertised as "sanitary," made of absolutely white-bodied semiporcelain fired at high temperatures to assure strength and durability. Hull's toilet ware and kitchenware were competitively priced, and trade catered to both residences and hotels alike. The company listed toilet ware sets in both "Hull shape" or "Rex Shape." Cuspidors were distinguished as either "hotel shaped" (having flat bases) or "parlor shaped" (having round bases). Hotel ware offered sugars in two sizes, 30 and 36; two sizes of oyster bowls, plain or decorated; and tapering and straight coffee mugs, either plain or decorated, along with what were referred to as Philadelphia coffee mugs.

Hull boasted of being the original producer of American White Body, an underglazed, raised-blue-banded kitchenware. Hull reported its "careful and constant study of the lines needed in the kitchen, together with excellent modeler to transform ideas to actual plaster model, and ceramic engineers to supervise the manufacturing processes in one of the most modern potteries, insures the buyer of Hull Ware, the most practical shapes possible, made of absolutely white body, with the deep blue raised bands under the glaze. The ware is strong and durable on account of the selection of clays in the body, and the high temperature attained in the kilns."

In Hull's words, the quality of hotel and toilet ware was "the same as the Blue Band Ware since the same body and glaze is used. Decorations are made over the glaze with decalcomania and color bands both selected for their pleasing colors and the fact that they fit nicely into the average color scheme of the ordinary room, be it hotel or residence." The glaze treatments were many, but some toilet wares included white, royal blue, or blue-mottled sets, ewers and basins, cuspidors, and chambers. Additional blue banding was offered to the plain or color glazed wares for an extra 50¢ per dozen. Toilet sets were offered in 5-, 6-, 7-, 8-, 9-, 11-, and 12-piece assortments.

Jugs, bake pans, mixing bowls, bean pots, teapots, and fluted nappies were also offered in white or blue-mottled glazes. "Decorated goods" referred to wares that were decorated in stamped or overglaze decalcomania, with or without color bands. The five-banded line was a refined semiporcelain kitchenware line that included several combinations of nested bowls, three teapots, and three coffee servers. This line was manufactured in a semiporcelain, high-fired white body, and featured a series of five overglaze bands that encircled the wares' midline or top edge. The lowest band was the thinnest, and the bands widened with each step of elevation.

Plate 10. Early Hull catalog page illustrating porcelain toilet ware.

Plate 11. Porcelain utility jars.

Cereal Ware Production

In 1915, original company advertising introduced cereal sets to the retail market:

The square cereal set has been sold heretofore as a general rule in sets of fifteen pieces. We have decided to establish a new method in regard to the marketing of our standard square cereal set. Now, the buyer may make up his own set composition or buy open stock as he pleases. We offer seven decorations from which to choose, which are representative as to designs and colorings. The following names will be furnished in any of our decorations in any quantity. For cereal jars we have coffee, tea, rice, cereal, flour, sugar. For spice jars: cinnamon, ginger, pepper, allspice, mustard, nutmeg. For bottles either oil or vinegar. Salt boxes are furnished in every decoration. These sets are made by the casting process from the white body, used for our Blue Band Ware, which insures a close, durable body.

The May 31, 1917, issue of *Pottery, Glass, and Brass Salesman*, further praised Hull's cereal sets:

The popularity of cereal sets still continues. The demand is growing every day and the manufacturers are hard pressed to keep abreast of it. In spite of this, the A. E. Hull Pottery, of which Guy Cooke, 200 Fifth Avenue, is the New York representative, has found time to work on four new decorations — a parrot in dark blue in a yellow panel, with dark blue bands on either side; a scroll effect in terra cotta color on both the top and bottom of the jars; a vine treatment in a combination of colors, including dark blue and green; and a classic design in green, blue and golden brown. In these new decorations the concern has gotten away from the old stereotyped forms usually seen on cereal sets. The ware is white, high fired and sanitary. Each set contains fifteen pieces, including large and small jars, vinegar and oil jugs, and salt box.

Cereal ware was not limited to square designs as Hull also produced round stoneware and round semiporcelain cereal sets. These sets, banded in blue, gold or yellow with black lettering, consisted of large jars for rice, beans, prunes, tapioca, cereal, sugar, coffee, and tea. Also available were jars in ½-gallon and 1-gallon sizes that were offered separately from the actual cereal set. The larger jars were complimented by spice jars for ginger, allspice, cloves, nutmeg, cinnamon, and pepper, and teamed with matching salt boxes. Additionally, banded round semiporcelain utility jars were manufactured in 2-, 4-, 8-, and 12-quart sizes that were lettered "flour," "bread," "cakes," "lard," "sugar," etc. Complimenting round storage and preserve jars were available in 2-, 3-, or 4-gallon sizes.

Ceramic Engineer William McClellan delineated his formula for "A. E. Hull White Body" on this early Hull statement form, dating about 1915.

Plate 12. Thirteen-piece porcelain round cereal ware set.

No. 150—Ship Scene Delft Cereal Ware

Plate 13. Original company brochure page from the American Clay Products Company illustrating 15-piece porcelain cereal ware set.

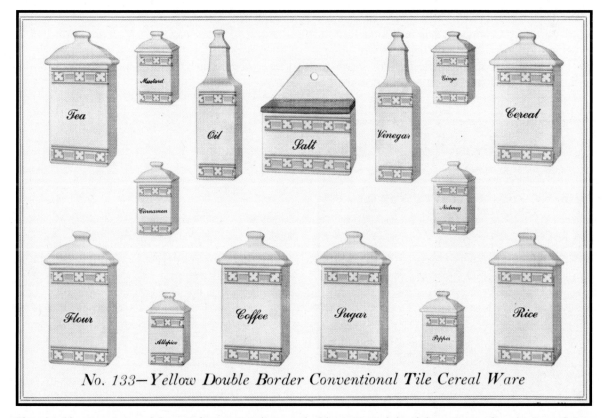

No. 133—Yellow Double Border Conventional Tile Cereal Ware

Plate 14. The square porcelain cereal ware was decorated with a prepared decal that was transferred prior to firing. Hull used innovative and time-saving methods that were soon copied by other area potteries.

The American Clay Products Company

In the early 1920s, there was unprecedented activity in all circles in this section of Ohio, and this boom in business was overshadowed only by the promised activity to come. A great campaign was drafted to accentuate the region's bountiful natural resources in an effort to entice businessmen to move into the area. Local reports boasted that never in this region's history had conditions been better than they were in the early 1920s. The potteries were all running, and laborers were receiving a living wage much superior to that paid before the World War.

Karl Langenbeck, a chemist of note among potters and tile makers, and a possessor of practical experience as a manufacturer, appealed to the business world by stating that "100 or more flourishing local clay-working industries could be added to those existing."

In existence as early as 1920, The American Clay Products Company, at 416 Masonic Temple, Zanesville, Ohio, marketed Hull's Zane Grey stoneware items along with nested banded bowls, yellow ware, hotel ware, toilet ware, and semi-porcelain cereal sets. The American Clay Products Company was such a large distributor of Hull products that Hull invoices of accounts receivable were imprinted with ACP's name.

The American Clay Products Company's stoneware plant covered three acres and was said to have had a greater capacity than any company of its kind in the world. The American Clay Products Company boasted that its member companies were the world's finest potters, being composed of the A. E. Hull Pottery Company, Star Stoneware, Ransbottom Bros. Pottery, Logan Pottery, Muskingum Pottery, Crooksville Pottery, Nelson McCoy Sanitary Stoneware Company, Burley Pottery Company, Burley Winter Pottery, and perhaps others. All formed in an effort to share orders. Frank Ransbottom of Ransbottom Bros. Pottery served as president, and Addis E. Hull, Sr., served as vice president of The American Clay Products Company. The company advertised "flower pots, all kinds of glazed specialties and high grade stoneware."

This formation served as a distribution campaign, and any one salesman could represent the ware of any firm involved. A common catalog was shared, and early on, the firms involved manufactured at least a portion of the same products, none being identified by actual manufacturer.

This practice eventually evolved into specific production styles being manufactured by individual companies. Catalogs were separated by companies, meaning the combined effort now shifted to sales. A fleet of salesmen existed that had access to all company catalogs which enabled them to sell for any one of the companies involved in this group. An early business card reads, "W. L. Brannon, Special Representative, The A. E. Hull Pottery Co. Lines, Crooksville, Ohio, for The American Clay Products Co., Zanesville, Ohio."

The American Clay Products Company was strictly a profit-making merchandising campaign that was formed much earlier than the Depression years. This was not a "beggar's plea" for sales during slow economic times, as sales during the 1920s were reportedly extremely brisk and profitable. This was absolutely a money-making formation to monopolize orders and promote business for this group of businessmen, and perhaps more importantly, for advertising and promoting the area as a whole. There was an active campaign taking place to illustrate Zanesville and the surrounding area as a profitable mecca in order to bring new businesses to the area. Promotion included the Zanesville Chamber of Commerce's printed booklet entitled *Zanesville — For the Manufacturer, Merchant, and Home Seeker*. The American Clay Products was dissolved in 1926 by the government, which declared its existence a monopoly.

A. E. Hull Pottery Co. Factory No. 2
CROOKSVILLE, OHIO

Sold to THE AMERICAN CLAY PRODUCTS CO. DATE
ZANESVILLE, OHIO

Acct.

Shipped to   J. Lowenstein & Sons,
                  Valparaiso, Ind.

If cash in advance order place "X" here_____

QUANTITY		DESCRIPTION
1½	Doz No. 21 Cuspidors	
1½	" No. 30 "	

Orders for The American Clay Products Company originated in both plants. This particular order for three dozen cuspidors was generated in Hull's Plant No. 2, the porcelain factory. Another portion of the invoice provided a place for Hull to designate how the shipment was to be packed: crates, barrels, boxes, or kegs.

Hull's Rising Market Demands Met by Importation of European Wares

James Felz managed the New Jersey warehouse, the dimensions of which were 86' x 225'. Guy Cooke served as Hull's New York representative. Cooke later took over the position of vice president of the company and manager of Hull's eastern branch, a vacancy left by F. H. Griswold. L. A. Springer headed up Hull's team as sales manager. D. W. Worthington worked out of the Chicago office. G. E. McKeever, a director of the company, served as a salesman and manager of the branch house in Detroit, Michigan. Western and northern sales areas were represented by G. W. Springer, and western and southern territories were represented by N. W. Leland. Also serving as a traveling salesman was V. D. Kinnon, a member of the board of directors.

Five-and-dimes, decorative shops, and florists were buying massive volumes of artware throughout the teens, and by the early 1920s, interest in artwares was so great that in order to supply the increasing market, Addis Hull traveled to Europe and arranged to purchase decorative earthenware, china, pottery, and tile from England, Italy, France, Czechoslovakia, and Germany.

The foreign items were delivered to New York at half the cost of local production. Hull continued to import foreign products until 1929, and sent a company representative to Europe each year to procure pottery items and arrange for their shipment. This early account indicates just how successful Hull had become in this particular business aspect:

The import division of the A. E. Hull Pottery Co., has made an auspicious start in the matter of its new importations for the fall trade, and as a result, a visit to its showrooms in the Fifth Avenue Building discloses an excellent display of items to tempt the buyer. They have the most interesting range of animal figures, consisting of dogs, elephants and cats. They are in both earthenware and china and present a varied range of sizes from small ones, which predominate to the larger animals.

They offer real values, which will be realized when it is stated they are priced to retail from 19 cents to $1.25. All of the animals are exceptionally true to life in every detail and they are all in natural colors. Scotties, wire-haired terriers, bull dogs, police dogs and sheep dogs are shown in the assortment. In addition to those mentioned above, the firm is also showing grotesque animals. These are in solid colors of red, dark gray and white. The little animals are comic and yet at the same time are quite artistic, having been designed by one of the leading European animal artists.

In addition to the new animals, the company has a number of other surprises. Naturally, when the name Hull is mentioned, one immediately thinks of kitchenware and the new samples in this respect are the very latest and most exclusive to be received from Europe. In fact, any line shown by Hull is classic in style and these newest importations are so exclusive that one cannot discourse upon them at very great length at this time. We can say, however, that they are most original and beautiful, and one can also comment upon their colors. Tints that are brand new and never shown before are included in their range, in addition to the other well known Hull colors.

The eastern warehouse, located at 57 Hudson Street in Jersey City, New Jersey, provided storage for imports, which numbered more than the entire output of domestic wares. The New York City office and showroom, located at 200 Fifth Avenue, Room 207, became the main headquarters and served as the distribution center for both domestic and imported wares. Hull also had a branch house in Detroit and a Chicago office located at the Morrison Hotel, both of which assisted in marketing both domestic and foreign wares. Foreign wares were sold alongside Hull's domestic production for nearly eight years. Hull wisely closed the doors of the Jersey City warehouse in 1929, due to the declining economy of the Depression years.

Meanwhile, Back in Crooksville

Pottery was such a profitable business that it was not uncommon for the area's pottery leaders to have multiple interests in the pottery trade. By the 1920s, Addis E. Hull, Sr., in addition to managing the two Hull plants, served as president and director of the Crooksville Pottery. Hull, and his director and sales manager, L. A. Springer, were both stockholders in the Muskingum Pottery Company. Springer additionally held the title of general manager of the Muskingum Pottery.

The increase in demand for art lines of the 1920s necessitated some major changes of equipment on the homefront, and Hull installed the first continuous tunnel kiln during this period. The new kiln was 310 feet in length and cost nearly $75,000, but proved to promote larger produc-

tion numbers of artwares. In 1925, the pottery announced production totalling three million pieces per year. This number excluded miscellaneous kitchenware items such as jugs, jars, custard cups, and salt boxes. Hull remained constantly involved in market analysis and soon noticed that interest in stoneware items was decreasing slightly, due to improved canning and preserving methods for food staples. Keeping with movements dictated by the market, Hull in 1926 converted Plant No. 1 to tiling operations. However, the pottery continued to manufacture stoneware items in very respectable numbers, making changes and improvements along the way.

Hull updated designs and decorations of its stone kitchenware items and produced large numbers of stoneware vases, jardinieres, flower pots, and hanging baskets in plain or multicolored blended glazes. Hanging pots and baskets were accompanied by chains. A miscellaneous assortment of art pottery consisting of jardinieres, flower pots, and vases were glazed regularly in the matte colors Bermuda Green and Lotus Blue. Special orders of matte Oyster White and Autumn Brown were available when ordered in large quantities. Other typical color glazes of the day were Maize Yellow, Eggshell White, and turquoise.

In 1928, Hull offered newly designed kitchenware based upon previously used designs, with updated features such as greater depth, projecting feet or bases, neater and more precise decorations, and spherical bottoms. New shapes replaced old shapes of white blue-banded bowls, and the No. 701 shape yellow ware bowls with brown bands replaced the No. 700 shape. White decorated luster-band bowls were offered with the choice of a wide red band with small blue stripes, wide Ivory Brown band with small blue lines, or a wide green band with small black lines. Hull stated they were "without doubt the finest appearing bowls we have produced in the past twenty-five years."

Hull's nursery ware was offered in both new and old styles. This semiporcelain nursery line included baby plates, cups, saucers, and bread and milk sets in two sizes with a companion child's mug. Semiporcelain cuspidors available in hotel, parlor, or low parlor shapes were banded with gold, blue, green, maroon, or luster colors. Also available were cuspidors that had been decorated with decals of rose or bird designs, or in glazed mahogany with gold line trim.

Due to the failed economy, Hull was prudent in closing the Jersey City warehouse in 1929. There were lessened workforces and sales staffs in the eastern and northern areas. Hull had no recourse but to upgrade local production by concentrating efforts on manufacturing only the highest quality domestic wares, now centering on stoneware and semiporcelain kitchenware and artware, and tile production. Markets indicated that new courses of production needed to be explored in order for the company to remain solvent, and Hull continued to keenly watch manufacturing activities and retailing trends.

Hull knew that good business practice involved more than producing a quality item. He took great pride in providing orders in a timely manner, and in his efforts to process orders more easily, provided customers the following classification systems for the bodies they purchased. Earthenware, which was of white semiporcelain body, was represented by a prefix number of three digits, such as 300/13 Casserole or 610/33 Vase.

Stoneware classification, which was of buff body, was represented by a prefix number of two digits — 34/30 Jardiniere, or 34/35 Flower Pot.

Hull's marketing system included a second number, which related to style. The number 30 represented jardinieres; 31, hanging pots and baskets; 32, flower and bulb bowls; 33, vases; 34, flower pots with unattached saucers; and 35, flower pots with attached saucers.

Hull's Plant No. 2, illustrated on this early letterhead of the mid-1920s, shows the extra kiln smokestacks, those attributed to the first continuous kiln, which was installed in 1923 at a cost of $75,000.00.

The Hull Company, composed of many adept leaders and salesmen, could not have survived the years without a loyal staff of frontline pottery craftsmen, such as illustrated in this photo dated 1928. During this period, Hull employees numbered 285, and while Hull consistently had 25 to 30 salesmen stationed at various offices throughout the nation, 7 salesmen traveled regularly from the home office in Crooksville.

Tile Production

A Zanesville, Ohio, man by the name of F. H. Hall saw the opportunity in 1875 to utilize local clays for tile and soon patented his process. Several area tiling plants followed: The American Encaustic Tiling Company, the Mosaic Tile Company, Empire Tile, and Standard Tile. In 1926, Hull, who was always conscious of current market trends and demands, obtained fire clay in Crooksville's Mineral Addition and converted operations in Plant No. 1 to tile production. Operations in Plant No. 1 were mainly devoted to production of floor and wall tile.

J. D. Young, an able and experienced man thoroughly schooled in his profession, and who had been associated with the company since 1905, served as superintendent of Plant No. 1. Young, born in 1863, had married Minnie Watts, a native of Perry County, Ohio. They were the parents of six children, one being Earl Watts Young, who served as assistant to his father. Tony Donluvy was enlisted as a tile designer, and William A. McClellan continued to head the company's glaze formulas for both plants, inclusive of Hull's tile manufacture.

A Hull company catalog of 1928 boasted of Hull's two large modern factories with floor space totalling four acres. At that time Hull advertised:

Matte glazed buff body and faience floor and wall tile...Bathroom and kitchen accessories in colors to match tile...Special plastic faience installations...Garden pottery — vases, urns, birdbaths, jadinieres, pedestals, etc. Kitchen pottery — bowls, pitchers, nappies, salt boxes, butter jars in semiporcelain and yellow ware.

This catalog included 14 mantel designs, 16 arch designs, and a variety of decorative inserts, stripes, and grilles. The company offered ninety standard colors and indicated that it was "prepared to make any ceramic color that it is possible to make."

Hull's two plants employed a total of 285 craftsmen from an annual payroll of $300,000.00. While Plant No. 1 employed 125 tile and stoneware workers and had a total payroll of $150,000.00, Plant No. 2 employed 160 craftsmen for its utility and artware output and had a payroll of $175,000.00. When operating normally, Plant No. 1 produced 3,800 square feet of floor, wall, and ornamental tile daily, or approximately 1,400,000 square feet annually. Plant No. 2's capacity was 650,000 dozens, or 7,800,000 pieces, of utility and artware annually.

Decorative tiling for floors, walls, fireplace mantles, etc., was made in a wide array of colors, both solid and stippled, and included pastels and black, in both high-gloss and matte finishes. Accessory items such as towel bars and soap dishes were made in coordinating colors. Much of the company's tile business was on a special order basis, with two types of tiles manufactured, plain and faience, either being available with a "cushioned," or rounded, surface.

Faience tile was characterized by a thicker body that usually contained grog, a mixture of dust made by pounding and sifting broken pieces of biscuit, or unglazed pottery. Faience was usually distinguished by a coarse, porous body covered by a heavy opaque enamel instead of a translucent glaze. Tile was pounded or pressed into the mold and then trimmed with a wire drawn across the bottom. The surface of the tile could be made smooth with a dampened finger or given a sandy finish by sprinkling with fine grog. A tile body too moist would crack due to unequal shrinkage. Tile had to dry slowly and evenly to avoid warping and cracking. Edges were dampened if they were drying faster than the center of the tile. Shrinkage was lessened by mixing about a fourth part of fine grog dust with the clay.

The architects and decorators of the William H. Jackson Company of New York were Hull's largest tile customers. However, Hull also supplied buyers in the Chicago, Detroit, and Cincinnati areas. McClellan's personal notebooks include tile formulas and their glazes and refers to supplying the William H. Jackson Company in Chicago as well as New York. Other tile buyers referred to include Star, Drake, Shaw, and Hawkinson, and specific notations refer to orders such as "356-W for Cran Brook School."

Specific notations regarding the W. H. Jackson Company include "Jackson #1, blue trile good, outside on top — #1, 3 hrs. grinding," "Jackson #2 blue green outside on top, 3 hrs. grinding," "#4 turquoise trile Jackson, trile muffle kiln, OK," "Blue Green Hi-fire Cone 10, W. H. Jackson Co., Chicago, Y.M.C.A. Job, OK," "W. H. Jackson, Chicago, #171 good," "#211-1 Detroit," and "81-1 Detroit."

McClellan's notations in a notebook inscribed, "For Trile For Tile — 1926" encompassed tile glaze colors in "gold, matt black, Blue Enamel, Enamel Green, matt blue, new black, yellow stain, pink stain, blue hi-fire, orange red, black enamel, MTC red glaze, lavendar, white matt, blue, slater blue, red brown, orange brown, copper, soft green, shamy yellow, Canary yellow, dark yellow, autumn leafe, crimson staine, olive green, rose, grey, bright red, blue green matt, yellow matt, ivory matt, brown bright, green bright, tan bright, Victoria green, blue green glaze — W. H. Jackson — YMCA, blood red, coral red, apple green, Hawthorne," and others. Tile bodies noted are "Mosaic body, one fire body, Dust Pressed body, and Faience."

Interesting to note is the tile body composition, noted in McClellan's own hand, that consisted of "63 buckets grog, 9 buckets ball clay, 13 wheel-barrow Ader H. Clay and 3 wheel-barrow Scott's ball clay," while the casting body (used for casting bath accessories and perhaps used for garden ware, statuary, and the like) was listed as "65 gal. water, 52 buckets clay, 3 lb. soda ash and 3 lb. sil. soda."

Further instructions, for the "Pressing Body," were noted as "24 shovel of body, 7 shovel of grog."

Instructions were penciled in the margins of McClellan's threadbare books: "#40 red bright, trile in muffle kiln apple green, hand fire," "Lt 107-1 samples OK, samples for Jackson in Chicago," "P.O. Watts wall tile body, grinde to go thru 200 mesh screen," "bright glaze for Shaw," "new green Lt 101, outside kiln," "Lt Blue Colson Cone 8," "sample 505-2 Drake," and "rec'd #1336A Special Bright Red, L. Reusche Co."

Special orders were taken in Hull's few years of tiling operations. Reproductions of art designs, along with free-form and original art designs, were executed in embossed clay tiles. Douglas Young, now deceased, described a tiling mastery of *The Lord's Supper* many years ago during an interview. Another artistic tiling work, thought to have been executed and installed in a Catholic church, illustrated the Stations of the Cross, the fourteen images or pictures that form the successive scenes of the Passion of Christ and before which devotions are performed. This information has been researched through the Roman Catholic Property Administration, thus far, to no avail. While the locations of these works have not been verified, it is interesting to note that McClellan's notebooks contain the glaze formula "Red for Christ's Robe."

In the 1930s, building construction declined and demand for tile decreased. Some tiling companies made attempts to lessen the costs of manufacturing faience tile in order to be competitive with others and to make their operations more profitable. The market price of dust-pressed 4¼" x 4¼" flat tile, which had previously been 65 – 70¢ per square foot, faltered to a mere 18¢ per foot. The Hull Pottery Company would not succumb to this type of operation, and rather than compromise quality, tile production was discontinued by 1931. Discontinuing tile production was Addis Jr.'s, foresight, as Addis, Sr., had died in 1930, leaving the company to be run by his eldest son. Hull had most assuredly inherited his father's keen business sense, as the decision to end tiling operations was a very wise one. The nearby American Encaustic Tile, the largest tiling operation in the world, closed in 1935.

Plant No. 1, which had earlier converted almost exclusively to tiling operations, now housed outdated equipment in need of many modifications. This, combined with the sluggish economy, prompted Hull, by 1933, to close the doors of Plant No. 1. Until that time, however, there was a unified effort by both plants to continue production of sizeable volumes of stoneware and semiporcelain.

Hull's Luster Glazes

Hull had been experimenting with luster glazes since 1927. By the close of the 1920s, lusters were being used for banded bowls, and Hull was working on a newly designed line of semiporcelain art ware that was to sport luster finishes. Special expertise was needed when glazing in luster treatments, and special care was necessary in the firing processes. Lusters, with two exceptions, were all the same color before being fired, a dark brown in the vial and a light yellow-brown when applied. Lusters positively could not be successfully mixed in the liquid form, nor could one be painted over another without firing between the applications.

Alcohol was used as a thinner for luster glazes, as turpentine left a greasy film on the surface and caused streaks. Luster glazes could be fired on any type of clay, from domestic to finer clays, but lusters did pose problems that weren't typical to other glaze techniques. Each fingerprint showed after firing a luster, and a coat too thick cracked or peeled off. Humidity was also an enemy to luster glazes, and some wares had to be fired while the lusters were still wet, while others needed to dry before lusters were applied.

The firing temperatures of luster colors had to be monitored at different levels for the various color techniques. Certain colors had to have light firing, while others required heavier firing. Some items had to be fired at once, so the luster color didn't sink into the initial glaze color, while others had to air dry before they were fired. A kiln that had not been heated very slowly at first, so that oils could be driven out gradually and fumes could be allowed to escape before the kiln became too hot, dulled the lusters and also caused them to rub off easily after being fired. Hull's semiporcelain lusterware items were decorated in colors the company described as orange, Shammy, Lavender, Slate, Emerald, light blue, iridescent dark blue, and Golden Glow. These lusters served as standard luster treatments. 10" luster artware vases wholesaled for $15.00 per dozen.

As you know, William A. McClellan was employed as Hull's ceramic engineer during the luster glaze period. Pottery historians know too that William McClellan also obtained employment with the American Encaustic Tiling Company. Some of the luster colors Hull used match identically with those used by A. E. Tile. This, coupled with the fact that luster pieces were usually not marked by either firm, causes much confusion in the marketplace. It was not uncommon for engineers, designers, modelers, and tradesmen to take employment at several different potteries during their lifetimes. Nor was it uncommon for a ceramic engineer that moved to another firm to take his livelihood with him, the formulas for bodies and glazes, which he carefully guarded.

McClellan noted, on the reverse sides of company invoices, the luster colors as he knew them: "New Dec. P.LB Mother P., P.LG Mother P., PLY Mother P., CT Coffee Tone, L.R. Red Silvery, ST Flash; Old Dec. LC shammy, LO Orange, LM Mulberry, L Gr Green Lt., L Gr Green Dk.," which translates as "New Decorations: plain light blue Mother-of-Pearl, plain light green Mother-of-Pearl, plain light yellow Mother-of-Pearl, coffee tone, red silver or silvery, gold flashes. Old Decorations: light Shammy, light orange, light mulberry, light green, dark green."

As part of themes designed outside the company (perhaps the Hommel Company), additional luster lines, Persian and Chinese Red Cracquell, were sold to the distributors in the Chicago area. One dozen of the same 10" vases used in the previous example cost $24.00 in the special luster glazes. It is believed that Persian refers to a turquoise-blue luster and that, of course, Chinese Red Cracquell refers to a red luster. McClellan's glaze books refer to several reds: bright reds, red stains, and red mattes. The blues recorded ranged from light blues to cobalts to Peacock blues and turquoises. If Persian actually referred to a blue-green shade of luster, it would have needed to have been applied in two or more applications in order to acquire something other than a gray tone. Gold luster glaze, when used in two paintings, provided a very rich purple; however, when a third painting used was a "covering" for gold luster, a pigeon-blood ruby was attained. This covering for gold luster was not used for any other purpose, as it had little or no color when fired alone. In pure speculation, any of these colors, combinations thereof, numerous applications of the gold lusters, or formulas contained in McClellan's glaze books could have been likely candidates for the special lusters. Cost alone tells us that Hull was using more expensive glazes, indicative of gold content or the application and firing of wares in several stages.

A letter directed to McClellan, dated April 21, 1927, from the O. Hommel Co., "Importers and Manufacturers, Bronze Powders, China Colors, Oxides and Ceramic Chemicals, Bronzing Liquids, Metal Leaf, Gold Paints, Enamels, Etc.," 209 – 213 Fourth Avenue, Pittsburgh, Pennsylvania, is no doubt in reference to Hull's luster glazes:

Dear Friend Bill:

You may think that I forgot my promise which I made you to send you the recipe for the Crystaline Glazes, but this is not the case. I have hunted a dozen times or more for the recipe but I have not been able to find it until just a short time ago. Ernest no doubt mentioned to you that I have not been well either and had been away on a trip so that for six weeks I did not attend to very much business. I am feeling considerably better again.

Hope you will let me hear from you what success you have with the crystalines. With many kind regards.

Another letter directed to McClellan from the Hommel Company is dated March 29, 1934, and may have referred to the color needed for the No. 300 line semiporcelain kitchenware decorated in overglaze Pimento Red stripes:

We have matched the specimen of Overglaze Red, submitted, and are sending, under separate cover, sample of Overglaze Red #3154-A which you will find firing out very close to the desired shade.

We would like to receive your business for this color and would appreciate it if you could arrange to have this tried soon and favor us with your next order.

We assure you we would appreciate your kind consideration and would give your orders our very best attention.

In this company photo, dated 1933, craftsmen are identified as follows:
Row 1 (bottom): Elmer Heskett, Billy Ansel, Don Lauterbach, William Woods, Ray Conaway, Jake Ansel, Ken Haymen, Harold Smith, Junior Williams, William Houk, Noah Watts. **Row 2**: Clifford Oliver, Burley Channel, Guy Eveland, Ralph Passon, Jay Young, Arthur Bayes, Lewis Woods, Pat Mooney, Orvil Bonifant, Guy Allen, Dick Cantor, Marshall Hall, Henry Tysinger. **Row 3**: Phyllis Rogers Stephenson, Grace Levering, Kathryn Mooney, "Click" Hinkle, Leona Orr, Grace Spung, Julia Dunn, Irene Williams, Loretta Presgrave, Elmer Conaway, Effie Ferguson, Cecila Adams, Zetta Wilson, Helen Bailey, Bertha McGuire, Ruth Russell, Cecil Hull. **Row 4**: Richard Rosser, Gerald Zinn, Tom Conaway, Gerald Conaway, Russell Lee, Dugan Kemmer, Cyril Burns, Raymond Underwood, Frank Stephenson, Bill Corbett, Clyde Allen, George Young, Arthur Levering, Cecil Wilson, Ralph Sherlock, Henry Russell.

The 1930s: A Time of Turmoil

Addis Emmet Hull, Sr.'s, accomplishments were many in his lifetime; he had been named postmaster of Rendville and was elected by his fellow townsmen to the town council. Hull served many years on the school board, taking an active interest in the education of his six children, Addis Emmet, Jr., James Brannon, Robert, Byron, Joy, and Jane. Hull, who supported the Democratic party, was elected to the Ohio legislature in 1898 in a Republican district, and in 1907/08 represented Perry County in the Ohio General Assembly. Hull, who had resided in Zanesville at 1245 Maple Avenue since 1911, proved instrumental in all aspects of advancement of community, schools, and legislation. Hull married Etta Brannon, born in 1873 in Morgan County, Ohio. Mrs. Hull was very active in social, civic, and church work, and served as director and trustee of the Bethesda Hospital in Zanesville.

Hull died in 1930, leaving the pottery trade in the experienced hands of his two eldest sons, Addis Emmet Hull, Jr., and James Brannon Hull. Robert was attending Ohio State University, taking courses related to factory management, and Byron had not been long out of high school at this time. Hull's two eldest sons were experienced in the pottery trade, having previously worked for their father. At the time, Addis, Jr., was serving as assistant manager of the Hull, and James Brannon held the position of accountant and bookkeeper in charge of the order department. Neither son was a stranger to the pottery business, and each had inherited his father's keen market sense and decision-making prudence.

Both sons had graduated from Ohio State University. Addis, Jr., held the degree of Ceramic Engineer. Following their father's footsteps and the family tradition, both sons would become successful presidents of the Hull Pottery Company. Addis Hull, Jr.'s, position of top management came soon after the death of his father in 1930, but James Brannon Hull had to wait nearly twenty years for the same managerial advancement.

Addis E. Hull, Jr., resided in Zanesville at 1252 Euclid Avenue and commuted to the village of Crooksville, where he kept the pottery steadfast and strong during the Great Depression. Hull had married Lois Barnett in 1917, and he had two children, A. E. III and Richard D. A veteran of the World War, in 1918 Addis, Jr., served as chief inspector in the explosive section, army ordnance. He was honorably discharged in 1919.

James Brannon Hull, a student at Ohio University during the late war, was attached to the federal reserve. Hull married Marie Hannum in 1924, and was eager to devote his full attention to the family pottery business.

Imports had halted, and the doors of the Jersey City warehouse had closed in 1929. After taking the helm of the family operation in 1930, Addis, Jr., ended tiling operations by 1931 and further closed Plant No. 1 in 1933. The major tiling manufacturers who remained in business faltered within the next few years. The American Encaustic Tiling Company, the largest tile company in the world, closed its doors completely by 1935. Interesting to note is that Addis, Jr., later acquired the A. E. Tile Company in 1937 and was instrumental in organizing another pottery on the premises, the Shawnee Pottery Company.

Although there was a definite movement to produce larger volumes of art pottery, as indicated by the company's importation of nearly 20% of its clay for special items and glazes, the largest output continued to be stoneware, kitchenware, garden ware, and florist ware.

There was no guesswork involved regarding marketplace demands. The Hulls who headed company production were very well versed in their trade. Economics and market trends ruled the ceramic industry, and the Hull Pottery Company throughout its history, met demands by maintaining quality and diversity at pleasing prices.

By 1935, Hull felt the lessening demand for stoneware, and decreased its production of stoneware utility items and kitchenware. Hull also closed the doors of the New York showroom. While the company continued to manufacture some stoneware pieces in the form of vases, jardinieres, and hanging pots, Hull's production emphasis was definitely taking a strong turn towards artware.

At this time, the preferred body for kitchenware items was nearly always porcelain. It was also increasingly clear that this medium was fast becomming the preferred body for the company's production of artware.

The 1930s proved to be a season of change. Addis E. Hull, Jr., successfully carried the company through the turbulent lean years of the 1930s.

By the mid-1930s, Hull employees had organized with the National Brotherhood of Operative Potters. The Hull Pottery and the Brush Pottery were the only two union-operated plants

Addis E. Hull, Sr., died in 1930, leaving the Hull Pottery Company in the capable and experienced hands of his two eldest sons, Addis E. Hull, Jr., and James Brannon Hull.

in the pottery region. This was also a time when Addis Hull, Jr., was interested in moving on. Hull had made the decision to accept a management position outside the family pottery.

Hull's earlier insight concerning the declining stoneware market had lead him to decrease company production of these wares. Now, in 1937, the stoneware business in general was dead. Hull not only offered stable guidance such as this when in charge of the company, but at other times too. When confronted with outside business interests, Hull very carefully provided for the future employment of company personnel and for the continuous flow of future production lines at his father's firm. Hull accomplished this by accepting a long-term contract with Shulton of New York for production of pottery cosmetic and soap product containers. Hull left the company knowing it was secure; jobs and production would continue under the direction of the company's new president, Gerald Watts, governed by provisions of this contractual agreement with Shulton.

While Plant No. 2's utility ware and artware production continued, the company made new space for the Shulton operations. Hull increased its 285-person workforce to 450 people and worked around the clock in three shifts.

The Hull Pottery Company manufactured in excess of eleven million Old Spice shaving mugs and aftershave lotion, cologne, and aftershave talc bottles over the next nine years.

Shulton created a reproduction of an old shaving mug for Old Spice mug soap. A small colonial pottery medicine jar was the design inspiration for Old Spice men's cologne, aftershave lotion, and aftershave talc bottles. These Hull pottery containers were decorated with fired-on illustrations of famous eighteenth-century sailing vessels: the *Mount Vernon*, the *Grand Turk*, the *Recovery*, and the *Friendship*. The original illustration used was a sketch of a clipper ship.

William Lightfoot Schultz, who had been in the soap business since 1910, was continually searching for *the* idea that would create the product appeal that would sell millions. The famous ship replicas on Hull's bottles and shaving mugs created that level of success.

The advent of World War II and the resulting redirection of raw materials into the war effort, plus Shulton's need to advance to automatic filling and closing operations when the demand for talc and shaving lotion rose to millions of bottles, forced a container material change. Shulton gave up the ceramic containers manufactured for them by Hull in 1944.

Hull manufactured millions of containers during the contract period; however, it never fully met Shulton's specifications for the bottles and mugs. The requirements Shulton demanded for capacity control and neck tolerances were so stringent that quality control measures became almost impossible to implement. Soon this venture proved to be a profitless operation. It was vital that Shulton's requirements be fully met in order for the pottery wares to survive Shulton's machine production filling operations. Inaccurate fills due to irregularities of the containers, the percentage of leakers, and the porosity of the pottery made handling and costs prohibitive on a large volume basis.

Both Hull and Shulton were relieved to see the "pottery-glass" bottles and mugs adopted. These had first been experimented with in late 1943, by the T. C. Wheaton Co. of Millville, New Jersey.

By 1944, all containers were being produced by Wheaton in an opaline glass that simulated the pottery made previously by Hull. Ceramic materials were added to the glass to give it a realistic clay-colored lustre that closely resembled the sheen of pottery. The glass containers duplicated the appearance of Hull's pottery containers and could be produced closer to desired specifications. The new bottles better tolerated the mechanical filling and packaging operations.

In March 1937, A. E. Hull, Jr., became the Shawnee Pottery Company's president and general manager. The May 6, 1937, prospectus of the Shawnee Company assigned Hull to make an immediate appraisal of the works at Zanesville, purchased from American Encaustic Tile Company, Inc. Hull "was considered by the Company best qualified to make an appraisal of such machinery and equipment." The Shawnee Pottery Company anxiously awaited the time it could reorganize the plant for use of new and improved techniques devised by Hull. Further scrutiny of the Shawnee Pottery Company's prospectus clarifies how very highly regarded Hull was in the field of ceramics:

Addis E. Hull, Jr., of Zanesville, Ohio, the President and General Manager, is a graduate of Ohio State University and holds the degree of Ceramic Engineer. He has been actively engaged in the pottery manufacturing business for more than twenty years, the last six as President and General Manager of A. E. Hull Pottery Company of Crooksville, Ohio, which was founded by his father and five associates in 1903. Mr. Hull has been devoting part of his time and attention to the affairs of the Company since its organization. His resignation from Hull Pottery Company will be effective not later than March 14, 1937, or at such prior time as may be convenient to Hull Pottery Company.

Mr. Hull has been employed by the Company as General Manager under an agreement terminating December 31, 1941, at a salary of $6,000 annually, plus 5% of the net profits for each fiscal year, resulting after deduction of all operating charges, including interest, depreciation and taxes, but excluding state and Federal income, excess profits and undistributed profits taxes. It is expected that life insurance in the amount of $100,000 payable to the Company will be placed on his life.

Mr. Hull will devote his entire time to the affairs of the Company. His principle activities will be market research by contact in the field with buyers and the design and development of new products. The success of pottery manufacture is greatly dependent upon the design and development of products having popular appeal, so that current sales trends may be anticipated and guided. Mr. Hull has outstanding ability as a designer and is thoroughly acquainted with the buyers of the large chain and department stores and wholesalers of pottery products.

With Hull having moved on to accept the presidency at Shawnee, Gerald F. Watts, the son of William Watts, became the president of the Hull Pottery firm. This was the first time in the history of the company that it was headed by someone outside the Hull family. The company had previously been clearly established as a giant in the field of ceramics by A. E. Hull, Sr., and A. E. Hull, Jr. Watts continued to project the same strong and diverse image for Hull by encouraging a major infusion of the fluid and lovely pastel art lines for which this pottery is most famous.

In the late 1920s, Hull, as well as many other American companies, dealt in voluminous sales of foreign imports. Now, ten-plus years into this practice, the flood that overcame the market was nearly disastrous for local manufacturers. U.S. importers of foreign wares had created their own monster. Hull was seriously in need of a great number of artware designs, to compete not only with local competitors, but also with foreign competition. Times demanded American wares with a distinctively local look and feel. Necessity demanded that local manufacturers out design, out merchandise, and out distance all foreign competition.

Area competition remained constant; every pottery attempted to keep its corner of the market. Labor and materials were scarce during World War II; however, money was plentiful, and the company was able to market all the artware that could be produced. A minimum of fifty spray gun operators (for tinting) and twenty-five decorators were needed for coloring the artware lines; the numbers of trimmers and finishers were even greater. There was a separate "cold room" filled with additional decorators in which masked and free-hand designs were painted. Kiln operators, ceramic engineers for clay and glaze preparation, die makers, mold makers, casters, jiggermen, maintenance men, and the like composed an additional 100 workmen.

America reclaimed its retail market when the war abruptly halted any desire or demand for imported wares. The growing resentment toward both Japan and Germany saw American-produced items outdistancing the sales of all foreign imports. "Buy American" campaigns were pushed by every available medium — radio, newspaper, and magazine. Hull, along with other local competitors, could sell all the American-made artware and kitchenware that could be produced.

This was both good news and bad news, since the redirection of raw materials into the war effort created problems, and modelers and other experienced craftsmen were scarce. The Hull Pottery Company remained open for production during the war years, while other companies were used for armed services headquarters, offices, and warehouses. Hull produced casseroles for food provisions for the Navy while it kept as many of its regular lines in operation as it could with its decreased number of employees. Hull pottery officials proudly recognized those employees who left their pottery worktables to join the war effort. From 1942 to 1946, the Hull Pottery Company allotted each employee serviceman $10.00 per month during the period he served his country.

Hull did its best to keep as many artware lines on the market as was possible. Perhaps because it was necessary during the war years, many shapes of the day were repeated three, and sometimes four times in a single pattern, gradually enlarging (e.g., Orchid, Tulip, Iris, and Poppy). Although the pottery firm was determined that each design keep its individual identity, it was not uncommon for shapes, ideas, and molds to be shared.

The massive movement towards art pottery was definite and positive competition for other art pottery manufacturers, and soon vases, baskets, ewers, wall pockets, rose bowls, console bowls, and other items were abundant. The pastel-tinted artwares of Hull, embossed with realistic floral sprays, virtually flooded the market. These are the lines for which the Hull Pottery Company is best remembered, soothing to the senses and simplistic in style. Hull's artware was airbrush-blended in predominantly matte colors of pink, blue, yellow, and green. Hull was noticed in the marketplace to repeat these pastel colorations. This, combined with the pottery's distinctive look and feel, proved to be Hull's trademark look in the forties. It was an important time to keep everything American in appearance, and there definitely were no foreign-looking designs coming from this factory during war years. The realistic floral sprays that decorated Hull wares were taken straight from the American garden path or walkway, i.e., irises, camellias, and calla lilies.

Some art and novelty designs were supplied by Hull's potential buyers and chain store representatives. The company was guaranteed sales by allowing the buyers to supply the ideas and gather packages and assortments of their own liking for their sales campaigns. T. K. Kirkpatrick of S. S. Kresge Co., W. W. Dixon of McCrory Stores Corp., H. H. Lindquist and Van Overschelde of F. W. Woolworth Co., and H. W. Smith of S. H. Kress Co. were instrumental in supplying basic production ideas to Hull and other pottery companies. Sears, Roebuck & Co. had a staff that assisted in designing kitchenware items and included Jane Miller, housewares stylist; James Butler, pottery buyer; and F. R. Henniger, the division merchandise manager. Ideas were transformed by a Hull modeler, and then dies and molds were made. Due to this merchandising assistance, there was very little need for a full-time designer at the plant.

However, additional design work was contracted through Louise Bauer, who was freelancing for many of the local potteries at the time.

Chain stores such as Mattingly, G. C. Murphy, F. W. Woolworth, McCrory, Federated Stores, Ben Franklin, and Kresge were leaders in Hull sales. Original price tags that remain on Hull wares show that the matte Woodland hanging basket retailed for $2.69; the Wild Flower vase 52-6" for $1.49; the Calla Lily 11" ewer for $1.98; and the Dogwood low bowl 521, 7" for 98¢. Merchants were guaranteed to double their investments, since Hull set minimum retail prices for pottery leaving the plant. Higher rates were established for areas west of the Rocky Mountains. Hull's marketing of assortment packages included a system in which the assortment number was, in fact, the wholesale price, e.g., assortment #6502 cost $65.02 and assortment #4690 cost $46.90.

Many prototype art lines came from the 1920s and 1930s, as did novelty items such as the Dancing Girl and Peasant Lady planters. The Sueno lines of Tulip, Calla Lily, and Thistle were introduced as early as 1938 and marked the beginning of Hull's most important artware years. Although the lines of Hull were many and varied, and all are worthy of mention, those best remembered are the matte pastels of the forties. Hull art lines represented the best of two worlds; function combined with art and form. Hull's many intricate and flowing designs emerged thereafter.

Floral artlines flooding the markets simultaneously included Tulip, Orchid, Calla Lily, and Iris. Here we saw a handful of shapes in graduated sizes. Intricacy of the embossed floral made these simple lines appear rich in detail.

Hull's Sueno line was predominately made up of Tulip designs, but also carried Calla Lily designs. Add to this the four Thistle vases and the lone Pine Cone vase.

Company information advertised three color combinations for Tulip: blue base and pink top, blue base and blue top, and blue base and cream top.

The somewhat plain, yet refined, Orchid art line was dec-

orated in muted colors of blue and rose. Artistic lines with little use of handle designs made this line a classic, at home in almost any setting. Much to collector dismay, Orchid offered only one size ewer and one size basket. This is the only early art line known to offer a set of bookends. Company information listed Orchid's color combinations as "Dec. No. 1 — blue green bottom and pink top. Dec. No. 2 — blue green bottom and top, and Dec. No. 3 — pink bottom and ivory top."

Calla Lily was decorated in earth tones as well as muted pastels. Sophisticated angular shapes and handles were customary of this line.

Iris design showcased a classic combination, from the plain lines used for the rose bowls and jardinieres to the more intricately scalloped vase tops and handles. Iris was offered in three color variations: blue base and rose top, peach base and peach top, and rose base and peach top.

These early art lines were complimented by the refined mattes of the company's earliest Mardi Gras lineup. Alongside were numerous novelty planters, and stoneware, yellow ware, and semiporcelain utility wares ranging from stacked bowl sets to cookie jars to colorful flower pots and hanging baskets. The general transition from stoneware to semiporcelain bodies for for utilitarian as well as art production was being made.

A. E. Hull Pottery Company Casting Room employees, dated July 17, 1941.

Poppy, Camellia, Dogwood, and Wild Flower (a number series) headed up the next series of art lines.

Shapes of the Poppy design were quite ordinary, and centered on bulbous designs. Poppy continued in the tradition of shapes in graduated sizes. Intricacy in the embossed floral enriched the design. Poppy was matte glazed in three color combinations: blue base and pink top, pink base and peach top, and pink base and blue top.

Camellia, often referred to as Open Rose, was Hull's most fanciful art design. There were no duplications in graduated sizes; each item in this line possessed an individual personality. There were vases with leafy handles, baskets with bows, jardinieres with rams' heads, hand-held fan vases, candle holders flanked by perched doves, a reclining mermaid with shell planter, and more. The stark white color treatments were somewhat chalky in comparison to the pink and blue combinations offered; however, no other line illustrated such a wide diversity of styles, which more than compensated for the white infiltration. Familiar colorations for Camellia were green base and rose top, and rose base and blue-green top.

Dogwood, also dubbed Wild Rose, featured a double duo-colored floral on most items. Color combinations included cream base and cream top, blue base and pink top, and turquoise base and cream top.

The handles and lines of the numbered Wild Flower design made this ware the most delicately intricate of all art lines manufactured by Hull. In this line, handles were more than functional, being extra lacy in double and triple forms and high-standing on the tea set, vases, and ewers. In addition to the lovely raised floral design, butterflies graced certain shapes. Two baskets, a handled bon-bon dish, and double candle holders were featured. Company information listed color combination A as having a pink top and a brown base, and B as having a mauve top and a green base. There is also an allover cream coloration.

The Red Riding Hood cookie jar, patented June 29, 1943, immediately and most assuredly made great impact on the novelty and kitchenware market. Design Patent Number 135,889 was issued to Louise E. Bauer of Zanesville, Ohio, assignor to the A. E. Hull Pottery Company, Inc., of Crooksville, Ohio, for "Cookie Jar." "Red" stole the heart of everyone she came in contact with. The storybook character proved to be a tremendous seller, and soon, various complementing accessories appeared, which continued to be made well into the 1950s. And while Hull began the livelihood of this bestseller with the assignment at the patent, the largest numbers of Red Riding Hood items were manufactured by the Regal China Corporation of Chicago, Illinois.

Also, many of the Hull-produced Red Riding Hood items were decorated by the Royal China and Novelty Company, a division of Regal China Corporation. Louise Bauer modeled additional Red Riding Hood characters for Regal China during the two seven-year terms of patent assignment. It appears some type of contractual agreement existed between Hull and Regal, since it appears the patent number remained assigned to Hull until June 29, 1957. It is possi-

ble, however, that the patent number was sold or legally transferred entirely by Hull to Regal.

Although matte-finished lines dominated this period of art pottery production, there were exceptions. In 1946, the Rosella pattern offered a high-gloss ivory or coral finish. Rosella's term of production was relatively short, due partly to the expense incurred in producing its special clay formula. The pink-based clay of Coral Rosella was produced of imported clay ingredients mixed in the factory.

The excitement surrounding the new Rosella line was apparent in advertising campaigns, which were launched immediately. The company's pride of master craftsmenship was advertised, and an expected allure to buyers of this new, modern ware was promoted:

An eloquent tribute in pottery to modern American homes. The beauty of your home will be enhanced by the smoothness and warmth of texture in Rosella — exquisitely designed, with the charming floral motif sculptured on a body of flawless coral. Pottery in its finest sense must have qualities of velvet-like feel to produce an emotional stir and justify a place among your finest possessions. This is a dominant characteristic in our new Rosella pattern. In Rosella there is a balance of subdued color and style seldom obtained but always sought. See and feel the actual piece of ware to become as keenly enthused as were the inspired craftsmen producing them. Your best gift displays will show this ware as rapidly as it can be produced.

Rosella was produced at a time when the company was torn between the comfort and stability of the old and the need to move on with updated, innovative new styles and glazes. The Hull Pottery Company was somewhat ahead of its time, as Rosella was produced in that small span of time before highly glazed artware items were truly trendy. While Hull tested its markets with Rosella, it at the same time maintained constant production of matte wares. On the retailers' shelves, Rosella competed not only with Hull matte wares, but also with Hull's competitors' products. Rosella did not take the retail market by storm; matte designs prevailed.

Hull Pottery cut its losses and commenced producing a full regiment of matte pastels in Wildflower W series and Magnolia lines, with the additional matte line, Water Lily, waiting in the wings. The company did not attempt another major gloss line for nearly two years, that being New Gloss Magnolia.

The Wildflower W series design was a second-generation line. The earlier line marked in numerical sequence was changed in name by joining the words *wild* and *flower*. The company was apparently in need of a completely new and inexpensive line, or perhaps it was the demanded volume of artware that dictated the immediate need for the new retail market lineup. Whatever the reasons, Hull found it necessary to bring back a previously used line with added newness, and described it as "fashionable foundations for your favorite flowers hand-painted in the gay colors of Spring to brighten the Fall and Winter months of indoor living...styled to dwell in graceful harmony with any interior."

The earlier Wild Flower number series had 29 shapes,

while the newer Wildflower listed only 22. Six of the earlier molds remained nearly the same, some with different cutouts or laces on the handles. A few molds were used with only slight modifications of floral design. Some of the molds disappeared altogether, as did the butterfly used for the Wild Flower numbered series line. Additional molds used for the Wildflower line were redesigned and updated. Simpler, more angular shapes appeared, and many of the fanciful handles used earlier were lost.

Matte glazes dominated, and Magnolia emerged with 27 newly designed molds. Although new colors seemed to have appeared in Wildflower and Magnolia, they were actually toned-down versions of the previously used pink and blue standards of earlier lines such as Orchid, Iris, Dogwood, and Poppy. The russet and yellow glazes were newly formulated glazes. Hull took control of a market with new ideas, colors, and concepts by way of using tried-and-true ideas, colors, and concepts with a special touch of added newness that captured and amazed its wholesale and retail audiences, yet all the while assured its past customers' comfort by allowing them to reacquaint with old friends.

For Hull's embossed duotone pastels, leaves and flowers were first decorated by brushwork. Paint glaze was thinned by Epsom salt when it thickened and was difficult to work with. Wares were then transferred to spray gun operators, who spray tinted first the top and then the base of the item being decorated. Wares were carried on boards through the pottery and to a hand-decorating room. From there the items moved to tinting, drying, and firing areas. Daine Neff recalled the day he disastrously dropped five 15" vases from the board he carried.

A small group of glaze books that belonged to Edgar McClellan (who followed in his father's footsteps as ceramic engineer for Hull) remain and offer but a glimpse into the years of prosperity in which Hull flourished during the forties and fifties. Glaze records inscribed in McClellan's own hand record a history in itself. His artistry relating to Magnolia included "Pink paint for Magnolia underglaze," "yellow/green for Magnolia," "Brown tint Magnolia," "Pink flower engobe," "Rose tint," "Lt. blue tint," "New Yellow underglaze for Magnolia," "Oct. 28, 1946 — New Blue Tint," "New Green Tint — Nov. 15, 1946," "Trial Pink Tint #20," "Green Tint Magnolia," "Peach Tint," "Silver Grey Tint Trial," "Blue Green Tint #2 — Trial Feb. 11, 1947, O.K.," and "Pink Tint #2 — Trial Feb. 11, 1947."

As directed by Hull, the Wildflower and Magnolia designs took the front-row seat of the nation's art pottery market and truly became major successes in the company's history. As in other times of Hull's prosperity, the conservative and traditional nature of the company came to light, and with this we gain insight into the men behind the scenes in how they used this to their advantage. Gerald Watts seemed to possess the same sixth sense as prior Hull managers regarding the current market trends of a nation of consumers. Crooksville, centered at the hub of pottery production, was surrounded by major potteries producing tremendous volumes of art lines.

Hull had wisely chosen to keep its personal identity of pink and blue tones, a trademark that most assuredly helped the company prevail while others faltered.

In 1947, Hull ventured to present another high-gloss artware line in the midst of the retail market's matte wares. However, instead of creating a newly designed mold system, as Hull had done when creating Rosella, the company opted to use shapes already familiar to the public. This proved to be a less expensive venture for the company, with exceedingly less risk. The known shapes of Magnolia in updated glazes proved to be far more comforting to the buying audience and were advertised as "Gracefully styled, handsomely decorated with hand-painted florals...glazed overall for shimmering, enduring beauty." Any speculation of failure on the company's part regarding this high-gloss artware and its timeliness would have been unfounded, as Hull's New Magnolia was a success.

Even with the major success of this high-gloss artware, Hull's conventional nature emerged again in 1948. Hull used the basic molds of Wild Flower numbered series #58 cornucopia, #53 vase, #71 vase, and #55 pitcher (although already redesigned for Wildflower) for the new Water Lily matte line. Flower pots with attached saucers were apparently back in vogue after being absent from the market for several years, and there was also a reemergence of the large jardiniere. Water Lily, consisting of 28 shapes, was decorated in matte colors of Walnut and Apricot or Turquoise and Sweet Pink. Company ads listed Water Lily as "practical, useful and handsome sculptural beauties, each with hand-painted floral, each in a choice of two duo-tone pastel combinations to assure complete harmony with your home's decorative motif."

Hull's well-known "theory of diversification," which kept two or three new and different lines on the market at all times, was truly a carefully planned strategy to assure that the company neither completely rid itself of the old, nor fully embraced the new. Although Hull's designers were capable of mastering completely new concepts in every aspect of artware, it's apparent the company chose not to. The conservative, well-thought-out management plans dictated differently; these plans allowed the Hull Pottery Company to prosper years longer than local competitors.

Production of the late 1940s was fully centered on artware; however, Hull continued to manufacture down-to-earth utilitarian kitchenware items, which also emerged in redesigned shapes and updated glazes. Kitchenwares continued to remain in the market alongside Hull's art designs. Throughout all manufacturing years, Hull remained in a position to please not only the retail buyer of artware, but also the customer needing utility wares and kitchenware. In 1948, the Cinderella Blossom and Bouquet lines of kitchenware, hand painted under the glaze, entered the market.

The years 1948 and 1949 saw an interesting combination of artware and kitchenware in the Sun-Glow line. The assortment was composed of kitchenware nested bowls, a casserole, a grease jar, and shakers, along with art and novelty styles that included four different wall pockets, a basket, assorted vases, and two styles of tea bells. Decorations offered were allover yellow gloss with pink decor, or allover pink with yellow decor. The Sun-Glow line's mold numbers, digits in the 50s and digits in the 80s, divided the artware and kitchenware shapes.

In 1949, the introduction of Bow-Knot proved to be a completely new concept in Hull artware. This apparently overnight change in form and content was due to the genius of designer Louise Bauer, who was responsible for modeling the line. The company saw the need for refining artware productions and made major changes in operations, and offered Bauer, a freelance modeler who had earlier been responsible for designing individual Hull items, full-time employment. Bow-Knot shapes included Sun-Glow's molds for wall pockets and the small basket. The company advertised Bow-Knot as "the epitome of smartness...beautiful new art pottery to match the natural beauty of your favorite flowers. Styled in twenty-nine pieces, including novel hanger pieces for unusual wall decorations." Bow-Knot was offered in duotone matte pastels of blue and pink or turquoise and blue.

During this same period, Louise Bauer created yet another full artware line, Woodland. This design's thirty shapes were billed as "an artware creation of the A. E. Hull Pottery Co. in gay, hand-painted florals, in a choice of Dawn Rose or Harvest Yellow body pastels." Hull continued its marketing campaign by describing the tea set as "from the pages of the 'Arabian Nights'...from the wonderful lamp of Aladdin come the graceful, flowing lines of this exquisite 3-piece Tea Set."

Again, kitchenwares flanked artware lines. A news account dated May 1, 1950, reported an ovenproof modern kitchenware in green or red plaid decoration. The items offered included a four-piece bowl set, ranging in width from 5" to 8", the largest bowl having a lip for pouring, retail price about $2.65 a set; a cookie jar, $1.69; a casserole,

$1.29; a range set, $1.89; a cream and sugar set, 98¢; and a cereal or vegetable bowl, 39¢.

While the nation's major art pottery companies had shown deficits in their bookkeeping departments since the end of World War II, the Hull Pottery Company remained steadfast and strong. The company identified known trends and anticipated and guided future markets. This anticipation, an art form in itself, was neccessary in order to survive a marketplace that had been overflowing with foreign competition for several years.

Hull remained cautious, because potteries that had been in business for decades concluded their clay histories at this very time. The Weller Pottery had faltered for more than a decade, finally closing its doors in 1948. The Roseville Pottery, which had declined steadily after the World War, maintained only a fragment of the market it had earlier held. Roseville had switched to several high-gloss lines of artware and kitchenware (some were revived shapes from the past), none of which attracted the attention of retail buyers. Roseville closed in 1952.

Hull's decision to employ full-time designer Louise Bauer proved to be not only a wise, but also a profitable, market strategy. The new designs of Bow-Knot and Woodland attained acceptance in numbers that astounded even Hull company officials. More importantly, Hull Pottery had most assuredly captured the attention of a nationwide art pottery market with its new designer and its new creations. The future seemed promising in all respects...

Louise E. Bauer, modeler and designer for the Hull Pottery Company.

Hull Pottery Destroyed by Flood and Fire

Fire and flame, the potter's most impairing plague, became a reality at the Hull Pottery on June 16, 1950. The *Columbus Evening Dispatch* reported:

Cloudburst and flash flood caused an avalanche of water which started from Black Fork Creek rushed northward in Jonathan Creek, south of Crooksville, and then poured into the three communities of Crooksville, Roseville and Rose Farm. Cascading water rushed up a narrow valley, smashed five homes in Rose Farm (also called Tropic) and caused an explosion and fire which destroyed the Acme Pottery.

A four-hour downpour changed Hull history. The Jonathan and Moxahala creeks poured over their banks, flooding a 25-square-mile area in Muskingum, Perry, and Morgan counties. In the village of Crooksville, water ran 7' deep on Main Street and stood 4' deep inside the Hull plant. When covered by water, the fiery pottery kiln of the Hull Company exploded, setting the plant ablaze. The tremendous pressure from the combination of rising waters and the great tunnel kiln firing at 2000 degrees caused the pottery's roof to ignite when expansion joints bolted apart.

The *Zanesville Times Recorder* reported that the downpour began at about 10:00 p.m., and flames broke out at the pottery after the kiln blew up about midnight. Between 30 and 35 persons who had taken refuge in the Hull pottery to escape flood waters were safely rescued after the fire started. One man waded through water up to his neck to get out of the plant.

The deep waters kept most firemen from being able to get close enough to fight the fire, and the few firemen able to reach the scene stood by helplessly without equipment. The firemen, as well as local townspeople and employees of the pottery, were forced to stand by and watch the pottery burn.

By dawn, it was certain that the Hull Pottery was no more than a rubble of smoke and ashes. In a matter of a few hours, earth's elements had rendered the pottery totally useless. The kiln had exploded, the roof was gone, and fire had razed the entire plant. All that remained were structural walls and charred waste within.

Brannon Hull, vice president of the company, declined to make an immediate estimate of the damage

This aerial view of the A. E. Hull Pottery was taken June 17, 1950, when all that remained were structural walls, billows of smoke, and flood waters that had partially receded.

for reporters; however, Gerald F. Watts, president of the pottery, told newsmen the loss would run at $500,000. News headlines proclaimed that "The Acme at Crooksville" was completely destroyed. Harold Showers, plant superintendent, had earlier given an estimate of $1,000,000. Showers stated the pottery was a complete loss and that all that was left standing was a portion of the walls. All areas of the plant, including the offices, which housed important documents, accounts receivable, and even payroll records, were affected by the flood and fire. The flood waters rose so rapidly that even the few workmen inside who operated the kiln had little, if any, notice of the impending tragedy.

A total of 1,500 pottery workers in the region were affected by the flood; 350 of them were employed by Hull. Payroll was carried out immediately by having employees line up in a vacant room on Main Street in Crooksville to declare what was due them.

Hull's foundation of goodwill was sound. Hull creditors felt an obligation to the company, and many satisfied customers rushed to pay their bills before they were due. One hundred thousand dollars came in immediately after the fire.

The flood devastated the small villages of Crooksville and Roseville. Only one pottery in Crooksville was unaffected by the high water and retained the use of its kiln.

By June 19, 1959, leaders of the community met in the offices of the Nelson-McCoy Pottery and estimated the Roseville loss at $136,000 to business places and $182,000 to residences. The loss in Crooksville, excluding the loss of the Hull plant, was believed to be even greater.

Industrial firms and many area potteries sent their employees to assist with cleanup.

Still, even with the added assistance, cleanup was slow. Many businesses and residences were destroyed, traffic was jammed as onlookers traveled through observing the storm damage, several miles of roadbed were damaged, and the Ohio Power Company transformer station had been thrown out of commision when it exploded. For several days, the only lighting in the area was from autos and emergency equipment.

The first shipment of pottery from Crooksville after the disasterous flood was sent on the Pennsylvania Railroad by the Worthington Pottery. Life resumed, and other potteries recovered one by one, while the Hull Pottery contemplated its future.

A New, Modern Pottery Rises from the Ashes

Potteries were typically plagued by fires; they were a fact of life to workers in this industry. Few burned-out potteries survived, but still fewer had the dynamic forces that Hull was afforded. The people behind this pottery proved to all that they were survivors and that this company would rise from the ashes. Hull's foundation was sound, its support was strong, and its reputation was unquestioned. Nearby towns quickly offered incentives to secure the business. Hull stockholders felt bound by moral obligation to remain in Crooksville, where the firm had been founded. The skilled craftsmen Hull employed and their families lived in this tiny village. Ninety-five percent of the stockholders voted to rebuild a new and modern pottery plant. While the Hull Pottery Company's president, Gerald F. Watts, was not in favor of rebuilding, the vice president of the firm, James Brannon Hull, vigorously declared his conviction that it was indeed essential to reconstruct the factory.

"Bump" Showers, son of one of the original founders of the Acme Pottery, took on the job of rebuilding the pottery, a job for which he asked for shares of company stock rather than pay. The firm was able, through insurance provisions, to keep company officials, ceramic engineers, and select key staff on the payroll during reconstruction of the new plant. This group staffed a pilot plant that remained operational during the months of reconstruction. Here new bodies and glazes were formulated expeditiously.

While architects and engineers were busy designing future processes of the modern plant, Hull salesmen were far from idle. The Hull Company maintained typical display space at all shows. Salesmen had little to display until mid-1951, but they met customers and promised resumption of production.

Byron Hull

Much credit rightfully belongs to the salesmen who were stationed far away from life in Crooksville. J. B. Hull's brother Byron continued the family pottery tradition and worked consistently throughout his lifetime as a salesman in the New York office. "Bike," concerned not only with Hull sales, kept a watchful eye on current market trends as reflected by the items competitors were selling and the prices of those items. He periodically shipped wares produced by other companies back to Crooksville, to inform Hull of new products being sold in New York.

No doubt Byron's extra duty in the field was greatly appreciated, and certainly the company was fortunate to have such expert assistance. Byron's salesmanship and marketing abilities were especially beneficial during the time the company was under reconstruction.

Byron Hull's skillful marketing strategy is evident in a letter he wrote "Brannie," dated September 15, 1951, regarding a sample of a "nicely shaped salad bowl" made by Taylor Smith and Taylor, a "part of their Luray shape which has been a good selling line for a number of years." Byron further states:

This piece is just under 10 inches in diameter but I think that ours should be a full 10 inches. It seems foolish to me to make something 9⅞" unless it is done because of a tremendous difference in cost when by adding an eighth you can list the item as a full 10 inches. Mr. Burgheimer

suggests very strongly that we emboss, or as he put it, "engrave" on the bottom the size of the bowl, and definitely put the name salad bowl in large letters. He says we should be sure that people know it is a salad bowl, not a nappy or low mixing bowl. I think he is correct about this and we should put in good sized letters "salad bowl."

This salad bowl, referred by a salesman, rather than by designers or modelers, was added to the production lines of Just Right Kitchenwares (Floral and Vegetable patterns), being sampled in Crooksville at the time.

If this wasn't design inspiration enough, Byron continued his letter:

I also sent you two planters, one a duck with a hat on and the other a pig, that sell for 39 cents in McCrory Stores. Orrie Yonkers showed me these about a month ago and said their price was $2.16 a dozen. They are made by Vogue China. The guy that owns this company is related to Lou Butler. He makes, as you can see, bigger pieces for the money than Lou. In fact, his are the largest in the field. Only his limited production and poor colors permit others to even be in the field. I only hope his prices are low enough that he will silently fold his tent, but I guess this won't happen as he has been in the business for a good number of years now.

I think we should send samples to the various firms in the following order: Woolworth, Newberry, Grant, McCrory, Kress, Murphy, Fishman, Green, McLellan, Neisner, Fisher-Beer.

Keep me posted on the progress. It sounded good to hear that our clay making machinery was going to work. Also will be anxious to hear what Stewart has to say. How about Sears or Montgomery Ward?

J. B.'s answer to Byron dated September 28, 1951, reads:

You are no doubt anxious to learn about the progress being made in our operation not only for yourself, but for the trade you have already contacted and is now waiting for samples.

We are now casting a limited amount of ware on all three machines together with quite a number of open benches, all being the Hand Decorated Woodland pattern together with the three planters namely: Lady Basket, Lamb and big Kitten. Today we were able to light the booster portion of our kiln which throws heat into the jigger units and by the middle of next week, at least a portion of the samples will be released to your trade covering Kitchenware in the order indicated.

You inquired about Kresge's reaction to samples which were only submitted on Tuesday the twenty-fifth, on which day we received a telephone call from Everett in Detroit, indicating an unusual and happy reaction from Mr. Stewart the buyer. He insisted that Everett leave all of his samples after the girls in his office admired what they claimed were California colors with emphasis upon the Coral. He has definitely stated that both complete lines of Kitchenware, the Vegetable and Floral, together with the Green banded bowls, would be placed on a listing at an early date and he requested colored illustrations covering all of this merchandise. The single exception is the pitcher in the Kitchenware line which he claims is overpriced. This is a very unusual reaction from Mr. Stewart, who is an extremely tough buyer, and I am still keeping my fingers crossed because they have always worked very closely with the Nelson McCoy Co.

Note: Company information indicates the Just Right Kitchenware pitcher, said by a prospective buyer to be overpriced, was reduced in price from $8.10 to $7.50 per dozen.

J. B. continued:

The strange thing is that the Nelson McCoy bowl set 4-piece that retails around a dollar seemed to present no particular problem to him. This is his reaction in front of John the salesman, and what might develop later remains to be seen. I am definitely a pessimist regarding this account, although the reaction is pleasing and might possibly work out to our advantage.

We liked very much the salad bowl you purchased and have already produced this shape in both the Vegetable and Floral pattern samples of which might possibly be ready by the middle of next week and forwarded to you. We will attempt to establish prices by that time also.

You will be glad to learn that we have received in excess of ninety five thousand dollars worth of orders on the Woodland pattern with only a limited number of samples and it is entirely likely that there will be in our hands for the holiday season an approximate one hundred fifty thousand dollars worth by the time the first order is released from our plant which we hope will be the week of October 14. Orders that are coming to us at this time should not be anticipated before the middle of November. We are passing this word along to several of the largest jobbing sources who have not started making inquiry.

This amount of business has come to us even before Butler's catalog reaches the trade, which will be within the next few days and we can at that time anticipate a considerable volume of business. In other words, our neck is out plenty far, so far as promising holiday shipments is concerned. One thing in our favor is that Butler Brothers has assured us that they will continue to sell this line all through the year 1952, and that they expect to sell a lot of merchandise for release following the holiday season. This kind of word could be passed along to other trade since they are all in the habit of selling this type of merchandise simply for a holiday period.

Just as soon as we get suitable Kitchenware samples which certainly will be by the middle of next week, we are going ahead with the production of color plates for colored illustrations to be placed in the hands of your syndicate operators. Since all of the catalogue information was destroyed in the fire we will have to get that detailed word from you again as soon as listings can be prepared.

The letter continued with regard to Boris Elias of Elias Brothers of Montreal, Canada, and a possible method of distribution in that country. Ware was already being distributed in Canada, but according to Byron, not at a large enough volume. Brannie answered, "hoping that we can develop more business across the border in the future than we had in the past."

Byron was always very modest about his accomplishments for the pottery, and in conversations, nearly always made comments about being away in New York, stating he was "not really aware of the happenings in Crooksville." He kept the company alive with ideas, was a designer of sorts, with the added knowledge of what was trendy and what the customer was willing to pay. Byron also seemed to be quite good at directing, perhaps even prodding, his brother Brannie, not only to the right sources, but also to the right pieces. And Byron, in New York, so close to the Canadian border, couldn't resist — Hull trade was in Canada both before and after 1950, compliments of Bike.

Salesmen were armed with a retail pricelist, dated July 1, 1951, listing 21 pieces of the New Woodland design. As they were before the plant fire, they were available in the matte glazes of Dawn Rose or Harvest Yellow. This same price listing of July 1951 included the #65 Lady Basket, the #66 Lamb, and the #68 Kitten planter.

Production was a reality by August 29, 1951. Hull's Just Right Kitchenware in Floral and Vegetable patterns, along with Blue Ribbon Bowls, headed up the utility lines. By September of 1951, the company's salesmen had secured in excess of $95,000.00 in orders of Woodland pattern alone. The first Woodland shipment was made in mid-October, 1951. Hull was assured that $150,000.00 of Woodland orders for the holiday season would follow.

A photo of the Hull plant shortly after reopening.

On October 24, 1951, additional items were placed on pricelists, including the novelty pieces #90 City Girl, #91 Country Boy, #92 Baby, #93 Elephant, #60 Parrot, #61 Pheasant, #86 Pig, #87 Boy with Dog, #88 Pup with Yarn, and #89 Kitty with Spool. A listing for December 10, 1951, featured the new novelty items #71 Ribbon wall pocket, #72 Fan vase, #73 Peacock vase, #78 Flamingo vase, and #79 Floral-decorated Daisy

Basket. Following closely were additional lines Parchment and Pine and Crescent dinnerware.

A year and a half was necessary for architects and builders to complete construction of the plant. January 1, 1952, the pottery was officially fully restored and the name changed from the A. E. Hull Pottery Company to the Hull Pottery Company.

Hull Pottery: Behind the Scenes

Hull's new plant was built for in-line pottery production, with only the latest and most modern equipment installed. Only air-floated clay was used, which prevented imperfections in the finished ware, and two 50-ton ram presses were installed, which formed ware many times faster than the old jigger and mold methods.

Hull's disasterous flood and fire enabled the plant to reconstruct with the assurance that its new pottery contained only the most organized methods for ease and speed of pottery production and handling. This organization was shown in mold making, casting, pressing, finishing, glazing, firing, sorting, and packaging.

Electric conveyor belts carried ware through various stations within the plant where workers finished and glazed it. Additional conveyor belts lifted ware to overhead drying ovens. The circular Allied continuous kiln fired at 2000 degrees and operated 24 hours a day, seven days a week. Up to 52 cars entered the kiln per day; one car entered and another exited every 25 minutes, turning out nearly 100,000 pieces of ware per week. Booster portions of the kiln threw heat to the press units and drying ovens.

Hull used a liquid form of clay to cast much of its product. This liquid clay, called either slip or soup, was poured into plastic molds. A wall of solid material gradually built up

along the face of the mold. When this wall reached the desired thickness the excess slip was poured out, leaving an essentially solid item for further processing. In this state, prior to its firing, an item is termed greenware.

Hull's earlier process of production for forming flatware and holloware, known as jiggering, was replaced in the new plant by the addition of compression machinery called ram presses.

The earlier process of jiggering flat pieces and bowls was similar to hand-turning clay, but was faster and easier due to a wheel that held the plaster mold in place while a pull down, or paddle, pressed clay against sides of the mold. An experienced clay worker was needed for this time-consuming task.

The ram presses compressed clay into the molds using great pressure. Quality, consistency, and speed were affected by the use of this manufacturing technique.

Many experienced clay workers besides those manning ram presses and pouring slip were necessary in the company's manufacture.

Mold makers were busy constructing molds for not only the original form to be cast, but also separate molds for any lids, feet, handles, knobs, or other ornamental attatchments.

Hull turned over its working molds three times during a single eight-hour shift. The life of a production mold was usually 150 "pours." In some cases, the mold cracked or

Increased production was made possible by the kiln installed after Hull's fire. Shown with J. B. Hull is Douglas Thomas. The circular continuous kiln operated 24 hours a day, seven days a week. The "cars" remained on a track and were continually in motion. One section of the circle was open, and this space was used to load and unload the cars as they slowly passed by. With the modern equipment in place, Hull was able to manufacture nearly 100,000 pieces of ware per week. Considered the most modern and efficient kilns of the day, tunnel kilns such as this were in almost universal use by 1947.

broke during use. The work of a die maker and mold maker was constant.

Finishing processes included trimming and removing waste material, moistening and rounding rims, scraping and smoothing cast lines and mold marks with a knife, sponging and streamlining joints, filling tiny air holes and bubbles; attaching handles, spouts, and knobs, by use of either clay slip or a modeling tool, and any other function necessary to provide quality and consistency to pottery wares. All finishing processes were completed on damp unfired greenware, which was very susceptible to crumbling and breakage.

Decorators were in great demand even with mass-produced items of the 1950s. While hand decorating gradually began being phased out, most every art line between 1950 and 1959 required some type of special hand decorating. These decorating needs included the sprayed effects of Parchment and Pine and Ebb Tide to the necessary hand detailing of New Woodland, Blossom Flite, Butterfly, and Serenade, and continued into lines of the late 1950s such as Tropicana, Tokay, and Tuscany, and additionally included many novelty items.

Tinters or spray gun operators remain active in the company longer than the hand decorators. These operators continued to decorate art, novelty, and florist lines through the late 1950s.

Production Lines of the 1950s

Hull proclaimed the theory of "security in diversification," and it certainly had the right designer and the right head salesman for the job. Hull produced a minimum of three new and different designs each year to cultivate profitable sales. New ideas, referred from Byron in New York, were designed in Crooksville. Samples were fired and returned to New York in a matter of a few weeks, ready to be shown to prospective buyers. This course continued in a pattern of one artistic design followed by another and another, in a seemingly unending line. The new, modern plant called for new, modern designs and finishes, and during the fifties, we saw everything from striking, high-gloss finishes to subtle, textured pastels.

An any given time, there were as many as half a dozen different designs in various stages of completion in the plant. Woodland, Parchment and Pine, Floral, Blue Ribbon green-banded bowls, Crescent, Swans, and novelties, along with other items, were all in production during the same period.

Woodland, introduced in thirty shapes in 1949 (listed as numbers 1 – 31, with number 20 omitted), prior to destruction of the plant, again surfaced. The company, however, was no longer carrying mold numbers 1, 5, 12, 17, 19, 21, 23, 25, and 31. This reemergence of matte Woodland in 1951 proved the delicate soft-bodied pastel glazes of Dawn Rose and Harvest Yellow could not be quickly and successfully duplicated, and Hull, with little time to spare in claiming its portion of the market, and with the urgent need to get its shipments out, decided it was time to move on and leave behind the glazes that were giving them problems.

August 29, 1951, also saw the kitchenware lines Vegetable and Floral, along with Blue Ribbon bowls, being manufactured, as well as novelty planters. The Lady basket and Lamb planters, which had been introduced in the early 1940s, were back. These novelties were underglazed in pink with red trim or ivory with blue trim. Other figural planters included three-piece Swan sets, Kitten, Parrot, Pheasant, Pig, Elephant, Country Boy, City Girl, Pup with Yarn, Kitten with Spool, a Wishing Well planter, a Ribbon wall pocket, Peacock, Flamingo vases, and others.

Parchment and Pine was manufactured beginning in 1951. Production lines began soon after the reopening of the plant. Hull advertised Parchment and Pine by saying, "Parchment...repeatedly varnished to preserve priceless contents, rolled, and yellowed with age...lends its gracefully curved beauty to this fine art pottery, with just the right touch of texture and color provided by clusters of pine and cones." Parchment and Pine remained in production until 1954.

From 1951 to 1954, Parchment and Pine, Ebb Tide, and Matte Two-Tone and Hi-Gloss Woodland headed the art market. The novelties that had been introduced in 1951 remained in production through 1952 and 1953, and a number of new items were added in late 1951 and early 1952. These items included the Bandana Ducks, Bird of Paradise and Hippo flower inserts, Unicorn and Flying Goose vases, Poodle and Giraffe vases, and others.

In 1952, Woodland entered the market in classy high-gloss glazes and was advertised as New Hi-Gloss Woodland. Brochure pages illustrated the Hi-Gloss Woodland as duotone-tinted pieces, reminiscent of earlier wares, while Two-Tone Woodland was illustrated as a one-color glazed ware with a contrasting interior color. The company later classified both decorations of Woodland in the same category, that being Hi-Gloss Woodland. Woodland headed the art market, in mattes and high glosses, from the reopening of the plant until 1954. Many of the novelty planters listed above prevailed. Just Right Floral dinnerware remained in production while Crescent was added in solid green or wine, and Debonair was presented in chartreuse and wine.

Next in line was Ebb Tide, available on January 1, 1954. The company described it by saying, "The shapes that inhabit the seas...shells, coral, fish, and plants...set the motif. Hull has captured them, in glowing colors, and fashioned them into art pottery of great beauty." This exotic line included sixteen shapes that were decorated in high-gloss Seaweed and Wine or Shrimp and Turquoise.

Although Ebb Tide was still available in 1955, the year heralded the new art design of Blossom Flite, which presented a "distinctive new rendering yet stays within the bounds of the vastly popular floral theme." Blossom Flite was available in fifteen pieces. Decorations of charcoal gray on overall high-gloss pink or blue on overall high-gloss pink with metallic green interior were available. Many of the same chain store assortments remained available, with a few new additions: the Rooster planter, Colt figurine, Siamese Cat with Kitten planter, and Knight on Horseback, to name a few. Kitchenware of the day remained Just Right Floral, Debonair in updated two-tones with banding, and nested bowls in either pink with charcoal veiling or black with pink veiling. Florist ware, referred to as the "F1 list" and the forerunner of the Imperial line, was also included in the 1955 lineup in tinted, airbrush blended, and veiled decorations.

While Blossom Flite was still being offered, the art design Butterfly was the company's major attraction for the year 1956, and it made up "the newest entrancing collection by Hull. America's finest from the kilns of Hull." Butterfly was offered in 25 pieces and was decorated in a combined gloss and matte finish of white on white, or matte white with turquoise interiors.

In 1956, the novelty ware and chain store assortments were still in abundance, but the new rage was pottery with wrought iron and brass accessories. Assortments included jardinieres in metal stands, lavabo sets in hanging racks, ashtray and planter combinations in Royal Mist glazes of pink or turquoise, airbrushed blended glazes, white on white, and the veiled decorations that were still in vogue. Jardinieres with stands were advertised as "High Fashioned, Red Hot Year Around Best Sellers" for use as porch or patio containers, cemetery urns, ice buckets, or gift ideas. A softer side of Hull was shown with Sun Valley Pastels and the Royal line, referred to as "Mist," which both entered the market in 1956. Each line included items with metal accessories. During this time, several varieties of satin-finished Madonna planters were also available.

Serenade headed Hull's art market in 1957: "Chipper chickadees on colorful boughs are the motif; fine art pottery from the kilns of Hull is the medium. The result...Serenade ...is beautiful, functional and colorful." Items with metal accessories were still in demand, and available were all the same varieties of jardinieres, ashtrays, and planters offered earlier. Three new chain store assortments emerged, Fiesta, Jubilee, and Fantasy. Sun Valley Pastels were still available in 1957, as were the various satin Madonnas, accompanied at this time by the St. Francis planter.

Sharing molds and the artware spotlight for the year 1958 were Tokay, "the zest of a gypsy dance, the warmth of fiery tokay wine," and Tuscany, "ornamental in relief with grapes and leaves from the valley of the silver Arno, bringing the peasant art of Italy to the homes of America." Tokay, "each piece trimmed in bright pleasing tints of pink and green," was also available in Milk White and Forest Green. Tuscany was available in two decorations, Sweet Pink and Gray Green or Milk White and Forest Green. Tuscany was introduced only slightly after Tokay entered the market; the dual line was most likely necessitated due to Hull serving two different syndicated buyers. By January 1, 1959, three new and distinct pieces had been added to the Tokay/Tuscany lineup. The company, "influenced by a definite trend towards larger sizes," soon added the Caladium leaf dish, a 15" pedestal vase, and a 15" pitcher to the two grape lines. By mid-1959, Tokay's pink and green combination and Tuscany's pink and gray-green combination had been discontinued, leaving both grape designs available exclusively in white and Forest Green. In 1958, the Heritageware kitchen line and the chain store assortment Mayfair entered the market.

Carryover items included Fiesta and Fantasy, along with the jardiniere assortments and ashtray and planter combinations in metal stands.

By January 1, 1959, Tropicana, "hand decorated pieces...carefree and colorful like the happy days of a Caribbean Holiday," and Continental, with its sophisticated, modern shapes in rich bold colors, were introduced. The Continental line was first available in "two strikingly lucid colors from nature...accented with rich, bold stripes." Initial colors were Persimmon, "the completely captivating accent for today's interiors in the higher key of contemporary color," and Evergreen, "a delightfully subtle color that lends itself as a perfect foil to nature's own brilliant floral and leaf displays." A third color for Continental, Mountain Blue, followed, and was characterized as "twilight in the Blue Mountains — modernized with stripes of white haze." Mayfair was still offered, as were Tokay and Tuscany, which continued to be offered only in Milk White and Forest Green.

Gold-Medal Flowerware also made its debut in 1959, and jardinieres and ashtray and planter combinations continued to be on the 1959 retail lists. While Hull had produced special items for florists throughout its tenure, and lines since the mid-1950s had included "F lists," Imperial, the first line "made especially for florists," gained attention, and was listed in 32 shapes with a 12-color glaze key.

Imperial was advertised in the following manner:

New and colorful American ceramic designs by Hull to accentuate your beautiful flowers, and priced at preinflation levels through the medium of modern methods of production. This is our response to requests from many important suppliers. Months of exhaustive study and preparation have culminated in these pieces and colors to meet all your requirements. From ordinary low cost vehicles for transporting plants, to beautiful containers for luxurious floral arrangements, you'll find everything you need and want in Imperial.

The predominate line of 1960 was Continental, and Tokay and Tuscany were still available in Milk White with Forest Green. Gold-Medal Flowerware and a variety of jardinieres and planters with metal stands remained available.

Coronet, in a new line of smoker stands and planter combinations, emerged. Pagoda, with its Oriental flair, and previously introduced novelty planters, now marked "Regal," in Milk White with green trim, were new lines in 1960.

In 1961, Capri, "inspired by the Isle of the Sun," was the last assortment truly singled out as an artware with individual identity. The year 1961 saw also the introduction of Athena, "reflecting the classic beauty and perfect proportions of Greek architecture," named for "Pallas Athena, goddess of peacetime industry. The fluted shapes, the graceful pedestals, the scrolled details were inspired by the Ionic, Doric and Corinthian columns of ancient Greece." Athena was introduced in Lilac or Spring Green with White Lava. By 1962, Athena was also offered in satin white. Other artware pieces emerged from this point to the plant's closing, all seemingly falling into the Imperial category.

There were steady parades of chain store lines throughout Hull's history; however, during the 1950s there were more shared molds, referred to by alternate names, than at any other time. Identical designs with different line names were used to serve a variety of chain stores. Many times the glaze, being the only clue, dictated the line for which the piece was actually intended.

Chain store sales representatives chose from groups of novelty wares, then designed and printed brochure pages of the lines or items they intended to retail. Buyers from the chain stores either singled out certain items for their particular sales agendas, or in some cases, opted for the entire line that Hull presented. These brochure pages were issued to all their stores and also forwarded to Hull. The reverse sides of the brochure pages sometimes contained the actual order form and an agreement between buyer and seller.

In this agreement, Hull had already dictated the minimum retail price expected for its wares. In return, Hull guaranteed to ship merchandise that met requirements of existing state and federal laws and provide articles that could be introduced into interstate commerce, more or less assigning temporary trademark rights. Hull agreed to "hold harmless and defend at its expense, the seller against all damage and expense from all claims of infringement of patents, copyrights, trademarks, or of unfair competition or bodily injuries or property damage arising out of the use, possession, consumption, or sale of said merchandise."

Chain store sales brochures read like a who's who of buyers. W. T. Grant sold a line it dubbed Mayfair, which included familiar items of Imperial, Gold-Medal Flowerware, and Fiesta. McCrory Stores Corp. advertised both a 13-piece and a 17-piece Sun Valley Pastel line, Jubilee teamed up with jardinieres with metal accessories, and a combined line that included both Fiesta and Fantasy.

McCrory-McLellan marketed Gold-Medal Flowerware and Coronet, along with several additional items with metal accessories. H. E. Stewart, buyer for S. S. Kresge Co., made it his business to specialize in Sun Valley Pastels, Jubilee, Pagoda, Fantasy, Fiesta, Gold-Medal Flowerware, and a group of jardinieres, planters, and ashtrays with brass and wrought iron accessories.

J. J. Newberry Co. retailed Sun Valley Pastels and Coronet, as well as with a few Gold-Medal Flowerware items. McLellan Stores chose to sell Jubilee. S. H. Kress & Co. did a volume of business with Jubilee and a Regal and Coronet combination. B. M. Swarzwalder sold Athena, Coronet, Gold-Medal Flowerware, and a large assortment of Regal. Rose's 5-10-25 Cent Stores Inc. marketed Gold-Medal Flowerware and Coronet. F. W. Woolworth was a leader in the sales of Flower Club Ceramics, a mixture of florist and novelty ware. H. L. Green Co. chose a mixture of Coronet, Gold-Medal Flowerware, Fiesta, and Fantasy for its lineup.

By having interspersed plain, sophisticated Imperial-type lines with its art designs throughout the 1950s, the Hull Pottery Company procured a new and demanding market in florist ware. This proved to be a successful and profitable market, and by 1960, Hull, quick to follow market trends, made the move to change total plant production to a combination of House 'n Garden serving ware and the Imperial florist line.

Times Dictate Changes in Production

In 1960, Hull, who remained at the helm, having tremendous insight into current market trends and demands, convinced board members Robert Hull, Byron Hull, Harold Showers, and J. E. Everett to make major changes in production in order to retain the company's firm economic stance. The California movement toward the casual in nearly every aspect of daily living, along with the good fortune Pfaltzgraff Pottery laid at Hull's disposal, prompted Hull to make an abrupt change from artware to dinnerware. J. B. Hull knew what the nation's market demanded from this tiny little corner of the world known as Crooksville. He was acutely aware that past style developments had moved from west to east across the country. Hull's leadership was sure and steady, but all the while adaptable to change, and so began the 25-year success story of House 'n Garden oven-proof casual serving ware.

Pfaltzgraff Pottery, whose goods were being distributed in the early 1960s to finer department stores, declined marketing its dinnerware to chain stores such as J.C. Penney, Sears, Kresge's, and five-and-dimes. Representatives from J.C. Penney asked Hull to duplicate the ware it was unable to purchase from Pfaltzgraff. J. B. Hull quickly and easily made his move to control a major portion of the dinnerware market by providing what Pfaltzgraff would not, and Hull's House 'n Garden entered the retail market by mid-1960. Pfaltzgraff soon after changed its design, leaving Hull in the market's major position to continue with the production of Mirror Brown and the other lines that followed. Through the years, J.C. Penney remained loyal to Hull and proved to be the company's largest account.

The company's first mention of color was described as "Old Fashioned Mirror-Brown, decorated with White Flow." Designed with strong masculine lines and expected to withstand constant daily use in the home or on the patio, House 'n Garden was first manufactured in what the company later decided to call Mirror Brown trimmed with Ivory Foam. Many of the original shapes remained in production throughout the pottery company's remaining years. In Hull's own words, "a few months later tangerine was added and now many items are also available in green and butterscotch. Combination of the four colors produced a Rainbow table setting unsurpassed on today's market." Rainbow House 'n Garden was offered until 1967. The company further said of the evolution of Rainbow dinnerware:

Nationwide inquiries for the famous Mirror Brown House 'n Garden serving-ware continue to be sensational.

Imitations by many manufacturers of ceramics have not suppressed consumer desires for the originals as evidenced by the ever growing demands on our facilities.

House 'n Garden serving-ware (now more than fifty items) excels for casual living — breakfast, luncheon, the patio, barbeque, at the T.V. along with table service. This serviceable ware is made for the American way of life — you'll like it in the living room or under the sheltering sky.

For those who want a more colorful effect, many items are also available in Tangerine, Butterscotch, and Green which together with Mirror Brown produce a four color Rainbow Table.

Beginning with colors that could be mixed and matched, glazes were formulated for House 'n Garden colors that could be used as companions to the standard Mirror Brown, such as the Rainbow table setting in which Mirror Brown was teamed with Butterscotch, Tangerine, and Green Agate.

Two colors of Rainbow, Tangerine and Green Agate, graduated to become separate lines of dinnerware, available to the consumer as complete sets. Green Agate, in an entire set, became known as Country Squire. Tangerine, identified as the 900 series, was further billed as Burnt Orange in an assortment made specifically for J.C. Penney. For promotional sales, Tri-City Grocers advertised its 50th Anniversary gala with Tangerine House 'n Garden, which was referred to as Golden Anniversary.

Hull's casual, down-to-earth dinnerware line was an instant success, not only with J.C. Penney, but with other retailers as well, and new shapes were continually added to the more than 40 companion kitchenware items. By the late 1960s, House 'n Garden included over 100 items.

Provincial, which advertised improved features for "perfect mixing and refrigeration," was offered from January 1, 1961, through 1963. This was the name used for Hull's Mirror Brown House 'n Garden with Milk White interiors and lids. The faces of dinner plates and saucers were additionally glazed in white, while the reverse sides remained Mirror Brown. Provincial was inspired by another manufacturer's design called Brown-Stone, which was brown glazed ware with chartreuse-glazed interiors. The Caladium leaf was used in Provincial in stark white as a chip 'n dip. J.C. Penney, J. J. Newberry Co., and other major chain stores were the main customers of Provincial. New sales were cultivated from retail firms and grocers that used Hull's dinnerware as give-aways and promotional items.

Hull's House 'n Garden competed with other manufactured dinnerware lines at showrooms in most major cities, including the Atlantic City shows, the National Housewares Show, the Chicago Gift Show, and the New York Gift Show, year after year, for 25 years. Byron Hull was always in attendance at these shows as salesman for the company, accompanied by John Everett and Marvin Hoffman. Moderately priced House 'n Garden ware by Hull was advertised to buyers as "an invitation to bigger, more profitable sales."

Crestone, a newly designed casual line for 1965, entered the market in lovely high-gloss turquoise with ivory foam. Crestone was considered "the new and fashionable way of life, thirty beautiful items designed specifically for present day living habits in the breakfast nook, on the patio, at the T.V. or barbeque, as well as normal table service." The Crestone dinnerware line was in production for only two years.

Hull also entered into a campaign effort headed by the National Association of Variety Stores, Inc., for promotion of its products, which proved to result in, in Hull's own words, "extraordinary volume." In 1966, Hull's sales were equal to Pfaltzgraff's. Each company reported $1,000,000 in sales.

In 1961, a House 'n Garden display by S. H. Kress advertised "Today's Best Buys — Outstanding Money Saving Values" from 29¢ to $2.49 each, and illustrated the versatility of Hull's wares in a patio barbecue or picnic setting.

This photograph, taken May 2, 1965, by the *Zanesville Times Recorder*, shows President J. B. Hull in the conference room of the Hull plant, where wares were displayed in showcase fashion. Hull examines Crestone's chip 'n dip with vice president Robert W. Hull and secretary-treasurer E. D. Young. The shelved showcase in the background housed Mirror Brown House 'n Garden.

Mirror Brown was the standard for House 'n Garden for 25 years, while other colors danced their way in and out of Hull's production. Hull believed in, and followed, a pattern of adapting to change in order to maintain the status House 'n Garden dinnerware held in the market, and the company continuously added new items. J. B. Hull asked of his already established trade, "Why new items?" This question was best answered in his own words:

The new items illustrated are meant to make sure that the consuming public does not have to turn to any other source to complete its casual serving and kitchenware needs.

The sole object is to maintain consumer enthusiasm and preference for the nation's number one line, instead of the normal reason for offering new items, to stimulate sales, which we all realize would not contribute to our present welfare.

But we are taking nothing for granted so far as the future is concerned and we are fortunately in a position to be very selective in our choice of patterns. Time and the privilege to choose from innumerable ideas and sketches is on our side so long as consumer acceptance through willing buyers remains at, or near, its present level.

We are proceeding with dies and molds in anticipation of favorable reaction to these offerings.

In 1968, Avocado with ivory trim was a part of Hull's dinnerware lineup. Hull advertised its most popular shapes in this timely color, formulated surely in an effort to follow the trend of avocado kitchen appliances. Could there possibly be a homemaker who wouldn't be smitten by a lovely set of avocado dinnerware to match her appliances? Hull didn't think so, and his vision was correct, as Avocado continued in production until May 15, 1971.

Hull provided House 'n Garden to chain store buyers both large and small: F. W. Woolworth Co.; King's Dept. Stores; Victory Merchandise Mart; Meadow Sales Company; E. A. Hinrichs & Co.; Neisner Brothers, Inc.; Nobel, Inc.; The 2800 Shop; S. E. Nichols, Inc.; J. A. Tepper Co.; S. S. Pennock Co.; G. C. Murphy Co.; Standard Drug Co.; Ben Franklin Stores; and more.

Orders were being placed by Canadian customers as well. Thomas A. Ivey & Sons, Ltd., of Port Dover, Ontario, and D. H. Lisser & Company, Ltd., of Montreal, Quebec, were two of Hull's Northern buyers.

House 'n Garden glazes were tested and approved under the guidance of U.S.P.A. working with the Federal Food and Drug Administration, which permitted a lead emission of seven parts per million (7 ppm). Hull's dinnerware tested at one hundredth of one part per million (.01 ppm), which was next to nothing and was far below the established safety level.

J. B. Hull was spearheading an effort to upgrade ware leaving the plant and had extensive conveying equipment installed in order to accomplish all sorting of ware during the normal daytime hours. J. B. Hull reported, "A silly union inspired labor board decision prevented us from obtaining acceptable supervisory judgment by the former round-the-clock method."

The Hen on Nest casseroles entered the marketplace in 1968, and in 1969, Hull added the two larger bakers with figural chicken bases. These bakers, one 2" deep and the other 3" deep, each had an incised rooster design in the bowl of the dish. An oval individual salad bowl, with the same incised rooster, complimented.

To renew interest in sales, Hull also presented at this time a corn serving dish, a gravy boat with an extremely elongated handle, a double serving dish, and a tray that had been teamed with a sauce bowl to become a chip 'n dip. Several of these items had become obsolete by December 1, 1970: the tray and sauce bowl, the double serving dish, and the individual salad with rooster decor.

In 1970, Hull had more than one thousand customers who, collectively, disposed of nearly three million dollars worth of ware annually at retail prices. Despite labor and management disagreements and rising costs of raw materials, the company assumed and maintained an enviable sales position throughout J. B. Hull's tenure as president of Hull. In September 1970, House 'n Garden casual serving ware and kitchenware was available in over 60 shapes and constituted 70 percent of the company's total production.

Hull forwarded to distributors price quotations that became effective on December 1, 1971. Inflation was a fact of life, uncontrolled by any type of business or service; however, Hull felt a need to give customers an explanation for the rise in prices:

The enclosed quotations represent in large measure the increase granted labor the second year of our three-year union shop agreement.

Of course our sources of raw material are in the same bind and in many cases their increases now come to us on postal cards, seeming to take for granted that this is simply our new way of life.

All we can do is to ask that you please bear with us as we continue a policy of adjusting prices to meet conditions over which we have the most limited control.

January 1, 1972, saw J. B. Hull further reconciling any differences with customers with an additional notification:

Prices quoted are in compliance with Executive Order No. 11627, and if any price is found to be illegal, resulting in a price roll back, refund will be made of any such overcharge(s).

Established through collective bargaining the second year of our three year labor contract exceeds the government guide line but has been granted to labor by law.

We now find ourselves in the position of having to attempt next year's production on the basis of a 3% price increase which is less than half what is needed to continue the normal advancement of our business.

It is no secret that government guide lines were established on the basis of big business where labor is generally less than 30% of their costs but this does not apply to our business in which labor exceeds 50%. Nevertheless, we are caught in the process and will have to absorb the losses a price increase of only 3% will bring about. The increase will not become effective until March 1, 1972.

The investment and added yearly expense to improve the quality of ware combined with the fact that government controls prevent us from seeking equitable price adjustment establishes an unprecedented challenge to management.

Thank you very much for all past business and for whatever consideration you choose to extend to us at this time. We will surely do our best to justify your confidence whenever offered the opportunity.

Hull discontinued the larger chicken servers with incised decoration effective March 1, 1972, in order to make way for the introduction of items 5280, 5770, 5840, and 5950, the newly designed Chicken and Duck casseroles.

At the same time the success of Hull's dinnerware and florist ware was unquestioned by a nation of consumers, Hull Pottery Company employees began to question their employment rights. The company was plagued by employee strikes throughout the 1970s and 1980s, eight to be exact. Inflation created rising costs of the product, and this, along with plant shutdowns and workers' demands (which had to be met in some form), put the company in a precarious position. J. B. Hull begged the indulgence of consumers after a seven-week strike.

Wages, still under government control on November 1, 1974, prompted Hull to again appeal to his consumer audience for their continued consideration:

In spite of the good intentions of our national governing body and the degree of stability needed, the only thing that keeps a business going is the difference between costs and selling prices, now, not some time in the future.

This is true because we have consistently followed a conservative policy of pricing that prevented an accumulation of funds sufficient to carry us over a prolonged period of time.

Therefore, our well-intentioned plan to delay price adjustment to late next year must be interrupted to meet cost increases forced upon us by the raw material sources of supply necessary in our operation together with labor costs established under government guide lines (before they were removed) causing anticipated cost of production to be far out of line.

This explanation may seem as an apology, and indeed it is, since it causes you to, again, have to decide whether or not our line is worth the all-too-often revision of prices. Naturally, we hope it is worth both the inconvenience and new quotations.

We are definitely holding to a company policy of turning away from new potential trade, both national and international, and are putting great emphasis on the quality of ware being sent to your stores. Nobody can be perfect in the production and inspection of thousands of pieces daily, but we are resisting a trend, prevalent in the country today, to cheapen the line for any reason whatsoever. This puts a burden on supervisors and the ceramic department as we encounter both prices and shortages of raw materials.

Continued additional cost adjustments prompted the company to send Byron Hull to J.C. Penney representatives on September 15, 1975, with new price quotations. This was followed by a letter from J. B. Hull to John Fuchs, J.C. Penney Company, New York, dated October 1, 1975:

The necessity for price advancement causes us to restate an important part of our company policy.

We have consistently rejected the opportunity to substitute lower cost materials that have a bearing on quality in the belief that a better made and better appearing line will continue to lead over-the-counter sales. And we will pursue this policy so long as the consuming public through willing buyers decides that our line is worth the needed price adjustments.

Many years ago when industry appeared to exercise too much control over the economy, Federal Laws governing monopolies came into existence. And similar treatment will have to be exercised over organized labor if we are to prevent the never ending upward movement of prices.

Our past fiscal year dollar sales figure was up but profits down with full factory operation which means that we absorbed a greater portion of increased costs of both raw materials and labor than quotations were expected to produce. Therefore, this present increase represents the third year wage increase in our labor contract, along with an effort towards partial recovery of lost profits.

And this is important because there is no way under existing circumstances for us (a union shop) to acquire contracts without granting higher wages which means higher prices. And we need not point out that only profitable companies can continue as your sources of supply.

For more than six years we have turned away from new potential trade and will continue this policy until normal 30 day deliveries can be accomplished. Our principal concern is that the consuming public can be reached for final judgment as to the worth of our line which is only possible under our present policy through sources similar to the one you represent. And beyond this is the expectation that we will remain able to furnish readily saleable ware.

In 1975, the company's dinnerware production now totalled nearly 75 percent of the company's total output. The company continued its vigorous advertising campaigns: "Open stock House 'n Garden offers startersets, dinnersets, party-packs and many more appealing serving pieces and they are all ovenproof. The American homemaker has chosen Hull's House 'n Garden for today's casual way of life, its popularity has earned it its rightful place as a nation's number one line." At this time, 75 all-purpose pieces of House 'n Garden were available in Hull's extensive open stock.

In that same year, the village of Crooksville was accorded a certificate of official recognition by the American Revolution Bicentennial Administration as a bicentennial community. The Crooksville-Roseville area Pottery Festival Association agreed to sanction the 10th Annual Pottery Festival as a bicentennial event. The Hull Pottery Company produced a Mirror Brown line to honor the bicentennial; however, it was never in full production, nor did it enter the retail market. A company brochure page was designed, and Hull intended to sell this ware in 16-piece sets consisting of the plain Mirror Brown dinner and salad plates, and specially designed mugs and fruits with an embossed eagle and star decoration. Hull also planned to sell 12-piece sets that included the plain Mirror Brown dinner plates teamed with the bicentennial fruits and mugs. Additional accessory items included a creamer and covered sugar set, a shaker set, a jumbo stein, a 2-quart pitcher, a 4-pint casserole, and a 5-pint bean pot.

Although new colors and styles of dinnerware were being market tested all across the United States, the standard House 'n Garden in Mirror Brown, still a major seller in the States, was a new sensation in Australia, where it was being sold at in-home parties.

Popularity of the Mirror Brown glaze remained unquestioned, as Hull was contracted to glaze and fire porcelain drawer pulls by the thousands. Wisconsin Porcelain initially contracted for Hull to glaze and fire 10,000 drawer pulls, and second and third orders, for 30,000 and 50,000, followed. The company received the drawer pulls already molded and in greenware form. After the glazing and firing processes, Hull shipped them to the Amerock Corporation of Rockford, Illinois. There they were given metal accessories and marketed.

During experiments in the spring of 1978, the round canister set in Mirror Brown was on the firing line. A few months later production lines were ready, but not without much controversy over shape, size, and the fact the canisters had no handles; practicality was questioned. The Hull Pottery Company went so far as to invite ladies in to make certain they could easily lift and use the largest canister when it was filled to the brim with flour. There were additional problems related to production after the company made the decision to move forward. The sides caved in quite easily during the finishing processes of trimming and sponging. Workers found it nearly impossible to keep the canister bowls round, which of course led to still another problem — improperly fitting lids. The company was also responsible for the production of additional innovative accessory items such as a spoon rest, an egg plate, a fish platter, a Gingerbread Man server, and a handled tray. Problems within the plant did not keep J. B. Hull from issuing new items. Although Hull wasn't soliciting new customers, he was certainly attempting to offer updated styles to create a continuing interest in Mirror Brown.

J. B. Hull's Death Leaves Company with Unpredictable Future

The production move to the innovative idea of casual serving ware, combined with the massive Imperial florist line, served as J. B. Hull's final chapter in leading the company. J. Brannon Hull died June 23, 1978, leaving the Hull Pottery Company unprepared for what was to come. Although knowing all Hulls of the pottery region were decidedly aged, the company's stockholders had made no provisions that would provide strong leadership to move the family pottery tradition forward in time. At the time, the seventy-three-year-old company, in which the family's interest had prevailed, was naive, almost helpless, concerning outside enterprises. Security within the family had cushioned the pottery from the rest of the world; stockholders failed to realize that the interests of a family-owned operation would most likely not remain the same when outsiders entered this protected circle. After Hull's death, consumers and local craftsmen alike pondered the outcome of a company, not only famous for its artware production, but also a leader in the manufacture of dinnerware and florist ware.

J. B. Hull never forgot that the company's success was based on customer satisfaction, and adamantly regarded the customer as number one. He reminded his employees of this on a daily basis with an enlarged letter on posterboard that was positioned inside the plant workers' area very near the time clock. It read:

To All Employees:
Our customers are our life line for job security and continued happiness for our families.
Keeping customers satisfied is everybody's business.
As long as we continue to do the best we know how our customers will remain loyal. Customers respond to better products — better service with more business.
More business keeps each of us working.
There's real satisfaction for all of us when we keep customers satisfied.
Sincerely,
J. B. Hull

Although Marie Hannum (Mrs. J. Brannon) Hull had controlling stock in the company, in 1978 management shifted to the hands of Henry Sulens, named the new president. Robert W. Hull served as chairman of the board; Byron Hull, vice president and sales manager; and Harold Showers, vice president and plant manager.

This was only the second time in the company's history that a Hull had not personally headed the firm. Adapting to change was difficult for Hull employees, as they found it difficult to relate to outsider Sulens, who was not a pottery man and was not from the Ohio pottery region.

Management and personnel had many disputes, and despite negotiations, employee strikes increased. At times there was harmony within the pottery, and the firm was profitable; at other times, the company lost as much as $100,000 in a year. During this period, the loss of work due to employee strikes caused the company to lose ground with solid, repeat customers. Many major contracts were lost, never to be regained. Hull was at this time centering primary interest — nearly 90 percent, in fact — on the production of dinnerware.

Early 1981 began with a three-month employee strike, and Henry Sullens left his position as Hull president.

Larry Taylor replaced Henry Sulens on May 26, 1981. According to Taylor, the company had lost $10,000 in May 1981 alone and never made a profit after that time. Taylor reports that the reason the company became stagnate was because it had not taken on any new accounts for nearly seven years. J. B. Hull had stated that no major accounts had been recruited since 1969. Due to union disputes, labor strikes, and increased costs due to inflation, Hull wisely felt obligated to serve present customers before adding new customers, which would create even more delays in services. The company had been unable to provide timely services for several years, and Hull believed more business would have only added to the number of problems the pottery faced.

J. B. Hull carried the company successfully through many years of diverse production. He remained president of the company until his death in 1978. Hull is shown with the three-piece Swan set made throughout his tenure as president of the firm. These swans became as recognizable as the Hull logo itself, and continue to serve as symbols of the Hull Pottery Company.

The company needed leadership, but more than that, it needed to revive the pottery worker's spirit of craftsmanship and pride for a livelihood that had kept the Ohio Valley in business since the early bluebird potteries. Workers and retailers alike waited for a miracle, wondering if this much-needed revival would take place.

Taylor, the first to admit he was not a potter, set forth to build on the solid reputation and respect Hull had earned from past years as a major supplier of quality dinnerware and florist ware. What Taylor failed to realize was that at this time, Hull Pottery was enmeshed in problems that were far beyond his ability to solve.

No doubt the gravest situation involved a letter from the Environmental Protection Agency instructing the company to clean up lead wastes in and around the plant. According to Taylor, this letter, delivered in April 1981, remained unnoticed for nearly a year. With the EPA left unnoticed, Taylor focused his attention on employees and production.

Jack Frame came into the business as Taylor's vice president on July 13, 1981, and a short time later also served as plant superintendent, taking the place of Harold "Slim" Showers. Under new management, changes were made. In years past, company employees had been allowed to work far into their senior years; many worked well into their eighties. While new management allowed employees to remain gainfully employed for a number of years, mandatory retirement was set at age seventy, and tenured employees were released.

There were also major differences of opinion that kept the company from moving ahead. Although the company was responsible for 2,000 ware presses per day, Taylor believed the company's production could be more efficient with a semiautomatic jigger installed; the ram presses would then be left free for even greater output. Jack Frame, the plant superintendent, believed a smaller kiln was necessary for a more profitable year-end picture. With sales down, the great tunnel kiln was deemed worthless by Frame for a profitable operation. Once the kiln was lit, it burned continuously, 365 days per year. In the event of a kiln rack, in which the kiln cars came off the track, a complete cool-down was necessary while the cars were rebuilt. The company lost several production days due to any kiln rack. Operational costs to fire the kiln were in excess of $10,000 per month, and it was estimated that in order to justify its operation, it was necessary to make $3,000,000 in sales per year. Hull had not produced this sales volume since the early 1970s. Decisions for change were left unmade, and Hull struggled with current equipment and operations.

An inventory was made, and Taylor soon found several ideas for production that had been shelved with no follow-through, ideas that may have worked in an earlier day, but which were now considered out-of-date. Although a few of these designs, such as the souffle dish, were expanded upon and used, fresh, innovative ideas were imperative. Larry Taylor retained Louise Bauer as designer, but when converting production to entirely new dinnerware lines, the company hired freelance designer Maury Mountain, known for creating the popular Pfaltzgraff designs.

To compliment yet another trend in colored kitchen appliances, Taylor initiated dinnerware in a glaze of Mirror Almond with Caramel trim. First shipments were made in mid-1981, after a few minor problems of glaze bubbling had been solved. Although appreciative of the Almond glaze, Byron Hull didn't care for the contrasting caramel trim and asked for his dinnerware set to be without the decoration. Items such as a round one-piece sectional server, a rectangular bake dish, and squat condiment shakers without the caramel trim were marketed in Ohio's area pottery retail stores. These items were special orders for a restaurant chain and did not carry the Hull trademark. The sectional server was marketed with a metal base provided by Chromex of Cleveland, Ohio. The Almond glaze was produced and marketed for nearly two years.

In 1982, Don Foulds, a retired ceramic engineer from Cleveland, moved to the Crooksville area after his expertise was retained by Hull Pottery. Foulds had brought with him 29 years' experience in glaze formulas, and reportedly, there was no glaze this man could not formulate. By this time, the Environmental Protection Agency had made clear its demands for lead cleanup at the pottery, and since lead had been found in Hull's glazes, Foulds's first task was to formulate a glaze that was lead free.

The EPA spotlight posed problems that were immense. If the EPA's letter regarding the new legislation for the cleanup had been adhered to in a timely manner, all could have been saved. Hull would have been afforded the same time period for waste cleanup as other potteries. Regardless of management transition, and Taylor's good intentions to make up for lost time, the government considered the pottery's dealings concerning cleanup a blatant refusal to adhere to law. When the EPA tested, it found lead in Hull's glazes, the same glazes that were being poured down drains within the plant. The same lead glazes that eventually settled in the waste lagoon adjacent to the plant property.

Management centered major emphasis on the talented pottery craftsmen of the Ohio Valley, and credit given to fine craftsmen was enlisted in all phases of Hull's advertising campaigns. With a renewed meaning for the pride and craftsmanship of the potter, the Potter-at-Wheel logo was relied on even more in these modern times. The addition of "Crooksville, Ohio" or "Crooksville, O." to all newly designed molds and any molds that were updated or retooled further promoted the local pottery region.

The Ridge Collection was in production nearly three years. Shipments of Ridge began in the spring of 1982. Ridge was advertised as being "a unique blend of contemporary style and country flavor. This highly functional casual servingware is produced with much the same care and artful expertise as our other pottery items." Ridge's name was derived from its distinctive ridged edges and also from the various local geographical ridges found in the Crooksville, Ohio, area. For this line, the new glazes of Tawny Ridge (tan) and Flint Ridge (gray) joined Hull's standard brown, now referred to in this line as Walnut Ridge. Many molds were restyled; the flat pieces such as plates were a little deeper and were ridged on their outer edges. New shapes emerged for bowls and shaker sets. Taylor reported that accounts had been enlisted with J.C. Penney and Woolworth Stores — at that time, the only national chains involved with the company.

Due in part to lost business accounts, Hull's advertising campaigns found it necessary to prove a point, and once again appealed heavily to the consumer, as it had with the initial introduction of House 'n Garden:

The Hull Pottery Company was founded in 1903 [taking credit for Acme Pottery's beginning, rather than Hull's, which was 1905], producing kitchenware, florist-ware, and many patterns of artware. Hull Pottery has grown considerably since then, but continues many of the same traditions of craftsmanship and artful exper-tise. This new, highly functional, casual serving-ware is the culmination of many years of skill and knowledge.

Your Ridge Collection casual serving-ware is a natural for the freezer, the oven, the micro wave, conventional ovens, the dishwasher, and, of course, the table. All Ridge Collection pieces are dishwasher safe and resist marring from everyday use. If items do become moderately scratched or dull, the original gloss can be restored by using a mild, powdered cleanser. You will notice some minor differences in color, size, and shape. This is very normal and characteristic of handcrafted pottery such as your Ridge Collection serving-ware. Due to the nature of ceramics, care should also be taken to protect fine wood furniture from being scratched by the "foot" or bottom edges of your serving-ware. Care is taken at the factory to make the bottoms as smooth as possible.

Taylor took the 11" serving tray that was first introduced in 1978 and saw to it that it was glazed in colors other than Mirror Brown, those being Tawny Ridge and Flint Ridge. When first introduced, it was made to use in both microwave and conventional ovens. But alas, this item came to bear, almost as an instruction, the incised mark "Serving Tray" on its base due to consumer use on the range top, which often led to breakage. The earlier manufactured trays were not marked with the "Serving Tray" logo.

The Gingerbread Man server had been placed in produc-tion before Taylor's term of presidency. And now it too was being glazed in the Ridge colors. Taylor saw a need to expand this idea, and Louise Bauer designed the cookie jar as a companion piece in 1982. The cookie jar proved suc-cessful, and soon afterward, a bowl, a mug, and a coaster/spoon rest appeared on the market. This animated design soon gave way to production of a train canister set, with Taylor setting the mode. His idea included bulging, ani-mated characters that looked as though they had stepped straight from a comic strip. Taylor, although still not quite satisfied as to the animals' appearances, set out a limited production run, which was discontinued by employee strike. Taylor's next step, which had already been planned, was to

include Gingerbread Junction, a train station house, in the train canister set. Although dies and molds were made for both this and a candy dish, the pieces were never finalized or trialed for production within the plant.

Taylor further commissioned Maury Mountain to design an entirely new dinnerware, also referred to as part of the Hull Collection, glazed in Mirror Brown. This dinnerware was designed in fluid lines, with a concentric band of rings added to plates, cups, bowls, and other pieces. Hull lines Heartland and Country Belle also benefited from the banded molds, although each kept a separate and distinct glaze and color treatment.

Heartland, a hand-stamped brown heart design on a satin background of cream with gold shadings, exhibited a distinctive country look. In this line, the bulbous-shaped can-isters with banded tops were used, rather than the plain, cylinder-shaped Ridge canisters. Canister jars were stamped "flour," "sugar," "coffee," and "tea," and companion jars for baked beans, chowder, chili, and cookies were available. Embossed, or raised, lettering had been used in many previ-ous kitchenware designs; however, this was the first time in many years that stamped lettering appeared on shakers and jars. Heartland was in production from late 1983 to early 1985, with large volumes being sold to major chain stores such as Wal-Mart and J.C. Penney, neither of which, at this time, was listed as a syndicate buyer.

The final line produced by Hull, Country Belle, was glazed in a classic winter white, alleged by Taylor to match the glaze of Lenox china. This dinnerware line epitomized the combination of class and style. Country Belle had a clas-sic flair combined with an air of country serenity, and was decorated with a blue underglaze floral stamp of trailing blue-bell florals. The Lenox look of this glaze is most apparent in the No. 7 Swan, which complemented this line. Hull's Coun-try-Belle brochure pages had been photographed and a limit-ed number were produced. The complementary swan was also a part of the promotional advertising for this line, although it had first been introduced as part of the Medley chain store assortment in 1962. Country Belle was made in limited quantities and was in production no more than six months. There was little or no chance to promote this din-nerware before the company closed.

The Pfaltzgraff influence was quite apparent in Heartland and Country Belle, as both were designed by Maury Moun-tain, Pfaltzgraff's former designer. Some of Hull's old stan-dards, the casseroles with chicken and duck covers, were additionally decorated in the Heartland and Country Belle glaze treatments. The 32 oz. covered casserole came from a shelf of discontinued molds. This casserole had first been introduced in the 1965 Crestone line; the lid's handle provides the proof. The newly molded souffle and quiche dishes offered in these lines were further evidence of Pfaltzgraff's influence.

Stressed management and labor relationship continued to make all of Crooksville uneasy. This, combined with decreased production, loss in contracts, and the fact that foreign-made wares were less costly to manufacture, made any attempt of stability by providing new lines and new marketing strategies futile. The new lines introduced had promise of becoming successful under normal conditions. However, issues surrounding the company were anything but normal. Problems within the plant greatly affected production output, which could have been close to 50,000 pieces per day.

Hull faced continuing problems with the EPA, which ultimately, beginning in 1981, resulted in federal court litigation. The outcome resulted in a two-year cleanup effort that

cost $150,000. Additional to this expense were court costs and fees for attorneys, engineers, and expert witnesses. The final figures were staggering, and according to Taylor, an upwards of a quarter of a million dollars was necessary for this purpose. The funds needed for the EPA cleanup were taken from the operations money of the pottery plant. The drastic reduction of operations money put yet another hardship on the already strained economics of the firm.

The Hull Pottery Succumbs

After having navigated the early, uncertain years with numerous area competitors of the pottery trade, the uncertainty of the Depression years, reduced output and decreased materials necessary for the war effort, disastrous flood and fire, conflicts over reconstruction of the plant, shaken stability due to loss of family leaders, numerous employee layoffs and strikes, and monumental problems with the Environmental Protection Agency, the Hull Pottery Company could withstand no more.

Hopes that ran high were soon doused, and the fate of the pottery operations that once gave the village and surrounding area potters their much-needed employment was now certain. Hull Pottery would not regain its status in the pottery manufacturing field. There would be no more glaze fired after August 6th, 1985, when 25 employees began an eighth strike. This strike centered on negotiations for increased holiday and insurance benefits; it did not concern employee pay.

Whether it was a case of a company and its officials too weary to fight any longer, or just plain economics, a tired old company closed its doors. The walls within, as well as the townspeople in the small village of Crooksville, Ohio, continued to hope for a miracle, believing this was not a fitting end

to the pottery tradition or to the area craftsmen who had made Hull a showplace in the "pottery center of the world".

It was traditional for a pottery to fire the ware left inside a kiln, even during a strike. With pottery operations discontinued almost overnight, Hull's kiln was filled with ware that was reportedly fired by a handful of kiln workers in this pottery tradition.

The official letter that allowed the company to close down picket lines and gave employees the opportunity to receive unemployment benefits was drafted March 24, 1986.

My last glimpse of the pottery came in 1986, and the sight was foreign to me. Walking through the vacant plant, making sure to avoid the clay slip on the concrete floors, brought to mind those days of a busy and bustling pottery. While memories of sights and sounds were deafening, now all was silent and still. Gone was the factory's usual busy state of workmen pouring liquid slip into the molds, ram presses at work, ladies trimming and sponging ware, overhead conveyor belts loaded with pottery items, workmen busy with packaging for shipment, and of course, pottery craftsmen who took time to shut down their machines or just stop what they were doing, look up, smile, and explain their particular areas of expertise.

Color Album of Pottery

From the company's inception, with its production of stoneware and porcelain in art and utility lines, to its later

production of lusterwares, tile, and novelties, Hull Pottery encompassed American craftsmanship at its best.

Plate 15.
Row 1:
1 – 4. Decorated jardinieres, "534 (H)," 4½", $20.00 – 30.00 each.
Row 2:
1 – 2. Blended jardinieres, "364 (H)," 4½", $30.00 – 40.00 each.
3 – 5. Sweet Potato/Ivy jars, "544 (H)," 4", $95.00 – 140.00 each.
Row 3:
1 – 2. Flower pots and attached saucers, "539 (H)," 6½",
$40.00 – 60.00 each.
3 – 5. Flower pots and attached saucers, "534 (H)," 5½",
$35.00 – 45.00 each.
Row 4:
1. Jardiniere, "846 (H)," 7½", $80.00 – 120.00.
2. Jardiniere, "546 (H)," 4", $40.00 – 55.00.
3. Jardiniere, "546 (H)," 5½", $50.00 – 75.00.
4. Jardiniere, "546 (H)," 7½", $80.00 – 120.00.
5. Jardiniere, "551 (H)," 7½", $75.00 – 100.00.
6. Jardiniere, "550 (H)," 7½", $75.00 – 100.00.

Row 5:
1. Jardiniere, "536 (H)," 5½", $40.00 – 65.00.
2. Jardiniere, "536 (H)," 7½", $75.00 – 110.00.
3. Jardiniere, "536 (H)," 5½", $40.00 – 65.00.
4. Jardiniere, "536 (H)," 7½", $75.00 – 110.00.
5. Jardiniere, "536 (H)," 5½", $40.00 – 65.00.
6. Jardiniere, "536 (H)," 7½", $75.00 – 110.00.
Row 6:
1. Yellow ware bowls, "421 (H)," 5", $25.00 – 35.00; 6",
$25.00 – 35.00; 7", $35.00 – 45.00; 8", $40.00 – 60.00;
9", $40.00 – 60.00.
2. Porcelain bowls, "30 (H)," 4½", $25.00 – 30.00; 5½", $25.00 –
30.00; 6½", $25.00 – 40.00; 7½", $25.00 – 40.00.
3. Stoneware bowls, "429 (H)," 5", $25.00 – 35.00; 6", $25.00 –
35.00; 7", $35.00 – 45.00; 8", $40.00 – 60.00; 9",
$40.00 – 60.00.

No. 534. 4½ inch Jardinieres, Hand Decorated

No. 364. 4½ inch Blended Jardinieres

No. 544. Sweet Potato or Ivy Jar with Chains

No. 539. 6½ inch Flower Pots Saucers Attached

No. 534. 5½ inch Flower Pots with Saucers

No. 846. 7½ inch Jardiniere

No. 546. 4, 5½, 7½ inch Blended Jardinieres

No. 551. 7½ inch Jardiniere

No. 550. 7½ inch Jardiniere

No. 536. 5½ and 7½ inch Jardinieres

No. 421A. Bowls

No. 30. Bowls (Ovenproof)

No. 429. Bowls (Green)

Plate 15.

51

The Early Years
(1905 – 1940)

Hull's early years of utility wares, art forms, and tile showcased diversity, craftsmanship, and pride. First emphasis was on the manufacture of stoneware, used by most people every day. However, soon recognizing a nationwide trend towards cleaner lines, Hull began manufacturing porcelain wares. Embossed patterns were used interchangeably for stoneware and porcelain bodies. Solid and blended glazes were used in striking high glosses as well as satin mattes. By the late twenties, Hull's manufacture included floor, wall, and ornamental tile.

The thirties were a time of change, with emphasis moving to artwares in an effort to keep abreast with foreign trade. Kitchenware remained a staple, with artwares alongside in brilliant, colorful hues, rich with texture. By the latter thirties, art lines rose in number and were supplemented by novelty animals and planters.

Cereal Ware

PRODUCTION DATES: 1915 – 1935

TRADEMARKS: None.

These cereal ware items are unmarked; however, they consistently bear the same type of glazed bases.

The cereal ware illustrated is of white semiporcelain body; decals were underglazed and appeared only on the face side of the ware. Decals were used both in single and double border treatments. Company information indicated that double border decals were more costly than single border decals, that difference being $1.00 more per 15-piece set. Decal lettering is black in color and appears in script form. The illustrated square cereal sets consisted of 15 pieces: six canisters (sugar, flour, rice, cereal, coffee, and tea), six spice jars (ginger, nutmeg, cinnamon, allspice, mustard, and pepper), a vinegar cruet, an oil cruet, and a salt box. The square cereal ware sets were initially sold in sets of 12, 14, and 15 pieces. Later, cereal ware was available in open stock, and the consumer was able to choose specific desired items.

Decalcomania designs used on square cereal ware sets included, but were not limited to, Blue Bird in Flight, Perched Blue Bird, Conventional Rose, Conventional Tile, Conventional Vine, Delft, Drape and Festoon, Blue Grecian Border, Gold Grecian Border, Blue Star and Lattice, Gold Star and Lattice, Plain, Parrot, Scroll, and Classic.

Plate 16.
Row 1:
1. Blue Star and Lattice spice jar, "Ginger," 4¾",
   $40.00 – 55.00.
2. Blue Star and Lattice spice jar, "Allspice," 4¾", $40.00 – 55.00.
3. Blue Star and Lattice spice jar, "Nutmeg," 4¾", $40.00 – 55.00.
4. Blue Star and Lattice spice jar, "Cinnamon," 4¾", $40.00 – 55.00.
5. Blue Star and Lattice spice jar, "Pepper," 4¾", $40.00 – 55.00.
6. Blue Star and Lattice spice jar, "Mustard," 4¾", $40.00 – 55.00.
Row 2:
1. Plain spice jar, "Nutmeg," 4¾", $40.00 – 55.00.
2. Blue Grecian canister, "Cereal," 8½", $55.00 – 85.00.
3. Drape and Festoon spice jar, "Cinnamon," 4¾", $40.00 – 55.00.
4. Drape and Festoon spice jar, "Allspice," 4¾", $40.00 – 55.00.
5. Drape and Festoon spice jar, "Ginger," 4¾", $40.00 – 55.00.
6. Gold Grecian canister, "Cereal," 8½", $50.00 – 80.00.
7. Gold Grecian spice jar, "Mustard," 4¾", $40.00 – 55.00.
Row 3:
1. Flying Blue Bird spice jar, "Nutmeg," 4¾", $50.00 – 70.00.
2. Flying Blue Bird canister, "Coffee," 8 ½", $65.00 – 95.00.
3. Flying Blue Bird canister, "Tea," 8½", $65.00 – 95.00.
4. Flying Blue Bird canister, "Rice," 8½", $65.00 – 95.00.
5. Flying Blue Bird spice jar, "Ginger," 4¾", $50.00 – 70.00.
Row 4:
1. Conventional Rose spice jar, "Allspice," 4¾",
   $40.00 – 55.00.
2. Conventional Rose spice jar, "Ginger," 4¾", $40.00 – 55.00.
3. Conventional Rose spice jar, "Cinnamon," 4¾",
   $40.00 – 55.00.
4. Conventional Rose cruet, "Oil," 9¾", $100.00 – 150.00.
5. Conventional Rose salt box, "Salt," 6¾", $125.00 – 155.00.
6. Conventional Rose cruet, "Vinegar," 9¾", $100.00 – 150.00.
7. Conventional Rose spice jar, "Nutmeg," 4¾", $40.00 – 55.00.
8. Conventional Rose spice jar, "Pepper," 4¾", $40.00 – 55.00.
9. Conventional Rose spice jar, "Mustard," 4¾", $40.00 – 55.00.
Row 5:
1. Conventional Rose canister, "Flour," 8½", $55.00 – 85.00.
2. Conventional Rose canister, "Sugar," 8½", $55.00 – 85.00.
3. Conventional Rose canister, "Rice," 8½", $55.00 – 85.00.
4. Conventional Rose canister, "Cereal," 8½", $55.00 – 85.00.
5. Conventional Rose canister, "Coffee," 8½", $55.00 – 85.00.
6. Conventional Rose canister, "Tea," 8½", $55.00 – 85.00.

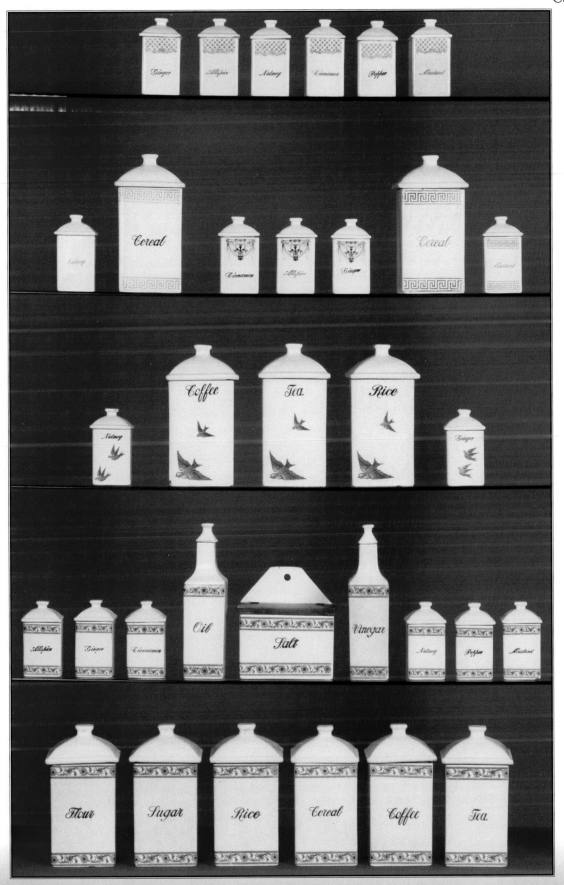

Plate 16.

Early Art

PRODUCTION DATES: 1925 – 1935

TRADEMARKS: Illustrations 5 – 8, appendix A.
Incised *H* in circle and mold number. Items are commonly unmarked.

These stoneware items are decorated in both high-gloss and matte glazes that are vertically striped, blended, or mottled. Colors include pink, mauve, blue, turquoise, green, and yellow, as well as others.

When pricing early art, mattes and variations to the blended-glazed mauve, blue, and turquoise combinations command highest prices.

Stoneware classification was used for that part of Hull production manufactured of buff body and represented by a prefix number of two digits — e.g., 34/30 jardiniere or 34/35 flower pot. Not all items fit this classification system, and those that do not are more than likely wares that were produced prior to the plan's formulation. This plan of identification was fully in place by 1935.

By 1935, the company's system further classified pieces as follows: 30, jardinieres; 31, hanging baskets and pots; 32, flower and bulb bowls; 33, vases; 34, flower pots with separate or unattached saucers; and 35, flower pots with attached saucers.

Plate 18.
Row 1:
1. Bulb bowl, matte finished, unmarked, 8", $75.00 – 125.00.
Row 2:
1. Vase, matte finished, "40 Ⓗ," 7", $75.00 – 125.00.
2. Vase, high gloss, "39 Ⓗ," 8", $125.00 – 165.00.
3. Vase, high gloss, "40 Ⓗ," 7", $75.00 – 125.00.
4. Vase, high gloss, unmarked, 5½", $65.00 – 85.00.
Row 3:
1. Vase, high gloss, "40 Ⓗ," 7", $75.00 – 125.00.
2. Vase, high gloss, "32 Ⓗ," 8", $75.00 – 125.00.
3. Vase, high gloss, "32 Ⓗ," 8", $75.00 – 125.00.
Row 4:
1. Vase, high gloss, "40 Ⓗ," 7", $75.00 – 125.00.
2. Vase, high gloss, "32 Ⓗ," 8", $75.00 – 125.00.
3. Vase, matte finished, "26 Ⓗ," 8", $75.00 – 125.00.
4. Vase, matte finished, "32 Ⓗ," 8", $75.00 – 125.00.

Plate 17. Early art stoneware jardiniere and pedestal, unmarked, 25½" overall. Jardiniere, 8½" x 12"; pedestal, 17". $350.00 – 400.00.

Plate 18.

EARLY ART
PRODUCTION DATES: 1925 – 1935

TRADEMARKS: Illustrations 5 – 8, appendix A.
  Incised *H* in circle and mold number. Items are commonly unmarked.

Plate 19.
Row 1:
1. Jardiniere, "23/30," 6½", $55.00 – 95.00.
2. Jardiniere, "20/30," 6½", $80.00 – 100.00.
3. Jardiniere, "22/30," 6½", $80.00 – 100.00.
4. Jardiniere, "36/30," 6½", $60.00 – 85.00.
5. Vase, "52/33," 7", $40.00 – 65.00.
Row 2:
1. Jardiniere, "34/30/2," 6½", $40.00 – 65.00.
2. Flowerpot and attached saucer, "34/35," 6½", $50.00 – 85.00.
3. Flowerpot and attached saucer, "34/35," 6½", $50.00 – 85.00.
Row 3.
1. Vase, "14/33," 5¾", $50.00 – 75.00.
2. Vase, "51/33," 6", $55.00 – 75.00.
3. Vase, "49/33," 6", $55.00 – 75.00.
Row 4.
1. Flowerpot and attatched saucer, "35/35," 6½", $55.00 – 95.00.
2. Flowerpot and attatched saucer, "35/35," 6½", $55.00 – 95.00.

Plate 20.
Row 1:
1. Stoneware jardiniere, matte finished, "Ⓗ 6"," $55.00 – 95.00.
2. Stoneware flower pot with saucer, matte finished, "Ⓗ," 5",
   $50.00 – 60.00.
3. Crab Apple semiporcelain vase, matte finished, unmarked, 5",
   $55.00 – 80.00.
4. Stoneware flower pot, matte finished, unmarked, 4¾", $35.00 –
   40.00.
5. Stoneware jardiniere, matte finished, unmarked, 7", $60.00 – 85.00.

Plate 21.
Row 1:
1. Stoneware hanging basket, matte finish, "25 Ⓗ 4"," $95.00 – 140.00.
2. Orange Tree stoneware jardiniere, "546 Ⓗ 4"," $40.00 – 50.00.
3. Stoneware hanging basket, unmarked, 6", $95.00 – 140.00.
4. Stoneware hanging basket, unmarked, 7", $135.00 – 225.00.
5. Orange Tree stoneware jardiniere, "546 Ⓗ 3"," $40.00 – 65.00.
Row 2.
1. Stoneware jardiniere, matte finished, "Ⓗ," 5", $40.00 – 65.00.
2. Stoneware jardiniere, matte finished, unmarked, 8", $75.00 – 110.00.
3. Stoneware jardiniere, "Ⓗ 8"," $75.00 – 110.00.
4. Stoneware jardiniere, "Ⓗ 5"," $40.00 – 50.00.
Row 3.
1. Stoneware jardiniere, "550 Ⓗ," 7", $75.00 – 100.00.
2. Stoneware jardiniere, "530 Ⓗ," 10", $90.00 – 120.00.
3. Stoneware jardiniere, "551 Ⓗ," 7", $75.00 – 100.00.

Plate 19.

Plate 20.

Plate 21.

The illustrated semiporcelain wares include matte white, matte yellow, and solid high-gloss colors of yellow or turquoise. Other colors were available. Illustrated stoneware items are solid brown and in blended high-gloss glazes.

Plate 22.
Row 1:
1. Vase, "660/33-5"," $25.00 – 40.00.
2. Vase, "650/33-9"," $75.00 – 100.00.

Plate 23.
Row 1:
1. Orange Tree semiporcelain jardiniere, "546 Ⓗ," 4", $40.00 – 55.00.
2. Orange Tree semiporcelain jardiniere, "546 Ⓗ," 5", $50.00 – 75.00.
3. Orange Tree semiporcelain jardiniere, "546 Ⓗ," 6", $60.00 – 90.00.
4. Stoneware jardiniere, "Ⓗ," 4½", $30.00 – 40.00.
Row 2:
1. Mardi Gras semiporcelain Spanish pot, unmarked, 4½", $18.00 – 22.00.
2. Crab Apple stoneware vase, "65/33" ink mark, 9", $75.00 – 100.00.
3. Crab Apple stoneware vase, unmarked, 9", $75.00 – 100.00.
4. Stoneware cuspidor, unmarked, embossed daisies, 7½", $70.00 – 95.00.
Row 3:
1. Streamline semiporcelain flower pot with attached saucer, unmarked, 6½", $30.00 – 40.00.
2. Streamline semiporcelain flower pot, unmarked, 8½", $30.00 – 40.00.
3. Semiporcelain vase, "660/33-8"," $40.00 – 60.00.
4. Semiporcelain vase, "Ⓗ," 5½", $55.00 – 75.00.
Row 4:
1. Tulip stoneware jardiniere, unmarked, 10", $90.00 – 125.00.
2. Tulip stoneware jardiniere, unmarked, 9", $90.00 – 125.00.
3. Love Birds stoneware jardiniere, embossed birds, unmarked, 7½", $75.00 – 100.00.

Crab Apple, in a 1935 company price list, was described as "art pottery vases, jardinieres, hanging baskets, available in matte Eggshell White, matte Peacock Blue on white semiporcelain body; hand painted flowers in rose, leaves in green on matte sun tan buff body; or bright white on white semi-porcelain body." This price list included eighteen shapes.

People of Crooksville have called this line "Acme" for years. (The locals have always had a habit of calling the Hull "Acme," since Hull moved into the Acme Building when expanding operations.) The line is not particularly scarce, it has just been ignored, the cruder pieces taking a back shelf to potteries that could be readily identified.

Although unmarked, this ware has been found with factory labels intact, and more importantly, some pieces bear permanent ink marks. The clay bodies and glaze colors correspond with company information, as do most of the labels and ink marks. Marking system and sizes correspond to Hull information as far as first digits of the series numbers are concerned; however, the last digit is dropped, i.e., 600/33 is 60/33, 670/30 is 67/30. This ware was produced in 1934 and 1935.

THE A. E. HULL POTTERY COMPANY, CROOKSVILLE, OHIO

TWO OUTSTANDING SHAPES FROM OUR CRAB APPLE LINE OF ART POTTERY. No. 660/33—5" VASE AND No. 650/33—9" VASE GLAZED IN PLAIN PEACOCK BLUE OR EGG SHELL WHITE.

Plate 22. Early Company
Advertisement for Crab Apple

Plate 23.

Early Art
PRODUCTION DATES: 1938 – 1948

TRADEMARKS: Illustrations 40 and 41, appendix A.
   Most of the novelty items illustrated carry impressed mold numbers, but no Hull designation. The Kitten and Lamb planters are impressed "Hull Art."

Plate 24.
Row 1:
1. Cat figural, "937," 5", $60.00 – 90.00.
2. Walking Elephant, "938," 5", $75.00 – 95.00.
3. Monkey planter, "939," 5", $40.00 – 60.00.
4. Monkey planter, "940," 4½", $40.00 – 60.00.
5 – 9. Swing Band set, 5½" – 6", $75.00 – 110.00.
    each.
Row 2:
1. Walking Elephant, "933," 6", $75.00 – 100.00.
2. Elephant, "934," 5¼", $30.00 – 40.00.
3. Rooster, "951," 7", $50.00 – 80.00.
4. Dog, "935," 6", $75.00 – 100.00.
5. Monkey, "936," 5½", $40.00 – 60.00.
Row 3:
1 – 3. Stoneware bowls, 5½", $25.00 – 35.00 each.
4. Batter bowl, "25-3-9"," $95.00 – 135.00.
5. Batter jug, "B-7-1 qt.," 6", $85.00 – 125.00.
6. Tumbler, "850-25-4½"," $25.00 – 35.00.
7. Oyster bowl, "190-23-6"," $10.00 – 20.00.
8. Mug, "190-25-3½"," $10.00 – 20.00.
Row 4:
1. Jardiniere, "690-30-6"," $15.00 – 20.00.
2. Cookie jar, "850-20-9"," $60.00 – 90.00.
3. Cookie jar, "22-20-9½"," $60.00 – 90.00.
4. Cookie jar, "300-20-11"," $90.00 – 125.00.
5. Ice-Lip pitcher, "850-29-7½"," $75.00 – 100.00.

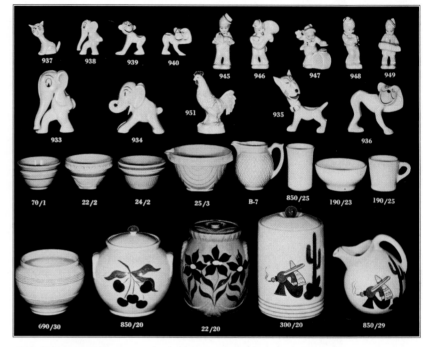

Plate 24.

Plate 25.
Row 1:
1. Rabbit, "952 USA," sample seal, 4½", $45.00 – 75.00.
2. Monkey, unmarked, 5½", $40.00 – 60.00.
3. Cactus Cat, "964," 2¾", $22.00 – 28.00.
4. Experimental monkey, unmarked, 3¾", $30.00 – 40.00.
Row 2:
1. Elephant, unmarked, 5¼", $30.00 – 40.00.
2. Rabbit, "968," 6", $30.00 – 40.00.
3. Rabbit, "968," 6", $30.00 – 40.00.
4. Rabbit, "968," 6", $30.00 – 40.00.
5. Elephant, unmarked, 5¼", $30.00 – 40.00.

Plate 26.
Row 1:
1. Basket Girl, "954," 8", high-gloss pink, $35.00 – 45.00.
2. Basket Girl, "954," 8", matte white, $50.00 – 75.00.
3. Basket Girl, "954," 8", high-gloss white, $35.00 – 45.00.
Row 2:
1. Kitten planter, "61," 7½", $40.00 – 55.00.
2. Pig planter, "60," 8½", 1940 – 1943, $30.00 – 45.00.
3. Lamb planter, "965," 7½", $40.00 – 60.00.
4. Cat doorstop, unmarked, 7¼", 1936, $275.00 – 375.00.

Plate 25.

Plate 26.

EARLY ART AND UTILITY

PRODUCTION DATES: 1925 – 1935

TRADEMARKS: Illustrations 5 – 8, appendix A.
Incised *H* in circle mark and mold number. Items are commonly unmarked.

Illustrated are solid high-gloss turquoise semiporcelain items embossed with the Orange Tree decoration, and early art stoneware in predominately blue, mauve, green, and turquoise solid and blended mattes as well as blended high-gloss glazes.
Acme wares are marked with a black shield and eagle ink stamp. (Trademark, see illustration 1, appendix A.) The Acme pieces illustrated and described are for historical reference only and have little monetary value in a Hull collection. Hull Pottery operations were conducted in the former Acme plant building.

Plate 28.
Row 1:
1. Lusterware vase, unmarked, 12", $80.00 – 120.00.
2. Acme plate, eagle ink stamp, 11", $35.00 – 45.00.
3. Acme plate, eagle ink stamp, 11", $35.00 – 45.00.

Plate 29.
Row 1:
1. Shell planter, "202," 5", $25.00 – 40.00.
2. Lusterware candleholder, unmarked, 9", $60.00 – 95.00.
3. Lusterware candleholder, unmarked, 9", $60.00 – 95.00.
4. Horse doorstop, tile body, deep indigo and black, 8¾", $175.00 – 225.00.
5. Vase, unmarked, 7½", $35.00 – 40.00.
6. Stoneware jardiniere, unmarked, 4¾", $30.00 – 40.00.

Plate 30.
Row 1:
1. Crab Apple stoneware jardiniere, unmarked, 6½", $75.00 – 100.00.
2. Donkey planter, advertised as 1940 campaign item, 6", $70.00 – 90.00.
3. Pleated stoneware utility pitcher "Ⓗ," 6½", $75.00 – 100.00.

Plate 31.
Row 1:
1. Orange Tree semiporcelain covered batter pitcher, "Ⓗ," 7", $275.00 – 375.00.
2. Orange Tree stoneware pitcher, "27 Ⓗ 30," 7", $375.00 – 475.00.
Row 2.
1. Orange Tree semiporcelain bowl, "26 Ⓗ," 6½", $35.00 – 45.00.
2. Orange Tree semiporcelain jardiniere, "546 Ⓗ," 7", $80.00 – 100.00.
3. Orange Tree semiporcelain covered bowl, "25 Ⓗ 4"," $65.00 – 90.00.

Plate 27. Crab Apple vase, semiporcelain, unmarked, 6½", $75.00 – 100.00.

Plate 28.

Plate 29.

Plate 30.

Plate 31.

Early Art and Utility

PRODUCTION DATES: Shulton product containers, 1937 – 1944; Banded semiporcelain, 1937 – 1942; Novelties, 1938 – 1940; Mardi Gras/Granada, 1938 – 1946

Hull produced Shulton product containers from 1937 to 1944. These highly glazed stoneware bottles and mugs have underglaze blue ship transfers and block red lettering — "After Shaving Lotion" and "Talcum for Men" — on bottles, and script red lettering — "Old Spice" — on bottles and mugs.

Shulton product containers carried an incised print "Early American, Made in U.S.A." trademak with incised script "Old Spice" in circle formation, or incised print "Early American Shaving Soap, Shulton, USA" with incised script "Old Spice" in circle formation (see trademark illustrations 30 and 31, appendix A). Kitchenwares, Novelties, and Mardi Gras/Granada bear no Hull designation but are incised numerically, indicating mold and dimension.

Swing Band items are unmarked and the bases are unglazed. Most items have a small hole in the base, part of the manufacturing process. There are several look-alikes on the market, in several compositions. One such set is marked "Coventry."

Swing Band items have an ivory matte finish and gold trim and hand-painted features. Some band sets have been entirely overglaze decorated. In 1940, Blackwell Wielandy Company retailed the five-piece set for $3.50.

Art and utility items pictured carried no Hull marks, but were incised with mold numbers and size identifications.

Plate 32.
Row 1:
1. Shulton "After Shaving Lotion" bottle with original pontil closure, "Ship Grand Turk," 5", $25.00 – 35.00.
2. Shulton mug, "Ship Friendship," 3", $16.00 – 24.00.
3. Shulton mug, in original box, "Ship Grand Turk," 3", $20.00 – 30.00.
4. Shulton "Talcum For Men" bottle, "Ship Grand Turk," 5", $20.00 – 30.00.
5. Shulton "Talcum For Men" bottle, "Ship Grand Turk," 5", $20.00 – 30.00.

Plate 33.
Row 1:
1. Swing Band Accordionist, unmarked, 6", $75.00 – 110.00.
2. Swing Band Clarinet Player, unmarked, 6", $75.00 – 110.00.
3. Swing Band Drummer, base unmarked, "Swing Band" incised on side of drum, 5½", $75.00 – 110.00.
4. Swing Band Band Leader, unmarked, 6½", $75.00 – 110.00.
5. Swing Band Tuba Player, unmarked, 5¾", $75.00 – 110.00.

Plate 34.
Row 1:
1. Banded semiporcelain nested bowls, "E-1," 5" to 10", $150.00 – 200.00.
2. Pitcher, "E-1-7"," $45.00 – 65.00.
3. Covered casserole, "E-13-7½"," $40.00 – 60.00.
4. Custard, "E-14-3½"," $12.00 – 15.00.
Row 2:
1. Head vase, "208-7½"," $75.00 – 130.00.
2. Mardi Gras/Granada vase, "216," 9", $50.00 – 80.00.
3. Mardi Gras/Granada cornucopia, "210," 5½", $30.00 – 40.00.
4. Basket Girl, matte finish, "954," 8", $50.00 – 75.00.
5. Mardi Gras/Granada vase, "215," 9", $50.00 – 80.00.
Row 3:
Bulb bowl, "532," 2¾", $40.00 – 60.00.
Row 4:
1. Streamline vase, "533-9"," $30.00 – 40.00.
2. Mardi Gras/Granada vase, "218-9"," $50.00 – 80.00.
3. Mardi Gras/Granada cornucopia, "211," $30.00 – 40.00.
4. Mardi Gras/Granada cornucopia, "209-9"," $35.00 – 45.00.
5. Mardi Gras/Granada vase, "214-9"," $50.00 – 80.00.
6. Mardi Gras/Granada vase, "219-9"," $50.00 – 80.00.

Plate 32.

Plate 33.

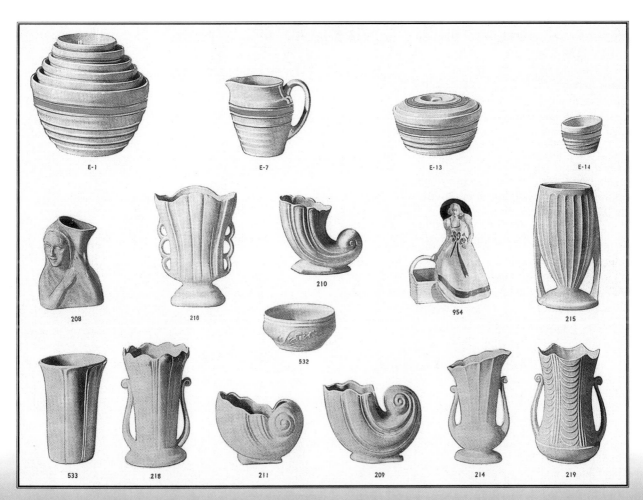

Plate 34. Original Hull advertising.

PRODUCTION DATES: 1925 – 1940

TRADEMARKS: Illustrations 5 – 8, appendix A.

Incised mold number, with or without *H* in circle mark and "USA." These items are also commonly found with only mold numbers and dimensions.

The illustrated solid glazed items, of both stoneware and semiporcelain bodies, encompass the rainbow colors of Rose Beige, Dust Rose, maroon, blue, yellow, seafoam green, rust, and a matte gray, with shapes ranging from plain to ribbed to floral embossed. For identification purposes, the cylinder vases contain thirteen raised ribs or bands.

Primrose, manufactured from 1937 – 1940, is a semiporcelain embossed floral kitchenware in high-gloss solid colors of maroon, green, white, yellow, and blue. This ware is marked with incised 400-series numbers and carries no Hull designation. Primrose was sold exclusively by Sears Robuck and Company.

The embossed floral spray wraps right to left on the ware. A similar line of semiporcelain, marked with 200-series numbers, features an embossed floral spray that wraps left to right, has arrow-shaped leaves, and has a pleat-type base pattern. This most likely represents an entirely different pattern, from a modified mold, that was distributed by another major chain store.

Plate 35.

Row 1:
1. Semiporcelain jardiniere, "95-4¼"," $15.00 – 20.00.
2. Stoneware flower pot, "Ⓗ," 4", $40.00 – 50.00.
3. Stoneware flower pot with separate saucer, "538 Ⓗ," 4", $45.00 – 60.00.

Row 2:
1. Stoneware custard, unmarked, 3¼", $12.00 – 15.00.
2. Mardi Gras semiporcelain Spanish pot, unmarked, 5", $12.00 – 16.00.
3. Streamline semiporcelain jardiniere, "690-6"," $35.00 – 45.00.
4. Mardi Gras semiporcelain Spanish pot, unmarked, 5", $12.00 – 16.00.
5. Stoneware custard, unmarked, 3¼", $12.00 – 15.00.

Row 3:
1. Primrose pitcher, "407," 5", $35.00 – 45.00.
2. Semiporcelain bean pot, "219-6"," $40.00 – 55.00.
3. Semiporcelain bean pot, "219-5"," $35.00 – 50.00.
4. Semiporcelain pitcher, "207," 5", $35.00 – 45.00.
5. Primrose custard, "414," 3½", $12.00 – 15.00.

Row 4:
1. Stoneware bowl, "300/1-8"," $35.00 – 40.00.
2. Mardi Gras semiporcelain jardiniere, unmarked, 7½", $35.00 – 45.00.
3. Mardi Gras stoneware bowl, unmarked, 10½", $35.00 – 45.00.

Row 5:
1. Stoneware bowl, "E-1-9"," $35.00 – 45.00.
2. Mardi Gras semiporcelain vase, unmarked, 6", $25.00 – 35.00.
3. Mardi Gras semiporcelain vase, unmarked, 10", $40.00 – 60.00.
4. Mardi Gras semiporcelain vase, unmarked, 6", $25.00 – 35.00.

Plate 35.

Early Art and Utility

Utility wares shown include semiporcelain, yellow ware, embossed Orange Tree items, and decaled kitchenware and cookie jars in both semiporcelain and stoneware. Hull's utility cookie jars were hand decorated in a variety of designs.

The cylinder cookie jars remained in production throughout the 1930s and 1940s. The only jars in this cylinder shape that contained Hull trademarks appear to be the Cinderella cookie jars (pages 100 – 101). Other jars were marked with number and size designations only. There are two sizes of jars, one being slightly taller than the other. Also, the lid's knob appears in two different styles. One knob is completely spherical, while the other knob is half round.

Plate 36.
Row 1:
1. Semiporcelain French-handed casserole, underglaze banding, unmarked, 6½", $25.00 – 35.00.
2. Semiporcelain covered bean pot, banding over glaze, unmarked, 4¼", $25.00 – 35.00.
3. Semiporcelain Nuline Bak-Serve/Pastel Rainbow Cross Point Pie Plate (also known as Diamond Quilt and Evangeline), "B-14-9½"," $30.00 – 40.00.
4. Semiporcelain pitcher, underglaze banding, "107 (H), 42," 4", $55.00 – 70.00.
Row 2:
1. Semiporcelain Spanish pot, "(H)," 3", $25.00 – 35.00.
2. Semiporocelain salt box, "(H)," incised groves, 5¼" x 4½", $65.00 – 95.00.
3. Semiporocelain casserole, unmarked, 8¼", $45.00 – 65.00.
4. Stoneware teapot, gray interior, unmarked, 6½", $65.00 – 80.00.
5. Stoneware mug, honeycomb pattern, unmarked, 3¼", $20.00 – 30.00.
Row 3:
1. Semiporcelain bowl, decal decorated, "50 (H) 6"," $20.00 – 25.00.
2. Orange Tree semiporcelain compote, "26 (H)," 10¼", $115.00 – 145.00.
3. Orange Tree semiporcelain custard, "(H)," 2¾", $15.00 – 20.00.
4. Primrose ice-lip pitcher, "429," 8¾", $65.00 – 95.00.
Row 4:
1. Yellow ware square shoulder bowl, underglaze banding, "USA," 9½", $45.00 – 65.00.
2. Harp stoneware jardiniere, unmarked, 7½", $65.00 – 95.00.
3. Yellow ware bowl, underglaze banding, "421 (H) 9," $40.00 – 60.00.
Row 5:
1. Stoneware square-footed cookie jar,* minus lid, blue matte with hand-painted cold color fruit and blossom decor, "USA," 9½", $60.00 – 90.00.
2. Semiporcelain cookie jar, high-gloss turquoise, unmarked, 11", $45.00 – 65.00.
3. Semiporcelain cookie jar, white gloss with decoration apple, pear, and strawberries over the glaze, unmarked, 11", $45.00 – 65.00.
4. Stoneware square-footed cookie jar,* matte turquoise with hand-painted floral over the glaze, unmarked, 9½", $60.00 – 90.00.

* The square-footed cookie jars characteristically have red glaze covering the unglazed stoneware edge of the top of jar and tip of lid's handle.

Plate 36.

PRODUCTION DATES: 1915 – 1930

TRADEMARKS: Illustrations 5 – 8, appendix A.
Incised *H* in circle with or without mold number and size identification. Items are commonly unmarked.

The utility stoneware and artware items illustrated are decorated in both solid and blended high glazes. The tankard and mugs are glazed in tones that add dimension to the relief-form Alpine scene.

Plate 38.
Row 1:
1. Mug, "(H)," 4½", $25.00 – 35.00.
2. Mug, "(H)," 3¾", embossed "Chocolate Soldier," $75.00 – 100.00.
3. Mug, "497 (H)," 5", embossed "Happy Days Are Here Again," $30.00 – 40.00.
Row 2:
1. Mug, "491 (H)," 5", $20.00 – 25.00.
2. Mug, "494 (H)," 4¼", embossed "Rhein Stein, Burg, Cochem, Stolzenfels," $45.00 – 60.00.
3. Mug, "491 (H)," 5", $20.00 – 30.00.
4. Mug, "497 (H)," 5", embossed "Happy Days Are Here Again," $30.00 – 40.00.
5. Mug, "265 (H)," 4½", embossed "Happy Days Are Here Again," $30.00 – 40.00.
Row 3:
1. Alpine tankard, "492 (H)," 9½", $185.00 – 275.00.
2. Alpine stein, "492 (H)," 6½", $40.00 – 60.00.
3. Stein, "496 (H)," 6½", embossed deer, "BPOE," $75.00 – 100.00.
4. Stein, "498 (H)," 6½", embossed "American Legion,"
      $75.00 – 100.00.
5. Alpine pretzel jar, "(H)," 9", $200.00 – 300.00.
Row 4:
1. Mug, "499 (H)," 5", $30.00 – 40.00.
2. Mug, "499 (H)," 5", $30.00 – 40.00.
3. Tankard, "499 (H)," 8½", $125.00 – 160.00.
4. Mug, "499 (H)," 5", $30.00 – 40.00.
5. Mug, "499 (H)," 5", $30.00 – 40.00.
Row 5:
1. Jardiniere, "536 (H)," 9", $80.00 – 110.00.
2. Flower pot with attached saucer, "539 (H)," 6", $60.00 – 85.00.
3. Jardiniere, "551 (H)," 7", $75.00 – 100.00.
4. Flowerpot, unmarked, 4", $30.00 – 40.00.

Plate 37. Original company brochure page. Stoneware cookie jars were cold-color decorated as shown, left to right: Poppy, Poinsettia, and Rose. These designs, as well as others, were painted over transparent yellow glazes.

Plate 38.

Early Utility

PRODUCTION DATES: 1915 – 1935

TRADEMARKS: Illustrations 4 – 8 and 13, appendix A.
   Incised *H* in circle, with or without mold number and size identification, or an incised *H* in diamond. Items are commonly found unmarked.

   Hull's early utility production included both stoneware and semiporcelain items. Illustrated are solid highly glazed finished wares. The incised banded items were glazed in white, green, yellow, blue, and gray. The *H* in a diamond–marked cereal ware canisters, spice jars, cruets, and salt box all have an embossed wheat sheaf decor and have been found in yellow, green, blue, and tan solid high-gloss glazes.
   Company information indicated the stoneware teapot was referred to as a "6-cup French-process coffee maker." The teapot was marketed with an aluminum insert. Please refer to plate 37 to view the complete set, including the aluminum insert.

Plate 40.
Row 1:
1. Semiporcelain individual covered bean pot,* "Ⓗ," 3", $30.00 – 45.00.
2. Semiporcelain bowl, "Ⓗ," 6", $25.00 – 35.00.
3. Semiporcelain pitcher, unmarked, gray interior, 6½", $100.00 – 165.00.
4. Stoneware bowl, "106 Ⓗ," 5", $18.00 – 30.00.
5. Stoneware pitcher, "107 Ⓗ 42," 3¾", $50.00 – 70.00.
Row 2:
1. Wheat semiporcelain cruet, unmarked, embossed "Vinegar," 6½", $90.00 – 135.00.
2. Wheat semiporcelain salt box, unmarked, embossed "Salt," 5¾", $80.00 – 110.00.
3. Semiporcelain covered bean pot,* "Ⓗ," 4½", $50.00 – 75.00.
4. Semiporcelain pitcher, "Ⓗ," 4¾", $60.00 – 80.00.
5. Stoneware custard, "60 Ⓗ," 2½", $14.00 – 18.00.
Row 3:
1. Wheat stoneware spice jar, incised *H* (in diamond), "Spice," 3½", $70.00 – 95.00.
2. Wheat stoneware spice jar, incised *H* (in diamond), "Pepper," 3½", $70.00 – 95.00.
3. Stoneware salt box, "111 Ⓗ," 6", $125.00 – 165.00.
4. Wheat stoneware canister, incised *H* (in diamond), "Sugar," 6½", $130.00 – 165.00.
5. Wheat stoneware canister, incised *H* (in diamond), "Coffee," 6½", $130.00 – 165.00.
Row 4:
1. Stoneware teapot, "Ⓗ," 6¼", $75.00 – 100.00.
2. Semiporcelain bowl "25 Ⓗ," 7", $35.00 – 45.00.
3. Semiporcelain bowl, "25 Ⓗ," 6",
   $20.00 – 25.00.
Row 5:
1. Stoneware bowl, "421 Ⓗ," 7",
   $35.00 – 50.00.
2. Stoneware bowl, "421 Ⓗ," 10",
   $60.00 – 90.00.
3. Semiporcelain bowl, "30 Ⓗ," 7",
   $25.00 – 35.00.

*Lids sit inside deeply recessed rims.

Plate 39. Stoneware Batter Bowl, incised "PAT APL FOR, USA, 25-3-9"," $95.00 – 135.00.

Plate 40.

PRODUCTION DATES: 1910 – 1935

TRADEMARKS: Illustrations 5 – 8, and 13, appendix A.

Incised *H* in circle, with or without mold number and size identification. It is not unusual for items to be unmarked, and some items bear an incised patent designation.

Hull's stoneware and yellow ware banded items comprised many different shapes and designs. These items were banded both underglaze and overglaze, in a rainbow of colors that included blue, pink, dark green, lime green, ivory, brown, white, gold, yellow, red, black, mauve, peach, and others. The illustrated yellow ware items are banded underglaze. The nested bowls have four incised bands, and have traces of their original green and orange overglaze, or cold-color paint.

Plate 41.
Row 1:
1. Fawn planter, "941," 5", $30.00 – 40.00.
Row 2:
1 – 5. Yellow ware bowls, "Ⓗ," 4½", $32.00 – 50.00; 5½", $35.00 – 55.00; 6½", $35.00 – 55.00; 7½", $40.00 – 60.00; 8½", $40.00 – 65.00.
Row 3:
1 – 3. Yellow ware bowls, "Ⓗ," 9½", $40.00 – 65.00; 10½", $60.00 – 95.00; 11½", $65.00 – 95.00.

Plate 42.
Row 1:
1. Yellow ware batter bowl, incised "PAT APL FOR, USA, 25-3-9"," $95.00 – 135.00.
Row 2:
1. Stoneware bowl, "428 Ⓗ," 5", $20.00 – 30.00.
2. Stoneware bowl, "428 Ⓗ," 6", $25.00 – 40.00.
3. Yellow ware covered casserole, "455 Ⓗ," 9", $100.00 – 145.00.
Row 3:
1. Yellow ware pitcher, "107 Ⓗ 36," 4¾", $75.00 – 100.00.
2. Yellow ware covered casserole, "113 Ⓗ," 7", $45.00 – 75.00.
3. Yellow ware bowl, "106 Ⓗ," 6", $25.00 – 35.00.
4. Yellow ware custard, "114 Ⓗ 2," 3¼", $15.00 – 20.00.
Row 4:
1. Yellow ware bowl, "421 Ⓗ," 12", $60.00 – 95.00.
2. Yellow ware covered casserole with metal bail, "455 Ⓗ," 9", $165.00 – 200.00.

Plate 43.
Row 1:
1. Cookie jar, unmarked, 10¾", decal decorated, 1940, $45.00 – 65.00.
2. Duck cookie jar, "966," 11½", decorated over the glaze, 1940, $75.00 – 100.00.
3. Cookie jar, "9½"-30," actual size 10¾", decorated under glaze, 1940, $75.00 – 100.00.

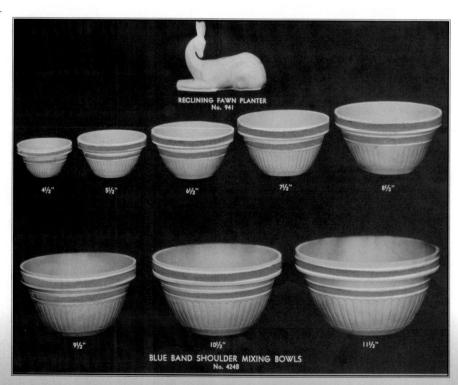

Plate 41. Original company brochure page.

Plate 42.

Plate 43.

Early Utility
PRODUCTION DATES: 1915 – 1935

TRADEMARKS: Illustrations 5 – 8, appendix A.

Banded items, rows 1 – 3, are marked with an incised *H* in a circle and mold number. These items are also commonly found unmarked. Remaining items are incised with an E-series mold number and "USA.," and are also commonly found unmarked. "Heat Resisting, Cold Resisting, Ovenproof" foil labels were also used for this utility ware. Refer to illustrations 16 – 18, appendix A, for examples.

Advertised as "pantry and cooking essentials for the American home," utility wares composed a large volume of Hull production. The wares illustrated are both overglaze and underglaze banded. Slight inconsistencies are common in the banding decorations, which are blown. The salt boxes are pictured with semiporcelain and wooden lids; both are original to the ware. The semiporcelain salt box paired with the semiporcelain lid is the more difficult to locate.

Plate 44.
1. Crab Apple vase, unmarked, 5", $40.00 – 65.00.
2. Cookie jar, semiporcelain with overglaze decoration, unmarked, 9", $50.00 – 80.00.
3. Five-band utility pitcher with overglaze decoration, unmarked, 8", $70.00 – 100.00.
4. Tankard, "499, (H)," 8½", $125.00 – 160.00.

Plate 45.
Row 1:
1. Covered casserole, "113 (H)," 7½", $60.00 – 80.00.
2. Pie plate, unmarked, 9", $45.00 – 65.00.
Row 2:
1. Salt box, "111 (H)," 5", wooden lid, $115.00 – 140.00.
2. Covered casserole, "(H)," 7½", $45.00 – 65.00.
3. Pitcher, "107 (H), 36," 4¾", $40.00 – 55.00.
4. Salt box, "(H)," 5¾", porcelain lid, $165.00 – 225.00.
Row 3:
1. Bowl, "(H)," 8", $25.00 – 35.00.
2. Bowl, "100 (H)," 8", $35.00 – 45.00.
3. Covered casserole, unmarked, 10", $115.00 – 145.00.
4. Spice jar, "118 (H)," embossed "Spices," 3¾", $55.00 – 75.00.
5. Spice jar, "118 (H)," embossed "Spices," 3¾", $55.00 – 75.00.
Row 4:
1. Pitcher, "E-7"," $45.00 – 65.00.
2. Covered casserole, "E-13-7½"," $40.00 – 60.00.
3. Bowl, "E-1-7"," $22.00 – 32.00.
4. Bowl, unmarked, 6½", $16.00 – 22.00.
Row 5:
1. Bowl, unmarked, 7", $25.00 – 30.00.
2. Custard, "E-14," 3½", $12.00 – 15.00.
3. Bowl, "E-1," 9½", $30.00 – 40.00
4. Custard, "E-14," 3½", $12.00 – 15.00.
5. Bowl, "E-1-10"," $45.00 – 65.00.

Plate 44.

Plate 45.

TRADEMARKS: Illustrations 7, 17, 33, 34, and 38, appendix A.

Utility items in row 1 are incised script "Hull Ware, USA" with an A-series mold number and size identification. Additional early banded wares are marked with an incised *H* in a circle, or a foil label that indicated the ware was "Heat and Cold Resisting." Additional label examples used for early utility ware are illustrations 16 and 18, appendix A.

Items shown illustrate Hull's underglaze and overglaze banding techniques. Few over-the-glaze-banded, or "cold-colored," items will be as showroom condition as those illustrated in rows 3 and 4. This particular line, which included casseroles, pie plates, bean pots, jugs, ramekins, and custard cups, was available with overglaze banding in Pimento Red or Nubian Black, and underglaze banding in Spring Green or Alice Blue.

The Hull Ware cookie jars illustrated are exceptional, each being decorated over the glaze. Both jars are difficult to locate and will most likely be on cookie jar collectors' want lists.

Plate 46.
1. Little Boy Blue cookie jar, incised "Hull Ware, Boy Blue, U.S.A. 971-12½"," 1940, $275.00 – 400.00.
2. Hen and Chick cookie jar, incised "Hull Ware, 968-11½", U.S.A. 1940," $350.00 – 550.00.

Plate 47.
Row 1:
1. Blue Ribbon bowl, "Hull Ware A-1-9½"," $35.00 – 45.00.
2. Blue Ribbon bowl, "Hull Ware A-1-7½"," $25.00 – 35.00.
Row 2:
1. Pitcher, unmarked, 3½", $25.00 – 35.00.
2. Bowl, unmarked, 7½", $25.00 – 40.00.
3. Bowl, unmarked, 7½", $25.00 – 40.00.
4. Pitcher, unmarked, 3½", $25.00 – 35.00.
Row 3:
1. Bowl, "30 Ⓗ," 6½", $25.00 – 40.00.
2. Bowl, "30 Ⓗ," 5½", $20.00 – 30.00.
3. Custard, unmarked, 3½", $12.00 – 15.00.
4. Custard, unmarked, 3½", $12.00 – 15.00.
5. Pitcher, unmarked, 6¼", $60.00 – 85.00.
Row 4:
1. Bowl, "30 Ⓗ," 7½", $25.00 – 40.00.
2. Bowl, "30 Ⓗ," 8½", $25.00 – 40.00.
3. Bowl, "30 Ⓗ," 9½", $30.00 – 45.00.

Plate 46.

Plate 47.

PRODUCTION DATES: 1937 – 1940

TRADEMARKS: Illustrations: 14, 16, 17, and 18, appendix A.

Impressed block "A. E. HULL, USA" or "HULL, USA" followed by appropriate "B," "C," or "D" and mold number with size identification. Many times the identification of this kitchenware was concealed during the glazing method when the too-thick glaze filled the impressions of the trademarks. Foil labels indicating "Heat and Cold Resisting" were also used for these kitchenware lines.

The NuLine Bak-Serve Kitchenware was also known as Pastel Rainbow and Pastel Trend. Patterns B and C were primarily marketed as Pastel Rainbow, while D was marketed as Trend Pastel. This ovenproof embossed semiporcelain kitchenware line was available in three distinctive designs:

B series — an embossed diamond quilt design, also known as Cross Point and Evangeline
C series — an embossed fish scale design
D series — an embossed drape and panel design

In solid matte and high-gloss colors of blue, Seafoam Green, Rose Beige, rose, yellow, cream, and white, this line included at least 22 shapes.

Plate 48.
Row 1:
1. Diamond Quilt teapot, "B-5," 5½", $95.00 – 125.00.
2. Drape and Panel French-handled casserole, "D-15," 4½", $20.00 – 30.00.
3. Fish Scale mug, "C-25," 3½", $60.00 – 85.00.
4. Diamond Quilt teapot, "B-5," 5½", $95.00 – 125.00.
Row 2:
1. Diamond Quilt custard, "B-14," 2¾", $12.00 – 15.00.
2. Diamond Quilt covered casserole, "B-13-7½"," $45.00 – 65.00.
3. Drape and Panel covered casserole, "D-13-7½"," $45.00 – 65.00.
4. Drape and Panel mixing bowl, "D-1-9½"," $35.00 – 45.00.
5. Fish Scale custard, "C-14," 2¾", $12.00 – 15.00.
Row 3:
1. Fish Scale mug, "C-25," 3½", $60.00 – 85.00.
2. Fish Scale batter jug, "C-7-1 Qt.," 6", $85.00 – 125.00.
3. Diamond Quilt batter jug, "B-7-1 Qt.," 6", $85.00 – 125.00.
4. Diamond Quilt batter jug, "B-7," 5", $40.00 – 55.00.
5. Fish Scale mug, "C-25," 3½", $60.00 – 85.00.
Row 4:
1. Fish Scale ice-lip pitcher, "C-29," 8½", $150.00 – 185.00.
2. Fish Scale ice-lip pitcher, "C-29," 7", $80.00 – 115.00.
3. Diamond Quilt bean pot, "B-19-5½"," $45.00 – 65.00.
4. Diamond Quilt ice-lip pitcher, "B-29," 8½", $150.00 – 185.00.
Row 5:
1. Diamond Quilt nested mixing bowls, "B-1," 5", 6", 7", 8", and 9", $165.00 – 225.00.
2. Fish Scale cookie jar, "C-20-2 Qt.," 8", $125.00 – 150.00.
3. Drape and Panel cookie jar, "D-20-2 Qt.," 8", $125.00 – 150.00.
4. Diamond Quilt cookie jar, "B-20-2 Qt.," 8", $125.00 – 150.00.

Plate 48.

Lusterware

PRODUCTION DATES: 1927 – 1930

TRADEMARKS:
Lusterware items are usually found unmarked, although some pieces have incised mold numbers and size identification. Bases of unmarked items are glazed, some with the same splotchy colorations as the body of the ware, others to match the interior of the item.

Hull lusters are exceedingly brilliant and very iridescent when rainbow colorings play over the surface in changing lights. Intensities of luster colors vary, since some colors did not accept the sheens as readily as others and settled primarily on the surface. It is believed Hull used a technique that caused moisture to condense in drops, to show white spots or splotching after fire. This method, called water smoking, could have been achieved by not warming the kiln before stacking the ware or by covering the items during firing.

This modest artware line of vases, ashtrays, and jardinieres was decorated in high-glaze iridescent colors the company referred to as Shammy, orange, lavender, Slate, emerald, light blue, iridescent dark blue, and Gold Glow, and at least 35 items were available. Chinese Red Cracquelle, a brilliant red, and Persian, an unidentified color (most likely blue or turquoise), were two additional Lusterware lines and were offered in 15 shapes.

Plate 49.
Row 1:
1. Lusterware bulb bowl, unmarked, 7½", $60.00 – 75.00.
2. Lusterware flower frog, unmarked, 4½", $20.00 – 30.00.
3. Lusterware candleholder, unmarked, 9", $60.00 – 95.00.
4. Lusterware bulb bowl, unmarked, 9½", $65.00 – 85.00.
5. Lusterware candleholder, unmarked, 9", $60.00 – 95.00.
Row 2:
1. Lusterware vase, unmarked, 10", $60.00 – 80.00.
2. Lusterware vase, unmarked, 13", $100.00 – 140.00.
3. Lusterware console bowl, unmarked, 10", $85.00 – 120.00.
4. Lusterware vase, unmarked, 13", $100.00 – 140.00.

Plate 50.
Row 1:
1. Lusterware candleholder, unmarked, 3", $30.00 – 40.00.
2. Lusterware candleholder, unmarked, 3", $30.00 – 40.00.
3. Lusterware candleholder, unmarked, 3", $30.00 – 40.00.
4. Lusterware pitcher, unmarked, 4", $40.00 – 65.00.
Row 2:
1. Lusterware pitcher, unmarked, 4", $40.00 – 65.00.
2. Lusterware vase, unmarked, 9", $75.00 – 100.00.
3. Lusterware vase, unmarked, 10", $60.00 – 80.00.
4. Lusterware vase, unmarked, 9", $75.00 – 100.00.
5. Lusterware vase, unmarked, 8", $50.00 – 65.00.
6. Lusterware vase, unmarked, 3½", $75.00 – 100.00.
Row 3:
1. Lusterware pitcher, unmarked, 5¾", $65.00 – 85.00.
2. Lusterware vase, unmarked, 8", $30.00 – 40.00.
3. Lusterware vase, unmarked, 12", $80.00 – 120.00.
4. Lusterware jardiniere, incised "91-7½"," $75.00 – 100.00.

Plate 49.

Plate 50.

TILE AND EARLY ART

PRODUCTION DATES: Tile, 1926 – 1931; Early Art, 1927 – 1938

TRADEMARKS: Illustrations 9 – 12, appendix A.
Hull marked tiles in both raised and incised form, and the designation of "faience" or "cushion" was usually noted. Most of the novelty items illustrated are unmarked; however, a few do bear incised mold numbers and size identification.

Plate 51.
Row 1:
1. Tile,* satin green, hand painted, incised "Hull Faience, Cushion," ink stamped "360," 4¼" x 4¼", $18.00 – 25.00.
2. Tile, Crest design, featuring six satin colors, incised "Hull Faience," 6" x 6". This was the only Hull item, tile or pottery, housed in the famous Purviance Collection at White Pillars, Norwich, Ohio. $125.00 – 175.00.
3. Advertising tile, embossed Potter-at-Wheel and "TILE BY HULL, INSTALLED BY A. SCHIRMER, CINCINNATI," 4¼" x 4¼", satin gray, $400.00 – 600.00.
4. Tile,* satin lavender, hand painted, incised "Hull Faience Tile, Cushion," ink stamped "349," 4¼" x 4¼", $18.00 – 25.00.
Row 2:
1. Tile, satin turquoise and cream, raised "Hull Tile," 2¾" x 6", $45.00 – 65.00.
2. Tile, satin turquoise and cream, raised "Hull Tile," 2¾" x 6", $45.00 – 65.00.
3. Tile, matte blue and gold, incised "Hull Faience," 2¾" x 2¾", $35.00 – 45.00.
4. Tile, matte orange, incised "Hull Faience, Cushion" in crisscross form, 2" x 2", $25.00 – 35.00.
5. Tile, dolphin decor, matte pink and blue, incised "Hull Faience," 2¾" x 2¾", $75.00 – 100.00.
6. Tile, boat decor, matte pink and blue, incised "Hull Faience," 2¾" x 2¾", $75.00 – 100.00.
7. Tile, boat decor, matte blues, raised "Hull Tile," 2¾" x 6", $100.00 – 150.00.
Row 3:
1. Puss 'n Boots, decorated bisque, unmarked experimental, 5½", 1936, $75.00 – 100.00.
2. Pig, decorated bisque, unmarked experimental, 5½", 1936, $75.00 – 100.00.
3. Crab Apple semiporcelain jardiniere, unmarked, 4", 1934 – 1935, $35.00 – 45.00.
4. Vase, unmarked, 5½", $25.00 – 35.00.
5. Monkey, unmarked experimental, 5¼", 1938, $35.00 – 50.00.
6. Jardiniere, unmarked, 3", 1938, $25.00 – 35.00.
7. Crab Apple semiporcelain vase, 3", 1934 – 1935, $35.00 – 45.00.
Row 4:
1. Lusterware pitcher, unmarked, 4¾", 1927 – 1930, $40.00 – 65.00.
2. Sueno vase, "930/33-1," 5", 1938, $25.00 – 40.00.
3. Lusterware wall pocket, unmarked, 8½", 1927 – 1930, $75.00 – 100.00.
4. Vase, "216-9"," 1938, $35.00 – 50.00.
5. Crazy Horse planter, "959," 5", 1938, $30.00 – 40.00.
6. Vase, unmarked, 5½", 1938, $60.00 – 80.00.

*These tiles were part of a sample set used by Hull retailing and order departments. The additional ink stamps referred to glaze color designations.

Plate 51.

THE FORTIES
(1938 – 1950)

By the late 1930s, Hull flooded the markets with matte pastel artware, an abundance of novelty figural planters, and up-to-date kitchenware.

Matte art lines continued to be produced until the Hull plant was destroyed by flood and fire in 1950.

The Potter-at-wheel logo became a mainstay promotional tool used in advertising Hull's pride in craftsmanship. It was used from Hull's earliest years to closing. First used on advertising materials and brochure pages, it later appeared in foil label form and was additionally used on company letterheads after 1950.

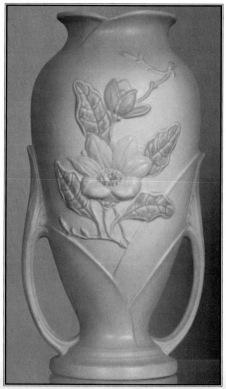

Pottery in its finest sense must have qualities of velvet-like feel to produce an emotional stir and justify a place among your finest possessions. This is a dominant characteristic...a balance of subdued color and style seldom obtained but always sought. See and feel the actual piece of ware to become as keenly enthused as were the inspired craftsmen.
Original Hull promotional material.

Magnolia vase, "15-16"," $475.00 – 600.00.

BOW-KNOT

PRODUCTION DATES: 1949 – 1950

TRADEMARKS: Illustrations 41 and 44, appendix A.

Bow-Knot carried an incised print "Hull Art, U.S.A.," a B-series mold number, and size identification. The line was additionally marked with the round black Potter-at-Wheel foil label, which had silver, gold, or gray lettering.

Bow-Knot's embossed floral decoration was produced in blue to pink or turquoise to blue combinations. Twenty-nine shapes appeared in catalog form. Add to this a rare wall pocket, in square form.

A Hull Company price list dated January 1, 1949, established minimum retail prices west of the Rockies at $6.49 each for the B-29-12" basket or console set, while the tea set retailed at $5.93 and the 10" plaque for $2.69. Wholesale prices were $3.00 each for the large basket, $2.90 per console set, $1.50 per tea set, and $1.25 per plaque. A Bow-Knot assortment package of 104 pieces wholesaled for $102.40, while 186 pieces sold for $184.90.

Trendy Bow-Knot's rising popularity and prices led to a number of 1970s reproductions. Having had early success with prime examples such as the B-29-12" basket, the B-15-13½" ewer, and the B-28-10" wall plaque, bootleggers continue to reproduce Bow-Knot tea sets, wall pockets, and large vases.

Reproduction Bow-Knot pieces are marked with a fairly convincing trademark. Once thought to be difficult to master, Hull's subtle matte pastels are considered by today's knowledgeable restoration artists to be one of the easiest glazes to simulate.

Plate 52. Ewer, "B-15-13½"," $900.00 – 1,100.00.

Plate 53.
Row 1:
1. Candleholder, "B-17," 4", $140.00 – 175.00.
2. Console bowl, "B-16-13½"," $375.00 – 475.00.
3. Candleholder, "B-17," 4", $140.00 – 175.00.
Row 2:
1. Pitcher wall pocket, "B-26-6"," $275.00 – 325.00.
2. Whisk Broom wall pocket, "B-27-8"," $275.00 – 325.00.
3. Cup and Saucer wall pocket, "B-24-6"," $275.00 – 325.00.
4. Iron wall pocket, unmarked, 6¼", $350.00 – 425.00.
Row 3:
1. Vase, "B-7-8½"," $300.00 – 365.00.
2. Jardiniere, "B-19-9⅜"," $950.00 – 1,200.00.
3. Vase, "B-9-8½"," $290.00 – 345.00.
4. Flower Pot with attached saucer, "B-6-6½"," $250.00 – 300.00.
Row 4:
1. Wall plaque, "B-28-10"," $950.00 – 1,250.00.
2. Basket, "B-29-12"," $1,400 – 2,200.00.
3. Vase, "B-14-12½"," $900.00 – 1,100.00.

Plate 53.

Bow-Knot

Plate 54.

Row 1:

1. Vase, "B-2-5"," $175.00 – 220.00.
2. Creamer, "B-21-4"," $200.00 – 225.00.
3. Teapot, "B-20-6"," $450.00 – 650.00.
4. Covered sugar, "B-22-4"," $200.00 – 225.00.
5. Ewer, "B-1-5½"," $210.00 – 250.00.

Row 2:

1. Basket, "B-25-6½"," $300.00 – 365.00.
2. Cornucopia, "B-5-7½"," $225.00 – 265.00.
3. Vase, "B-8-8½"," $260.00 – 340.00.
4. Jardiniere, "B-18-5¾"," $235.00 – 275.00.

Row 3:

1. Vase, "B-4-6½"," $245.00 – 275.00.
2. Double cornucopia, "B-13-13"," $350.00 – 450.00.
3. Vase, "B-3-6½"," $200.00 – 245.00.

Row 4:

1. Vase, "B-11-10½"," $550.00 – 700.00.
2. Basket, "B-12-10½"," $800 – 1,100.00.
3. Vase, "B-10-10½"," $500.00 – 625.00.

Magazine advertisement, 1949.

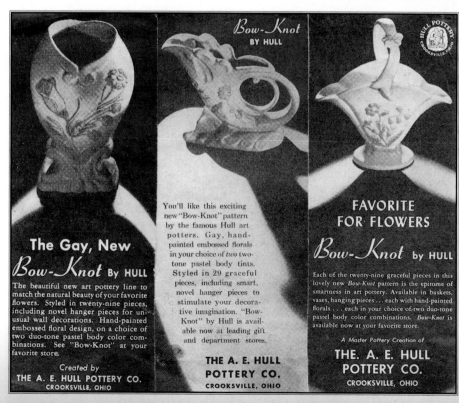

Magazine advertisement, 1949.

90

Plate 54.

Calla Lily
Thistle
Tulip

PRODUCTION DATES: 1938 – 1940

Calla Lily, Tulip, and Thistle are all shown as Hull's Sueno line, most likely an overall name for a chain store sales package. Tulip and Thistle were offered until 1941.

TRADEMARKS: Illustrations 22, 23, 24, 25, and 26, appendix A.

Calla Lily: Does not carry a Hull trademark in the mold. However, it carries an incised 500-series mold number and size identification.

Thistle: Incised 50-series mold number and size identification. There is no Hull trademark on the mold.

Tulip: Incised block "HULL, U.S.A.," 100-series mold number, and size identification.

Calla Lily, Tulip, Thistle, and the plain Sueno vases all bear the triangular or diamond foil labels that state "HULL POTTERY" in two lines. These seals are found with black or maroon background with gold or silver lettering.

Plate 55.

Row 1.

1. Vase, "502/33-6½"," $140.00 – 165.00.
2. Vase, "520/33-8"," $185.00 – 240.00.
3. Vase, "500/32-10"," $215.00 – 260.00.
4. Vase, "530/33-5"," $140.00 – 175.00.

Plate 56.

Row 1:

1. Candleholder, unmarked, 2¼", $100.00 – 130.00.
2. Console bowl, "500/32-10"," $215.00 – 260.00.
3. Candleholder, unmarked, 2¼", $100.00 – 130.00.

Row 2:

1. Vase, "503-33-6"," $100.00 – 135.00.
2. Vase, "530/33-7"," $175.00 – 235.00.

3. Vase, "530/33-5"," $140.00 – 175.00.
4. Vase, "550/33-7½"," $165.00 – 200.00.

Row 3:

1. Vase, "501-33-6½"," $90.00 – 125.00.
2. Vase, "520/33-8"," $185.00 – 240.00.
3. Vase, "500/33-8"," $190.00 – 250.00.
4. Vase, "540/33-6"," $140.00 – 165.00.

Row 4:

1. Vase, unmarked, 9½", $275.00 – 400.00.
2. Vase, "560/33-13"," $500.00 – 600.00.
3. Ewer, "506-10"," $380.00 – 480.00.

Plate 55.

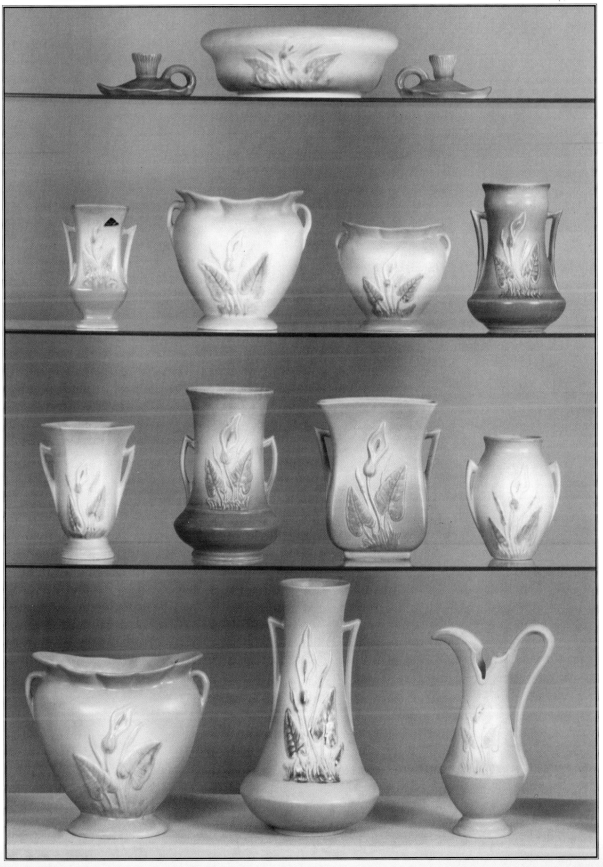

Plate 56.

Plate 57.
1. Calla Lily vase, "560/33-13"," $500.00 – 600.00.
2. Calla Lily ewer, "506-10"," $380.00 – 480.00.
3. Calla Lily vase, "560/33-13"," $500.00 – 600.00.
4. Calla Lily ewer, "506-10"," $380.00 – 480.00.
5. Calla Lily vase, "560/33-13"," $500.00 – 600.00.
6. Calla Lily ewer, "506-10"," $380.00 – 480.00.
7. Calla Lily vase, "560/33-13"," $500.00 – 600.00.
8. Experimental Calla Lily ewer, stoneware glaze, "506-10"," $550.00 – 750.00.
9. Calla Lily vase, "560/33-13"," $500.00 – 600.00.

Plate 58.
Row 1:
1. Sueno vase, "920-33-1-5"," $30.00 – 40.00.
2. Calla Lily console bowl, "590/32," 13", $175.00 – 225.00.
3. Sueno vase, "930-33-3-5"," $30.00 – 40.00.
Row 2:
1. Tulip jardiniere, "117-30-5"," $135.00 – 160.00.
2. Tulip bud vase, "104-33-6"," $140.00 – 165.00.
3. Tulip jardiniere, "115-33-7"," $295.00 – 345.00.
4. Tulip vase, "100-33-6½"," $130.00 – 150.00.
5. Tulip vase, "100-33-4"," $60.00 – 90.00.
Row 3:
1. Thistle vase, "#51-6½"," $90.00 – 125.00.
2. Thistle vase, "#52-6½"," $90.00 – 125.00.
3. Thistle vase, "#53-6½"," $90.00 – 125.00.
4. Thistle vase, "#54-6½"," $90.00 – 125.00.
Row 4:
1. Tulip vase, "105-33-8"," $265.00 – 310.00.
2. Tulip ewer, "109-8"," $265.00 – 300.00.
3. Tulip vase, "101-33-9"," $295.00 – 360.00.
4. Sueno vase, "750-33-9½"," $115.00 – 150.00.

Plate 58.

Camellia

PRODUCTION DATES: 1943 – 1944

TRADEMARKS: Illustrations 26, 28, and 29, appendix A.

Raised "HULL, U.S.A.," 100-series mold number, and size identification. This line bears the triangular foil label, which states "HULL POTTERY" in two lines. This seal is found with black or maroon background with gold or silver lettering.

This line is also referred to as Open Rose by collectors; however, Camellia is the correct company name. Featured are hand-decorated embossed florals on shaded pastel backgrounds of matte pink and blue, or allover matte white. At least 44 pieces were cataloged.

Collectors need to be aware that there are Camellia reproductions in today's marketplace. While Hull reproductions are being made in various lines, those reproduced in Camellia are the most convincing. Reproduced items carry the same Hull mark as the originals, and the differences in size, color, and weight are subtle. Your best defense is use of a reputable dealer. However, with Camellia this is of little help, because the reproduced ware is so similar to the original that some of the best dealers have been fooled. Camellia's tea set and Mermaid planter are prime reproduction targets.

Plate 60.

Row 1:
1. Basket, "142-6¼"," $295.00 – 395.00.
2. Creamer, "111-5"," $125.00 – 150.00.
3. Teapot, "110-8½"," $350.00 – 425.00.
4. Open sugar, "112-5"," $125.00 – 150.00.

Row 2:
1. Candleholder, "117-6½"," $180.00 – 225.00.
2. Console bowl, "116-12"," $300.00 – 375.00.
3. Candleholder, "117-6½"," $180.00 – 225.00.
4. Hanging basket, "132-7"," $260.00 – 325.00.

Row 3:
1. Vase, "118-6½"," $175.00 – 215.00.
2. Low bowl, "113-7"," $145.00 – 175.00.
3. Jardiniere, "114-8¼"," $325.00 – 395.00.
4. Basket, "140-10½"," $900.00 – 1,200.00.
5. Ewer, "128-4¾"," $130.00 – 165.00.

Row 4:
1. Wall pocket, "125-8½"," $400.00 – 525.00.
2. Vase, "103-8½"," $165.00 – 205.00.
3. Vase, "124-12"," $400.00 – 500.00.
4. Ewer, "115-8½"," $245.00 – 295.00.
5. Ewer, "105-7"," $230.00 – 275.00.

Plate 59. Mermaid with Shell planter, "104-10½"," $1,800.00 – 2,600.00.

Plate 60.

The Forties (1938 – 1950)

Camellia

Plate 61.
Row 1:
1. Sugar, "112-5"," $125.00 – 150.00.
2. Teapot, "110-8½"," $350.00 – 425.00.
3. Creamer, "111-5"," $125.00 – 150.00.
4. Candleholder, "117-6½"," $180.00 – 225.00.
5. Console bowl, "116-12"," $300.00 – 375.00.
6. Candleholder, "117-6½"," $180.00 – 225.00.
Row 2:
1. Vase, "127-4¾"," $80.00 – 110.00.
2. Ewer, "128-4¾"," $130.00 – 165.00.
3. Vase, "130-4¾"," $80.00 – 110.00.
4. Vase, "131-4¾"," $80.00 – 110.00.
5. Basket, "107-8"," $350.00 – 425.00.
6. Hanging basket, "132-7"," $260.00 – 325.00.
Row 3:
1. Low bowl, "113-7"," $145.00 – 175.00.
2. Vase, "118-6½"," $175.00 – 215.00.
3. Vase, "120-6¼"," $130.00 – 160.00.
4. Vase, "121-6¼"," $130.00 – 160.00.
5. Vase, "122-6¼"," $130.00 – 160.00.
6. Bud vase, "129-7"," $135.00 – 160.00.
7. Basket, "142-6¼"," $295.00 – 395.00.
Row 4:
1. Vase, "133-6¼"," $130.00 – 160.00.
2. Vase, "134-6¼"," $135.00 – 155.00.
3. Vase, "135-6¼"," $130.00 – 150.00.
4. Vase, "136-6¼"," $135.00 – 160.00.

5. Vase, "137-6¼"," $130.00 – 160.00.
6. Vase, "138-6¼"," $135.00 – 160.00.
7. Vase, "123-6¼"," $145.00 – 175.00.

Plate 62.
Row 1:
1. Vase, "130-4¾"," $80.00 – 110.00.
2. Vase, "136-6¼"," $135.00 – 160.00.
3. Basket, "107-8"," $350.00 – 425.00.
4. Vase, "121-6¼"," $130.00 – 160.00.
5. Vase, "131-4¾"," $80.00 – 110.00.
Row 2:
1. Vase, "122-6¼"," $130.00 – 160.00.
2. Vase, "138-6¼"," $135.00 – 165.00.
3. Vase, "108-8½"," $210.00 – 270.00.
4. Vase, "120-6¼"," $130.00 – 160.00.
5. Vase, "134-6¼"," $135.00 – 155.00.
Row 3:
1. Cornucopia, "141-8½"," $175.00 – 225.00.
2. Vase, "135-6¼"," $130.00 – 150.00.
3. Vase, "126-8½"," $330.00 – 400.00.
4. Vase, "137-6¼"," $130.00 – 160.00.
5. Cornucopia, "101-8½"," $175.00 – 215.00.
Row 4:
1. Vase, "102-8½"," $215.00 – 280.00.
2. Lamp-shaped vase, "139-10½"," $350.00 – 450.00.
3. Ewer, "106-13¼"," $700.00 – 825.00.
4. Vase, "143-8½"," $200.00 – 260.00.

Plate 61. Original company brochure page.

Plate 62.

Cinderella
Blossom and Bouquet

PRODUCTION DATES: 1948 – 1949

TRADEMARKS: Illustrations 50, 51, 53, and 55, appendix A.

Incised bold "HULL" with a flourishing, incised "U.S.A." Sizes represented on molds identified volume in ounces. This kitchenware line carried a specially designed label, a blue and gold foil Cinderella label depicting horses and a carriage. Bouquet items beyond the 15 cataloged pieces were usually marked with the small brown script ink stamp.

Cinderella was Hull's overall line name for kitchenware it produced in two distinct designs known as Blossom and Bouquet. Each design had 15 illustrated cataloged shapes, while a company price list additionally specified the 9¾" salad bowl. Unlisted items that are so few that they are categorized as experimental include other dinnerware accessories, e.g., square cereal bowls, square dinner plates, and a compartment plate.

Blossom: Ovenproof kitchenware items, white gloss finish, with six-petal underglaze, hand-painted flower in pink or yellow with green leaves and banding. The Blossom line was first introduced with yellow florals, but changed ten months later to pink florals. The two Blossom decors are distinctively different in style.

Bouquet: Ovenproof kitchenware in white gloss finish, with yellow-tinted tops with underglaze hand-decorated floral spray of pink, yellow, and blue.

Plate 64.
Row 1:
1. Blossom creamer, "No. 28-4¼"," $45.00 – 70.00.
2. Blossom teapot, "No. 26-42 oz.," $140.00 – 180.00.
3. Blossom covered sugar, "No. 27-4½"," $45.00 – 70.00.
Row 2:
1. Blossom shaker, "No. 25-3½"," $20.00 – 30.00.
2. Blossom shaker, "No. 25-3½"," $20.00 – 30.00.
3. Bouquet grease jar, "No. 24-32 oz.," $50.00 – 75.00.
4. Bouquet covered casserole, "No. 21-8½"," $40.00 – 60.00.
5. Blossom pitcher, "No. 29-16 oz.," $45.00 – 70.00.
Row 3:
1. Bouquet pitcher, "No. 29-32 oz.," $25.00 – 35.00.
2. Blossom mixing bowl, "20-5½"," $25.00 – 35.00.
3. Blossom mixing bowl, "20-7½"," $35.00 – 50.00.
4. Blossom mixing bowl, "20-9½"," $50.00 – 75.00.
Row 4:
1. Bouquet bowl, brown ink stamp, 9¾", $100.00 – 125.00.
2. Bouquet cookie jar, unmarked, 10½", $140.00 – 180.00.
3. Bouquet ice-lip pitcher, "No. 22-64 oz.," $155.00 – 200.00.

Plate 63. Original company brochure page.

Plate 64.

Dogwood

PRODUCTION DATES: Dogwood, 1942 – 1943

TRADEMARKS: Illustrations 26 and 29, appendix A.

Dogwood items are marked with raised "HULL, U.S.A.," a 500-series mold number, and size identification. This line bears the triangular foil label, which states "HULL POTTERY" in two lines. This seal is found with black or maroon background with gold or silver lettering.

Known also as Wild Rose, this hand-decorated embossed single and double rose motif is shaded in duotone matte finishes of blue and pink, turquoise and cream, or overall cream, and was offered in 22 shapes.

Plate 65.
Row 1:
1. Dogwood vase, "517-4¾"," $80.00 – 110.00.
2. Dogwood vase, "516-4¾"," $75.00 – 95.00.
3. Novelty Dancing Girl, "955," 7", 1938, $50.00 – 75.00.
4. Sun-Glow tea bell, rare matte, unmarked, 6¾", 1949, $300.00 – 375.00.
5. Sun-Glow rope-handled tea bell, rare matte, unmarked, 6", 1949, $325.00 – 450.00.
Row 2:
1. Dogwood ewer, "520-4¾"," $135.00 – 160.00.
2. Dogwood jardiniere, "514-4"," $130.00 – 155.00.
3. Dogwood low bowl, "521-7"," $160.00 – 195.00.
4. Dogwood cornucopia, "522, 3¾"," $110.00 – 135.00.
Row 3:
1. Dogwood basket, "501-7½"," $295.00 – 350.00.
2. Dogwood window box, "508-10½"," $195.00 – 275.00.
3. Dogwood teapot, "507-6½"," $300.00 – 400.00.
Row 4:
1. Dogwood candleholder, "512, 3¾"," $135.00 – 155.00.
2. Dogwood console bowl, "511-11½"," $285.00 – 395.00.
3. Dogwood candleholder, "512, 3¾"," $135.00 – 155.00.

Plate 65.

Plate 66.
Row 1:
1. Dogwood vase, "509-6½"," $135.00 – 155.00.
2. Dogwood ewer, "505-6½"," actual height 8½", $245.00 – 300.00.
3. Dogwood vase, "513-6½"," $140.00 – 165.00.
Row 2:
1. Dogwood vase, "515-8½"," $150.00 – 210.00.
2. Dogwood ewer, "516-11½"," $400.00 – 525.00.
3. Dogwood vase, "502-6½"," $240.00 – 300.00.
Row 3:
1. Dogwood vase, "510-10½"," $325.00 – 425.00.
2. Experimental Dogwood vase, unmarked, 14", $700.00 – 900.00.
3. Dogwood ewer, "519-13½"," $675.00 – 785.00.

Plate 66.

Iris

PRODUCTION DATES: 1940 – 1942

TRADEMARKS: Illustrations 22 and 26, appendix A.

Incised "HULL, USA," 400-series mold number, and size identification. This line bears the triangular and diamond foil labels, which state "HULL POTTERY" in two lines. These seals are found with black or maroon background with gold or silver lettering.

Iris is made up of hand-decorated embossed florals on matte tinted backgrounds of blue and rose, rose and peach, or allover peach. There are 14 shapes cataloged, and several come in graduated sizes.

Plate 67.
Row 1:
1. Candleholder, "411-5"," $125.00 – 155.00.
2. Basket, "408-7"," $265.00 – 310.00.
3. Jardiniere, "413-5½"," $175.00 – 205.00.
4. Rose bowl, "412-7"," $220.00 – 275.00.
Row 2:
1. Console bowl, "409-12"," $280.00 – 340.00.
2. Candleholder, "411-5"," $125.00 – 155.00.
Row 3:
1. Vase, "414-16"," $450.00 – 600.00.
2. Ewer, "401-13½"," $500.00 – 625.00.
3. Vase, "403-10"," $325.00 – 410.00.
4. Vase, "402-7"," $150.00 – 200.00.
5. Vase, "404-8½"," $210.00 – 250.00.
Row 4:
1. Bud vase, "410-7½"," $165.00 – 210.00.
2. Vase, "406-8½"," $200.00 – 250.00.
3. Vase, "407-8½"," $215.00 – 270.00.
4. Vase, "405-8½"," $210.00 – 250.00.

Plate 68.
Row 1:
1. Candleholder, "411-5"," $125.00 – 155.00.
2. Console bowl, "409-12"," $280.00 – 340.00.
3. Candleholder, "411-5"," $125.00 – 155.00.
Row 2:
1. Vase, "407-8½"," $215.00 – 270.00.
2. Vase, "402-4¼"," $100.00 – 125.00.
3. Vase, "404-8½"," $200.00 – 250.00.
4. Vase, "403-4¾"," $120.00 – 145.00.
5. Vase, "402-8½"," $200.00 – 250.00.
Row 3:
1. Vase, "404-10½"," $325.00 – 410.00.
2. Vase, "414-16"," $450.00 – 600.00.
3. Ewer, "401-13½"," $500.00 – 625.00.

Plate 67. Original company brochure page.

Plate 68.

Plate 69.
Row 1:
1. Basket, "408-7"," $265.00 – 310.00.
2. Advertising plaque, "The A. E. Hull Co. Pottery," 5" x 11", 1938, $5,000.00 – 8,000.00.
3. Vase, "406-4¾"," $120.00 – 145.00.
Row 2:
1. Vase, "402-7"," $150.00 – 200.00.
2. Advertising plaque, "HULL," unmarked, 2¼" x 5½", 1938, $2,500.00 – 3,500.00.
3. Bud vase, "410-7½"," $165.00 – 210.00.
4. Vase, "405-8½"," $210.00 – 250.00.
5. Ewer, "401-8"," $245.00 – 295.00.
Row 3:
1. Rose bowl, "412-7"," $220.00 – 275.00.
2. Rose bowl, "412-4"," $120.00 – 145.00.
3. Jardiniere, "413-9"," $475.00 – 600.00.
4. Vase, "404-4¾"," $120.00 – 145.00.
5. Jardiniere, "413-5½"," $175.00 – 205.00.
Row 4:
1. Vase, "407-8½"," $200.00 – 250.00.
2. Ewer, "401-5"," $140.00 – 165.00.
3. Vase, "414-10½"," $325.00 – 410.00.
4. Vase, "407-4¾"," $130.00 – 150.00.
5. Vase, "403-7"," $175.00 – 225.00.

Plate 69.

LAMPS

PRODUCTION DATES: 1940s

TRADEMARKS:
 The lamps illustrated do not carry any Hull trademarks in their molds, although some do have an L-series system of numbering, and some carry an incised "USA." Please consult the index for lamps that appear in other sections of this volume.

DESCRIPTION:
 Buyer beware, lamps are at a premium and you must be sure you are purchasing a factory-made lamp. If the lamp has a metal base and/or top fitting, you would be wise to ask the owner's permission to disengage the lamp parts to assure it is factory made. The exceptions to this advice about metal fittings are the small Rosella and Classic lamps. These were either made at the factory or authorized by an agent; all fittings are consistently the same.
 In considering other lamps, a buyer's absolute dream is locating a lamp base that has never been wired and is without bothersome metal fittings. When the upper portion is factory filled in, sometimes even built up in a rounded or stairstep fashion, you no doubt have a lamp base produced within the factory. The drilled area for cord placement is the second most important area to check; make sure it was drilled first and then glazed, rather than drilled after the glazing process.
 With prices for lamps at a premium, expect to find home-fashioned items on the market. Also, there are some extremely close versions of the lamp shown in row 4, no. 3.

Plate 70.
Row 1:
1. Water Lily, gloss, unmarked, 7½", 1949, $295.00 – 400.00.
Row 2:
1, Classic, "T-1," 7¾", 1946, $175.00 – 235.00.
2. Classic, "T-2," 7¾", 1946, $150.00 – 200.00.
3. Classic, "T-1," 7¾", 1946, $175.00 – 235.00.
Row 3:
1. Experimental Rosella, dimpled body, unmarked, 10¾", 1946, $950.00 – 1,400.00.
2. Unnamed matte line, unmarked, 9", early 1940s, $400.00 – 550.00.
3. Rosella, decorated over glaze, "L3," 11", 1946, $260.00 – 395.00.
Row 4:
1. Rosella, unmarked, Rosella foil label, 6¾", 1946, $240.00 – 325.00.
2. Rosella, "L-3," 11", 1946, $260.00 – 395.00.
3. Picture-framed rose decal, "L2," 13", 1940, $200.00 – 250.00.
4. Rosella, "L3," 11", 1946, $260.00 – 395.00.
5. Rosella, unmarked, 6¾", 1946, $240.00 – 325.00.

This lamp was made by a specialty company from Kitten planter no. 61. The pottery section of this lamp is 7½". Its value is only minimally more than that of the planter itself since it was not factory produced. $40.00 – 60.00.

Plate 70.

LITTLE RED RIDING HOOD

PRODUCTION DATES: 1943 – 1957

TRADEMARKS: Illustrations 33 through 37, appendix A.

All Little Red Riding Hood pottery and china products have been referred to as Hull products for the past 20 years or more, even though very few items were actually produced by Hull. Hull's trademarks included the script "Hull Ware, Little Red Riding Hood, Patent Applied For U.S.A." and the script "Hull Ware, U.S.A." Regal China wares were marked with an incised Little Red Riding Hood script form; many carried only the patent design number 135889, and some were unmarked.

The Hull company originated the Little Red Riding Hood design, and U.S. patent number 135,889 was issued for its cookie jar. Interest was so great that this piece spurred demand for additional kitchenware characters. Regal China Company, not Hull, met this demand.

Actual Hull-produced Little Red Riding Hood wares were few, and limited to the open basket cookie jar, covered "bow" jars, and shakers. Although some of the same decals were used jointly by Hull Pottery and Regal China, identification of wares comes from the clay color and content.

The collecting audience for Little Red Riding Hood is voluminous, and most collectors begin their collections in good faith that this ware was of Hull manufacture. Even with the publication of Mark E. Supnick's book, *Collecting Hull Pottery's Little Red Riding Hood*, and further explanation of the ware's origins, Little Red Riding Hood is still referred to as Hull pottery, and is bought, sold, and traded as such.

The original seven-year patent 135,889 was assigned to A. E. Hull Pottery Company and Louise E. Bauer, designer of the cookie jar. The patent was filed April 12, 1943, and granted June 29, 1943. Interest was so great that the patent was extended once, expiring June 29, 1957. While Louise Bauer designed the cookie jar, and designed small and large shakers for the Royal China and Novelty Company of Chicago, Illinois (a division of the Regal China Corporation), most likely Regal China hired modelers to design the additional items. Hull and Regal obviously either had some type of contractual agreement, or the registered patent was sold and transferred totally to Regal. The Little Red Riding Hood advertising plaque, obviously produced by Regal China, incorporated the patent number into the design.

With the knowledge in hand that Hull Little Red Riding Hood is usually *not Hull*, Little Red Riding Hood collectors can continue to collect it and call it whatever they wish. Little Red Riding Hood items do have a rightful place in Hull's history and listings of lines of manufacture, since the design inspiration was, in fact, Hull's.

To make the collecting dilemma even more confusing, you will see illustrated in the next few photographs several additional items collectors value in their Little Red Riding Hood collections. It appears collectors gather various types of porcelain wares decorated with the same decal that was used on Hull and Regal Little Red Riding Hood items.

Many Little Red Riding Hood shapes have been reproduced. These reproductions are poor quality and can be spotted fairly easily. Smaller size, lighter overall weight, and poor paint (true red is extremely hard to produce) are indications of a reproduction. Marks on reproductions include "McCoy," "Cookie Jar Classics," various "China" markings, and ink-stamped "Little Red Riding Hood." It should be noted that the McCoy Pottery Company never manufactured a line of Little Red Riding Hood.

Plate 71.
Row 1:
1. Regal China advertising plaque, "Featuring Little Red Riding Hood, Covered By Pat, Des. No. 135889," 6½" x 11½", $4,500.00 – 6,500.00.
2. Regal China butter dish, 5½", $325.00 – 450.00.
Row 2:
1 & 2. Regal China shakers, 3¼", $65.00 – 90.00 each.
3. Regal China creamer, 5", $225.00 – 300.00.
4. Pope Gosser gravy with attached underplate, 9", $35.00 – 50.00.

5. Regal China sugar, 5", $225.00 – 300.00.
6. Regal China mustard with spoon, 5¼", $375.00 – 460.00.
Row 3:
1. Hull covered jar, 9", $300.00 – 425.00.
2. Pope Gosser platter, 13½", $35.00 – 50.00.
3. Regal China teapot, 8", $375.00 – 475.00.
Row 4:
1. Regal China cookie jar, 13", $375.00 – 400.00.
2. Lamp, maker unknown, 12", $45.00 – 65.00.
3. Hull cookie jar, 13", $450.00 – 650.00.

Plate 71.

Little Red Riding Hood

Plate 72.

Row 1:

1. Regal China crawling sugar, unmarked, 3", $350.00 – 450.00.

2. Regal China tab-handled creamer, unmarked, 3½", $275.00 – 375.00.

Row 2:

1. Hull covered jar, "Hull Ware 932," 9", $550.00 – 700.00.

2. Regal China canister, "Pretzels," "Pat, Des. 135889," 10", $1,200.00 – 1,500.00.

3. Regal China pitcher, "Pat. Des. 135889," 8", $400.00 – 500.00.

Row 3:

1. Regal China canister, "Coffee," "Pat. Des. 135889," 10", $900.00 – 1,200.00.

2. Regal China covered sugar, unmarked, 3½", $350.00 – 400.00.

3. Regal China head-pour creamer, unmarked, 3½", $350.00 – 450.00.

4. Regal China canister, "Tea," "Pat. Des. 135889," 10", $900.00 – 1,200.00.

Plate 72.

Plate 73.
Row 1:
1. Regal China shaker, unmarked, 5¼", $100.00 – 150.00.
2. Regal China hanging matchbox, "Pat. Des. No. 135889," 5¼", $450.00 – 650.00.
3. Regal China shaker, unmarked, 5¼", $100.00 – 150.00.
Row 2:
1. Regal China canister, "Cereal," "Pat. Des. No. 135889," 10", $1,000.00 – 1,400.00.
2. Regal China canister, "Flour," "Pat. Des. No. 135889," 10", $900.00 – 1,400.00.
3. Regal China canister, "Sugar," "Pat. Des. No. 135889," 10", $900.00 – 1,400.00.
Row 3:
1. Regal China cookie jar, "Pat. Des. No. 135889," 13", $600.00 – 900.00.
2. Regal China shaker, unmarked, 4½", $95.00 – 140.00.
3. Regal China canister, "Salt," "Pat. Des, No 135889," 10", $1,200.00 – 1,500.00.
4. Regal China wall hanging planter, "Pat. Des. No. 135889," 9", $600.00 – 800.00.

Plate 73.

Little Red Riding Hood

Plate 75.

Row 1:

1. Regal China shaker, unmarked, 5¼", $95.00 – 140.00.
2. Regal China shaker, unmarked, 5¼", $95.00 – 140.00.
3. Regal China hanging matchbox, unmarked, 5½", $300.00 – 400.00.
4. Regal China wolf jar, "USA," 6", $750.00 – 900.00.
5. Hull shaker, unmarked, 5½", $400.00 – 500.00.
6. Hull shaker, unmarked, 5½", $400.00 – 500.00.

Row 2:

1. Regal China pitcher, unmarked, 7", $400.00 – 500.00.
2. Hull covered jar, 9", $530.00 – 700.00.
3. Regal China covered jar, unmarked, 8½", $550.00 – 700.00.
4. Regal China standing bank, unmarked, 7", $750.00 – 1,000.00.

Row 3:

1. Chic Pottery wall pocket, 4¾", $35.00 – 45.00.
2. Pope Gosser creamer, 3½", $20.00 – 30.00.
3. Pope Gosser dinner plate, 10", $6.00 – 8.00.
4. Pope Gosser covered sugar, 4½", $20.00 – 30.00.
5. Chic Pottery iron wall pocket, 5½", $35.00 – 50.00.

Row 4:

1. Hull cookie jar, 13", $450.00 – 650.00.
2. Lamp, maker unknown, 13", $45.00 – 65.00.
3. Lamp, maker unknown, 12½", $45.00 – 65.00.
4. Hull cookie jar, 13", $450.00 – 650.00.

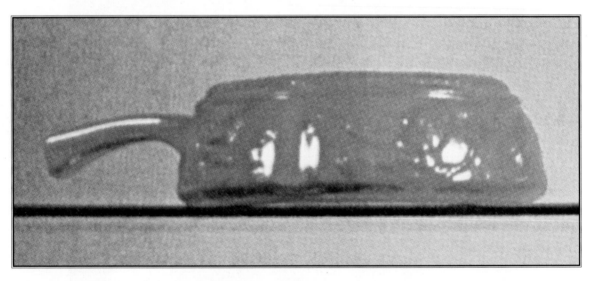

Plate 74. Regal China handled casserole, "Pat. Des. No.135889," 11¾", $1,800.00 – 2,200.00.

Plate 75.

MAGNOLIA

PRODUCTION DATES: 1946 – 1947

TRADEMARKS: Illustrations 44 and 48, appendix A.
Raised print "Hull Art, U.S.A.," mold number, and size identification. This line carried the round black Potter-at-Wheel foil label, which had silver, gold, or gray lettering.

Magnolia can be identified by its hand-decorated embossed florals on shaded matte pastels of pink and blue or dusty rose and yellow. Twenty-seven items were included in this line, with vase 21-12½" being available with either open or tab handles.

Plate 77.
Row 1:
1. Creamer, "24-3¾"," $55.00 – 80.00.
2. Teapot, "23-6½"," $240.00 – 275.00.
3. Open sugar, "25-3¾"," $55.00 – 80.00.
Row 2:
1. Vase, "12-6¼"," $75.00 – 100.00.
2. Double cornucopia, "6-12"," $205.00 – 255.00.
3. Vase, "3-8¼"," $155.00 – 200.00.
4. Vase, "15-6¼"," $70.00 – 85.00.
Row 3:
1. Vase, "8-10½"," $200.00 – 240.00.
2. Ewer, "14-4¾"," $75.00 – 105.00.
3. Vase, "9-10½"," $235.00 – 275.00.
4. Vase, "13-4¾"," $50.00 – 75.00.
5. Vase, "21-12½"," open handles, $400.00 – 500.00.
Row 4:
1. Ewer, "18-13½"," $375.00 – 435.00.
2. Vase, "21-12½"," (tab handles), $350.00 – 450.00.
3. Vase, "17-12¼"," $300.00 – 385.00.
4. Vase, "22-12½"," $300.00 – 365.00.

Plate 76. Magnolia, first produced in matte pastels, was later replaced by a more modern high-gloss version named New Magnolia. Due to current collector preference, prices of New Magnolia remain slightly lower for most pieces than they do for the matte counterparts. The exceptions would be for the New Magnolia 10½" basket and 13½" ewer, which are more difficult to locate in gloss.

Plate 77.

Plate 78.

Row 1.
1. Cornucopia, "19-8½"," $155.00 – 210.00.
2. Basket, "10-10½"," $375.00 – 425.00.
3. Vase, "7-8½"," $155.00 – 200.00

Row 2:
1. Candleholder, "27-4"," $65.00 – 95.00.
2. Console bowl, "26-12"," $200.00 – 250.00.
3. Candleholder, "27-4"," $65.00 – 95.00.

Row 3:
1. Vase, "4-6¼"," $70.00 – 90.00.
2. Ewer, "5-7"," $175.00 – 225.00.
3. Vase, "1-8½"," $175.00 – 215.00.
4. Vase, "2-8½"," $175.00 – 215.00.
5. Vase, "11-6¼"," $70.00 – 90.00.

Row 4:
1. Vase, "20-15"," $475.00 – 600.00.
2. Lamp, 15" pottery section, not factory produced, $375.00 – 500.00.
3. Vase, "16-15"," $475.00 – 600.00.

Original Hull advertisements from *House Beautiful* and *Better Homes and Gardens*, 1947 – 1948.

Plate 78.

New Magnolia

PRODUCTION DATES: 1947 – 1948

TRADEMARKS: Illustrations 44 and 49, appendix A.
Raised print "Hull Art, U.S.A.," H-series mold number, and size identification. This line carried the round black Potter-at-Wheel foil label, which had silver, gold, or gray lettering.

New Magnolia showcases a hand-painted embossed floral decoration of blue or pink, with allover transparent pink high glaze. Many items were detailed in gold outside the factory, not uncommon for this line. Twenty-four pieces were included in the company catalog.

Hull, in 1947, made the decision to place another high-gloss artware line in the midst of the retail market's matte wares. Instead of creating a newly designed mold system (as it had when creating its high-gloss Rosella), the company opted for using shapes already familiar to the public. Here was seen a less expensive venture, with exceedingly less risk to the company. The known shapes in updated glazes proved to be far more comforting to Hull's wholesale and retail audiences. Hull's New Magnolia was a success.

Plate 81.
Row 1:
1. Vase, "H-5-6½"," $50.00 – 70.00.
2. Candleholder, "H24," 4", $50.00 – 65.00.
3. Console bowl, "H-23-13"," $125.00 – 165.00.
4. Candleholder, "H24," 4", $50.00 – 65.00.
5. Vase, "H-1-5½"," $40.00 – 60.00.
Row 2:
1. Vase, "H-2-5½"," $40.00 – 60.00.
2. Creamer, "H-21-3¾"," $50.00 – 70.00.
3. Teapot, "H-20-6½"," $175.00 – 225.00.
4. Covered sugar, "H-22-3¾"," $50.00 – 70.00.
5. Ewer, "H3-5½"," $60.00 – 85.00.

Row 3:
1. Cornucopia, "H-10-8½"," $115.00 – 155.00.
2. Basket, "H-14-10½"," $400.00 – 450.00.
3. Double cornucopia, "H-15-12"," $150.00 – 200.00.
Row 4:
1. Vase, "H-8-8½"," $120.00 – 165.00.
2. Vase, "H-6-6½"," $65.00 – 90.00.
3. Ewer, "H-11-8½"," $145.00 – 175.00.
4. Vase, "H-7-6½"," $45.00 – 65.00.
5. Vase, "H-9-8½"," $120.00 – 165.00.
Row 5:
1. Vase, "H-17-12½"," $240.00 – 310.00.
2. Vase, "H-16-12½"," $240.00 – 265.00.
3. Vase, "H-13-10½"," $140.00 – 180.00.
4. Ewer, "H-19-13½"," $370.00 – 465.00.

Plate 79. Magazine advertisement, May 1947.

Plate 80. Original company brochure page.

Plate 81.

MARDI GRAS
GRANADA

PRODUCTION DATES: 1938 – 1946

TRADEMARKS: Illustrations 26, 45, 46, and 61, appendix A.

Mardi Gras and Granada are incised with mold numbers and size identification, but do not carry the Hull trademark. They usually carry Hull labels. While Mardi Gras and Granada carry the triangular black or maroon foil label stating "HULL POTTERY" in gold or silver lettering, Mardi Gras and Granada also have a foil labels designed specifically for the lines.

Mardi Gras is marked with a vase-shaped black foil Potter-at-Wheel label that states "Mardi Gras" in silver or gold lettering. The company reports another foil label in white or silver, featuring a black silhouette of a female flamenco dancer with mask.

Granada is marked with a vertically rectangular black foil Potter-at-Wheel label that states "GRANADA" in silver or gold lettering.

Mardi Gras and Granada are lines with shared molds that were sold in assortments to a variety of chain stores. Mardi Gras/Granada items spanned many years of Hull production, from the 1930s throughout the 1950s. Items ranged from utility kitchenware items to artwares in both gloss and matte colors. The items illustrated are from Hull's most central years. These items are plentiful and are collected widely and mix well with Hull's floral designs. The dual line items illustrated include matte-finished items with embossed florals and deco-styled wares finished in solid matte or gloss whites and pastels. Another variation is the duotone matte body of blue and pink.

Plate 82.
Row 1:
1. Mardi Gras/Granada candleholder, unmarked, 3¼", $25.00 – 35.00.
2. Novelty planter, "204-5"," 1938, $55.00 – 80.00.
3. Mardi Gras/Granada candleholder, unmarked, 3¼", $25.00 – 35.00.
Row 2:
1. Morning Glory* ewer, "63," 11", $175.00 – 225.00.
2. Morning Glory* basket, "62," 8", $175.00 – 225.00.
3. Mardi Gras/Granada ewer, "31-10"," signed "'Grany Shafer," $300.00 – 350.00.
Row 3:
1. Mardi Gras/Granada basket, "32-8"," $140.00 – 195.00.
2. Mardi Gras/Granada teapot, "33-5½"," $235.00 – 310.00.
3. Mardi Gras/Granada basket, "65-8"," $100.00 – 145.00.
Row 4:
1. Mardi Gras/Granada ewer, "31-10"," $135.00 – 160.00.
2. Novelty cornucopia, "200," 9", 1938, $35.00 – 45.00.
3. Mardi Gras/Granada ewer, "66-10"," $125.00 – 160.00.

*Collectors have named this line Morning Glory because of the embossed trumpet-shaped floral design. It has further been speculated by collectors that it is an experimental or trialed design. However, the number of pieces in circulation, their varied locations of purchase, and the fact these pieces are usually mold marked make it easy to discount this theory. It is just as easy to theorize that they belong to the Mardi Gras/Granada line.

Plate 82.

Plate 83.
Row 1:
1. Pinecone vase, "55-6½"," $175.00 – 225.00.
2. Mardi Gras/Granada vase, "207-7½"," $50.00 – 80.00.
3. Pinecone vase, "55-6½"," $175.00 – 225.00.
Row 2:
1. Mardi Gras/Granada vase, "216-9"," $50.00 – 80.00.
2. Mardi Gras/Granada vase, "47-9"," $85.00 – 110.00.
3. Mardi Gras/Granada vase, "215-9"," $50.00 – 80.00.
Row 3:
1. Mardi Gras/Granada vase, "49-9"," $85.00 – 110.00.
2. Mardi Gras/Granada vase, "219-9"," $50.00 – 80.00.
3. Mardi Gras/Granada vase, "48-9"," $85.00 – 110.00.
Row 4:
1. Lamp, "L-1, USA," 13", $360.00 – 460.00.
2. Lamp, "L-1, USA," 13", $360.00 – 460.00.
3. Lamp, "L-1, USA," 13", $360.00 – 460.00.
4. Mardi Gras/Granada vase, "750-13½"," $75.00 – 125.00.

Original Florist's Ware company brochure page.
Row 1:
1. Vase, "750-9½"," $40.00 – 60.00.
2. Vase, "750-11½"," $55.00 – 80.00.
3. Vase, "750-13½"," $75.00 – 125.00.
Row 2:
1. Spanish pot, "71-10"," $30.00 – 40.00.
2. Spanish pot, "71-7"," $20.00 – 25.00.
3. Spanish pot, "71-5"," $15.00 – 22.00.
4. Spanish pot, "71-3¾"," $15.00 – 22.00.
5. Dancing Girl, "955-7"," $50.00 – 75.00.
Row 3:
1. Vase, "215-9"," $50.00 – 80.00.
2. Vase, "218-9"," $50.00 – 80.00.
3. Basket Girl, "954," 8", matte finish, $50.00 – 75.00.
Row 4:
1. Vase, "219-9"," $50.00 – 80.00.
2. Vase, "216-9"," $50.00 – 80.00.
3. Lamb, "965," 7½", $40.00 – 60.00.
4. Kitten, "61," 7½", $40.00 – 55.00.

Plate 83.

Orchid

PRODUCTION DATES: 1939 – 1941

TRADEMARKS: Illustrations 22, 23, and 26, appendix A.

Incised "HULL, U.S.A.," 300-series mold number, and size identification. This line bears the triangular and diamond foil labels, which state "HULL POTTERY" in two lines. These seals are found in black or maroon background with gold or silver lettering.

Hand-decorated embossed Orchid on duotone shaded matte backgrounds. Hull described the color combinations this way: "Dec. No. 1, blue green bottom and pink top; Dec. No. 2, blue green bottom and top; and Dec. No. 3, pink bottom and ivory top." At least 15 shapes were cataloged, and many were offered in graduated sizes.

Plate 85.
Row 1:
1. Vase, "303-4¾"," $120.00 – 145.00.
2. Vase, "308-4¼"," $120.00 – 145.00.
3. Bulb bowl, "312-7"," $150.00 – 200.00.
4. Bud vase, "306-6¾"," $175.00 – 225.00.
Row 2:
1. Vase, "307-6½"," $135.00 – 175.00.
2. Vase, "307-4¾"," $95.00 – 130.00.
3. Basket, "305-7"," $600.00 – 800.00.
4. Vase, "303-6"," $150.00 – 180.00.
5. Vase, "302-6"," $150.00 – 180.00.
Row 3:
1. Vase, "304-6"," $150.00 – 180.00.
2. Candleholder, "315," 4", $135.00 – 160.00.

3. Console bowl, "314-13"," $340.00 – 440.00.
4. Candleholder, "315," 4", $135.00 – 160.00.
5. Vase, "308-6"," $150.00 – 180.00.
Row 4:
1. Vase, "302-8"," $180.00 – 220.00.
2. Jardiniere, "310-9½"," $325.00 – 450.00.
3. Jardiniere, "310-6"," $225.00 – 265.00.
4. Jardiniere, "310-4¾"," $155.00 – 200.00.
5. Vase, "301-8"," $150.00 – 180.00.
Row 5:
1. Vase, "301-10"," $350.00 – 450.00.
2. Lamp base, unmarked, 10", $450.00 – 550.00.
3. Vase, "304-10¼"," $350.00 – 450.00.
4. Ewer, "311-13"," $625.00 – 725.00.

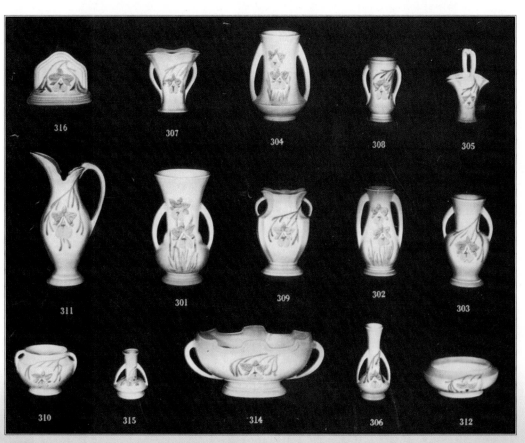

Plate 84. Original company brochure page.

Plate 85.

Poppy

PRODUCTION DATES: 1943 – 1944

TRADEMARKS: Illustrations 26, 28, and 29, appendix A.

Poppy is marked with a raised "HULL, U.S.A.," a 600-series mold number, and size identification. This line bears the triangular foil label, which states "HULL POTTERY" in two lines. This seal is found in black or maroon background with gold or silver lettering.

This line is composed of hand-decorated embossed florals on duotone pastel backgrounds of blue to pink or pink to cream, or on allover cream backgrounds. There are at least 12 shapes available, many in graduated sizes.

Listed under "gifts for the house," Spiegel of Chicago, Illinois, advertised on page 431 of its 1943 fall and winter catalog the $1.10 Poppy vase, 607-10½", as "pottery vase, ornate shape with convenient side handles. Cream colored with gold flower on each side. 7 inches wide, 11 inches high."

Plate 86.
Row 1:
1. Vase, "607-6½"," $125.00 – 160.00.
2. Basket, "601-9"," $600.00 – 700.00.
3. Ewer, "610-4¾"," $165.00 – 200.00.
Row 2:
1. Jardiniere, "603-4¾"," $165.00 – 240.00.
2. Wall pocket, "609-9"," $310.00 – 410.00.
3. Low bowl, "602-6½"," $225.00 – 275.00.
4. Jardiniere, "608-4¾"," $165.00 – 200.00.
Row 3:
1. Vase, "607-8½"," $235.00 – 275.00.
2. Vase, "605-8½"," $235.00 – 275.00.
3. Vase, "606-8½"," $235.00 – 275.00.
Row 4:
1. Vase, "607-10½"," $400.00 – 500.00.
2. Ewer, "610-13½"," $800.00 – 1,000.00.
3. Vase, "606-10½"," $400.00 – 500.00.

Plate 86.

Rosella

PRODUCTION DATE: 1946

TRADEMARKS: Illustrations 40 and 43, appendix A.

Raised print "Hull Art, U.S.A.," R-series mold number, and size identification. Cornucopia vases and ewers carry an "L" (left) and "R" (right) designation. Rosella was an expensive line to produce, with its specially mixed clay, and further carried a foil label designed specifically for this ware. The banner and flower-form foil label is brown with gold accents.

Original advertising described Rosella as "distinctively designed by Hull master craftsmen: with the sculptured wild rose pattern hand-tinted under the glaze on a choice of ivory or coral body." The Rosella design included 16 shapes, with an additional pitcher, teapot, three lamps, dimpled vase, and window box. The lid to Rosella's sugar is absent in many cases. The lid increases value of the sugar bowl by $100.00.

Rosella was produced at a time when the company was torn between the comfort and stability of past designs and the need to move on with updated, innovative styles and glazes. Hull tested its markets with gloss Rosella, but at the same time, retained production of matte wares.

Hull was a little ahead of its time, as Rosella was produced in that short span of time before high-gloss artware items were truly trendy. Rosella did not take the market by storm; it was being teamed on retailers' shelves with matte wares belonging not only to Hull, but also the company's competitors, Roseville and Weller. Matte designs prevailed, and Rosella was neglected. The Rosella line was short-lived; the market numbers are deceptive. Rosella pieces that are taking a backseat to matte pastels are few in number, and only appear plentiful because they are being overlooked.

Plate 88.
Row 1:
1. Basket, "R-12-7"," $260.00 – 310.00.
2. Vase, "R-2-5"," $70.00 – 95.00.
3. Basket, "R-12-7"," $260.00 – 310.00.
Row 2:
1. Creamer, "R-3-5½"," $45.00 – 65.00.
2. Covered sugar, "R-4-5½"," $150.00 – 170.00.
3. Creamer, "R-3-5½"," $45.00 – 65.00.
4. Covered sugar, "R-4-5½"," $150.00 – 170.00.
Row 3:
1. Ewer, "R-11-7½" L," $140.00 – 175.00.
2. Vase, "R-6-6½"," $70.00 – 90.00.
3. Wall Pocket, "R-10-6½"," $150.00 – 175.00.
4. Vase, "R-5-6½"," $70.00 – 90.00.

5. Ewer, "R-11-7" R," $140.00 – 175.00.
Row 4:
1. Cornucopia, "R-13-8½" R," $125.00 – 165.00.
2. Ewer, "R-9-6½"," $75.00 – 125.00.
3. Vase, "R-8-6½"," $135.00 – 175.00.
4. Vase, "R-1-5"," $70.00 – 95.00.
5. Cornucopia, "R-13-8½" L," $125.00 – 165.00.
Row 5:
1. Vase, "R-15-8½"," $135.00 – 165.00.
2. Vase, "R-7-6½"," smooth, $70.00 – 90.00.
3. Vase, "R-14-8½"," $135.00 – 165.00.
4. Experimental vase, "R-7-6½"," rare dimpled, $350.00 – 515.00.
5. Ewer, "R-7-9½"," $1,200.00 – 1,500.00.

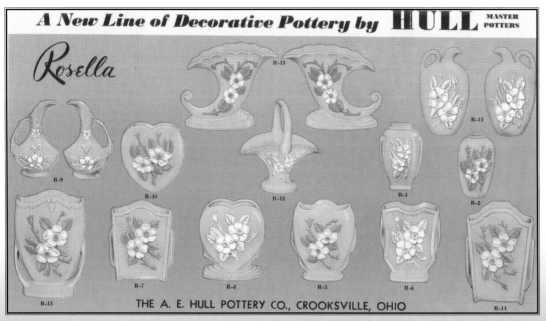

Plate 87. Original Hull company brochure page.

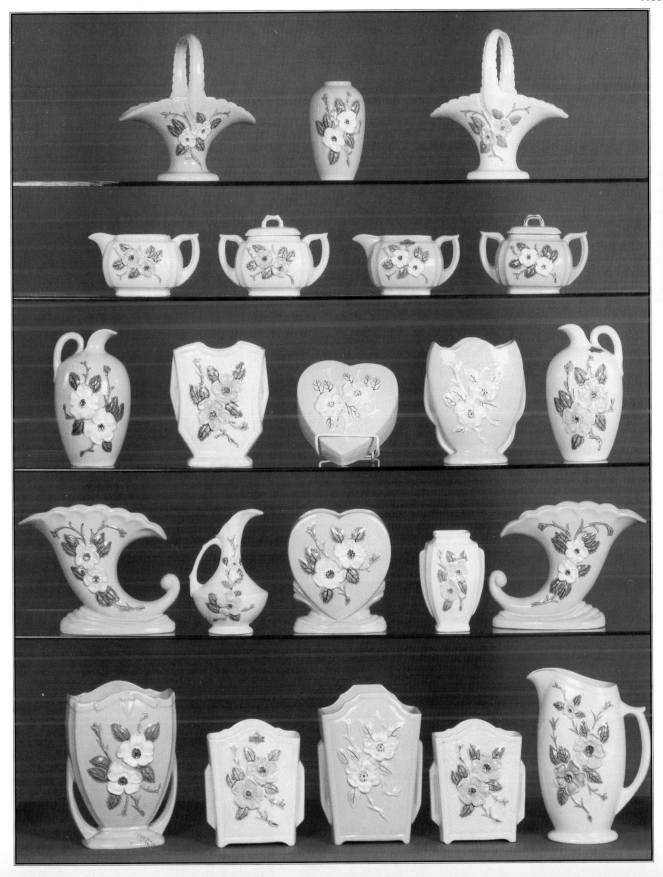

Plate 88.

SUN-GLOW

PRODUCTION DATES: 1948 – 1949

TRADEMARKS:

Sun-Glow does not carry the Hull trademark or a Hull label, most likely because it was used for chain store sales. Items are impressed with the mold number and size identification.

This line included hand-decorated embossed florals in solid high-gloss backgrounds of either pink or yellow. Two distinctly different florals appeared on this line, an embossed straw-like daisy and an embossed pansy, sometimes with an additional butterfly decoration. Gold detailing outside the factory was not unusual for these items. There were 29 available shapes.

Plate 89.
Row 1:
1. Mixing bowl, "50-9½"," $35.00 – 45.00.
2. Mixing bowl, "50-7½"," $25.00 – 35.00.
3. Mixing bowl, "50-5½"," $16.00 – 25.00.
4. Cup and Saucer wall pocket, "80," 6¼", $135.00 – 165.00.
5. Jug wall pocket, "81," 5½", $135.00 – 165.00.
6. Whisk Broom wall pocket, "82," 8½", $135.00 – 165.00.
Row 2:
1. Covered caserole, "51-7½"," $60.00 – 80.00.
2. Pitcher, "52-24 oz.," $45.00 – 65.00.
3. Iron wall pocket, unmarked, 6", $165.00 – 210.00.
4. Basket, "84," 6¼", $95.00 – 145.00.
5. Vase, "85," 8½", $45.00 – 70.00.
Row 3:
1. Shaker, "54," 2¾", $15.00 – 20.00.
2. Grease jar, "53," 5¼", $50.00 – 75.00.
3. Shaker, "54," 2¾", $15.00 – 20.00.

4. Rope-handled tea bell, unmarked, 6¼", $100.00 – 125.00.
5. Tea bell, unmarked, 6½", $100.00 – 125.00.

Plate 90.
Row 1:
1. Cornucopia, "8½"-96," $75.00 – 110.00.
Row 2:
1. Iron wall pocket, unmarked, 6", $165.00 – 210.00.
2. Basket, "84," 6¼", $95.00 – 145.00.
3. Ewer, "90-5½"," $40.00 – 55.00.
Row 3:
1. Jug wall pocket, "81," 5½", $135.00 – 165.00.
2. Hanging basket, "99-6"," $85.00 – 120.00.
3. Vase, "89-5½"," $35.00 – 50.00.
Row 4:
1. Vase, "94-8"," $75.00 – 100.00.
2. Covered casserole, "51-7½"," $60.00 – 80.00.

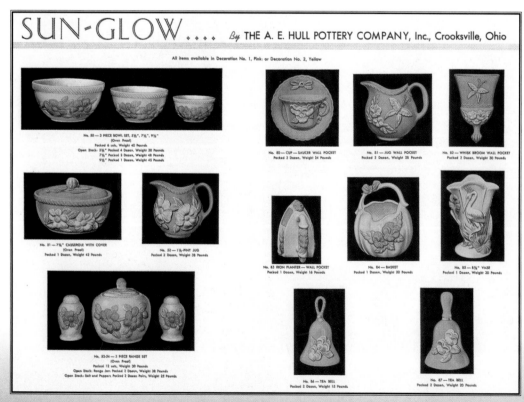

Plate 89. Original company catalog page.

Plate 90.

SUN-GLOW
Classic

PRODUCTION DATES: 1942 – 1945

CLASSIC TRADEMARK: Illustration 47, appendix A.

Classic does not bear the Hull trademark, but is incised with the mold number and "USA." Classic wares are additionally marked with a gold or silver banner and shield foil label with "Classic" printed on a green banner.

Plate 91.
Row 1.
1. Sun-Glow rope-handled tea bell, unmarked, 6¼",
   $100.00 – 125.00.
2. Sun-Glow rope-handled tea bell, unmarked, 6¼",
   $100.00 – 125.00.
3. Classic vase, "T-1-6½"," $25.00 – 35.00.
4. Classic vase, "T-2-6½"," $20.00 – 30.00.
5. Classic vase, "T-3-6½"," $25.00 – 35.00.
6. Sun-Glow tea bell, unmarked, 6½", $100.00 – 125.00.
Row 2.
1. Cornucopia, "203-5½"," $30.00 – 40.00.
2. Classic vase, "4-6"," $25.00 – 35.00.
3. Classic vase, "5-6"," $25.00 – 35.00.
4. Classic ewer, "6-6"," $25.00 – 35.00.
5. Cornucopia, "201," 5", $30.00 – 40.00.

Plate 92.
Row 1:
1. Shaker, "54," 2¾", $15.00 – 20.00.
2. Grease jar, "53," 5¼", $50.00 – 75.00.
3. Shaker, "54," 2¾", $15.00 – 20.00.
Row 2:
1. Vase, "100-6½"," $50.00 – 70.00.
2. Pitcher, "52-24 oz.," $45.00 – 65.00.
3. Vase, "93-6½"," $45.00 – 65.00.
Row 3:
1. Mixing bowl, "50-9½"," $35.00 – 45.00.
2. Mixing bowl, "50-7½"," $25.00 – 35.00.
3. Mixing bowl, "50-5½"," $16.00 – 25.00.
4. Whisk Broom wall pocket, "82," 8½", $135.00 – 165.00.
Row 4:
1. Cup and Saucer wall pocket, "80," 6¼", $135.00 – 165.00.
2. Ice-lip pitcher, "55," 7½", $155.00 – 200.00.
3. Jardiniere, "98-7½"," $50.00 – 70.00.
4. Jardiniere, "97-5½"," $40.00 – 55.00.

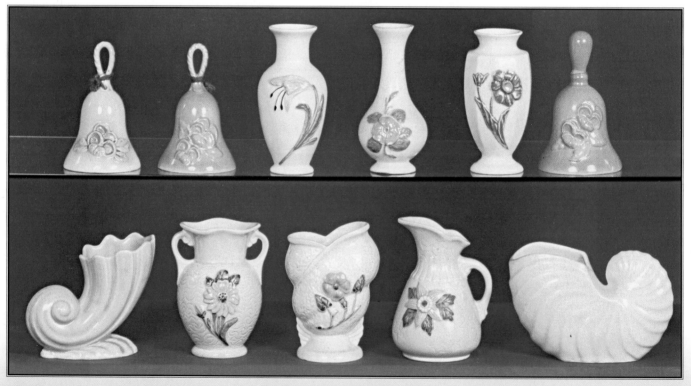

Plate 91.

Plate 92.

Tulip

PRODUCTION DATES: 1938 – 1941.

TRADEMARKS: Illustrations 22, 23, and 26, appendix A.
    Incised with "HULL, U.S.A.," 100-series mold number, and size identification.

Hand-decorated embossed tulips on duotone matte pastels of blue and pink, blue and cream, or allover blue. There were 15 cataloged shapes, and many were offered in graduated sizes.

Plate 93.
Row 1:
1. Tulip flower pot with attached saucer, "116-33-4¼"," 1938 – 1941, $135.00 – 165.00.
2. Camellia factory lamp, top filled rather than open for use as a vase, base is open, side drilled for cord, unmarked, 10½", $750.00 – 900.00.
3. Camellia vase, "123-6½"," $145.00 – 175.00.
Row 2:
1. Orchid bookend, "316-7"," 1939 – 1941, $500.00 – 700.00.
2. Dogwood vase, "504-8½"," 1942 – 1943, $140.00 – 225.00.
3. Morning Glory vase, "61-8½"," 1940, $145.00 – 200.00.
4. Orchid bookend, "316-7"," 1939 – 1941, $500.00 – 700.00.

Plate 94.
Row 1.
1. Calla Lily cornucopia, "570/33-8"," $100.00 – 135.00.
2. Tulip flower pot with attached saucer, "116-33-6"," $175.00 – 210.00.
Row 2.
1. Tulip vase, "108-33-6"," $130.00 – 150.00.
2. Tulip basket, "102-33-6"," $275.00 – 350.00.
3. Tulip vase, "111-33-6"," $145.00 – 175.00.
Row 3.
1. Tulip vase, "107-33-6"," $135.00 – 160.00.
2. Tulip vase, "110-33-6"," $140.00 – 165.00.
3. Tulip suspended vase, "103-33-6"," $265.00 – 340.00.
4. Tulip vase, "106-33-6½"," $130.00 – 150.00.
Row 4.
1. Tulip vase, "100-33-8"," $160.00 – 230.00.
2. Tulip ewer, "109-33-13"," $465.00 – 540.00.
3. Tulip vase, "100-33-10"," $275.00 – 325.00.

Plate 93.

Plate 94.

WATER LILY

PRODUCTION DATES: 1948 – 1949

TRADEMARKS: Illustrations 40, 44, and 48, appendix A.

Water Lily's trademark was usually raised, but was occasionally incised, and was a print "Hull Art, U.S.A." with L-series mold number and size identification. This line carried the round black Potter-at-Wheel foil label, which had silver, gold, or gray lettering.

Hand-decorated embossed Water Lily floral on duotone matte backgrounds of Walnut and Apricot or turquoise and Sweet Pink. Many items were detailed in gold outside the factory, not uncommon for this line. There were 28 cataloged shapes.

Plate 96.
Row 1:
1. Creamer, "L-19-5"," $80.00 – 110.00.
2. Teapot, "L-18-6"," $245.00 – 300.00.
3. Covered sugar, "L-20-5"," $80.00 – 110.00.
Row 2:
1. Vase, "L-1-5½"," $55.00 – 80.00.
2. Cornucopia, "L-7-6½"," $115.00 – 160.00.
3. Vase, "L-4-6½"," $95.00 – 130.00.
Row 3:
1. Vase, "L-9-8½"," $255.00 – 315.00.
2. Vase, "L-A-8½"," $240.00 – 275.00.
3. Vase, "L-10-9½"," $210.00 – 265.00.
Row 4:
1. Vase, "L-12-10½"," $250.00 – 330.00.
2. Vase, "L-15-12½"," $475.00 – 600.00.
3. Vase, "L-13-10½"," $250.00 – 330.00.

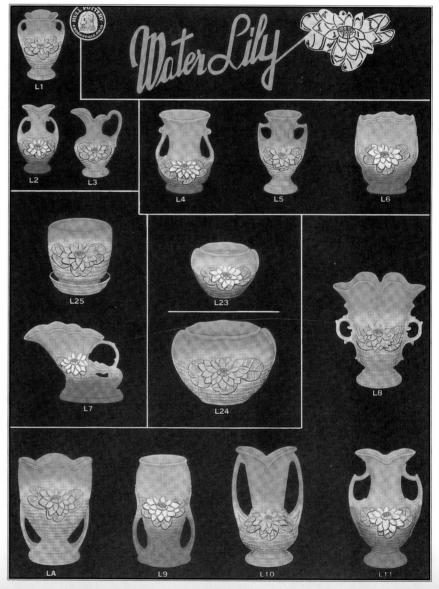

Plate 95. Original company brochure page.

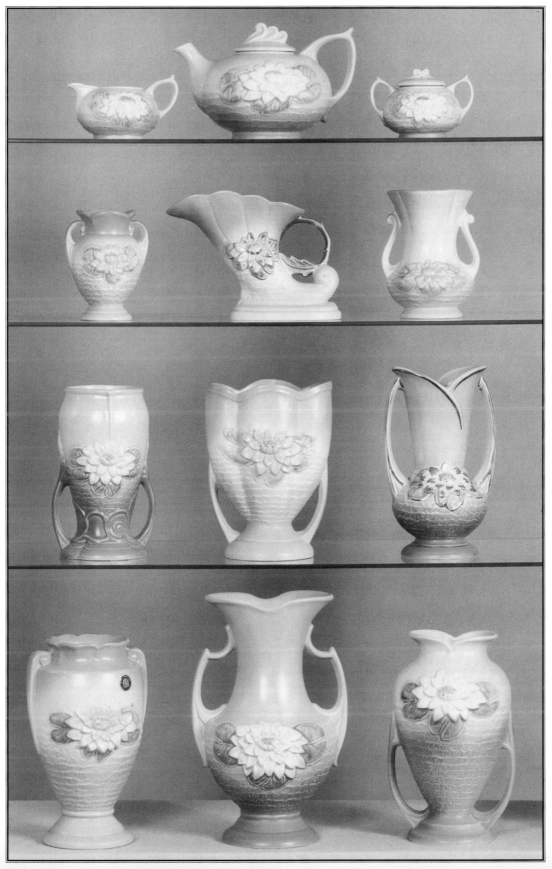

Plate 96.

WATER LILY

Plate 97.
Row 1:
1. Vase, "L-12-10½"," $250.00 – 330.00.
2. Vase, "L-13-10½"," $250.00 – 330.00.
3. Candleholder, "L-22-4½"," $85.00 – 125.00.
4. Candleholder, "L-22-4½"," $85.00 – 125.00.
5. Candle bowl, "L-21-13½"," $260.00 – 300.00.
Row 2:
1. Basket, "L-14-10½"," $400.00 – 510.00.
2. Double cornucopia, "L-27-12"," $230.00 – 295.00.
3. Covered sugar, "L-20-5"," $80.00 – 110.00.
4. Creamer, "L-19-5"," $80.00 – 110.00.
5. Teapot, "L-18-6"," $245.00 – 300.00.
Row 3:
1. Vase. "L-16-12½"," $400.00 – 525.00.
2. Ewer, "L-17-13½"," $400.00 – 510.00.
3. Vase, "L-15-12½"," $475.00 – 600.00.

Plate 98.
Row 1:
1. Candleholder, "L-22, 4½"," $85.00 – 125.00.
2. Console bowl, "L-21-13½"," $260.00 – 300.00.
3. Candleholder, "L-22, 4½"," $85.00 – 125.00.
Row 2:
1. Ewer, "L-3-5½"," $115.00 – 140.00.
2. Vase, "L-6-6½"," $75.00 – 120.00.
3. Vase, "L-2-5½"," $60.00 – 85.00.
4. Vase, "L-5-6½"," $90.00 – 125.00.
Row 3:
1. Jardiniere "L-23-5½"," $130.00 – 170.00.
2. Jardiniere, "L-24-8½"," $365.00 – 425.00.
3. Vase, "L-11-9½"," $210.00 – 265.00.
4. Flowerpot with attached saucer, "L-25-5¼","
   $175.00 – 225.00.
Row 4:
1. Vase, "L-16-12½"," $400.00 – 525.00.
2. Basket, "L-14-10½"," $400.00 – 510.00.
3. Ewer, "L-17-13½"," $525.00 – 650.00.

Magazine advertisement from a 1948 *House Beautiful*.

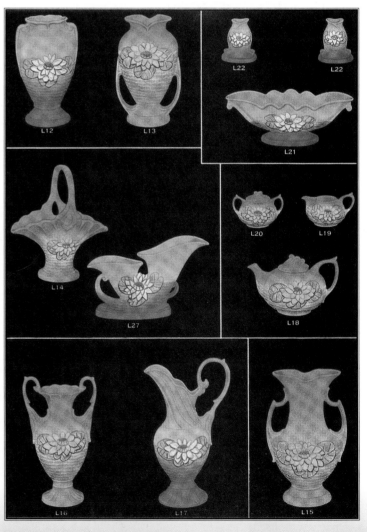

Plate 97. Original company brochure page.

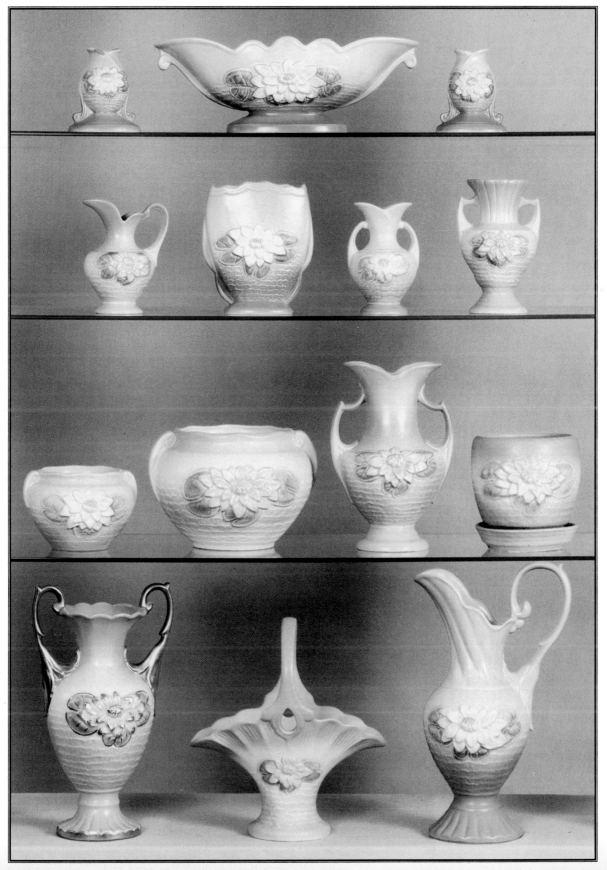

Plate 98.

Wildflower

PRODUCTION DATES: 1946 – 1947

TRADEMARKS: Illustrations 44 and 48, appendix A.

Raised print "Hull Art, U.S.A.," W-series mold number, and size identification. This line carried the round black Potter-at-Wheel foil label, which had silver, gold, or gray lettering.

Hand-decorated embossed floral spray of Trillium, Mission, and Bluebell in two-tone matte pastel body shades of pink and blue or yellow and dusty rose. There were 22 cataloged shapes.

Plate 99.
Row 1:
1. Vase, "W-1-5½"," $65.00 – 90.00.
Row 2:
1. Ewer, "W-2-5½"," $105.00 – 140.00.
2. Vase, "W-4-6½"," $70.00 – 95.00.
3. Vase, "W-5-6½"," $95.00 – 135.00.
4. Basket, "W-16-10½"," $375.00 – 425.00.
Row 3:
1. Vase, "W-3-5½"," $55.00 – 80.00.
2. Vase, "W-6-7½"," $95.00 – 130.00.
3. Cornucopia, "W-7-7½"," $80.00 – 110.00.
4. Vase, "W-8-7½"," $85.00 – 115.00.
Row 4:
1. Vase, "W-9-8½"," $190.00 – 245.00.
2. Cornucopia, "W-10-8½"," $165.00 – 215.00.
3. Ewer, "W-11-8½"," $175.00 – 225.00.

Plate 100.
Row 1:
1. Candleholder, "W-22," 2½", $60.00 – 85.00.
2. Console bowl, "W21-12"," $225.00 – 265.00.
3. Candleholder, "W-22," 2½", $60.00 – 85.00.
Row 2:
1. Cornucopia, "W-7-7½"," $80.00 – 110.00.
2. Vase, "W-5-6½"," $95.00 – 135.00.
3. Vase, "W-8-7½"," $85.00 – 115.00.
Row 3:
1. Basket, laced handle, "W-16-10½"," $375.00 – 425.00.
2. Vase, "W-13-9½"," $200.00 – 240.00.
3. Basket, "W-16-10½"," $375.00 – 425.00.
Row 4:
1. Vase, "W-18-12½"," $275.00 – 350.00.
2. Vase, "W-20-15½"," $450.00 – 600.00.
3. Vase, "W-17-12½"," $275.00 – 350.00.

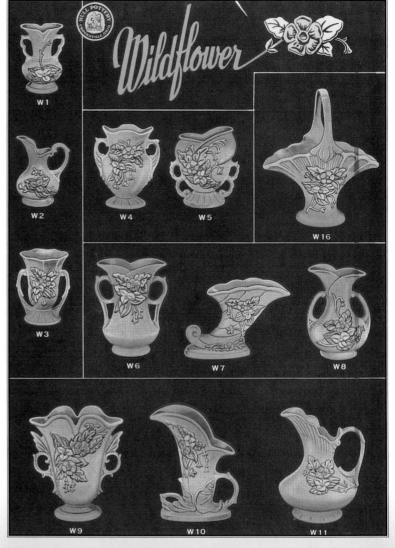

Plate 99. Original Hull catalog page.

Plate 100.

Plate 101.
Row 1:
1. Vase, "W-12-9½"," $225.00 – 275.00.
2. Vase, "W-13-9½"," $200.00 – 240.00.
3. Vase, "W-14-10½"," $260.00 – 315.00.
Row 2:
1. Candleholder, "W-22," 2½", $60.00 – 85.00.
2. Console bowl, "W-21-12"," $225.00 – 265.00.
3. Candleholder, "W-22," 2½", $60.00 – 85.00.
4. Vase, "W-15-10½"," $250.00 – 300.00.
Row 3:
1. Vase, "W-17-12½"," $275.00 – 350.00.
2. Vase, "W-18-12½"," $275.00 – 350.00.
3. Ewer, "W-19-13½"," $450.00 – 550.00.

Plate 102.
Row 1:
1. Vase, "W-1-5½"," $65.00 – 90.00.
2. Vase, "W-3-5½"," $55.00 – 80.00.
3. Ewer, "W-2-5½"," $105.00 – 140.00.
Row 2:
1. Vase, "W-6-7½"," $95.00 – 130.00.
2. Vase, "W-9-8½"," $190.00 – 245.00.
3. Vase, "W-4-6½"," $70.00 – 95.00.
Row 3:
1. Cornucopia, "W-10-8½"," $165.00 – 215.00.
2. Vase, "W-14-10½"," $260.00 – 315.00.
3. Vase, "W-12-9½"," $225.00 – 275.00.
4. Ewer, "W-11-8½"," $175.00 – 225.00.
Row 4:
1, Ewer, "W-19-13½"," $450.00 – 550.00.
2. Vase, "W-15-10½"," $250.00 – 300.00.
3. Lamp, not factory, 12½", $200.00 – 250.00.

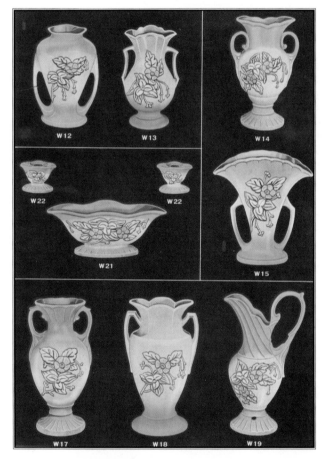

Plate 101. Original Hull catalog page.

Magazine advertisements from *Better Homes and Gardens*

Plate 102.

Wild Flower Number Series

PRODUCTION DATES: 1942 – 1943

TRADEMARKS: Illustrations 40 and 44, appendix A.
Raised print "Hull Art, U.S.A.," mold number, and size identification. This line bears the triangular foil label, which states "HULL POTTERY" in two lines. This seal is found with either black or maroon background with gold or silver lettering.

Embossed hand-decorated florals on matte duotone tinted backgrounds of blue and pink or Russet and pink, or on allover cream background. Several of the items have an embossed butterfly motif included in the lid, on the handle, or within the body of the embossed decoration. There are 29 cataloged items available.

Plate 103.
Row 1:
1. Vase, "52-6¼"," $150.00 – 175.00.
Row 2:
1. Sugar, "74-4¾"," $240.00 – 275.00.
2. Teapot, "72-8"," $850.00 – 1,150.00.
3. Creamer, "73-4¾"," $240.00 – 275.00.
4. Vase, "62-6¼"," $140.00 – 165.00.
5. Vase, "61-6¼"," $135.00 – 160.00.
Row 3:
1. Ewer, "57-4½"," $100.00 – 145.00.
2. Jardiniere, "64-4"," $140.00 – 165.00.
3. Vase, "56-4½"," $140.00 – 170.00.
4. Vase, "60-6¼"," $150.00 – 180.00.
5. Vase, "54-6¼"," $150.00 – 175.00.
Row 4:
1. Double candleholder, "69-4"," $175.00 – 225.00.
2. Console bowl, "70-12"," $400.00 – 495.00.
3. Double candleholder, "69-4"," $175.00 – 225.00.
4. Handled bon-bon dish, "65-7"," $375.00 – 475.00.

Plate 104.
Row 1:
1. Jardiniere, "64-4"," $140.00 – 165.00.
2. Creamer, "73-4¾"," $240.00 – 275.00.
3. Teapot, "72-8"," $850.00 – 1,150.00.
4. Open sugar, "74-4¾"," $240.00 – 275.00.
5. Vase, "56-4½"," $140.00 – 170.00.
Row 2:
1. Vase, "52-6¼"," $150.00 – 175.00.
2. Vase, "67-8½"," $400.00 – 450.00.
3. Vase, "52-6¼"," $165.00 – 210.00.
4. Cornucopia, "58-6¼"," $195.00 – 235.00.
Row 3:
1. Vase, "51-8½"," $300.00 – 350.00.
2. Vase, "59-10½"," $300.00 – 350.00.
3. Ewer, "55-13½"," $900.00 – 1,200.00.
4. Vase, "76-8½"," $350.00 – 440.00.

Plate 103. Original company brochure page.

Plate 104.

Wild Flower Number Series

Plate 105.
1. Vase, special decoration,* "77-10½"," $240.00 – 325.00.
2. Vase, "54-6¼"," $150.00 – 175.00.

Plate 106.
Row 1:
1. Double candleholder, "69-4"," $175.00 – 225.00.
2. Handled bon-bon dish, "65-7"," $375.00 – 475.00.
3. Double candleholder, "69-4"," $175.00 – 225.00.
Row 2:
1. Double candleholder, "69-4"," $175.00 – 225.00.
2. Console bowl, "70-12"," $400.00 – 495.00.
3. Double candleholder, "69-4"," $175.00 – 225.00.

Plate 107.
1. Ewer, "57-4½"," $100.00 – 145.00.
2. Ewer, "63-7¼"," $185.00 – 235.00.

Plate 108.
1. Poppy basket, "601-12"," $800.00 – 1,000.00.
2. Experimental Dogwood suspended vase,* white with gold decor, "502-6½"," $175.00 – 250.00.
3. Basket, "66-10¼"," $850.00 – 1,000.00.

*Additional information regarding specials and experimentals can be found on pages 288 and 289.

Plate 105.

Plate 106.

Plate 107.

Plate 108.

Woodland

PRODUCTION DATES: 1949 – 1950

TRADEMARKS: Illustrations 44 and 54, appendix A.

Raised script "Hull, USA," W-series mold number, and size identification. Woodland was also marked with the black Potter-at-Wheel foil label, which had silver, gold, or gray lettering.

Hand-decorated embossed florals in matte finished duotones of pastel Dawn Rose or Harvest Yellow. An allover stark white high-gloss ware with contrasting hand-painted floral decoration was also part of the pre-1950 Woodland design. The white gloss items many times included gold detailing done outside the factory. There were 30 cataloged shapes of pre-1950 Woodland wares, which were numbered 1 – 31, with number 20 being skipped.

After the fire of 1950, Hull had ceramic engineers experimenting with glazes, most being substandard to those the market had become accustomed to. Even though the molds were retooled, the company was unable to quickly regain the quality of the pre-1950 Woodland glaze.

Plate 109.
Row 1:
1. Ewer, "W6-6½"," $180.00 – 240.00.
2. Planter, "W19-10½"," $175.00 – 235.00.
Row 2:
1. Creamer, "W27," 3½", $165.00 – 225.00.
2. Teapot, "W26," 6½", $450.00 – 550.00.
3. Covered sugar, "W28," 3½", $165.00 – 225.00.
Row 3:
1. Vase, "W1-5½"," $110.00 – 135.00.
2. Vase, "W8-7½"," $140.00 – 175.00.
3. Basket, "W9-8¾"," $250.00 – 300.00.
4. Vase, "W16-8½"," $230.00 – 295.00.
5. Cornucopia, "W2-5½"," $105.00 – 145.00.
Row 4:
1. Double cornucopia, "W23," 14", $530.00 – 700.00.
2. Vase, "W18-10½"," $260.00 – 350.00.
3. Jardiniere, "W21-9½"," $900.00 – 1,100.00.

Original company advertising.

Plate 109.

Woodland

Plate 110.

Row 1:
1. Ewer, "W3-5½"," $130.00 – 175.00.
2. Cornucopia, "W10-11"," $170.00 – 230.00.
3. Cornucopia, "W5-6½"," $100.00 – 125.00.

Row 2:
1. Flower pot with attached saucer, "W11-5¾"," $165.00 – 215.00.
2. Vase, "W4-6½"," $95.00 – 135.00.
3. Jardiniere, "W7-5½"," $175.00 – 230.00.

Row 3:
1. Wall pocket, "W13-7½"," $250.00 – 300.00.
2. Candleholder, "W30," 3½", $140.00 – 170.00.
3. Console bowl, "W29," 14", $375.00 – 475.00.
4. Candleholder, "W30," 3½", $140.00 – 170.00.

Row 4:
1. Double bud vase, "W15-8½"," $225.00 – 265.00.
2. Hanging basket, "W12-7½"," $500.00 – 600.00.
3. Vase, "W17-7½"," $325.00 – 425.00.

Row 5:
1. Vase, "W25-12½"," $575.00 – 675.00.
2. Basket, "W22-10½"," $600.00 – 800.00.
3. Ewer, "W24-13½"," $650.00 – 900.00.

The Pages of the "Arabian Nights" Inspired This Gay Tea Set in

WOODLAND ARTWARE BY HULL

From the wonderful lamp of Aladdin come the graceful, flowing lines of this exquisite 3-piece Tea Set. These and 27 other exciting pieces in this new *Woodland* artware pattern are now available at your favorite store—each with hand-painted flowers, in your choice of two body colors. An artware creation of THE A. E. HULL POTTERY CO., CROOKSVILLE, OHIO.

Magazine advertisement, 1949.

Smart—New—Styled for You . . .

WOODLAND ARTWARE BY *HULL*

This lovely double horn is just one of the 30 graceful, smart pieces of *Woodland*—now available at your favorite store. Gay hand-painted florals, in a choice of Dawn Rose or Harvest Yellow body pastels. Styled by THE A. E. HULL POTTERY CO., CROOKSVILLE, OHIO.

Magazine advertisement, 1949.

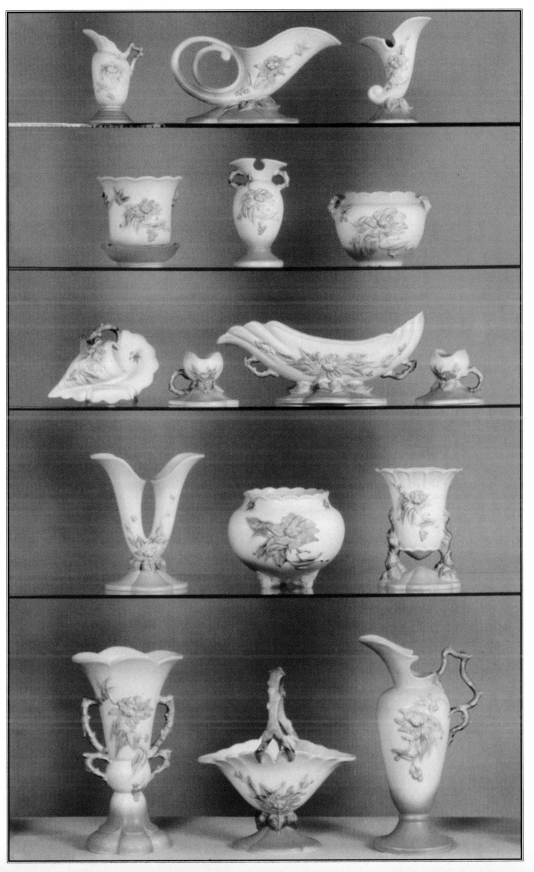

Plate 110.

WATER LILY GLOSS
WOODLAND GLOSS

PRODUCTION DATES: 1949 – 1950

TRADEMARKS: Pre-1950 Gloss Water Lily, illustration 48, appendix A; pre-1950 Gloss Woodland, illustration 54, appendix A.
Pre-1950 Gloss Water Lily: Raised print "Hull Art, U.S.A.," L-series mold number, and size identification.
Pre-1950 Gloss Woodland: Raised script "Hull, U.S.A.," W-series mold number, and size identification.

Water Lily items, high-gloss and matte, were made prior to the 1950 company disaster. Company glaze treatments over-lapped, and one glaze treatment at a glance is similar to the colorations of the Sun-Glow line. Gloss Water Lily items typically have gold detailing that was done outside the factory.

The only gloss Woodland from pre-1950 years is that which was glazed in high-gloss colors of stark white, ivory, or pale pink. These glazes appeared on the 30 mold shapes used before the flood and fire. Pay attention to the open floral and the side used for that floral; those are the basic keys for identification of pre-1950 wares. Many of these glazed Woodland pieces have gold detailing from area artists, not unusual for these particular items. Hull also produced Woodland in high-gloss white ivory and pale pink after reconstruction of the company.

Plate 111.
Row 1:
1. Woodland vase, "W1-5½"," $75.00 – 100.00.
2. Woodland jardiniere, "W7-5½"," $135.00 – 210.00.
3. Woodland ewer, "W3-5½"," $80.00 – 120.00.
Row 2:
1. Water Lily vase, "L-5-6½"," $70.00 – 100.00.
2. Water Lily vase, "L-2-5½"," $55.00 – 70.00.
3. Water Lily ewer, "L-3-5½"," $80.00 – 120.00.
Row 3:
1. Water Lily creamer, "L-19-5"," $60.00 – 80.00.
2. Water Lily teapot, "L-18-6"," $175.00 – 225.00.
3. Water Lily covered sugar, "L-20-5"," $60.00 – 80.00.
Row 4:
1. Woodland double cornucopia, "W23-14"," $235.00 – 335.00.
2. Experimental Water Lily vase, "L-15-12½"," $375.00 – 475.00.
3. Water Lily vase, "L-A-8½"," $130.00 – 195.00.

FOR YOUR HOUSE BEAUTIFUL, THE ART POTTERY BEAUTIFUL
Water Lily BY HULL

Make your cut flowers even more lovely with the perfect setting of "Water Lily" art pottery. There's a variety of twenty-seven graceful pieces—each with hand-painted floral, each in a choice of two duo-tone pastel combinations to assure complete harmony with your home's decorative motif. "Water Lily" is available at leading stores; crafted by master potters at THE A. E. HULL POTTERY CO., CROOKSVILLE, OHIO.

Magazine advertisement, 1949.

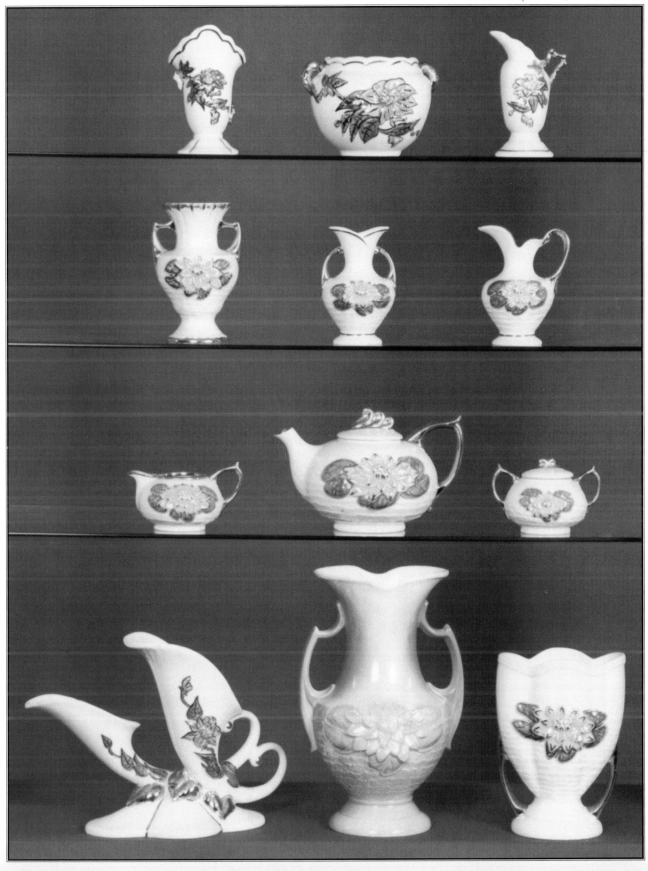

Plate 111.

The Fifties
(1950 – 1960)

Construction of a new plant that had only the most modern equiptment enabled the Hull Company to bettter compete in the national market of pottery manufacture. Outdated ways and wares were left behind in search of updated designs and glazes.

This new era of artware production included embossed birds, butterflies, florals, and clusters of fruit. Kitchenware remained in steady production alongside artware. Novelty wares proved to be the third component in Hull's marketing strategy, and helped keep business booming for the next ten years.

Original company promotional material for Tokay, circa 1958. Sophisticated, artful graphics were used throughout the fifties for marketing artware.

Serenade
by Hull

Chipper chickadees on colorful boughs are the motif; fine art pottery from the kilns of Hull is the medium. The result . . . Serenade . . . is beautiful, functional and colorful. Each piece is available in either of three color combinations: Decoration 1 — Jonquil Yellow outside, Willow Green inside; Decoration 2 — Regency Blue outside, Sunlight Yellow inside; Decoration 3—Shell Pink outside, Pearl Gray inside.

Coronet By HULL

By HULL

IY, Crooksville, Ohio

The Hull Pottery Company strived for product diversity, a practice that successfully carried the company through the fifties. At any given time during this era, Hull produced at least three unique lines.

Animals and Novelties

PRODUCTION DATES: 1951 – 1954

TRADEMARKS: Illustrations 57, 59, and 69, appendix A.
Marks most commonly used for items illustrated included incised script "Hull, USA" and incised script "Regal, USA."

Hull's striking high-gloss dark green and wine combinations included a wide variety of figural shapes and designs. Although some novelty items were in production for several years, most can be accurately dated by their color treatments. The glazes of the day are the key to dating Hull's 1950s wares. By referring to the glazes of the major 1950s artware lines, you will be able to identify dates for the company's novelty items that were glazed in that same treatment. The bulk of novelties with chartreuse glazes and trims was produced shortly after the company's reopening, right along with chartreuse Woodland. The deep green tones were also characteristically used after the reopening of the plant. Some of the novelty items illustrated also reflect the 1954 tones of the wine glaze used for Ebb Tide.

Plate 112.
Row 1:
1. Window box, unmarked, 11", $16.00 – 25.00.
2. Basket, unmarked, 6", $25.00 – 35.00.
Row 2:
1. Flying Goose wall pocket, "67," 6", $55.00 – 75.00.
2. Clover-shaped planter, "121," 4½", $20.00 – 28.00.
3. Regal rectangular flower dish, "124," 10", $15.00 – 20.00.
4. Rectangular vase, "116," 6", $18.00 – 24.00.
Row 3:
1. Giraffe planter, "115," 8", $50.00 – 75.00.
2. Deep oval flower bowl, unmarked, 10", $25.00 – 30.00.
3. French Poodle planter, "114," 8", $50.00 – 75.00.
Row 4:
1. Bandana Duck planter, "75," 7", $50.00 – 70.00.
2. Bandana Duck planter, "74," 9", $80.00 – 115.00.
3. Bandana Duck planter, "76," 3½", $30.00 – 40.00.
4. Bandana Duck candle holder, 3½", $60.00 – 85.00.
Row 5:
1. Flying Duck planter, "104," 8½", $75.00 – 105.00.
2. Low flower bowl, "85," 13", $35.00 – 45.00.
3. Bird of Paradise flower frog, unmarked, 10½", $115.00 – 155.00.
4. Suspended vase, "110," 9¼", $70.00 – 105.00.

Plate 112.

of the illustrated novelty wares were made for two to three years. The dates listed refer to introductory dates of manufacture.

TRADEMARKS: Illustrations 57 and 59, appendix A.

These items are commonly unmarked; wares that do have a trademark bear an incised script "Hull," a mold number, and "USA."

While novelty items were sometimes placed in use more than once, perhaps for different chain store lines, most can be identified by color glaze treatments. Some of these novelty items crossed over from pre-1950 lines to post-1950 lines. The Sun-Glo Flamingo No. 85 vase, introduced in 1948, was referred to as the No. 78 vase in 1951 and was placed in production a third time in 1960, as No. 309 in the Regal line.

Plate 113.
Row 1:
1. Parrot with cart planter, "60," 6", $45.00 – 65.00.
2. Fan vase, "72," 8½", 1951, $30.00 – 40.00.
Row 2:
1. Jubilee garden dish, "402," 8½", $10.00 – 15.00.
2. Peacock vase, "73," 10½", 1951, $35.00 – 50.00.
3. Jubilee garden dish, "401," 6¾", $10.00 – 15.00.
Row 3:
1. Jubilee jardiniere, "425," 4", 1957, $12.00 – 16.00.
2. Flower dish, "81," 10", 1957, $15.00 – 20.00.
3. Sun-Glo Flamingo vase, "85," 8½", 1948 – 1949, $45.00 – 70.00.
Row 4:
1. Unicorn vase, "99," 11½", 1952, $95.00 – 110.00.
2. Unicorn vase, "98," 9½", 1952, $65.00 – 95.00.
3. Jubilee ashtray, "407," 11½", 1957, $30.00 – 45.00.

Plate 113.

TRADEMARKS: Illustrations 57, 59, and 69, appendix A.
   Items illustrated are most commonly found with the incised script Hull trademark and mold number, along with "USA."

Plate 116.
Row 1:
1. Colt figurine, unmarked, 5½", 1954, $90.00 – 115.00.
Row 2:
1. Regal Parrot with Cart planter, "313," 12½", 1960, $75.00 – 100.00.
2. Colt on flower bowl, 7", 1953, $60.00 – 85.00.
Row 3:
1. Knight on Horseback planter, "55," 8", 1953, $90.00 – 130.00.
2. Double bud vase, "103," 9", 1951, $50.00 – 75.00.
3. Rooster planter, "54," 7½", 1953, $115.00 – 150.00.
Row 4:
1. Love Birds planter, "93," 6", 1953, $40.00 – 60.00.
2. Rooster planter, "53," 5¾", 1953, $100.00 – 135.00.
3. Flying Duck planter, "79," 6", 1953, $45.00 – 60.00.
Row 5:
1. Flying Goose vase, "97," 11¾", 1953, $55.00 – 75.00.
2. Fiesta Fan vase, "50," 9", 1956, $80.00 – 110.00.
3. Twin Deer vase, "62," 11½", 1953, $60.00 – 80.00.

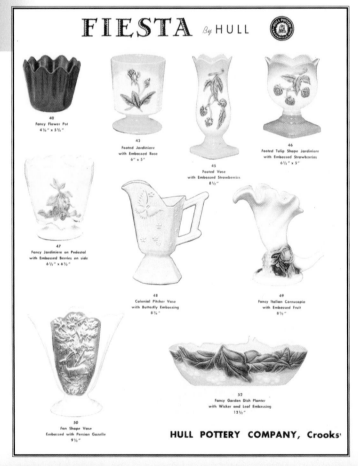

Plate 114. Original company brochure featuring Fiesta, circa 1956. This ware was embellished with fruits, florals, butterflies, and deer.

Plate 115. Original company brochure featuring fifties novelties.

Plate 116.

PRODUCTION DATES: 1951 – 1962

While most of the illustrated novelty wares were made for two to three years, dates listed refer to introductory dates of manufacture.

TRADEMARKS: Illustrations 57, 59, and 73, appendix A.

Items illustrated are most commonly marked with an incised script Hull trademark, a mold number, and "USA." Urn-Vases from Imperial's 400-series bear "Urn-Vase" in incised print, along with "USA."

Apparently another firm produced dachshund figurals in the 1950s. On the retail market is a molded dachshund that very closely resembles Hull's. The Hull dachshund is only slightly larger and has a tail in a flipped-up or curved fashion. The look-alike dachshund's most conspicuous difference is a tail that curls under the back leg. The clay content of both is nearly the same, as is the weight. The colors of the look-alike dachshunds are very similar to Hull's pinks, blacks, and charcoals. The look-alikes even bear a slight indication of glazed-over mold marks in the same position as Hull's.

Plate 117.
Row 1:
1. Vase, "110," 9½", $35.00 – 45.00.
2. Window box, unmarked, 10½", $30.00 – 40.00.
3. Basket, unmarked, 12½", $45.00 – 65.00.
Row 2:
1. Poodle planter, "114," 8", $50.00 – 75.00.
2. Giraffe planter, "115," 8", $50.00 – 75.00.
3. Vase, "116," 6", $18.00 – 24.00.
Row 3:
1. Planter, unmarked, 4", $15.00 – 20.00.
2. Planter, unmarked, 10", $25.00 – 35.00.
3. Planter, "121," 4½", $20.00 – 28.00.
Row 4:
1. Basket, unmarked, 6", $25.00 – 35.00.
2. Planter, "124," 10", $15.00 – 20.00.
3. Double Hippo flower frog, unmarked, $200.00 – 250.00.

Plate 118.
Row 1:
1. Caladium leaf dish, 14", 1957, $25.00 – 35.00.
Row 2:
1. Urn-Vase, "418," 5", 1962, $15.00 – 20.00.
2. Dachshund planter, 14", 1952, $150.00 – 200.00.
3. Bubble vase, "109," 9", 1952, $25.00 – 35.00.
Row 3:
1. Wishing Well planter, "101," 7¾", 1951, $40.00 – 60.00.
2. Candle holder, "455," 4½", 1963, $15.00 – 20.00.
3. Single Hippo flower frog, "83," 3½", 1951, $200.00 – 250.00.
4. Twin Geese planter, "95," 6½", 1951, $50.00 – 80.00.
5. Flower Club planter, "823," 5½", 1963, $15.00 – 20.00.
Row 4:
1. Gold-Medal Flowerware Egyptian vase, "103," 12", 1959, $45.00 – 70.00.
2. Dachshund figural, 14", 1952, $175.00 – 225.00.
3. Urn-Vase, "410," 7", 1962, $20.00 – 30.00.

Plate 117. Original company brochure page.

Plate 118.

PRODUCTION DATES: 1951 – 1962

Keep in mind that most of these novelty wares were in production two to three years, and dates listed refer to initial introductory dates of manufacture.

TRADEMARKS: Illustrations 57 and 59, appendix A.

Although many of these novelty items were commonly distributed unmarked, those that are marked most often bear an incised script "Hull, USA."

The Swan planters, produced from 1951 through the 1970s, were so plentiful that they became symbols of the Hull Pottery Company, acting as Hull trademarks themselves. There were several variations of high-gloss color treatments, but by 1961, the Swan set was available only in Satin White. The Swan centerpiece planter was first introduced shortly after the reopening of the plant in 1951. The small Swan, 70, was introduced in price lists first as an ashtray. Later it was referred to as an ashtray/planter.

Plate 119.
Row 1:
1. "The Dutchess" planter, "411," 12¼", $55.00 – 85.00.
2. Swan planter, "413," 10½", $55.00 – 85.00.
3. "The Dutchess" planter, "412," 5", $25.00 – 35.00.
4. Window box, "404," 13½", $25.00 – 35.00.
5. Basket, "418," 8¾", $45.00 – 70.00.
6. Caladium leaf, "405," 14", $25.00 – 40.00.
Row 2:
1. Planter, "402," 8½", $10.00 – 15.00.
2. Planter, "403," 9¼", $25.00 – 35.00.
3. Jardiniere, "425," 4", $12.00 – 16.00.
Row 3:
1. Vase, "421," 11½", $50.00 – 70.00.
2. Jardiniere, "426," 8", $40.00 – 60.00.
3. Jardiniere, "427," 10", $45.00 – 75.00.
4. Ashtray, "407," 11½", $30.00 – 45.00.
5. Planter, "401," 6¾", $10.00 – 15.00.
6. Ashtray, "408," 13", $30.00 – 45.00.

Plate 120.
Row 1:
1. Console planter, "F-3," 4", 1957, $15.00 – 20.00.
2. Mayfair planter, "87," 10", 1958, $20.00 – 30.00.
3. Footed planter, "410," 5", 1958, $10.00 – 15.00.

Row 2:
1. Daisy basket, "70," 6½", 1951, $80.00 – 120.00.
2. Ribbon wall pocket, "71," 6", 1951, $80.00 – 115.00.
3. Kitten with Spool planter, "89," 6", 1951, $25.00 – 35.00.
4. City Girl planter, "90," 5½", 1951, $30.00 – 40.00.
Row 3:
1. Pig planter, "86," 6¾", 1951, $25.00 – 35.00.
2. Medley window box with metal stand, "603," 13", 1962, $20.00 – 30.00.
3. Pup with Yarn planter, "88," 5½", 1951, $30.00 – 40.00.
Row 4:
1. Baby with Pillow planter, "92," 5½", 1951, $25.00 – 35.00.
2. Swan ashtray/planter, "70," 4", 1951, $14.00 – 20.00.
3. Swan planter, "80," 6", 1951, $35.00 – 45.00.
4. Swan centerpiece planter, "69," 8½", 1951, $50.00 – 75.00.
Row 5:
1. Mayfair leaf dish, "86," 10", 1958, $20.00 – 30.00.
2. Jubilee "The Duchess" planter, "411," 12¼", 1957, $55.00 – 85.00.
3. Jubilee "The Duchess" ashtray/planter, 5", 1957, $25.00 – 35.00.
4. Fantasy vase, "71," 9", 1957, $25.00 – 35.00.

Plate 119. Original company brochure page.

Plate 120.

TRADEMARKS: Illustrations 57 and 59, appendix A.

Although many of these novelty items were commonly distributed unmarked, those that are marked most often bear an incised script "Hull, USA."

Experimental tumblers were used to test the day's glazes to assure quality control. These test pieces usually bear inscribed alphanumeric markings, in the base or on the side of the tumbler, that related to a certain glaze formula or color batch identification. These test tumblers were used from the reopening of the plant in 1950 to the plant's closing. Date of production is determined by the glaze treatment.

The novelty items shown were glazed in both matte or satin finishes and high glosses; the Rooster planter was decorated in matte finish. The novelty Pig and Poodle planters were decorated in matte underglaze with airbrush decoration and hand-painted detail.

Baby head vase no. 62, illustrated in plate 122, row 2, item 3, is currently being reproduced in a satitn-finished glaze. The baby has blonde hair, blue eyes, and a blue-trimmed bonnet. This vase has found its way into antique malls as well as eBay, and thus far, remains unmarked.

Pink and charcoal glazes, very popular from 1955 to 1957 for novelty and dinnerware items, were most often used in high-gloss finishes, but also for matte backgrounds. Decoration treatments of items illustrated included airbrush blending and line veiling.

Another popular glaze treatment used in the mid-1950s and illustrated in the brochure page is webbed ware. It characteristically has a heavy, thick glaze with a rough, raised texture in contrasting color to the glaze beneath. Webbing was used for both kitchenware and artware items. The jardiniers illustrated in the brochure page have black background with pink webbing and pink background with blue webbing.

Plate 122.
Row 1:
1. Experimental tumbler, inscribed "36," 3½", $20.00 – 30.00.
2. Experimental tumbler, inscribed "68, 93, 94," 3½", $20.00 – 30.00.
3. Experimental tumbler, inscribed "54," 3½", $20.00 – 30.00.
4. Experimental tumbler, inscribed "12-7, 55," 3½", $20.00 – 30.00.
5. Rooster, "951," 7", 1938 – 1942, $50.00 – 80.00.
6. Experimental tumbler, inscribed "116," 3½", $20.00 – 30.00.
7. Experimental tumbler, inscribed "174," 3½", $20.00 – 30.00.
8. Experimental tumbler, inscribed "9-29, 175-V-31," 3½", $20.00 – 30.00.
9. Experimental tumbler, inscribed "5-24-1-10," 3½", $20.00 – 30.00.
Row 2:
1. Vase, "38," 6½", 1955, $140.00 – 180.00.
2. Vase, "37," 6½, 1955, $140.00 – 180.00.
3. Vase, "62," 6½", 1938 – 1940, $30.00 – 40.00.
4. Vase, "39," 6½", 1955, $140.00 – 180.00.

Plate 123.
Row 1:
1. Cornucopia, "64," 10", $30.00 – 40.00.
2. Scroll window bowl, "71," 12½", $30.00 – 40.00.
Row 2:
1. Bowl, "No. 10," 8½", $25.00 – 35.00.
2. Covered divided casserole, "35," 8½", $45.00 – 65.00.
3. Individual French-handled casserole, 5", $15.00 – 22.00.
Row 3:
1. Scroll basket, "56," 6", $50.00 – 80.00.
2. Telephone vase, "90," 9", $80.00 – 110.00.
3. Scroll basket, "72," 8", $80.00 – 125.00.

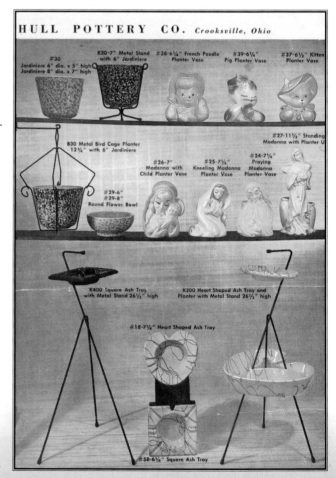

Plate 121. Original company brochure page.

Plate 122.

Plate 123.

The Fifties (1950 – 1960)
Animals and Novelties

TRADEMARKS: Illustrations 57, 59, 64, and 78, appendix A.

Items shown are most commonly found marked with an incised script "Hull," a mold number, and "USA." It is not unusual to find these novelty items unmarked. The latest Hull production illustrated is marked with an incised "hull" and a mold number.

Plate 124.

Row 1:
1. Imperial vase/candleholder, "67 U.S.A.," 4", 1957, $15.00 – 20.00.
2. Swan, unmarked, 8". (This is from a previously used Medley mold from 1962 and was glazed to compliment the Country-Belle dinnerware line in 1985.) $25.00 – 35.00.
3. Imperial planter, "405 U.S.A.," 8¼", 1958, $8.00 – 10.00.

Row 2:
1. Athena flower bowl, "601, USA," 5¾", 1960, $5.00 – 8.00.
2. Pigeon planter, "91," 6", 1955, $35.00 – 50.00.
3. Modern flower bowl, "Hull USA," 11½", 1955, $15.00 – 22.00.
4. Capri basket, "F38," 6½", 1961, $40.00 – 60.00.

Row 3:
1. Mayfair Candle Lite flower bowl, "88," 11", 1958, $10.00 – 15.00.
2. Vase, "414 USA," 10½", 1958, $10.00 – 15.00.
3. Dove ashtray/planter, unmarked, 4¼", $10.00 – 15.00.
4. Imperial leaf planter, "F24," 12½", 1955, $15.00 – 20.00.

Row 4:
1. Imperial basket, embossed basketweave decor, unmarked, 8", 1985, $40.00 – 60.00.
2. Imperial Frog, unmarked, 6½", 1985, $75.00 – 100.00.
3. Ashtray, "H.P. Co. Pat. Pend.," 6¼", 1960, $20.00 – 30.00.
4. Imperial planter, unmarked, 5", 1985, $10.00 – 15.00.
5. Imperial basket, embossed strawberry decor, unmarked, 7½", 1985, $40.00 – 60.00.

Row 5:
1. Jubilee Top Hat basket, "418," 8½", 1957, $45.00 – 70.00.
2. Gold-Medal Flowerware gladiolus vase, "112," 10", 1959, $30.00 – 40.00.
3. Tokay/Tuscany vase, "20," 15", 1959, $200.00 – 250.00.
4. Pagoda vase, "P5," 12½", 1960, $30.00 – 40.00.
5. Gold-Medal Flowerware vase, "101," 8", 1959, $20.00 – 25.00.

Plate 124.

Ashtray/Planter Combinations

TRADEMARKS: Illustrations 57, 70, and 71, appendix A.

Incised script "Hull," mold number, and "USA." The Coronet smoker set base is marked with an incised script "Coronet, USA," while the ashtray is incised with only the mold number and "USA."

Ashtray/Planter combinations were offered in a variety of glaze treatments beginning in 1956. While some stands were offered only in wrought iron, others were available in brass. The Coronet smoke stands were introduced in 1959. Glazed treatments of combination stands ranged from gloss to matte finishes, which were additionally airbrushed, edged with foam, and line veiled. Styles ranged from square or cylinder to heart or star shaped. All metal stands are original to these Hull items.

In the mid-1950s, Hull saw the trend towards pottery items with metal stands. The introduction of such wares started on the West Coast and moved west to east. Hull joined the bandwagon and from mid-1950 through early 1960 produced jardinieres, ashtrays, planter with ashtray combinations, lavabos, and more. Hull advertised them as "Red Hot, Year Around Sellers!"

Plate 125.
1. Ashtray/Planter, veiled decoration, ashtray 18", planter 19", 26" overall, 1955, $75.00 – 100.00.
2. Royal Lantern jardiniere with stand, "75-7"," 19" overall, 1955, $50.00 – 75.00.

Plate 126.
1. Jardiniere in stand, jardiniere 8", 15" overall, classic shape in Willow Green Mist, $30.00 – 40.00.
2. Jardiniere in stand, jardiniere 10", 21" overall, crimped jardiniere in high-gloss black with white foam, $75.00 – 100.00.
3. Coronet ashtray/planter, star-shaped ashtray "A5," planter "204," 24½", $85.00 – 110.00.
4. Ashtray/Planter, ashtray 18", planter 19", 26" overall, $75.00 – 100.00.

Plate 127.
1. Ashtray/Planter, ashtray 22", planter 23", 26" overall, 1955, $75.00 – 100.00.
2. Coronet ashtray/planter, star-shaped ashtray "A5," planter "204," 24½", 1959, $85.00 – 110.00.
3. Ashtray/Planter, ashtray 22", planter 23", 26" overall, 1956, $75.00 – 100.00.
4. Jubilee ashtray/planter, ashtray "T20," planter "T21," 26", matte-finished embossed basketweave with charcoal edge, 1957, $130.00 – 165.00.

Plate 125.

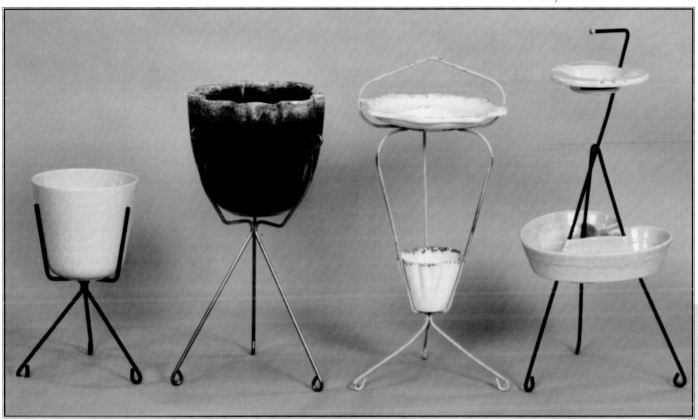

Plate 126.

Plate 127.

Athena
Coronet
Mayfair
Regal

PRODUCTION DATES: Athena, 1960; Coronet, 1959; Mayfair, 1958 – 1959; Regal, 1960

TRADEMARKS: Illustrations 57, 69, 70, 71, and 78, appendix A.
   Some items shown are unmarked, and some have an incised script "Hull, USA" or an incised "hull, USA." Regal and Coronet are each marked with an incised script form of its line name, "USA," and a mold number.

DESCRIPTIONS:
   Athena: Eleven items were offered in this chain store vase and planter assortment that was decorated in overall high-glaze Lilac or Spring Green and trimmed with White Lava. Items were additionally glazed in Satin White.
   Coronet: A line of vases, jardinieres, dish gardens, ashtray and planter combinations, etc., manufactured specifically for chain store sales. Wares were decorated in solid and tinted high glazes, with or without contrasting foam edges. While assortments varied per retailer, at least 13 items were available, along with the high-styled ashtray and planter combinations in brass and wrought iron stands.
   Mayfair: Composed a chain store novelty and florist assortment in solid high-gloss pastels and black, all with white foam trim. At least 16 shapes were available.
   Regal: A line designed exclusively for chain store sales. Items offered included novelty planters, vases, and florist ware items in a variety of high glazes, some with contrasting trim.

Plate 128.
Row 1:
1. Imperial vase, "F1," 4", 1961, $15.00 – 20.00.
2. Siamese Cat planter, "63," 12", 1953, $110.00 – 165.00.
3. Imperial vase, "F1," 4", 1961, $15.00 – 20.00.
Row 2:
1. Regal planter, "301," 3½", $10.00 – 15.00.
2. Regal bowl, unmarked, 6½", $10.00 – 15.00.
3. Regal planter, 6½", $10.00 – 15.00.
4. Regal planter, "303," 5", $10.00 – 15.00.
Row 3:
1. Athena cornucopia vase, "608," 8½", $30.00 – 40.00.
2. Athena low flower bowl, "602," 9", $15.00 – 20.00.
3. Mayfair Hand with Cornucopia vase, "83," 7¾", $50.00 – 70.00.
4. Athena oval picture frame/wall pocket, "611," 8½", $130.00 – 150.00.
Row 4:
1. Regal Flying Duck vase, "310," 10½", $40.00 – 65.00.
2. Vase, "B14," 10½", 1958, $40.00 – 60.00.
3. Coronet Queen with Crown vase, "209," 9", $75.00 – 100.00.
4. Regal Flamingo vase, "309," 9", $40.00 – 65.00.

Plate 128.

Banks
Leeds Bottles

PRODUCTION DATES: Banks, 1940 – 1985; Leeds Bottles, 1940s

TRADEMARKS: Banks, illustrations 63 and 68, appendix A; Leeds bottles, illustration 32, appendix A.

Corky Pigs are marked, in script, "Corky Pig, ©57, USA." This mold was used from 1957 to the plant's closing in 1985.

The largest pig banks from 1940 were marked "USA" only, and there is absolutely no way to identify the one absent of embossed florals unless you buy it straight from a Hull family member or a Hull employee. McCoy produced this pig bank too. The smallest pig, the dime bank, produced in the 1950s, was marked "USA" only. Hull employees boasted there was nothing small about these banks, since they proved they held $75.00 in dimes.

The sitting pig banks were manufactured from mid-1960 to the plant's closing in 1985. In production almost the same length of time was the razorback hog bank.

Leeds bottles are incised "LEEDS, USA."

These banks are as fun to display as they are to collect. Even though there was a limited number of mold shapes, the company was imaginative in its use of color combinations. You'll have your work cut out for you trying to gather one in each color. Shown is a representative sampling, but colors shown are not inclusive of all those available.

The Leeds bottles were airbrush decorated in high-gloss pastels of pink and blue. The liquor bottles were made in the 1940s, and many Crooksville citizens can relate stories of the many hundreds of bottles that floated through their village during the flood of 1950.

Plate 129. Dinosaur bank, premium for Sinclair Oil Company, 7", 1960, $1,200.00 – 1,800.00.

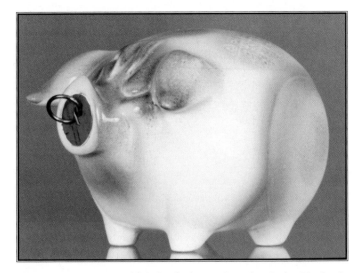

Plate 130. Expermental pig bank, larger than the Corky Pig Bank, incised X's and O's pattern on back, unmarked, 6" x 9", 1957, $400.00 – 600.00.

Plate 131.
Row 1:
1. Pig lamp, "196," 6", $250.00 – 350.00.
2. Pig bank, "196," 6", Tawny Ridge, $350.00 – 500.00.
3. Pig bank, "196," 6", $85.00 – 125.00.
Row 2:
1. Corky Pig bank, 5", Tawny Ridge, $350.00 – 500.00.
2. Leeds elephant liquor bottle, 7¾", 1939 – 1944, $60.00 – 80.00.
3. Corky Pig bank, 5", $75.00 – 115.00.
4. Leeds pig liquor bottle, 7¾", 1939 – 1944, $60.00 – 80.00.
5. Corky Pig bank, 5", Flint Ridge, $350.00 – 500.00.

Row 3:
1. Corky Pig bank, 5", $140.00 – 175.00.
2. Corky Pig bank, 5", $140.00 – 175.00.
3. Corky Pig bank, 5", $140.00 – 175.00.
Row 4:
1. Pig dime bank, 3½", $275.00 – 360.00.
2. Corky Pig bank, 5", $140.00 – 175.00.
3. Pig bank, underglaze decorated, 14", $160.00 – 225.00.
4. Pig dime bank, 3½", $275.00 – 360.00.
Row 5:
1. Pig bank, embossed floral, decorated over the glaze, 14", $160.00 – 225.00.
2. Pig bank, razorback, "197," 8", $200.00 – 300.00.

Plate 131.

Blossom Flite

PRODUCTION DATES: 1955 – 1956

TRADEMARK: Illustration 59, appendix A.
Incised script "Hull USA," T-series mold number, and size identification.

Glaze treatments for Blossom Flite included charcoal gray on overall high-gloss pink with pink interior, or blue on overall high-gloss pink with metallic green interior. A multicolored relief spray of florals decorated this line of 15 pieces.

Some of these molds can be found in transitional stages, e.g., with different placement or numbers of blossoms. These and additional pieces not cataloged represent experimental items. There were several experimental glazes considered for this line. According to company literature, this "enchanting art pottery presents a distinctive new rendering, yet stays within the bounds of the vastly popular floral theme."

Company advertising described the embossed decor as "a windblown pattern with blossoms of various colors," and an ad began, "As a summer storm subsides, the land is flooded with the rosy light of the reappearing sun, and a final gust of wind detaches flower petals from their stems to fill the air with form and color.

"This magic, fleeting moment in nature has been captured permanently by Hull to set the theme for Blossom Flite."

Company literature for this line additionally advertised the company's 50th anniversary and celebrated the company's years of operation, 1905 – 1955.

Plate 133.
Row 1:
1. Honey pot, "T1," 6", $65.00 – 105.00.
2. Teapot, "T14," 8", $140.00 – 195.00.
3. Basket, "T2," 6", $65.00 – 105.00.
Row 2:
1. Candleholder, "T11," 3", $45.00 – 65.00.
2. Console bowl, "T10," 16½", $115.00 – 165.00.
3. Candleholder, "T11," 3", $45.00 – 65.00.
Row 3:
1. Basket vase, "T4," 8½", $170.00 – 210.00.
2. Cornucopia, "T6," 10½", $90.00 – 145.00.
3. Planter flower bowl, "T12," 10½", $90.00 – 135.00.
Row 4:
1. Ewer, "T13," 13½", $165.00 – 210.00.
2. Handled low bowl, "T9," 10", $175.00 – 235.00.
3. Ewer, "T13," 13½", $165.00 – 210.00.

Magazine advertisement for Blossom Flite, 1955.

Plate 132. Original company brochure page.

Plate 133.

Butterfly

PRODUCTION DATE: 1956

TRADEMARKS: Illustrations 44 and 57, appendix A.

Has an incised script "Hull, USA" and is impressed with "© 56" and a B-series mold number. Sizes do not appear on the molds. The round black foil Potter-at-Wheel label was used for this ware.

Original company description: "Raised pastel butterfly and flower motif in a combined gloss and matte finish of white on white, or matte transparent white with turquoise inner surfaces." Gold detailing was not uncommon, but was done outside the factory. There were 25 cataloged items in the Butterfly line.

Plate 134.
Row 1:
1. Creamer, "B19," 5", $65.00 – 95.00.
2. Teapot, "B18," 8½", $150.00 – 200.00.
3. Sugar, "B20," 5", $65.00 – 95.00.
Row 2:
1. Serving dish, "B23," 11½", $115.00 – 165.00.
2. Vase, "B9," 9", $60.00 – 85.00.
3. Bowl, "B16," 10½", $70.00 – 100.00.
Row 3:
1. Basket, "B17," 10½", $265.00 – 350.00.
2. Candleholder, "B22," 2½", $20.00 – 30.00.
3. Console bowl, "B21," 10", $125.00 – 165.00.
4. Candleholder, "B22," 2½", $20.00 – 30.00.

Plate 135.
Row 1:
1. Lavabo, "B24" and "B25," in original hanger, 16", $200.00 – 250.00.
Row 2:
1. Jardiniere, "B5," 5", $50.00 – 70.00.
2. Vase, "B10," 7", $55.00 – 80.00.
Row 3:
1. Candleholder, "B22," 2½", $20.00 – 30.00.
2. Candleholder, "B22," 2½", $20.00 – 30.00.
3. Ashtray, "B3," 7", $40.00 – 60.00.
4. Cornucopia, "B2," 6¼", $35.00 – 55.00.
Row 4:
1. Cornucopia, "B12," 10½", $100.00 – 160.00.
2. Serving dish, "B23," 11½", $115.00 – 165.00.
3. Ewer, "B15," 13½", $165.00 – 235.00.

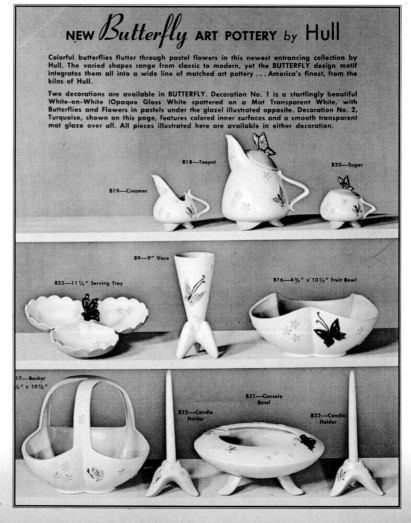

Plate 134. Original company brochure page.

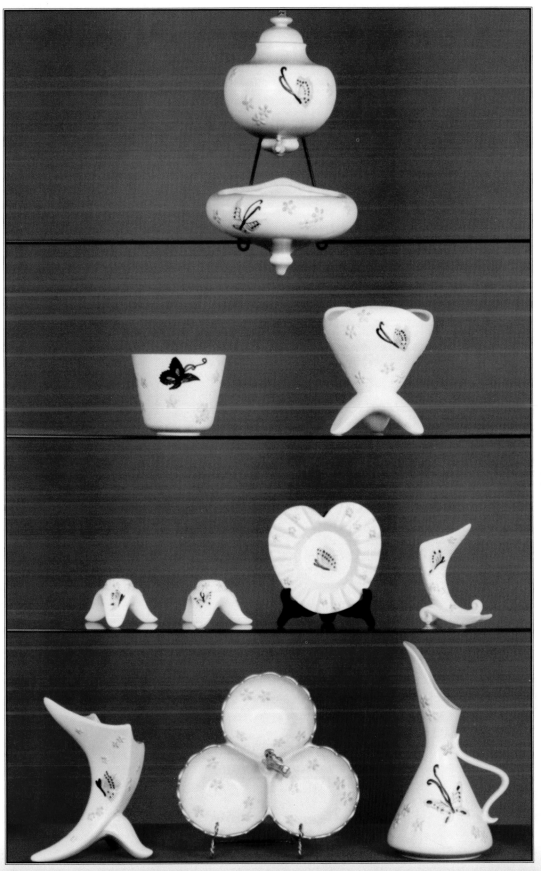

Plate 135.

The Fifties (1950 – 1960)

Butterfly

Plate 136.

Row 1:
1. Bud vase pitcher, "B1," 6¼", $40.00 – 60.00.
2. Cornucopia, "B2," 6¼", $35.00 – 55.00.
3. Ashtray, "B3," 7", $40.00 – 60.00.
4. Bon-bon dish, "B4," 6½", $20.00 – 25.00.
5. Jardiniere, "B5," 5", $50.00 – 70.00.

Row 2:
1. Flower dish, "B7," 9¾", $40.00 – 60.00.
2. Window box, "B8," 12¾", $40.00 – 60.00.
3. Urn, "B6," 5¼", $25.00 – 40.00.

Row 3:
1. Vase, "B10," 7", $55.00 – 80.00.
2. Basket, "B13," 8", $140.00 – 180.00.
3. Ewer, "B11," 8¾", $155.00 – 215.00.

Row 4:
1. Lavabo, "B24" and "B25," 16", $200.00 – 250.00.
2. Vase, "B14," 10½", $95.00 – 145.00.

3. Cornucopia, "B12," 10½", $100.00 – 160.00.
4. Ewer, "B15," 13½", $165.00 – 235.00.

Plate 137.

Row 1:
1. Creamer, "B19," 5", $65.00 – 95.00.
2. Teapot, "B18," 8½", $150.00 – 200.00.
3. Covered sugar, "B20," 5", $65.00 – 95.00.

Row 2:
1. Basket, "B-13," 8", $140.00 – 180.00.
2. Basket, "B17," 10½", $265.00 – 350.00.
3. Ewer, "B11," 8¾", $155.00 – 215.00.

Row 3:
1. Vase, "B14," 10½", $95.00 – 145.00.
2. Console bowl, "B21," 10", $125.00 – 165.00.

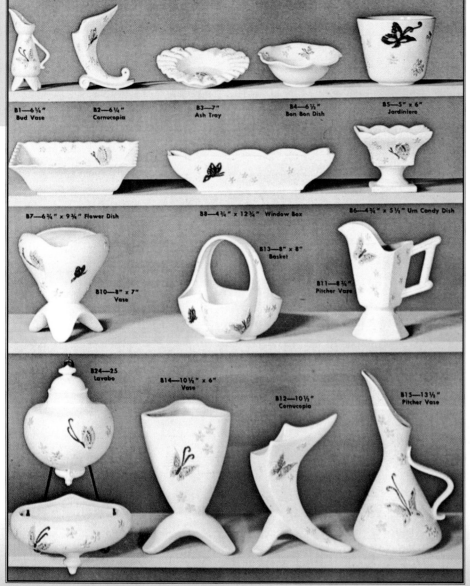

Plate 136. Original company brochure page.

Plate 137.

Capri
Imperial Golden Mist

PRODUCTION DATES: Capri, 1961; Imperial Golden Mist, 1967

TRADEMARKS: Illustrations 57 and 78, appendix A.
Capri was marked with incised script "Hull, USA," while Imperial items were usually marked with an incised "hull, USA." It is not uncommon to find items of either line unmarked.

The company described Capri as "satin finished bowls and planters in Coral with weathered limestone effect, or Sea-green to represent sea-washed rock formations." The Capri line consisted of 30 shapes.
The Imperial items illustrated with Capri are decorated in what Hull called Golden Mist. While items from the Imperial brochure page are all inviting, the items glazed in Golden Mist have a special mystique.

Plate 138.
Row 1:
1. Capri Swan, "23," 8½", $50.00 – 75.00.
Row 2:
1. Imperial Golden Mist Chickadee planter, "F473," 6", $18.00 – 25.00.
2. Capri leaf basket, "48," 12¼", $50.00 – 75.00.
3. Imperial Golden Mist Praying Hands planter, "F475," 6", $20.00 – 30.00.
Row 3:
1. Capri ewer, "87," 12", $135.00 – 185.00.
2. Capri covered candy, unmarked, 8½", $50.00 – 75.00.
3. Imperial Golden Mist Eagle flower bowl, 5¾", $18.00 – 22.00.
4. Imperial Golden Mist Swirl ewer, "F480," 10¾", $65.00 – 100.00.
Row 4:
1. Imperial Golden Mist Gurgling Fish ewer, "F480," 11", $85.00 – 125.00.
2. Capri vase, "58," 13¾", $55.00 – 75.00.
3. Capri Lion Head urn-vase, "50," 9", $45.00 – 65.00.

Plate 138.

CONTINENTAL

PRODUCTION DATES: 1959 – 1960

TRADEMARK: Illustration 57, appendix A.
Incised script "Hull, USA," with a 50-series mold identification number and the "© 59" designation. Many items did not carry the Hull trademark.

Modern shapes in the brilliant high-gloss colors of Evergreen, Persimmon, and Mountain Blue, with contrasting vertical stripes, or "run." Items with Evergreen and Mountain Blue glazes were decorated with contrasting white stripes, while Persimmon-glazed items were striped with yellow. There were 26 cataloged items. It is typical that some of these very bright shades vary in intensity.

The Continental line, first introduced in 1959, consisted of 14 items in "two strikingly lucid colors from nature ... accented with rich, bold stripes." Initial colors were Persimmon, "the completely captivating accent for today's interiors in the higher key of contemporary color," and Evergreen, "a delightfully subtle color that lends itself as a perfect foil to nature's own brilliant floral and leaf displays." The Continental line later included additional sophisticated, modern shapes that were offered in the earlier-mentioned colors, along with a third color scheme, Mountain Blue with White Haze.

Plate 139.
Row 1:
1. Vase, "64," 10", $50.00 – 80.00.
2. Bud vase, "66," 9½", $35.00 – 50.00.
3. Consolette, "70," 13¼", $65.00 – 95.00.
4. Vase, "28," 9¾", $40.00 – 60.00.
5. Vase, "29," 12", $50.00 – 80.00.
Row 2:
1. Flower bowl, "69," 9¼", $40.00 – 60.00.
2. Candleholder/Planter, "67," 4", $25.00 – 35.00.
3. Planter, "68," 8½", $25.00 – 30.00.
4. Candleholder/Planter, "67," 4", $25.00 – 35.00.
Row 3:
1. Ashtray, "A3," 12", $40.00 – 60.00.
2. Ashtray, "A40," 13", $65.00 – 95.00.

Plate 140.
Row 1:
1. Vase, "53," 8½", $35.00 – 45.00.
Row 2:
1. Candleholder/Planter, "67," 4", $25.00 – 35.00.
2. Flower dish, "51," 15½", $25.00 – 40.00.
3. Candleholder/Planter, "67," 4", $25.00 – 35.00.
Row 3:
1. Ewer, "56," 12½", $145.00 – 225.00.
2. Basket, "55," 12¾", $145.00 – 215.00.
3. Bud vase, "66," 9½", $35.00 – 50.00.
Row 4:
1. Bud vase, "66," 9½", $35.00 – 50.00.
2. Bud vase, "66," 9½", $35.00 – 50.00.
3. Basket, "55,"12¾", $145.00 – 215.00.
4. Ewer, "56," 12½", $145.00 – 225.00.

Plate 139. Original company brochure page.

Plate 140.

Cook 'N' Serve Ware

PRODUCTION DATES: 1952 – 1953

TRADEMARK: Illutration 57, appendix A.
Sometimes marked with incised script "Hull, USA," and also commonly found marked only by mold number.

Skillet trays were available in two sizes and are found in a variety of high-gloss color treatments. They are both overglaze and underglaze decorated. While some of these glaze treatments are considered experimental and may have been made for whimsies, others glazes were formulated for accessories to the Cook 'N' Serve dinnerware line. The Cook 'N' Serve line is a combination of Cinderella and Just Right Kitchenware shapes. Glaze treatments included high-gloss yellow and brown, pink and charcoal, green with brown flow, and white with contrasting black trim, with other color combinations possible. There were 22 ovenproof pieces in this line. A total of 19 items were cataloged, exclusively for A. H. Dorman, New York.

Plate 141.
Row 1:
1. Planter, "403," 9¼", $25.00 – 35.00.
2. Planter, "402," 8½", $10.00 – 15.00.
3. Planter, "401," 6¾", $10.00 – 15.00.
Row 2:
1. Vase, "421," 11½", $50.00 – 70.00.
2. Jardiniere, "426," 8", $40.00 – 60.00.
3. Jardiniere, "427," 10", $45.00 – 75.00.
Row 3:
1. Jardiniere, 6"; in brass stand, 7½" overall; $30.00 – 50.00.
2. Jardiniere, 8"; in brass stand, 15" overall; $75.00 – 100.00.
3. Jardiniere, 7"; in brass stand, 19" overall; $50.00 – 75.00.
4. Jardiniere, 10"; in brass stand, 21" overall; $75.00 – 100.00.

Plate 142.
Row 1:
1. Skillet tray, cold color decor, "No. 27," 9½", $40.00 – 65.00.
2. Experimental skillet tray, unmarked, 9¼" x 15½", $40.00 – 65.00.
Row 2:
1. Skillet tray, "No. 27," 9¼" x 15½", $40.00 – 65.00.
2. Skillet tray, 9¼" x 15½", $40.00 – 65.00.
Row 3:
1. Skillet tray, cold color decor, "No. 30," 5" x 10", $30.00 – 40.00.
2. Experimental skillet tray, unmarked, 9¼" x 15½", $140.00 – 170.00.
3. Skillet tray, "No. 30," 5" x 10", $30.00 – 40.00.
Row 4:
1. Skillet tray, "No. 27," 9¼" x 15½", $75.00 – 125.00.
2. Experimental skillet tray, 9¼" x 15½", $140.00 – 170.00.

Plate 141. Hull's belief in security through diversification was evident throughout the fifties, with planters and novelties displayed as companions to kitchenware.

Plate 142.

CORONET
FIESTA
Gold-Medal Flowerware

PRODUCTION DATES: Coronet, 1959; Fiesta, 1957 – 1958; Gold-Medal Flowerware, 1959; Imperial, 1955 – 1985; Jubilee, 1957; Mayfair, 1958 – 1959

TRADEMARKS: Illustrations 57, 70, 71, 77, and 78, appendix A.

Items shown are most commonly found marked with an incised script "Hull," a mold number, and "USA." Coronet line is marked with incised script "Coronet," a mold number, and "USA." It is not unusual to find these novelty items unmarked. Imperial items were marked with either an incised script "Hull" or an incised "hull, USA."

The green glazes of Hull ware were many, and varied in intensity from chartreuse to olive. Some mid-1950s novelty wares were characterized by the chartreuse and yellow-to-green combinations. Coronet items were manufactured in high-gloss solid glazes of turquoise, gray, green, orange, and white, and many had contrasting black, gray, or white foam edges. Items from the Fiesta line featured embossed floral and berry decorations, somewhat reminiscent of earlier embossed themes. Jubilee consisted of a line of jardinieres with metal accessories, along with a number of novelty items.

Plate 144.
Row 1:
1. Wall pocket, "112," 10½", 1952, $40.00 – 60.00.
2. Coronet Swan, "213," 6½" x 10", $45.00 – 65.00.
3. Coronet planter, "207," 8", $15.00 – 20.00.
Row 2:
1. Flower pot, unmarked, 3¾", 1958, $8.00 – 12.00.
2. Mayfair consolette, "91," 13½", $30.00 – 40.00.
3. Imperial basket, "F38," 7", 1958, $25.00 – 35.00.
Row 3:
1. Basket, unmarked, 12½", 1952, $45.00 – 65.00.
2. Imperial basket, "B36," 9", 1971, $25.00 – 35.00.
3. Bulb bowl, unmarked, 10½", 1952, $30.00 – 40.00.

Row 4:
1. Fiesta basket, "51," 12½", $125.00 – 150.00.
2. Madonna, "24," 7", 1956, $35.00 – 45.00.
3. Fiesta window box, "52," 12½", $30.00 – 40.00.
Row 5:
1. Imperial pitcher with bowl, "#A50" and "#A51," 7½", 1971, $25.00 – 40.00.
2. Clover vase, "110," 9½", 1952, $35.00 – 45.00.
3. Jubilee vase, "421," 11½", $50.00 – 70.00.
4. Gold-Medal Flowerware Bucket jardiniere, "94," 9", $65.00 – 100.00.

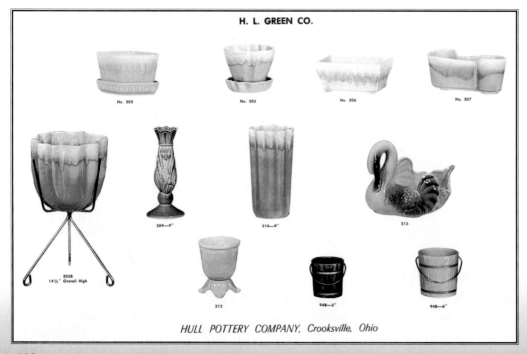

Plate 143. Hull catered to five-and-dimes by constructing assortments to meet customers' needs. H. L. Green's assortment consisted of coronet, Jubilee, and brass planters.

Plate 144.

CRESCENT

PRODUCTION DATES: 1952 – 1954

TRADEMARK: Illustration 57, appendix A.

This kitchenware line most commonly carried the incised script "Hull, USA," along with a mold number and size identification. Crescent had B-series numbers.

This kitchenware line was named for its crescent-shaped lids and handles, and a crescent moon was incorporated into the company's advertising. This ovenproof line was decorated in solid high-gloss color combinations of chartreuse with dark green trim, or high-gloss strawberry with maroon trim. Twelve shapes were available in the Cresent line.

Plate 145.
Row 1:
1. Cookie jar, "B-8-9½"," $65.00 – 90.00.
2. Mug, "B-16," 4¼", $15.00 – 20.00.
3. Ice jug, "B-13," 7½", $45.00 – 70.00.
Row 2:
1. Covered casserole, "B-2," 10", $50.00 – 75.00.
2. Individual casserole, "B-7," 5", $18.00 – 25.00.
3. Creamer, "B-15," 4½", $16.00 – 22.00.
4. Covered sugar, "B-14," 4½", $16.00 – 22.00.
Row 3:
1. Shaker, "B-4," 3½", $12.00 – 18.00.
2. Shaker, "B-4," 3½", $12.00 – 18.00.
3. Teapot, "B-13," 7½", $65.00 – 95.00.
Row 4:
1. Bowl, "B-1-9½"," $30.00 – 40.00.
2. Bowl, "B-1-7½"," $25.00 – 35.00.
3. Bowl, "B-1-5½"," $12.00 – 18.00.

Plate 146.
Row 1:
1. Crescent creamer, "B-15," 4¼", $16.00 – 22.00.
2. Crescent teapot, "B-13," 7½", $65.00 – 95.00.
3. Crescent sugar, minus lid, "B-14," 4¼", $16.00 – 22.00.
4. Crescent individual casserole, "B-7," 5", $18.00 – 25.00.
Row 2:
1. Crescent covered casserole, "B-2," 10", $50.00 – 75.00.
2. Crescent mug, "B-16," 4¼", $15.00 – 20.00.
3. Crescent shaker, "B-4," 3½", $12.00 – 18.00.
4. Crescent shaker, "B-4," 3½", $12.00 – 18.00.
Row 3:
1. Crescent bowl, "B-1-5½"," $12.00 – 18.00.
2. Crescent bowl, "B-1-7½"," $25.00 – 35.00.
3. Crescent bowl, "B-1-9½"," $30.00 – 40.00.
Row 4:
1. Crescent cookie jar, "B-8-9½"," $65.00 – 90.00.
2. Spatter Ware bowl, green over yellow, yellow interior, "No. 10-9"," 1951, $20.00 – 30.00.
3. Debonair cookie jar, "0-8," 8¾", $75.00 – 105.00.

Plate 145. Original company brochure page.

Plate 146.

Debonair

PRODUCTION DATES: Wine and chartreuse, 1952 – 1954; pink and lavender with black banding, 1955

TRADEMARK: Illustration 57, appendix A.
Incised script "Hull, USA" followed by O-series mold number and size identification.

Debonair ovenproof kitchenware was manufactured in high-gloss wine and chartreuse or high-gloss duotone lavender (referred to as gray in company information) and pink with black center banding. Fifteen items were cataloged. The Spatter Ware bowls are a spin-off of the Just Right Kitchenware Floral and Vegetable lines, and may be experimental. They were attained from the collection of Byron Hull.

Plate 147.
Row 1:
1. Cookie jar, "O-8," 8¾", $75.00 – 105.00.
2. Creamer, "O14," 3½", $25.00 – 35.00.
3. Covered sugar, "O15," 4", $25.00 – 35.00.
4. Teapot, "O13," 8", $75.00 – 100.00.
Row 2:
1. Casserole, "O-2," 8½", $45.00 – 65.00.
2. Bowl, "O-10," 4", $12.00 – 18.00.
3. Shaker, "O4-5," $12.00 – 18.00.
4. Shaker, "O4-5," $12.00 – 18.00.
Row 3:
1. Divided casserole, $18.00 – 25.00.
2. Divided casserole, "O-17," $45.00 – 65.00.
3. Mug, "O16," 3¾", $10.00 – 15.00.
4. Pitcher, "O6," 5", $35.00 – 45.00.
Row 4:
1. Mixing bowl, "O-1-9"," $30.00 – 40.00.
2. Mixing bowl, "O-1-7"," $25.00 – 30.00.
3. Mixing bowl, "O-1-5"," $20.00 – 30.00.

Plate 148.
Row 1:
Debonair divided casserole, "O-17," 8½", $45.00 – 65.00.
Row 2:
1. Debonair shaker, "O4-5," 3½", $12.00 – 18.00.
2. Debonair shaker, "O4-5," 3½", $12.00 – 18.00.
3. Debonair teapot, "O13," 8", $75.00 – 100.00.
4. Debonair mug, "O16," 3¾", $10.00 – 15.00.
Row 3:
1. Debonair bowl, "O-1-5"," $15.00 – 20.00.
2. Debonair cookie jar, "O-8," 9", $130.00 – 180.00.
3. Debonair pitcher, "O6," 5", $35.00 – 45.00.
4. Debonair creamer, "O14," 3½", $25.00 – 35.00.
Row 4:
1. Charcoal Spatter Ware bowl, "No. 40," 7",
    1951, $20.00 – 30.00.
2. Charcoal Spatter Ware batter bowl, "No. 41-9","
    1951, $40.00 – 60.00.
3. Debonair bowl, "O-1-9"," $30.00 – 40.00.

Plate 147. Original company brochure page.

Plate 148.

Ebb Tide

PRODUCTION DATE: 1955

TRADEMARK: Illustration 57, appendix A.
Incised script "Hull, USA," E-series mold number, and size identification.

Ebb Tide is characterized by embossed fish and seashell designs in the high-gloss colors of Seaweed and wine (chartreuse and wine) or Shrimp and turquoise. Gold detailing was not uncommon, but was done outside the factory. There were 16 cataloged shapes in the Ebb Tide line.

Described in company literature, "Up from the sea comes the inspiration for Hull's newest, colorful, complete line of art pottery. In Ebb Tide, the shapes that inhabit the seas...shells, coral, fish, and plants...set the motif. Hull has captured them, in glowing colors, and fashioned them into art pottery of great beauty."

Plate 149.
Row 1:
1. Candleholder, "E-13," 2¾", $25.00 – 35.00.
2. Console bowl, "E-12," 15¾", $215.00 – 260.00.
3. Candleholder, "E-13," 2¾", $25.00 – 35.00.
4. Vase, "E-6," 9¼", $150.00 – 200.00.
Row 2:
1. Teapot, "E-14," 6½", $235.00 – 265.00.
2. Cornucopia, "E-9," 11¾", $175.00 – 210.00.
3. Mermaid cornucopia, "E-3," 7½", $170.00 – 225.00.
Row 3:
1. Creamer, "E-15," 4", $95.00 – 125.00.
2. Covered sugar, "E-16," 4", $95.00 – 125.00.

Plate 150.
Row 1:
1. Teapot, "E-14," 6½", $235.00 – 265.00.
Row 2:
1. Basket, "E-11," 16½", $210.00 – 265.00.
Row 3:
1. Cornucopia, "E-9," 11¾", $175.00 – 210.00.
2. Ewer, "E-10," 14", $210.00 – 275.00.

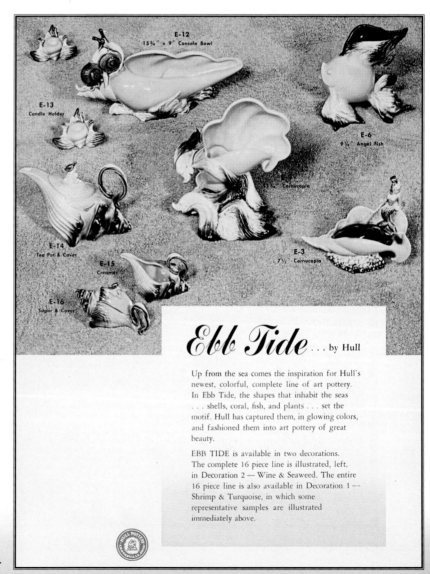

Ebb Tide ... by Hull

Up from the sea comes the inspiration for Hull's newest, colorful, complete line of art pottery. In Ebb Tide, the shapes that inhabit the seas . . . shells, coral, fish, and plants . . . set the motif. Hull has captured them, in glowing colors, and fashioned them into art pottery of great beauty.

EBB TIDE is available in two decorations. The complete 16 piece line is illustrated, left, in Decoration 2 — Wine & Seaweed. The entire 16 piece line is also available in Decoration 1 — Shrimp & Turquoise, in which some representative samples are illustrated immediately above.

Plate 149. Original company brochure page.

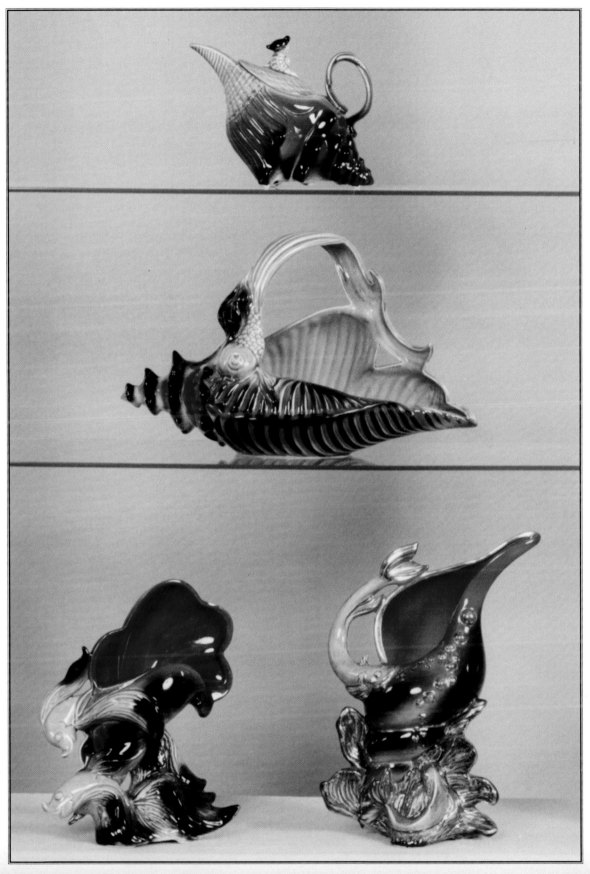

Plate 150.

Plate 151.
Row 1:
1. Cornucopia, "E-9," 11¾", $175.00 – 210.00.
2. Ewer, "E-10," 14", $210.00 – 275.00.
Row 2:
1. Console bowl, "E-12," 15¾", $215.00 – 260.00.
2. Candleholder, "E-13," 2¾", $25.00 – 35.00.
3. Candleholder, "E-13," 2¾", $25.00 – 35.00.
4. Basket, "E-5," 6¼", $140.00 – 195.00.
5. Basket, "E-11," 16½", $210.00 – 265.00.
Row 3:
1. Ashtray, "E-8," 5", $170.00 – 225.00.
2. Vase, "E-2," 7", $75.00 – 105.00.
3. Vase, "E-6," 9¼", $150.00 – 200.00.
Row 4:
1. Teapot, "E-14," 6½", $235.00 – 295.00.
2. Covered sugar, "E-16," 4", $95.00 – 125.00.
3. Vase, "E-7," 11", $175.00 – 210.00.
4. Ewer, "E-4," 8¼", $150.00 – 200.00.

Row 5:
1. Creamer, "E-15," 4", $95.00 – 125.00.
2. Bud vase, "E-1," 7", $75.00 – 105.00.
3. Mermaid cornucopia, "E-3," 7½", $170.00 – 225.00.

Plate 152.
Row 1:
1. Creamer, "E-15," 4", $95.00 – 125.00.
2. Teapot, "E-14," 6½", $235.00 – 295.00.
3. Covered sugar, "E-16," 4", $95.00 – 125.00.
Row 2:
1. Basket, "E-5," 6¼", $140.00 – 195.00.
2. Ashtray, "E-8," 5", $170.00 – 225.00.
Row 3:
1. Candleholder, "E-13," 2¾", $25.00 – 35.00.
2. Console bowl, "E-12," 15¾", $215.00 – 260.00.
3. Candleholder, "E-13," 2¾", $25.00 – 35.00.
4. Vase, "E-6," 9¼", $150.00 – 200.00.

Plate 151. Original company brochure page.

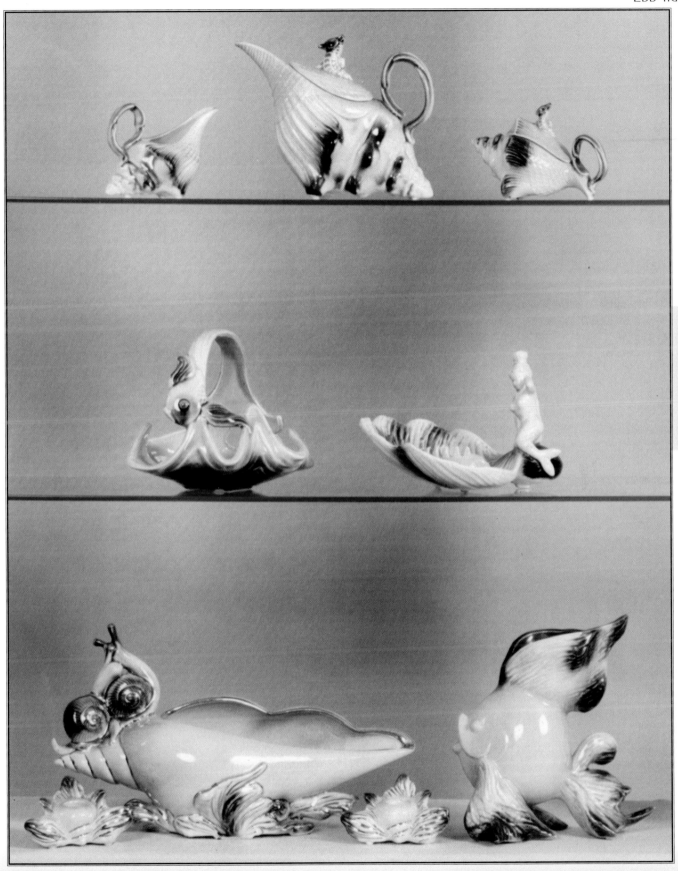

Plate 152.

Fantasy
Gold-Medal Flowerware
Mayfair

PRODUCTION DATES: Fantasy, 1957 – 1958; Gold-Medal Flowerware, 1959; Imperial, 1955 – 1985; Mayfair, 1958 – 1959

TRADEMARKS: Illustrations 57, 77, and 78, appendix A.

On this page, marking variations include an incised script "Hull" on the 1950s items and an incised "hull" on the later items. While the incised script "Imperial" appeared on many of the line's earliest items, the incised lowercase "hull" form became the trademark of choice. Items are commonly found without a Hull trademark.

The numbering system for Imperial is not fully consistent, most likely due to its many years of production and a number of items being retained each year while a number of new items were introduced. A consistent trait was the inclusion of the incised "F," which appeared in front of many mold numbers and signified florist ware.

The massive Imperial florist ware line, produced from 1955 to 1985, was first referred to by company salesmen as the "Fl list" and included planters, vases, flower bowls, and baskets. Many colors in both satin and high-gloss finishes appeared; some had contrasting foam or "run-down" trim. Earliest pieces of Imperial ware were veiled and webbed in free-form designs over contrasting color glazes.

Many of the 1950s designs, e.g., Fiesta, Fantasy, Jubilee, Mayfair, and others, are identified only by their color treatments, as shapes were used sometimes for more than one line. Color treatments assist in determining line names of many wares from the 1950s. As far as the Imperial line is concerned, identification of color treatments (usually other than Satin White) can be effectively used for determining dates of production.

Hull's Imperial line evolved from a variety of previously used designs of the 1950s. While Hull's earlier lines were separated from one another, the 1950s lines were characteristically combined for chain store sales, e.g., Fiesta teamed with Fantasy, Fantasy with Gold-Medal Flowerware, and others. Hull lines, which had initially kept sole identities, later mixed with other designs to form the chain store sales packages dictated by the pottery's retail markets.

By the late 1950s, assortments that had been known earlier as Medley, Mayfair, and others were simply referred to as "flowerware." Interesting to note is that first glimpses of Hull's Imperial line were interspersed in earlier variety packages. By the late 1950s, planters, jardinieres, flower bowls, flower vases, etc., were known as Imperial, and a short time later, the plant's entire output, other than the kitchenware that was being produced, was known as Imperial Florist Ware. While some of the Imperial items illustrated were manufactured for several years, only the initial dates of production will be listed.

Plate 153.
Row 1:
1. Imperial candleholder, "437," 2", 1970, $10.00 – 15.00.
2. Imperial Swan, "23," 8½", 1961, $25.00 – 35.00.
3. Imperial candleholder, "437," 2", 1970, $10.00 – 15.00.
Row 2:
1. Mayfair Mandolin wall pocket, "84," 7", $50.00 – 75.00.
2. Fantasy Cherub planter, "90," 7¼" x 9", $45.00 – 65.00.
3. Mayfair Violin wall pocket, "85," 7", $50.00 – 75.00.
Row 3:
1. Imperial Cherub Girl planter, unmarked, 5¾", 1969, $15.00 – 20.00.
2. Fantasy candleholder, "78," 6½", $15.00 – 20.00.
3. Imperial basket, "457," 6½", 1964, $40.00 – 60.00.
4. Fantasy candleholder, "78," 6½", $15.00 – 20.00.
5. Imperial baby planter, "F51," 5½", 1969, $12.00 – 18.00.

Row 4:
1. Imperial pitcher with bowl, "F91" and "F92," 6", 1974, $25.00 – 30.00.
2. Imperial Victorian basket, "B36," 9", 1974, $40.00 – 55.00.
3. Gold-Medal Flowerware Bucket jardiniere, "94B," 6", $25.00 – 35.00.
4. Gold-Medal Flowerware Bucket jardiniere, "94B," 5", $20.00 – 30.00.
Row 5:
1. Imperial vase, "413," 8¾", 1955, $15.00 – 20.00.
2. Fantasy vase, "73," 9½", $20.00 – 30.00.
3. Fantasy vase, "39," 12", $30.00 – 45.00.
4. Imperial vase, "F28," 9½", 1955, $15.00 – 20.00.
5. Imperial ewer, "461, USA," 12", 1964, $45.00 – 65.00.

Plate 153.

Floral

PRODUCTION DATES: 1951 – 1954.

TRADEMARKS: Illustrations 56 and 58, appendix A.
Incised script "Oven-Proof, Hull, USA," with 40-series mold number in a circle formation. Sizes were not included in the mold.

Floral wares were decorated in high-gloss with raised yellow airbrushed florals and yellow airbrushed lids with brown banding. Florals appear on only one side of the ware. Fifteen items were available.

Plate 154.
Row 1:
1. Shaker, "No. 44," 3½", $15.00 – 20.00.
2. Shaker, "No. 44," 3½", $15.00 – 20.00.
3. Grease jar, "No. 43," 5¾", $40.00 – 55.00.
4. Bowl, "No. 40," 5", $14.00 – 18.00.
5. Bowl, "No. 40," 6", $14.00 – 18.00.
6. Bowl, "No. 40," 7", $15.00 – 20.00.
7. Bowl, "No. 40," 8", $20.00 – 30.00.
8. Bowl, "No. 40," 9", $35.00 – 55.00.
Row 2:
1. Open individual casserole, "No. 47," 5", $15.00 – 20.00.
2. Covered individual casserole, "No. 47," 5", $18.00 – 25.00.
3. Cookie jar, "No. 48," 8¾", $110.00 – 160.00.
4. Covered casserole, "No. 42," 7½", $40.00 – 60.00.
Row 3:
1. Salad bowl, "No. 49," 10", $60.00 – 85.00.
2. Cereal bowl, "No. 50," 6", $14.00 – 18.00.
3. Pitcher, "No. 46," 1qt., $40.00 – 55.00.

Plate 155.
Row 1:
1. Floral salad bowl, "No. 49," 10", $60.00 – 85.00.
2. Floral mixing bowl, "No. 40," 9", $45.00 – 65.00.
Row 2:
1. Floral cookie jar, "No. 48," 8¾", $110.00 – 160.00.
2. Floral grease jar, "No. 43," 5¾", $40.00 – 55.00.
3. Floral salt shaker, "No. 44," 3½", $15.00 – 20.00.
4. Floral pepper shaker, "No. 44," 3½", $15.00 – 20.00.

Row 3:
1. Floral individual French-handled casserole, "No. 47," 5", $18.00 – 25.00.
2. Floral mixing bowl, "No. 40," 5", $14.00 – 18.00.
3. Cook 'N' Serve Ware mug, "No. 33," 3¾", $6.00 – 8.00.
4. Cook 'N' Serve French-handled casserole, 5", $15.00 – 20.00.
Row 4:
1. Cook 'N' Serve Ware divided covered casserole, "No. 35," 11½", $45.00 – 65.00.
2. Cook 'N' Serve Ware coffee server, "No. 32," 11", $40.00 – 60.00.
3. Cook 'N' Serve Ware French-handled casserole, "No. 28-8"," $25.00 – 35.00.

Plate 154. Original company brochure page.

Plate 155.

Fiesta
Sun Valley Pastels

PRODUCTION DATES: Fiesta, 1957 – 1958; Sun Valley Pastels, 1956 – 1957

TRADEMARK: Illustration 57, appendix A.
Illustrated items are most commonly found with the incised script Hull trademark with a mold number and "USA."

There were 24 items in the Fiesta line. Items included a varied assortment of high-gloss and satin-finished jardinieres with metal accessories, fancy vases, baskets and garden dishes with embossed fruit and floral decorations, classic flower bowls with candle holders, and more.

Sun Valley Pastels was a 17-piece vase assortment for chain store sales in which 11 items were offered in satin finish of pink exterior with high-gloss gray interior, or satin finish of turquoise exterior with high-gloss yellow interior. The additional items were offered in satin exterior finishes of pink, Willow Green, and white, with gloss interiors.

Plate 157.
Row 1:
1. Sun Valley Pastel flower dish, "152," 13", $25.00 – 35.00.
Row 2:
1. Sun Valley Pastel window box, "153," 12½", $25.00 – 35.00.
2. Sun Valley Pastel bulb bowl, "154," 8½", $15.00 – 22.00.
Row 3:
1. Fiesta tulip-shape jardiniere, "46," 6½", $85.00 – 125.00.
2. Sun Valley Pastel footed compote bowl, "159," 5¼", $30.00 – 45.00.
3. Fiesta jardiniere, "47," 6½", $35.00 – 45.00.
Row 4:
1. Sun Valley Pastel flower pot with stand, "150," 10", $25.00 – 35.00.
2. Fiesta vase, "45," 8½", $85.00 – 125.00.
3. Fiesta jardiniere, "43," 6", $40.00 – 65.00.
4. Sun Valley Pastel square candy dish, "158," 6¾", $35.00 – 50.00.
Row 5:
1. Sun Valley Pastel vase, "163," 11½", $20.00 – 30.00.
2. Sun Valley Pastel tulip vase, "162," 11½", $30.00 – 40.00.
3. Fiesta jardiniere, "92," 7", $40.00 – 60.00.
4. Fiesta cornucopia, "49," 8½", $75.00 – 105.00.

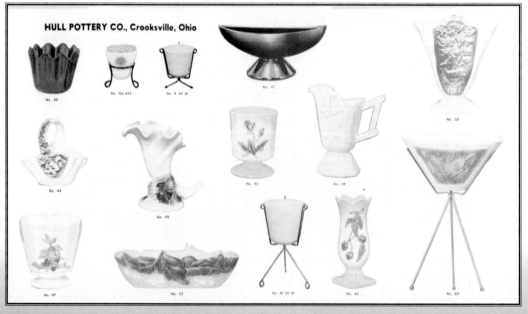

HULL POTTERY CO., Crooksville, Ohio

Plate 156. Original company brochure illustrating the diversity of wares marketed as assortment packages for chain stores.

Plate 157.

Heritageware
Marcrest

PRODUCTION DATES: Heritageware, 1958; Marcrest, 1958; Sun Valley Pastels, 1956 – 1957

TRADEMARKS: Heritageware, illustration 57, appendix A; Marcrest, illustrations 66 and 67, appendix A; Sun Valley Pastels, illustration 57, appendix A.

Heritageware: Incised script "Hull, U.S.A., © 58," with an A-series mold identification number

Marcrest: The "Marcrest Quality, Oven Proof" logo was incised into the mold and appeared on many Marcrest items. These items were used for premiums and grocers' giveaways. The Marcrest ashtrays were marked, "MARCREST, USA."

Marcrest was a trade name used by Marshall Burns, a distributor for the Chicago area, and was the name used on nearly all pottery and dinnerware items marketed by this firm. What is important to note is that Hull was not the only producer of Marcrest items; however, Hull appears to be the only producer of the pastel-colored dinnerware for Marshall Burns. Brown Marcrest dinnerware was produced by Western Stoneware of Monmouth, Illinois.

Sun Valley Pastels: Marked with an incised script "Hull," a mold number, and "USA."

Heritageware is an ovenproof kitchenware line the company described as high-gloss Mint Green or Azure Blue with a light touch of foam edge. An additional treatment was the textured or semimatte finished glaze with contrasting white lids or companion pieces, e.g., shakers or cruets. Company information illustrated 15 shapes.

Marcrest high-gloss ovenproof kitchenware items were used for grocery store giveaways, and were highly glazed in pastel colors of Mint Green, pink, yellow, Coral, and white. Marcrest items were not trimmed with foam, while Heritageware items were given the contrasting decoration. The Marcrest trademark in raised block form was used on the ashtrays, which were also sales premiums. They were glazed in both solid high-gloss and satin finishes.

Sun Valley Pastels was 17-piece assortment for chain store sales in which 11 items were offered in satin finish of pink exterior with high-gloss gray interior, or satin finish of turquoise exterior with high-gloss yellow interior. The additional items were offered in satin exterior finishes of pink, Willow Green, and white, and had gloss interiors.

Plate 158.
Row 1:
1. Marcrest ashtray, 7½", $15.00 – 20.00.
2. Sun Valley Pastel leaf tray, "31," 8¾", $15.00 – 20.00.
3. Marcrest ashtray, 7½", $15.00 – 20.00.
Row 2:
1. Heritageware shaker, 3½", $15.00 – 18.00.
2. Heritageware shaker, 3½", $15.00 – 18.00.
3. Heritageware pitcher, "A-7," 4½", $18.00 – 25.00.
4. Marcrest mug, 3¼", $8.00 – 10.00.
5. Heritageware mug, 3¼", $8.00 – 10.00.
6. Heritageware oil cruet, 6¼", $25.00 – 35.00.
7. Heritageware vinegar cruet, 6¼", $25.00 – 35.00.
Row 3:
1. Marcrest pitcher, 7½", $40.00 – 60.00.
2. Marcrest pitcher, 7½", $40.00 – 60.00.
3. Marcrest pitcher, 7½", $40.00 – 60.00.
Row 4:
1. Heritageware grease jar, "A-3-5¾"," $30.00 – 45.00.
2. Heritageware cookie jar, "0-18-9½"," $100.00 – 125.00.
3. Heritageware pitcher, "A-6-7"," $30.00 – 40.00.
4. Heritageware cookie jar, "0-18-9½"," $100.00 – 125.00.

Plate 158.

Imperial

PRODUCTION DATES: 1955 – 1985

TRADEMARKS: Illustrations 57, 61, 77, and 78, appendix A.

Trademark variations for items illustrated included incised script "Hull," incised lowercase "hull," and script "Imperial." These items are also commonly found unmarked.

The Imperial floristware line included planters, vases, flower bowls, and baskets produced from the mid-1950s through 1985. Several Gold-Medal Flowerware items were later included in the Imperial line. Both satin and high-gloss finishes were used, and illustrated are three vases decorated by Granville "Grany" Shafer, of the Shafer Pottery Company of Zanesville, Ohio. Two are decorated in lusters of blue and dark rose, while a third is a decoration Shafer referred to as his gold "daisy chain." Formulas for these decorations were Shafer's guarded secrets,

Hull's religious planters first entered the market in January, 1957, with Praying Madonna, 24; Kneeling Madonna, 25; Madonna with Child, 26; Standing Madonna with Urns, 27; and St. Francis planter, 89. Madonna planters were advertised in new satin finishes of yellow, ivory, and Carnation, with hand-painted underglaze features. While some Madonna planters were later glazed in high-gloss white, yellow, and pink, they eventually became available only in Satin White. Hull designer Louise Bauer, a devout Catholic, was responsible for modeling these and other religious planters for the firm.

The Imperial Spiral design of 1960 included a line of vases that doubled as pedestals for jardinieres. F83 vase and F84 Jardiniere together were 25" high. These items were distributed in glazes of Moss Green or mahogany with white flow and allover Satin White.

Plate 160.

Row 1:

1. Imperial Duck planter, "F69," 10", 1985, $25.00 – 35.00.

Row 2:

1. Imperial jardiniere, "F88," Shafer dark rose luster, 5¾", 1970, $50.00 – 75.00.
2. Imperial jardiniere, "F34," Shafer gold Daisy Chain, 5", $50.00 – 75.00.
3. Imperial jardiniere, "F88," Shafer blue luster, 5¾", $50.00 – 75.00.

Row 3:

1. Imperial Madonna, "F7," 7", 1974, $15.00 – 20.00.
2. Imperial Madonna, "417," 9½", 1960, $20.00 – 25.00.
3. Imperial ewer, "F480," 10½", 1965, $45.00 – 75.00.
4. Imperial Madonna, "25," 7", 1957, $30.00 – 40.00.

Row 4:

1. Imperial Victorian vase, "B37," 9", Shafer gold, 1974, $50.00 – 75.00.
2. Twin Swan planter, "81," 10½", 1970, $40.00 – 60.00.
3. Imperial Victorian vase, "B37," 9", 1974, $10.00 – 16.00.

Row 5:

1. Imperial spiral jardiniere, unmarked, 10" x 12", 1960, $155.00 – 210.00.
2. Gold-Medal Flowerware jardiniere, "105," 11", 1959, $30.00 – 40.00.
3. Gold-Medal Flowerware vase, "102," 11½", 1959, $20.00 – 30.00.

Plate 159. Original company advertising.

Plate 160.

Imperial

The Imperial line, first referred to as the "F1 list" in 1955, was manufactured in volume until the plant's closing in 1985. Imperial's color treatments were many, and included both satin and high-gloss finishes. Imperial glazes illustrated on the following page include Wild Honey, olive green trimmed in Willow Green, green trimmed in turquoise, Satin Avocado, Mirror Black, and Satin White.

Many Imperial wares were in production for several years; sometimes the same shape was produced in a variety of different glaze treatments. Certain glaze treatments for Imperial assist in determining production dates. While olive green, Green Agate, Moss Green, and Satin White were used for many years, other glazes, such as Satin Pink, Lilac, Coral, mahogany, and others were used during specific years of production.

Plate 161.
Row 1:
1. Imperial Victorian footed dish garden, "B32," 7", $8.00 – 10.00.
2. Imperial footed bowl, unmarked, 3½", 1982, $8.00 – 10.00.
3. Imperial footed pot, unmarked, 4½", 1982, $8.00 – 10.00.
Row 2:
1. Imperial pedestaled planter, "B26," 6½", $8.00 – 10.00.
2. Imperial jardiniere, "431," 6", 1968, $15.00 – 20.00.
3. Imperial fancy oval vase, "F33," 5¾", 1967, $6.00 – 8.00.
4. Dove ashtray/planter, unmarked, 4¼", 1965, $10.00 – 15.00.
Row 3:
1. Imperial Swirl pedestaled planter, "F57," 8¼", 1969, $8.00 – 10.00.
2. Gold-Medal Flowerware Chinese Sage Mask wall pocket, "120," 8", 1959, $130.00 – 165.00.
3. Vase, Mirror Black, 9", 1980, $20.00 – 30.00.
4. Vase, Mirror Black, 6", 1980, $15.00 – 20.00.
5. Gold-Medal Flowerware Chinese Sage Mask wall pocket, "120," 8", 1959, $130.00 – 165.00.
6. Imperial Usubata vase, "439," 9", 1968, $15.00 – 20.00.
Row 4:
1. Imperial Rose vase, 9", 1974, $10.00 – 15.00.
2. Experimental ashtray, unglazed base, 8", 1965, $40.00 – 50.00.
3. Imperial jardiniere, "F60," 5½", 1969, $15.00 – 20.00.
4. Imperial jardiniere, thunderbird decor, 4", 1978, $15.00 – 20.00.
Row 5:
1. Vase, 6", 1980, $15.00 – 20.00.
2. Vase, 9", 1980, $20.00 – 30.00.
3. Vase, 4", 1980, $10.00 – 15.00.
4. Jubilee caladium leaf, "405," 14", 1957, $25.00 – 40.00.

Plate 161.

Medley

PRODUCTION DATE: 1962

TRADEMARKS: Illustrations 57, 73, 78, and 79, appendix A.

While many novelty items were unmarked, some were marked with the incised script "Hull, USA," the incised "hull, USA," and with an incised "planter inc." The Medley urn vases are marked with an incised print "URN-VASE, USA" in circle form.

This chain store assortment of swirled urn vases; Dolphin, Swan, and Teddy Bear planters; a Cat vase; a Madonna planter; and items with metal accessories was decorated in Satin White, Green Agate with turquoise trim, and Persimmon with yellow trim. Twenty-five items were cataloged for the Medley assortment, some being shared Coronet and Imperial shapes.

For those who appreciate the high-gloss Tangerine glaze, illustrated are items in solids and spattered glazes and those edged with contrasting foam. The Jack-O-Lanterns were produced in at least two face styles.

Plate 162.
1. Urn-Vase, "801," 5", $15.00 – 20.00.
2. Urn-Vase, "802," 6", $15.00 – 20.00.
3. Urn-Vase, "803," 7", $18.00 – 22.00.
4. Urn-Vase, "804," 8", $20.00 – 25.00.
Row 2:
1. Flower bowl, "805," 5", $6.00 – 8.00.
2. Jardiniere, "806," 5¾", $10.00 – 12.00.
3. Vase, "807," 9", $16.00 – 20.00.
4. Vase, "808," 8", $22.00 – 30.00.
Row 3:
1. Cat vase, "809," 11", $75.00 – 100.00.
2. Dolphin vase, "810," 5¼"," $15.00 – 20.00.
3. Teddy Bear planter, "811," 7½", $40.00 – 65.00.
Row 4:
1. Swan, "812," 9 x 7½", $25.00 – 35.00.
2. Madonna, "813," 9", $20.00 – 25.00.
3. Flower bowl, "814," 11½", $12.00 – 18.00.

Plate 163.
Row 1:
1. Bulb bowl, "107," 7", 1952, $30.00 – 40.00.
2. Vase, "100," 9", 1952, $45.00 – 65.00.
3. Medley Swan, "815," 4", $8.00 – 10.00.
Row 2:
1. Imperial window box, unmarked, 14¾", 1960, $20.00 – 30.00.
2. Medley jardiniere, "806," 5", $10.00 – 15.00.
Row 3:
1. Jack-O-Lantern, unmarked, 5½", 1965, $25.00 – 30.00.
2. "Planter Inc." flower pot, "25-3¼"," 1962, $10.00 – 12.00.
3. Medley Teddy Bear planter, "811," 7", $40.00 – 65.00.
Row 4:
1. Medley Urn-Vase jardiniere, "801," 5", $15.00 – 20.00.
2. Double bud vase, "103," 9", 1952, $50.00 – 75.00.
3. Medley round flower bowl, "44," 4½", $15.00 – 20.00.

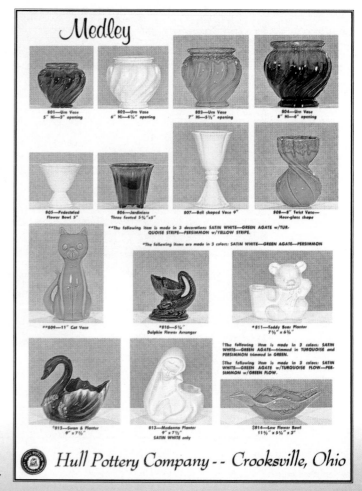

Plate 162. Original company brochure page.

Plate 163.

Mirror Black

PRODUCTION DATES: 1955 – 1957

TRADEMARK: Illustration 57, appendix A.
    Incised script "Hull," mold number, and "USA."

The high-gloss Mirror Black wares overlap from the Fiesta and Fantasy lines, and some are decorated with contrasting foam. The florist Fl collection, forerunner of the massive Imperial line, emerged in 1955, in tinted and veiled decorations. Kitchenware bowls in high-gloss solid black backgrounds with pink veiling also entered the marked in 1955. The wall pocket is from the varied Gold-Medal Flowerware line.

Plate 164.
Row 1:
1. Knight planter, "55," 8", $90.00 – 130.00.
2. Rooster planter, "53," 5¾", $110.00 – 135.00.
3. Goose wall pocket, "67," 6", $55.00 – 75.00.
4. Twin deer vase, "57," 8¾", $40.00 – 65.00.
Row 2:
1. Window box, "71," 12½", $30.00 – 40.00.
2. Flying duck planter, "79," 6", $45.00 – 60.00.
3. Flower bowl, "78," 12¼", $30.00 – 40.00.
Row 3:
1. Basket, "56," 6", $50.00 – 80.00.
2. Cotton flower bowl, "59," 7", $60.00 – 85.00.
3. Cornucopia, "64," 10", $30.00 – 40.00.
Row 4:
1. Planter, "F1," 6¾", $20.00 – 30.00.
2. Window box, "73," 14¾", $20.00 – 30.00.
3. Planter, "F3," 8¾", $20.00 – 30.00.
Row 5:
1. Siamese cat and kitten planter, "63," 12", $110.00 – 165.00.
2. Planter, "F2," 7¾", $20.00 – 30.00.
3. Swan, "80," 6", $35.00 – 45.00.

Plate 165.
Row 1:
1. Window box, veiled decoration, "82," 12½", 1955, $25.00 – 35.00.
Row 2:
1. Planter, veiled decoration, "F1," 6¾", 1955, $20.00 – 30.00.
2. Fiesta flower pot, "40," 4", 1957, $20.00 – 30.00.
3. Fantasy pedestaled planter, "38," 4¾", 1958, $18.00 – 24.00.
Row 3:
1. Bowl, ovenproof, veiled decoration, "16," 9", 1955, $35.00 – 45.00.
2. Bowl, ovenproof, veiled decoration, "16," 7", 1955, $25.00 – 35.00.
3. Bowl, ovenproof, veiled decoration, "16," 5", 1955, $15.00 – 20.00.
Row 4:
1. Fantasy candy dish, 8", 1958, $40.00 – 60.00.
2. Gold-Medal Flowerware vase, "111," 15½", 1959, $55.00 – 75.00.
3. Gold-Medal Flowerware Chinese Sage Mask wall pocket, "120," 8", 1959, $130.00 – 165.00.
4. Fantasy vase, "37," 8¼", 1958, $30.00 – 40.00.

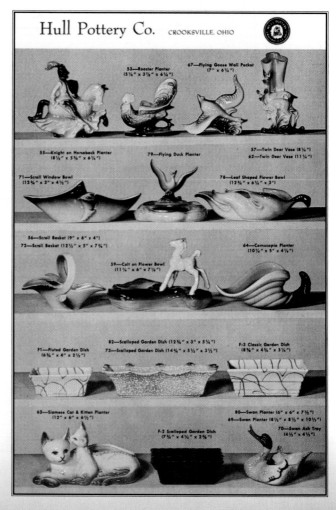

Plate 164. Original company brochure page.

Plate 165.

Pagoda
Continental

PRODUCTION DATE: 1960

TRADEMARKS: Illustrations 57 and 72, appendix A.
Pagoda: Incised script "Pagoda," along with a P-series mold number and "USA."
Continental: Incised script "Hull, USA," with a 50-series mold identification number.

Pagoda jardinieres, flower bowls, and vases have a distinct Oriental flair, offered in three high-gloss solid glazes, Persimmon or green with black trim, and white with gray trim. The company cataloged 12 shapes.

Plate 166.
Row 1:
1. Planter, "P1," 3¾", $12.00 – 15.00.
2. Planter, "P2," 10", $12.00 – 15.00.
Row 2:
1. Vase, "P3," 7½", $40.00 – 60.00.
2. Vase, "P4," 10", $45.00 – 60.00.
3. Vase, "P5," 12", $50.00 – 65.00.
4. Vase, "P6," 15", $55.00 – 75.00.
Row 3:
1. Jardiniere, "P7," 6", $16.00 – 20.00.
2. Jardiniere, "P8," 10", $40.00 – 55.00.
3. Jardiniere, "P9," 11½", $55.00 – 75.00.
Row 4:
1. Jardiniere, "P10," 6", $16.00 – 22.00.
2. Jardiniere, "P11," 10", $40.00 – 55.00.
3. Jardiniere, "P12," 11½", $60.00 – 85.00.

Plate 167.
Row 1:
1. Continental ashtray, "52," 10¼", $30.00 – 40.00.
2. Continental ashtray, "A-1," 7¾", $35.00 – 45.00.
3. Continental ashtray, "52," 10¼", $30.00 – 40.00.
Row 2:
1. Pagoda vase, "P3," 7½", $40.00 – 60.00.
2. Pagoda vase, "P4," 10", $45.00 – 60.00.
3. Experimental Pagoda vase, glazed in cobalt blue, unmarked, 7¾", $100.00 – 150.00.
Row 3:
1. Pagoda vase, "P5," 11½", $50.00 – 65.00.
2. Continental ashtray, "A-4," 13", $40.00 – 55.00.
3. Pagoda vase, "P5," 11½", $50.00 – 65.00.

Plate 166. Original company brochure page.

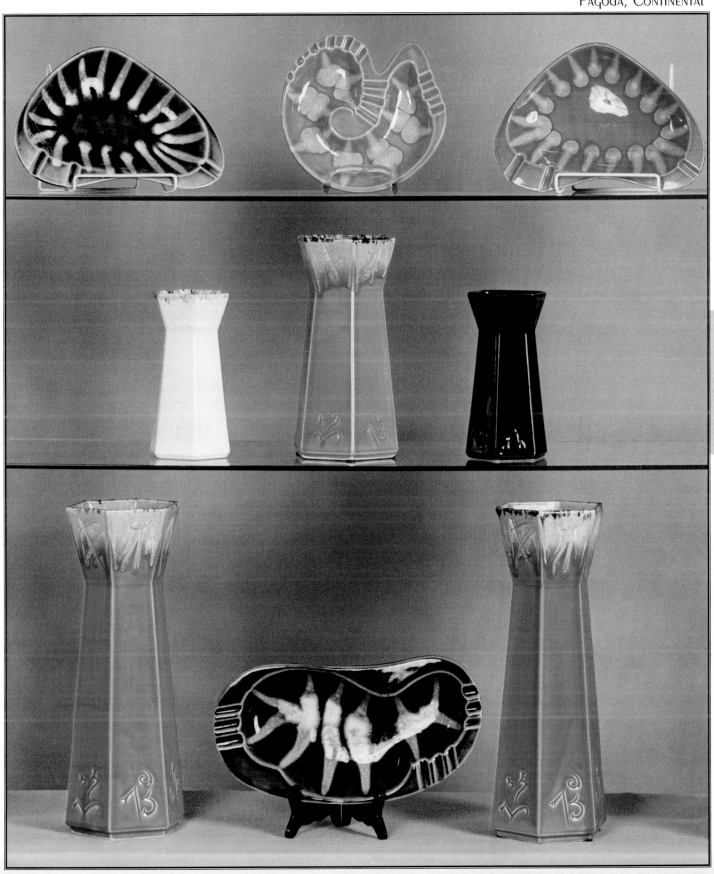

Plate 167.

Parchment and Pine

PRODUCTION DATES: 1951 – 1954

TRADEMARK: Illustration 57, appendix A.

Incised script "Hull, USA" and S-series mold number. Cornucopias carry "L" (left) and "R" (right) designations. Many pieces in this line do not carry a Hull trademark.

Parchment and Pine is decorated with realistic embossed pine sprays, decorated in Pine Green and Pearl Gray with brown or black trim and contrasting interiors. The company illustrated 15 cataloged shapes. Additionally offered were shapes noted as the 14" center bowl and the S15 instant coffee server. All shapes were offered through 1954, except the S14 center bowl, which was deleted from the company listing January 1, 1954.

Plate 168.
Row 1:
1. Candleholder, "S-10," 5", $25.00 – 35.00.
2. Basket, "S-8," 16½", $195.00 – 235.00.
3. Candleholder, "S-10," 5", $25.00 – 35.00.
Row 2:
1. Creamer, "S-12," 3¾", $20.00 – 35.00.
2. Teapot, "S-11," 6", $100.00 – 140.00.
3. Sugar, "S-13," 3¾", $20.00 – 35.00.
4. Basket, "S-3," 6", $90.00 – 130.00.

Plate 169.
Row 1:
1. Candleholder, "S-10," 5", $25.00 – 35.00.
2. Console bowl, "S-9," 16", $95.00 – 135.00.
3. Candleholder, "S-10," 5", $25.00 – 35.00.
Row 2:
1. Cornucopia, "S-2-L," 7¾", $45.00 – 70.00.
2. Window box, "S-5," 10½", $70.00 – 100.00.
3. Cornucopia, "S-2-R," 7¾", $45.00 – 70.00.
Row 3:
1. Center bowl, "S-14," 14", $85.00 – 135.00.
2. Vase, "S-4 10"," $75.00 – 100.00.

Plate 168. Original company brochure page.

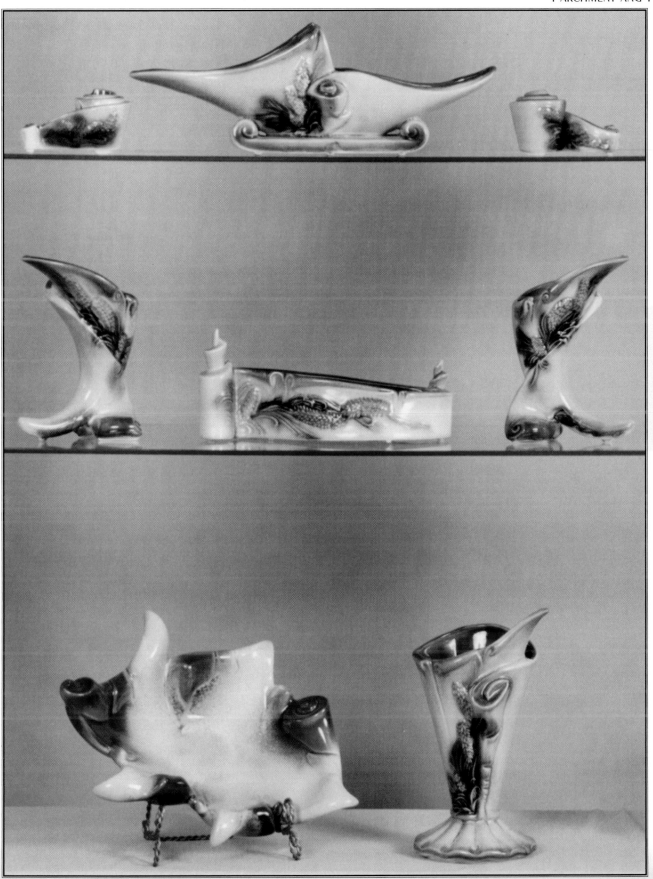

Plate 169.

Plate 170.
Row 1:
1. Basket, "S-3," 6", $90.00 – 130.00.
2. Cornucopia, "S-2" (left or right), 7¾", $45.00 – 70.00.
3. Console bowl, "S-9," 16", $95.00 – 135.00.
Row 2:
1. Creamer, "S-12," 3¾", $20.00 – 25.00.
2. Teapot, "S-11," 6", $100.00 – 140.00.
3. Sugar, "S-13," 3¾", $20.00 – 35.00.
Row 3:
1. Cornucopia, "S-6," 10½", $90.00 – 130.00.
2. Candleholder, "S-10," 5", $25.00 – 35.00.
3. Console bowl, "S-9," 16", $95.00 – 135.00.
4. Candleholder, "S-10," 5", $25.00 – 35.00.

Row 4:
1. Vase, "S-14," 14", $85.00 – 135.00.
2. Basket, "S-8," 16½", $195.00 – 235.00.
3. Ewer, "S-7," 14¾", $195.00 – 250.00.

Plate 171.
Row 1:
1. Teapot, "S-11," 6", $100.00 – 140.00.
Row 2:
1. Vase, "S-1," 6", $45.00 – 70.00.
2. Basket, "S-3," 6", $90.00 – 130.00.
3. Instant coffee server, "S15," 8", $175.00 – 225.00.
Row 3:
1. Basket, "S-8," 16½", $195.00 – 235.00.
2. Ewer, "S-7," 14¼", $195.00 – 250.00.

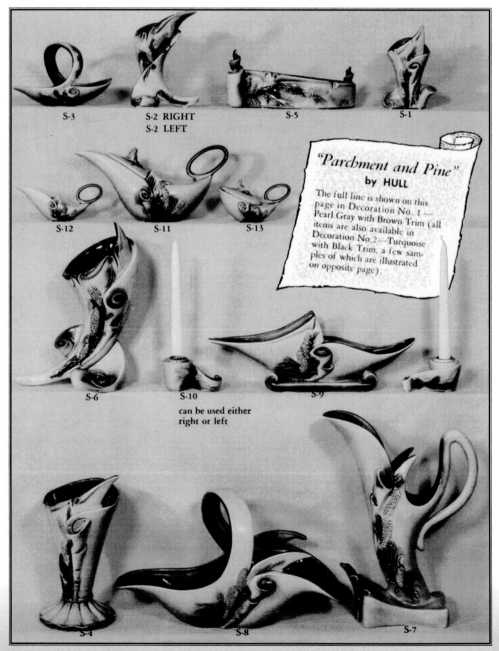

Plate 170. Original company brochure page.

Plate 171.

Plaidware
Vegetable

PRODUCTION DATES: Plaidware, 1950; Vegetable, 1951

TRADEMARKS: Illustrations 53 and 57, appendix A.

The Just Right Vegetable line most commonly bears the incised script "Hull, USA," along with a mold number and size identification. Plaidware does not carry the Hull trademark and was incised with mold numbers and size identification only. A foil label stating "A. E. Hull Pottery Co., Hull Ware, Crooksville, Ohio," in three lines accompanied Plaidware. The label had a light blue background with silver lettering.

Plaidware is an 11-piece ovenproof kitchenware line offered in decorations of green or red plaid on overall highly glazed white background with yellow horizontally striped decoration. Items included three nested bowls, a batter bowl, a cereal bowl, a casserole, a range jar, shakers, a cookie jar, and a creamer and a sugar.

Embossed Vegetable-pattern kitchenware is decorated in high-gloss solid colors of yellow, Coral, and green. Carrots, pea pods, radishes, and string beans were embossed in the design. "Cookies" was embossed on the cookie jar, and "S" (salt) and "P" (pepper) were embossed on the shakers. Fifteen Vegetable shapes were cataloged.

Plate 172.
Row 1:
1. Plaidware shaker, "64," 3¼", $25.00 – 35.00.
2. Plaidware shaker, "64," 3¼", $25.00 – 35.00.
3. Plaidware range jar, "63," 5½", $65.00 – 95.00.
4. Plaidware covered sugar, "68," 4", $40.00 – 60.00.

Plate 173.
1. Plaidware creamer, "67, USA," 3", $40.00 – 60.00.
2. Plaidware covered sugar, "68 USA," 4", $40.00 – 60.00.
3. Plaidware cookie jar, "66, Ovenproof USA," 9½", $150.00 – 210.00.
4. Plaidware bowl, "60-5", Ovenproof, USA," $25.00 – 35.00.
5. Vegetable batter bowl, "No. 21-9"," $105.00 – 165.00.
Row 2:
1. Debonair French-handled casserole, "18-8"," $45.00 – 75.00.
2. Experimental Plaidware cookie jar, unmarked, 9½". (This jar is decorated just the opposite of what the company placed on the market. Instead of brush-striped yellow on overall white with red crisscross, this jar is brush-striped red on overall white with yellow crisscross.) $150.00 – 250.00.
3. Cook 'N' Serve Ware French-handled casserole, "No. 28-8"," $25.00 – 35.00.

Plate 174.
Row 1:
1. Cook 'N' Serve Ware creamer, "No. 25," 3½", $15.00 – 20.00.
2. Cook 'N' Serve Ware covered sugar, "No. 24," 4", $15.00 – 20.00.
3. Experimental shaker, 3½", 1958, $30.00 – 40.00.
4. Experimental cookie jar, "18," 9½", 1958, $175.00 – 250.00.
Row 2:
1. Cook 'N' Serve Ware shaker, "No. 14," 4", $12.00 – 15.00.
2. Vegetable cookie jar, "28," 8¾", $165.00 – 225.00.
3. Vegetable salt shaker, "USA, 25," 3½", $30.00 – 40.00.
4. Vegetable pepper shaker, "USA, 25," 3½", $30.00 – 40.00.
5. Vegetable bowl, "20-5"," $30.00 – 40.00.

Plate 172.

Plate 173.

Plate 174.

Royal

PRODUCTION DATES: 1955 – 1957

TRADEMARKS: Illustrations 57 and 59, appendix A.

Raised or incised script "Hull, USA," with mold numbers and size identifications of the molds shared with Butterfly, Woodland, Ebb Tide, and Imperial. Since these pieces were designed for chain store sales, many carried no Hull trademark unless the trademark was already an existing part of the mold.

Royal, also referred to as Mist, is characterized by its high-gloss pink and turquoise glazes with overall white spattered decoration. Airbrushed charcoal gray appears on handles, lids, and bands. Hull noted this as its "W & E line" (Woodland and Ebb Tide) in pink or turquoise "mist" edged with Dove Gray.

Royal items were additionally offered with metal accessories, as illustrated by this Hull Pottery Company brochure. Shown are lantern jardinieres and classic straight-lined jardinieres in single, double, and triple stands, and a lavabo set.

Plate 175.
Row 1:
1. Lavabo, "86" and "87," 16" overall, $145.00 – 195.00.
2. Double jardiniere, "75-6,", 16" overall, $75.00 – 100.00.
3. Jardiniere, "75-7"," 19" overall, $50.00 – 75.00.
Row 2:
1. Jardiniere, 8", 15" overall, $30.00 – 40.00.
2. Triple jardiniere, 6" pots, 30" overall, $75.00 – 100.00.
3. Ashtray and planter, "18" and "19," 26" overall, $75.00 – 100.00.

Plate 176.
Row 1:
1. Royal Butterfly lavabo, "86" and "87," original hanger, 16", $145.00 – 195.00.

Row 2:
1. Royal Imperial window box, "82," 12½", $25.00 – 35.00.
2. Royal Woodland basket, "W9-8¾"," $95.00 – 150.00.
Row 3:
1. Royal Ebb Tide vase, unmarked, 7", $35.00 – 45.00.
2. Royal Imperial urn, unmarked, 5¾", $20.00 – 30.00.
3. Royal Ebb Tide bud vase, "E1," 7", $40.00 – 55.00.
Row 4:
1. Royal Woodland vase, "W18," 11", $90.00 – 120.00.
2. Royal Woodland basket, "W22," 10½", $225.00 – 295.00.
3. Royal Ebb Tide vase, unmarked, 11", $90.00 – 125.00.

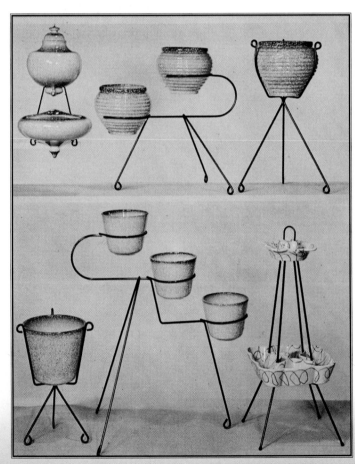

Plate 175. Original company brochure page.

226

Plate 176.

Royal

The chain store assortments included novelties as well as the Woodland and Ebb Tide mold shapes. The company brochure page illustrated shows that one such assortment also included the Telephone planter.

Plate 177.
Row 1:
1. Royal Woodland vase, "W4-6½"," $40.00 – 60.00.
2. Royal Woodland ewer, "W6-7"," $40.00 – 65.00.
3. Royal Ebb Tide vase, "E1," 7", $40.00 – 55.00.
4. Royal Ebb Tide cornucopia, "E3," 7½", $75.00 – 100.00.
5. Royal Ebb Tide vase, "E2," 7", $35.00 – 45.00.
Row 2:
1. Royal Woodland wall pocket, "W13-7½"," $100.00 – 135.00.
2. Royal Woodland vase, "W8-7½"," $50.00 – 70.00.
3. Royal Woodland basket, "W9-8½"," $95.00 – 150.00.
4. Royal Woodland vase, "W16-8½"," $60.00 – 80.00.
Row 3:
1. Royal Woodland candleholder, "W30," 3½", $40.00 – 55.00.
2. Royal Woodland console bowl, "W29," 14", $90.00 – 110.00.
3. Royal Woodland candleholder, "W30," 3½", $40.00 – 55.00.
Row 4:
1. Royal Ebb Tide vase, "E7," 11", $90.00 – 125.00.
2. Royal Ebb Tide vase, "E6," 9¼", $70.00 – 90.00.
3. Royal Woodland vase, "W18," 11", $90.00 – 120.00.
4. Telephone planter, "90," 9", $80.00 – 110.00.

Plate 178.
Row 1:
1. Royal Woodland cornucopia, "W10-11"," $65.00 – 95.00.
Row 2:
1. Royal Woodland candleholder, "W30," 3½", $40.00 – 55.00.
2. Royal Woodland console bowl, "W29," 14", $90.00 – 110.00.
3. Royal Woodland candleholder, "W30," 3½", $40.00 – 55.00.
Row 3:
1. Royal Woodland wall pocket, "W13-7½"," $100.00 – 135.00.
2. Royal Imperial jardiniere, "75-7"," $45.00 – 65.00.
3. Royal Woodland vase, "W4-6½"," $40.00 – 60.00.
Row 4:
1. Royal lazy Susan, sections marked "No. 81," center bowl marked "No. 83," 18" overall, $145.00 – 225.00.
2. Royal Woodland ewer, "W24-13½"," $175.00 – 225.00.

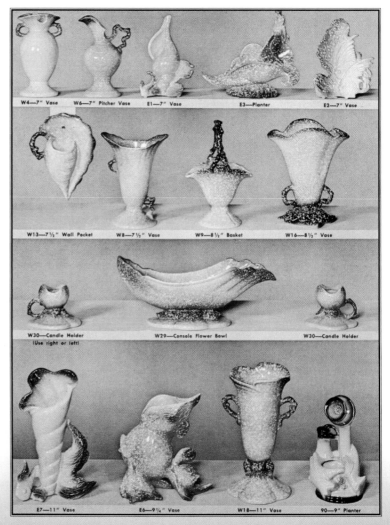

Plate 177. Original company brochure page.

Plate 178.

Serenade

PRODUCTION DATE: 1957

TRADEMARK: Illustration 57, appendix A.
   Incised script "Hull, USA, © 57" and S-series mold number.

The Serenade line incorporated an embossed bough and chickadee decoration. Solid pastel colors included textured matte Regency Blue with Sunlight Yellow gloss interior, textured matte Shell Pink with Pearl Gray gloss interior, and textured matte Jonquil Yellow with Willow Green gloss interior. Serenade included 24 cataloged shapes.
   Items from the Serenade molds were additionally produced in solid-textured pastel colors without further decoration of the embossed design. These items are not uncommon, and represent a separate line for chain store sales.

Plate 180.
Row 1:
1. Fruit bowl, "S15," 7", $140.00 – 180.00.
2. Ewer, "S2," 6½", $85.00 – 125.00.
Row 2:
1. Bud vase, "S1," 6½", $50.00 – 70.00.
2. Teapot, "S17," 5", $175.00 – 235.00.
3. Vase, "S-6," 8½", $50.00 – 100.00.

Row 3:
1. Covered casserole, "S20," 9", $120.00 – 165.00.
2. Puritan vase, "S4," 5¼", $65.00 – 90.00.
Row 4:
1. Vase, "S11," 10½", $100.00 – 125.00.
2. Basket, "S14," 12", $350.00 – 500.00.
3. Vase, "S11," 10½", $140.00 – 170.00.

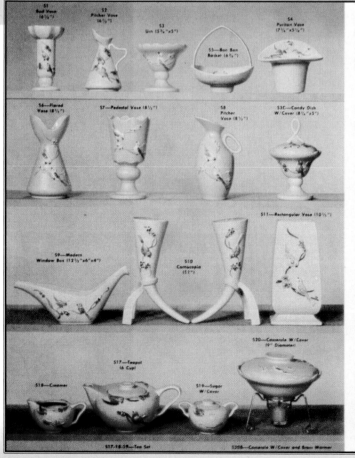
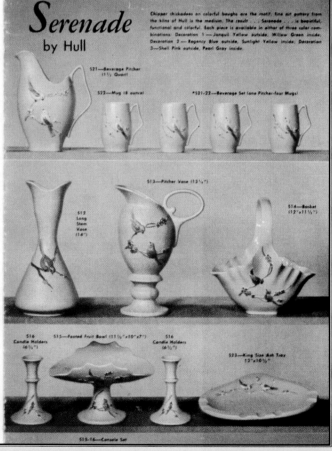

Plate 179. Original company brochure for Serenade.

Plate 180.

Serenade

Plate 181.

Row 1:
1. Candleholder, "S16," 6½", $70.00 – 85.00.
2. Candleholder, "S16," 6½", $70.00 – 85.00.
3. Window box, "S9," 12½", $90.00 – 110.00.

Row 2:
1. Beverage pitcher, "S21," 10½", $225.00 – 275.00.
2. Candy dish, "S3," 8¼", $155.00 – 200.00.
3. Cornucopia, "S10," 11", $90.00 – 110.00.

Row 3:
1. Basket, "S5," 6¾", $135.00 – 165.00.
2. Mug, "S22," 5½", $80.00 – 115.00.
3. Basket, "S5," 6¾", $90.00 – 115.00.

Row 4:
1. Vase, "S12," 14", $150.00 – 200.00.
2. Ashtray, "S23," 13", $115.00 – 155.00.
3. Ewer, "S13," 13¼", $360.00 – 460.00.

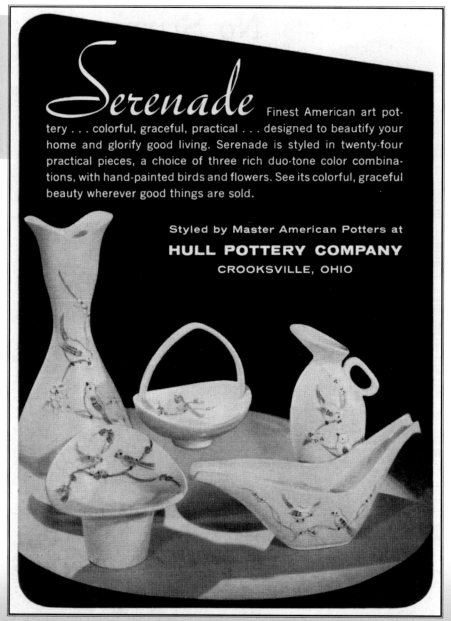

Advertisement from *Home and Garden* magazine, May 1957.

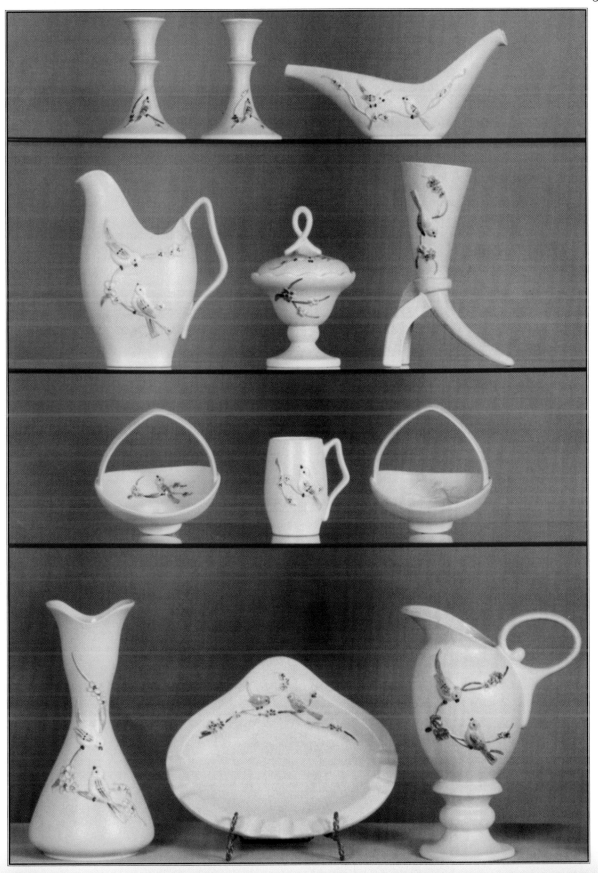

Plate 181.

Tokay
Tuscany

PRODUCTION DATES: Tokay, both color combinations, 1958; Tuscany, both color combinations, 1958; Tokay and Tuscany, Milk White and Forest Green, 1958 – 1960

TRADEMARKS: Tokay, illustration 65, appendix A; Tuscany, illustration 57, appendix A.
Tokay: Molds bear incised script "Tokay" and "USA" and mold number. The Hull name was not included on the Tokay mold.
Tuscany: Incised script "Hull, USA" and mold number. Items were commonly unmarked.

Tokay: Embossed leaf and grape decor in allover high-gloss background of Milk White with Forest Green grapes and leaves, or high-gloss duotoned spray tinted light green and Sweet Pink with pink grapes and green leaves. Eighteen shapes were catalogued.
Tuscany: Embossed leaf and grape decor in allover high-gloss backgrounds of Milk White or Sweet Pink, each with green grapes and leaves. Eighteen shapes were initially cataloged.
Additional items to the Tokay/Tuscany line included the 14" leaf dish, a 10" pedestaled vase, a 15½" pedestaled vase, and a 14" ewer.

Plate 182.
Row 1:
1. Basket, "No. 6," 8", $75.00 – 115.00.
2. Basket, "No. 15," 12", $165.00 – 225.00.
3. Ewer, "No. 3," 8", $80.00 – 115.00.
Row 2:
1. Cornucopia, "No. 10," 11", $55.00 – 85.00.
2. Planter, "No. 9," 8", $40.00 – 60.00.
3. Fruit bowl, "No. 7," 9½", $175.00 – 220.00.
4. Ewer, "No. 3," 8", $80.00 – 115.00.
Row 3:
1. Vase, "No. 8," 10", $105.00 – 135.00.
2. Moon basket, "No. 11," 10½", $120.00 – 170.00.
3. Vase, "No. 4," 8¼", $80.00 – 115.00.
Row 4:
1. Ewer, unmarked, 15", $265.00 – 325.00.
2. Leaf dish, "No. 19," 14", $30.00 – 50.00.
3. Ewer, "No. 13," 12", $265.00 – 325.00.

Plate 182.

Tokay, Tuscany

Plate 183.

Row 1:
1. Covered sugar, "No. 18," 3¼", $75.00 – 105.00.
2. Consolette, "No. 14," 15¾", $145.00 – 210.00.
3. Creamer, "No. 17," 3¼", $75.00 – 105.00.

Row 2:
1. Basket, "No. 6," 8", $75.00 – 100.00.
2. Vase, "No. 8," 10", $100.00 – 125.00.
3. Cornucopia, "No. 10," 11", $55.00 – 85.00.

Row 3:
1. Covered candy dish, "No. 9," 8½", $115.00 – 150.00.
2. Leaf dish, "No. 19," 14", $30.00 – 50.00.
3. Urn, "No. 5," 5½", $40.00 – 60.00.

Row 4:
1. Ewer, "No. 13," 12", $265.00 – 325.00.
2. Moon basket, "No. 11," 10½", $120.00 – 170.00.
3. Vase, "No. 12," 12", $95.00 – 145.00.
4. Ewer, "21," 14", $265.00 – 325.00.

Original company advertising. Left to right: Moon basket, no. 11, 10½", $120.00 – 170.00; covered sugar, no. 18, 3¼", $75.00 – 105.00; teapot, no. 16, 7½", $130.00 – 180.00; creamer, no. 17, 3¼", $75.00 – 105.00,

Original company advertising. Ewer, no. 21, 14", $265.00 – 325.00; vase, no. 20, 15", $100.00 – 150.00; leaf dish, no. 19, 14", $30.00 – 50.00.

Plate 183.

Tropicana

PRODUCTION DATE: 1959

TRADEMARK: Illustration 57, appendix A.
   Incised script "Hull, USA" and T-series mold number.

DESCRIPTION:
   Tropicana was produced in high-gloss white edged in Tropic Green. The ware is decorated with colorful Caribbean figures. The company offered seven cataloged shapes.
   Because Tropicana commands the highest prices of any post-1950 artware, it too is a target for current reproduction. Since reproduction Tropicana items can be found in antique malls sitting next to Hull reproductions in Camellia, Bow-Knot, and Little Red Riding Hood patterns, the general consensus is that it is produced by the same maker.
   The script Hull mark appears on Tropicana reproductions, but is usually blurred, either due to poor modeling, or as an intended part of the scheme. Overall coloration is poor. The background gloss white has a yellowish cast to it, and the green trim is off-color and poorly executed. The Tropicana figures are fairly convincing, so buyer beware.

Plate 185.
Row 1:
Flower bowl, "T51," 15½", $375.00 – 450.00.
Row 2:
1. Slender vase, "T54," 12½", $450.00 – 550.00.
2. Flat-sided vase, "T53," 8½", $355.00 – 460.00.
3. Ewer, "T56," 12½", $575.00 – 675.00.
Row 3:
1. Fancy basket, "T55," 12¾", $700.00 – 850.00.
2. Planter vase, "T57," 14½", $650.00 – 800.00.
3. Fancy basket, "T55," 12¾", $700.00 – 850.00.

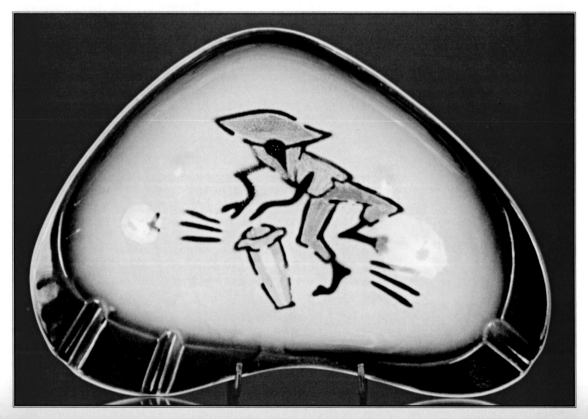

Plate 184. Ashtray, "T52," 10", $350.00 – 450.00.

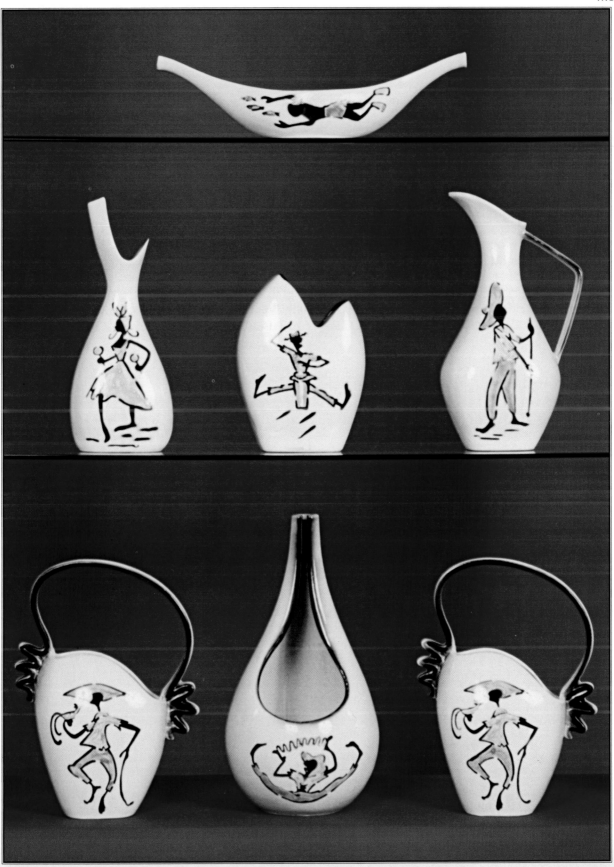

Plate 185.

Woodland

PRODUCTION DATES: Matte Woodland, 1951; Hi-Gloss Woodland, 1952 – 1954; Two-Tone Woodland, 1952 – 1954

TRADEMARKS: Illustrations 57 and 59, appendix A.
Raised script "Hull, USA," W-series mold number, and size identification.

DESCRIPTIONS:
Post-1950s items are identified first by mold use; treatment and color glaze is secondary. One definite characteristic of the post-1950s ware is the reversal of the mold; that is, the handles and decoration of the ware appeared on the opposite side from that used in earlier wares.

Matte production of Woodland in Dawn Rose and Harvest Yellow body pastels resumed after Hull's reconstruction. Most of these finishes were substandard. The color was usually satisfactory, but the glaze and finish themselves were coarser in most cases. After providing a short term of matte Woodland production, the company moved on to high-gloss color treatments. Twenty-one shapes appeared in post-1950 Woodland styles.

Woodland's gloss finishes included several two-toned glazes, such as rose and chartreuse, rose and peach, green and chartreuse, and green and blue, and allover green with either white or dark green interiors, and allover white or pastel pink. It is not unusual for the lighter colored items to have gold detailing that was done outside the factory. Glazes were first separated into the designations of Hi-Gloss Woodland and Two-Tone Woodland, but by January 1, 1954, all treatments were referred to as Hi-Gloss.

Plate 186.
Row 1:
1. Cornucopia, "W2-5½"," $45.00 – 70.00.
2. Ewer, "W3-5½"," $85.00 – 115.00.
3. Vase, "W4-6½"," $50.00 – 75.00.
4. Ewer, "W6-6½"," $95.00 – 115.00.
Row 2:
1. Cornucopia, "W10," 11", $80.00 – 110.00.
2. Flower pot with attatched saucer, "W11-5¾"," $100.00 – 145.00.
Row 3:
1. Wall pocket, "W13-7½"," $95.00 – 130.00.
2. Window box, "W14," 10", $60.00 – 90.00.
3. Basket, "W22," 10½", $250.00 – 300.00.
4. Ewer, "W24-13½"," $275.00 – 375.00.

Plate 187.
Row 1:
1. Candleholder, "W30," 3½", $130.00 – 160.00.
2. Console bowl, "W29," 14", $375.00 – 475.00.
3. Candleholder, "W30," 3½", $130.00 – 160.00.
Row2:
1.Covered sugar, "W28," 3½", $45.00 – 65.00.
2. Window box, "W14," 10", $60.00 – 90.00.
3. Creamer, "W27," 3½", $45.00 – 65.00.
Row3:
1. Jardiniere, "W7-5½"," $70.00 – 95.00.
2. Teapot, "W26," 6½", $140.00 – 185.00.
3. Cornucopia, "W10," 11", $80.00 – 110.00.
Row 4:
1. Vase, "W18-10½"," $115.00 – 165.00.
2. Vase, "W16-8½"," $230.00 – 275.00.
3. Ewer, "W24-13½"," $240.00 – 340.00.
4. Basket, "W9-8¾"," $135.00 – 215.00.

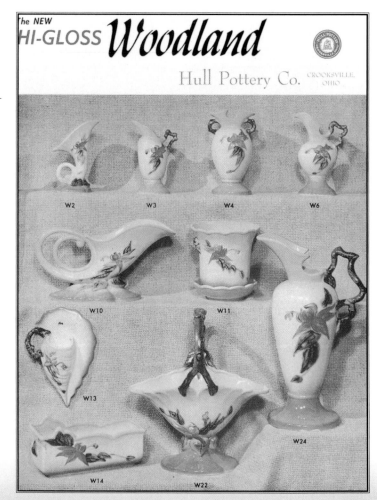

Plate 186. Original company brochure page.

Plate 187.

Woodland

Plate 189.

Row 1:
1. Ewer, "W6-6½"," $95.00 – 115.00.
2. Basket, "W9-8¾"," $135.00 – 200.00.
3. Vase, "W8-7½"," $100.00 – 125.00.
4. Ewer, "W6-6½"," $125.00 – 150.00.

Row 2:
1. Teapot, "W26," 6½", $145.00 – 185.00.
2. Vase, "W8-7½"," $60.00 – 80.00.
3. Console bowl, "W29," 14", $145.00 – 175.00.

Row 3:
1. Ewer, "W24-13½"," $275.00 – 375.00.
2. Candleholder, "W30," 3½", $275.00 – 375.00.
3. Vase, "W18-10½"," $115.00 – 165.00.
4. Candleholder, "W30," 3½", $35.00 – 55.00.
5. Ewer, "W24-13½"," $275.00 – 375.00.

The NEW HI-GLOSS *Woodland*

DECORATION No. 2

Pieces shown above are two of the 21 items comprising the full "Woodland" pattern in a new color combination. This "Decoration No. 2" has a blue-gray top, forest green handles and base. The original and still available No. 1 has a chartreuse top, forest green handles, and pink base.

Decorations may be assorted in standard packages at no extra charge.

Hull Pottery Co.

CROOKSVILLE, OHIO

Original company advertisement. Basket, "W22-10½"," $250.00 – 300.00, and ewer, "W24-13½"," $275.00 – 375.00.

Plate 188. Experimental Woodland lamp, unmarked, 15", $500.00 – 700.00.

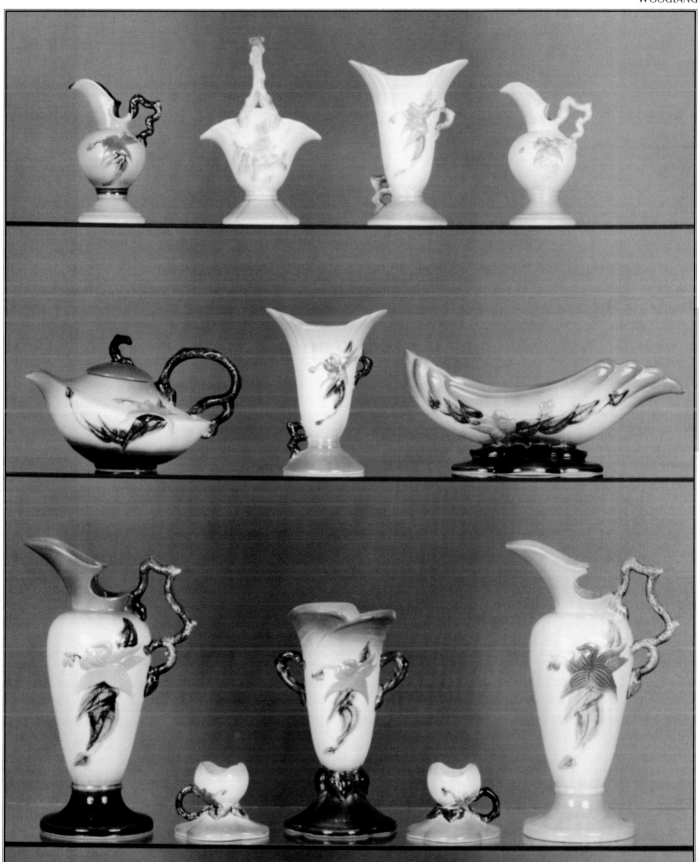

Plate 189.

The Fifties (1950 – 1960)
Woodland

Introduced before the plant's destruction, Woodland appeared in 30 cataloged shapes numbered 1 – 31, with number 20 skipped. The original 30 Woodland shapes were used prior to the company's flood and fire in 1950, with both matte and high-gloss wares. The earlier Woodland molds numbered 1, 5, 12, 17, 19, 21, 23, 25, and 31 were not remolded, and were seldom used for wares after 1950.

Plate 190.
Row 1:
1. Cornucopia, "W2-5½"," $45.00 – 70.00.
2. Ewer, "W3-5½"," $85.00 – 115.00.
3. Vase, "W4-6½"," $50.00 – 75.00.
4. Ewer, "W6-6½"," $95.00 – 115.00.
Row 2:
1. Cornucopia, "W10-11"," $80.00 – 110.00.
2. Flowerpot with attached saucer, "W11-5¾"," $100.00 – 145.00.
Row 3:
1. Wall pocket, "W13-7½"," $95.00 – 130.00.
2. Window box, "W14," 10", $60.00 – 90.00.
3. Basket, "W22-10½"," $250.00 – 300.00.
4. Ewer, "W24-13½"," $275.00 – 375.00.

Plate 191.
Row 1:
1. Ewer, "W3-5½"," $85.00 – 115.00.
2. Flowerpot with attached saucer, "W11-5¾"," $100.00 – 145.00.
3. Vase, "W8-7½"," $100.00 – 125.00.
4. Flowerpot, "W31-5¾"," $135.00 – 175.00.
5. Cornucopia, "W2-5½"," $80.00 – 100.00.
Row 2:
1. Vase, "W4-6½"," $50.00 – 75.00.
2. Double bud vase, "W15-8½"," $120.00 – 165.00.
3. Teapot lamp, unmarked, 8", $400.00 – 525.00.
4. Ewer, "W6-6½"," $95.00 – 115.00.
Row 3:
1. Basket, "W22-10½"," $250.00 – 300.00.
2. Free-form lamp, unmarked, 14", $500.00 – 700.000.
3. Experimental ewer lamp, incised into the clay "M. Wilson" (Sylvanus Burdette "Mose" Wilson), 14¾", $450.00 – 650.00.

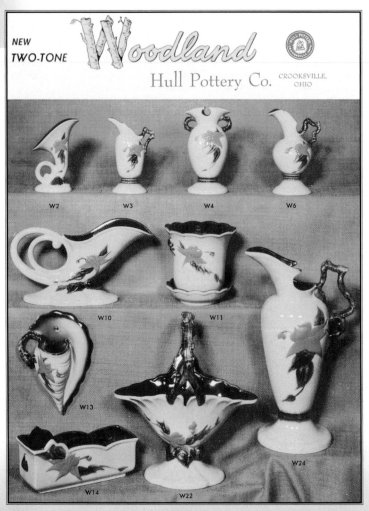

Plate 190. Original company brochure page.

Plate 191.

DINNERWARE
(1960 – 1986)

Always innovative and with the times, in 1960, Hull, aware of a general movement towards comfortable living and patio relaxation, introduced its House 'n Garden line. With modern shapes and glaze treatments, House 'n Garden carried the company through its final days of production.

Original company brochure pages representing lines from Hull's final twenty-five years of dinnerware production.

Avocado

PRODUCTION DATES: 1968 – 1971

TRADEMARK: Illustration 74, appendix A.
   Incised "hull, ovenproof USA."

This is House 'n Garden's casual serving ware offered in Avocado trimmed in ivory foam. Satin-finished Avacado was also manufactured during this same time period. It most often was not trimmed. Thirty items were available, including a cylinder-shaped cookie jar.

Plate 192.
Row 1:
1. Soup/Salad bowl, 6½", $4.00 – 6.00.
2. Dinner plate, 10¼", $8.00 – 10.00.
3. Mug, 3½", $5.00 – 7.00.
4. Fruit bowl, 5¾", $4.00 – 5.00.
5. Salad plate, 6½", $4.00 – 5.00.
Row 2:
1. Salt shaker, 3¾", $10.00 – 15.00.
2. Pepper shaker, 3¾", $10.00 – 15.00.
3. Creamer, 4½", $15.00 – 22.00.
4. Covered sugar, $15.00 – 22.00.
5. French-handled casserole, $16.00 – 20.00.
6. Fruit bowl, 6", $4.00 – 5.00.
7. Stein, 6", $6.00 – 10.00.
Row 3:
1. Coffee server, 11", $35.00 – 50.00.
2. Teapot, 6½", $40.00 – 65.00.
3. Pitcher, 7½", $25.00 – 40.00.
4. Chip 'n dip, 15" x 10½", $45.00 – 65.00.
Row 4:
1. Oval steak plate, 11¾", $20.00 – 25.00.
2. Divided vegetable dish, 10¾", $25.00 – 35.00.
3. Oval covered casserole, 2 qt., $30.00 – 40.00.

Original label from boxed House 'n Garden dinnerware set.

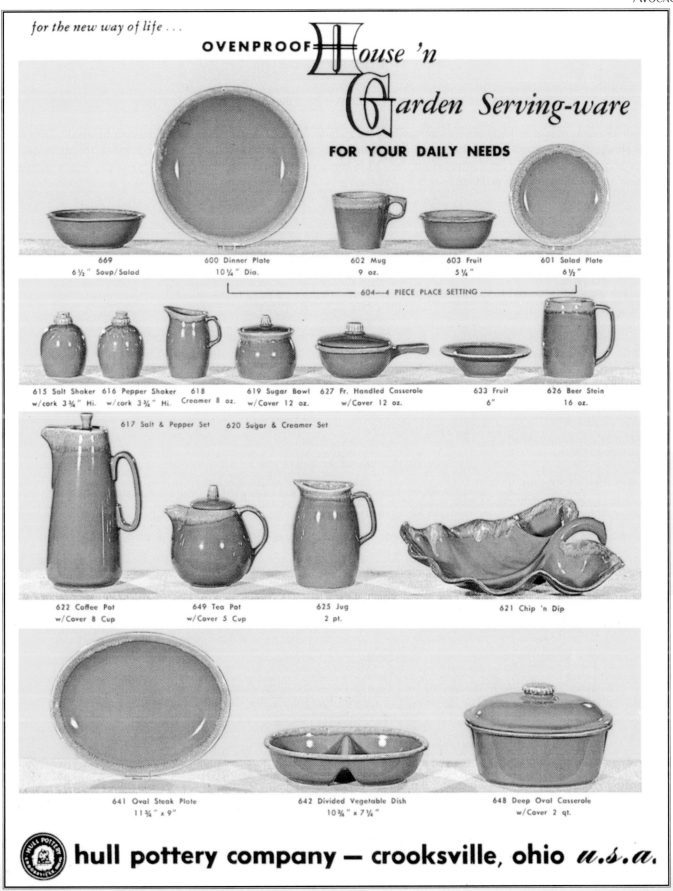

for the new way of life . . .

OVENPROOF House 'n Garden Serving-ware

FOR YOUR DAILY NEEDS

669
6½" Soup/Salad

600 Dinner Plate
10¼" Dia.

602 Mug
9 oz.

603 Fruit
5¼"

601 Salad Plate
6½"

604—4 PIECE PLACE SETTING

615 Salt Shaker
w/cork 3¾" Hi.

616 Pepper Shaker
w/cork 3¾" Hi.

618
Creamer 8 oz.

619 Sugar Bowl
w/Cover 12 oz.

627 Fr. Handled Casserole
w/Cover 12 oz.

633 Fruit
6"

626 Beer Stein
16 oz.

617 Salt & Pepper Set   620 Sugar & Creamer Set

622 Coffee Pot
w/Cover 8 Cup

649 Tea Pot
w/Cover 5 Cup

625 Jug
2 pt.

621 Chip 'n Dip

641 Oval Steak Plate
11¾" x 9"

642 Divided Vegetable Dish
10¾" x 7¼"

648 Deep Oval Casserole
w/Cover 2 qt.

hull pottery company — crooksville, ohio *u.s.a.*

Plate 192. Original company brochure page.

COUNTRY-BELLE

PRODUCTION DATE: 1985

TRADEMARKS: Illustrations 83 – 85, appendix A.
Incised "hull, Ovenproof, USA" and area of origin, "Crooksville, Ohio."

Country-Belle is glazed in high-gloss winter white with a hand-stamped blue decoration of trailing bluebells. Designed by Maury Mountain of Pfaltzgraff fame, this dinnerware boasted a glaze that Hull stated was identical to the glaze of Lenox China. In original advertising, Hull illustrated the No. 71 Swan as a centerpiece for this line. This swan, originally from the Medley line, was first introduced in 1962.

Plate 193.
Row 1:
1. Pitcher, 3½", $25.00 – 35.00.
2. Cheese shaker, 6½", $20.00 – 30.00.
3. Swan, unmarked, 8", $25.00 – 35.00.
4. Mug, clear glaze, no stamp, 5", $4.00 – 6.00.
5. Mug, 4¼", $8.00 – 10.00.
Row 2:
1. Pie plate, 11", $25.00 – 35.00.
2. Luncheon plate, 8½", $8.00 – 10.00.
3. Oval platter, 12", $15.00 – 22.00.
Row 3:
1. Canister, 5", $20.00 – 30.00.
2. Canister, 5", $20.00 – 30.00.
3. Canister, 6¼", $25.00 – 35.00.
4. Canister, 7¼", $30.00 – 40.00.
Row 4:
1. Bowl, 12", $40.00 – 60.00.
2. Rectangular baker, 14", $40.00 – 60.00.

Plate 193.

Country-Belle

Plate 195.

Row 1:

1. Covered sprout casserole, 7½", $55.00 – 75.00.

Row 2:

1. Salt shaker, 6", $20.00 – 25.00.
2. Pepper shaker, 6", $20.00 – 25.00.
3. Soup/Cereal bowl, 6¾", $8.00 – 15.00.
4. Mug, 5", $8.00 – 12.00.
5. Mug, 4¼", $8.00 – 10.00.

Row 3:

1. Beverage pitcher, 7½", $70.00 – 95.00.
2. Handled server, 11½", $45.00 – 65.00.

Row 4:

1. Mixing bowl, 8", $20.00 – 25.00.
2. Dinner plate, 10", $10.00 – 12.00.
3. Teapot/Coffee server, 9", $65.00 – 95.00.

Plate 194. Original company brochure page.

Plate 195. Original company brochure page.

COUNTRY SQUIRE

PRODUCTION DATES: 1963 – 1967

TRADEMARK: Illustration 74, appendix A.
  Incised "hull, Ovenproof USA."

Country Squire evolved from Hull's Rainbow dinnerware line and is also known as Green Agate. This separate line included at least 40 items. Remember that some lines, in identical or different mixes, were renamed primarily so they could be marketed to different retailers.

Plate 196.
Row 1.
1. Dinner plate, 10¼", $8.00 – 10.00.
2. Salad plate, 6½", $3.00 – 4.00.
3. Fruit bowl, 5¼", $3.00 – 4.00.
4. Mug, 4", $4.00 – 5.00.
5. Coffee server, 11", $35.00 – 50.00.
Row 2.
1. Mixing bowl, 5¼", $20.00 – 25.00.
2. Mixing bowl, 6¾", $20.00 – 25.00.
3. Mixing bowl, 8¼", $20.00 – 30.00.
4. Pitcher, 9", $40.00 – 60.00.
5. Pitcher, 7½", $30.00 – 40.00.
6. Pitcher, 4½", $15.00 – 22.00.
Row 3.
1. Bean pot, 6½", $30.00 – 40.00.
2. Individual bean pot, 3½", $15.00 – 22.00.
3. Covered sugar, 3½", $15.00 – 22.00.
4. Creamer, 3½", $15.00 – 22.00.
5. Covered casserole, 3 pt., $25.00 – 30.00.
6. Individual French-handled casserole, 5", $15.00 – 22.00.
7. Stein, 5", $5.00 – 6.00.
Row 4.
1. Ice-lip pitcher, 7½", $30.00 – 40.00.
2. Salt shaker, 3¾", $10.00 – 15.00.
3. Pepper shaker, 3¾", $10.00 – 15.00.
4. Chip 'n dip, 15", $40.00 – 50.00.
5. Cookie jar, 9", $50.00 – 85.00.

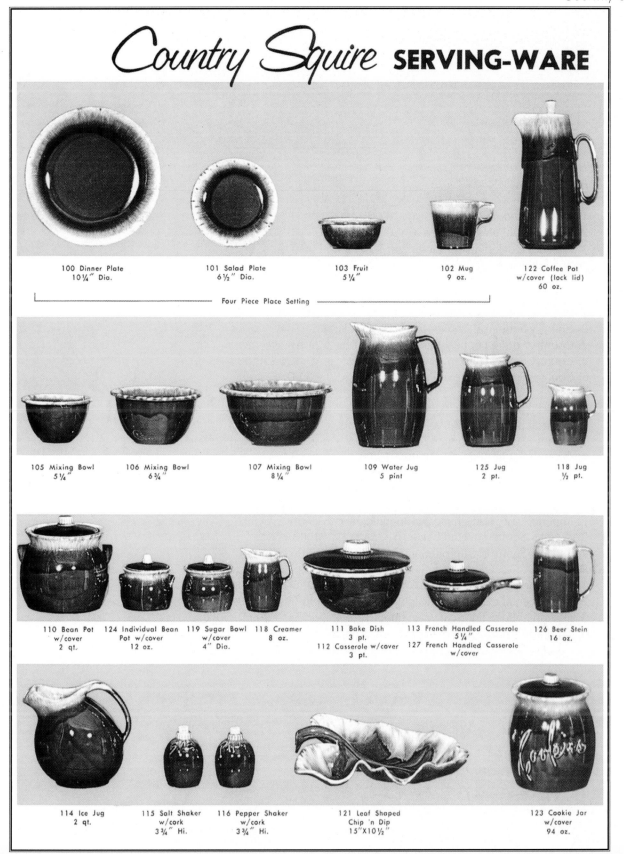

Country Squire **SERVING-WARE**

| 100 Dinner Plate 10¼" Dia. | 101 Salad Plate 6½" Dia. | 103 Fruit 5¼" | 102 Mug 9 oz. | 122 Coffee Pot w/cover (lock lid) 60 oz. |

—————————————— Four Piece Place Setting ——————————————

| 105 Mixing Bowl 5¼" | 106 Mixing Bowl 6¾" | 107 Mixing Bowl 8¼" | 109 Water Jug 5 pint | 125 Jug 2 pt. | 118 Jug ½ pt. |

| 110 Bean Pot w/cover 2 qt. | 124 Individual Bean Pot w/cover 12 oz. | 119 Sugar Bowl w/cover 4" Dia. | 118 Creamer 8 oz. | 111 Bake Dish 3 pt. 112 Casserole w/cover 3 pt. | 113 French Handled Casserole 5¼" 127 French Handled Casserole w/cover | 126 Beer Stein 16 oz. |

| 114 Ice Jug 2 qt. | 115 Salt Shaker w/cork 3¾" Hi. | 116 Pepper Shaker w/cork 3¾" Hi. | 121 Leaf Shaped Chip 'n Dip 15"X10½" | 123 Cookie Jar w/cover 94 oz. |

Plate 196. Original company brochure page.

Plate 197.

Row 1:

1. Imperial jardiniere, "F470," 4", $6.00 – 8.00.

2. Experimental glass in green agate, 3½", $20.00 – 30.00.

3. Imperial Duck planter, unmarked, 10", $30.00 – 40.00.

4. Imperial planter, unmarked, 3", $6.00 – 8.00.

5. Country Squire cup, 3¼", $4.00 – 6.00.

Row 2:

1. Country Squire jug/creamer, 4¼", $15.00 – 22.00.

2. Country Squire salt shaker, 3½", $8.00 – 12.00.

3. Country Squire pepper shaker, 3½", $8.00 – 12.00.

4. Country Squire soup 'n sandwich; mug, 5"; tray, 9½"; $20.00 – 25.00.

5. Country Squire deep-well saucer, 5¾", $2.00 – 3.00.

Row 3:

1. Imperial planter, unmarked, 3¾", $6.00 – 8.00.

2. Imperial planter, "F27," 4", $8.00 – 10.00.

3. Country Squire syrup/gravy boat, marked "Crestone," recessed lid and handle, 5", $45.00 – 65.00.

4. Country Squire stein, 5", $8.00 – 12.00.

5. Imperial planter, "F476," 4¾", $15.00 – 20.00.

Row 4:

1. Imperial Chickadee planter, "F474," 5", $12.00 – 16.00.

2. Imperial vase, lion's heads, unmarked, 6¾", $15.00 – 20.00.

3. Country Squire covered baker, 10", $40.00 – 50.00.

4. Country Squire ice-lip pitcher, 7½", $30.00 – 40.00.

Row 5:

1. Experimental cylindrical vase, unmarked, 6", $20.00 – 30.00.

2. Experimental cylindrical vase, unmarked, 9", $30.00 – 40.00.

3. Experimental cylindrical vase, unmarked, 4", $15.00 – 20.00.

4. Experimental low flower bowl, unmarked, 9¼", $75.00 – 100.00.

5. Country Squire dinner plate, 10½", $8.00 – 10.00.

Plate 197.

CRESTONE

PRODUCTION DATES: 1965 – 1967

TRADEMARKS: Illustrations 74 and 76, appendix A.
Crestone was marked with an incised "hull, USA," along with its incised script "Crestone" signature and "© 65."

Original company advertising describes Crestone as "ovenproof casual serving ware in high gloss turquoise with white foam edge." Thirty items were available.
The company advertised the ware's prominent features:
...extra deep, form fitting well in saucers of items like standard cups and the gravy boat; casserole covers have large deep rings as knobs to serve as glazed over trivets when inverted; platform type chimes prove far superior to ordinary handles; gravy boat is separate from saucer and is ideal as syrup pitcher, carafe holds 2 cups to start of neck — no need to burn fingers; same cover fits 9 oz. French handled casserole and soup-salad, duplication unnecessary.
Hull also advertised Crestone by saying, "Designed specifically for present day living habits in the breakfast nook, on the patio, at the T. V. or barbecue, as well as normal table service, only Crestone offers these features at prices all can afford."

Plate 198.
Row 1:
1. Pitcher, 38 oz., $25.00 – 35.00.
2. Stein, 14 oz., $16.00 – 25.00.
3. French-handled casserole, 9 oz., $12.00 – 16.00.
4. Cup, 7 oz., $4.00 – 7.00.
5. Saucer, 5⅞", $2.00 – 3.00.
6. Luncheon plate, 9⅜", $6.00 – 8.00.
Row 2:
1. Bowl, 10", $20.00 – 25.00.
2. Teapot, 7", $45.00 – 65.00.
3. Mustard/Jam jar, 8 oz., $25.00 – 30.00.
4. Butter dish, ¼ lb., $25.00 – 35.00.
5. Bowl, 9 oz., $2.00 – 3.00.
6. Carafe with cup and saucer, 8", $45.00 – 65.00.
Row 3:
1. Bowl, 10", $20.00 – 25.00.
2. Gravy boat with underplate, 10 oz., $15.00 – 22.00.

Plate 199.
Row 1:
1. Covered sugar, 4¼", $20.00 – 25.00.
2. Teapot, 7", $45.00 – 65.00.
3. Creamer, 4¼", $20.00 – 25.00.
Row 2:
1. Fruit bowl, 6", $4.00 – 5.00.
2. Shaker, 3¾", $10.00 – 20.00.
3. Shaker, 3¾", $10.00 – 20.00.
4. Carafe with cup, 8", $40.00 – 60.00.
5. Cup, 3½", $4.00 – 6.00.
Row 3:
1. Chip 'n dip leaf, 14½", $50.00 – 75.00.
2. Vegetable/Salad bowl, 10", $20.00 – 25.00.
Row 4:
1. Salad plate, 7½", $6.00 – 8.00.
2. Dinner plate, 10½", $8.00 – 10.00.
3. Coffee server, 11", $75.00 – 125.00.

Plate 198. Original company brochure page.

Plate 199.

CRESTONE
RAINBOW
RIDGE

PRODUCTION DATES: Crestone, 1965 – 1967; Rainbow, 1961 – 1967; Ridge, 1982 – 1984.

TRADEMARKS: Illustrations 74, 76, 83, 84, and 85, appendix A.

Crestone was marked with an incised "hull, USA," along with its incised script "Crestone" signature and "© 65." Ridge and Rainbow wares were marked with an incised "hull, Ovenproof, USA" and incised script "Hull, USA." Newly molded or remolded items had incised "Crooksville, Ohio" added to the trademark.

Casual servingware was glazed in allover turquoise with white foam trim. Crestone is the only forerunner dinnerware with molds specific to this line. Some Crestone molds were commonly used for House 'n Garden lines and can be found with Mirror Brown and Green Agate glazes. These Crestone molds in color glazes other than turquoise are not considered rare or experimental.

Hull's Rainbow consisted of ovenproof casual serving ware in solid high-gloss colors of Mirror Brown, Tangerine, Green Agate, and Butterscotch, all with contrasting foam edge. This ware was an assortment created to be mixed and matched. Only the combination of colors was referred to as Rainbow, for what the company advertised as a "rainbow" table setting. Rainbow's Tangerine became a spin-off dinnerware, and it was addionally known as Golden Anniversary when sold for Tri-State Grocer's 50th anniversary.

Additional Rainbow colors included Green Agate and Butterscotch. A full line of Green Agate became known as Country Squire.

Hull's Ridge dinnerware line was advertised as "a unique blend of contemporary style and country flavor, produced in three distinctly different colors." Ridge was created from previously used molds, updated molds, and completely new molds.

Ridge dinnerware was glazed in Tawny (Ridge), Flint (Ridge), and Walnut (Ridge). Tawny was a tan glaze, Flint was a gray glaze, and Walnut was Mirror Brown.

Ridge dinnerware place settings have distinct, deeply recessed rims. Newly designed bowls and cream and sugar bowls have recessed feet. The experimental flower bowl illustrated in plate 200 was also molded in this fashion.

Plate 200.
Row 1:
1. Tawny Ridge salt shaker, 3", $12.00 – 16.00.
2. Tawny Ridge pepper shaker, 3", $12.00 – 16.00.
3. Experimental glass in Tawny, inscribed "120," 3½", $20.00 – 30.00.
4. Experimental glass in flint, 3½", $20.00 – 30.00.
5. Flint Continental mug, 6", $15.00 – 22.00.
6. Flint ramekin, 1½", $20.00 – 30.00.
7. Rainbow mug, Butterscotch, 3½", $4.00 – 5.00.
8. Experimental glass in Butterscotch, inscribed "30," 3½", $20.00 – 30.00.
9. Leaf dish, 7½", $15.00 – 22.00.
Row 2:
1. Crestone butter dish, 7½", $25.00 – 35.00.
2. Crestone bread and butter plate, 6¾", $3.00 – 4.00.
3. Experimental glass in Crestone turquoise, inscribed "54," 3½", $20.00 – 30.00.
4. Crestone mug, 2¾", $4.00 – 6.00.
5. Crestone carafe, 6½", $30.00 – 40.00.
6. Crestone stein, 5", $16.00 – 25.00.
Row 3:
1. Flint Gingerbread Boy coaster/spoon rest, 5", embossed "Crooksville Bank 80th Year, 1982, " $25.00 – 35.00.
2. Tawny Gingerbread Boy coaster/spoon rest, 5", embossed "Crooksville Bank 80th Year, 1982," $25.00 – 35.00.
3. Experimental Tawny Ridge low flower bowl, unmarked, 9¼", $75.00 – 100.00.
4. Tawny Gingerbread Boy coaster/spoon rest, 5", $25.00 – 35.00.
5. Rainbow divided baker, 11", $25.00 – 35.00.
6. Experimental glass in Tangerine; inscribed "16," "117," and "114"; 3½", $20.00 – 30.00.
Row 4:
1. Tawny cookie jar, 9", $135.00 – 210.00.
2. Coronet ashtray, unmarked, factory drilled for metal accessory, 11¼", $20.00 – 30.00.
3. Tawny Duck covered casserole, 8", $175.00 – 250.00.

Plate 200.

GINGERBREAD MAN

PRODUCTION DATES: Gingerbread Man Server, 1978 – 1985; Gingerbread Man Cookie Jar, 1982 – 1984

TRADEMARKS: Illustrations 74, 81, and 82, appendix A.

Incised "hull, Ovenproof, USA." Newly molded or remolded items had the incised "Crooksville, Ohio" added to the trademark. Gingerbread Man items proudly carry the Gingerbread name in incised script form. The handled server bears an incised "Server" designation.

The adorable Gingerbread Man character was the animated design used for serving pieces that accompanied House *n Garden dinnerware. The cookie jar was designed by Louise Bauer and first produced in 1978. The Gingerbread Man concept was later expanded to include a mug, bowl, and coaster/spoon rest. A four-piece train canister set was trialed in 1985, but was never placed on the retail market.

The Gingerbread Boy coaster/spoon rests with the Crooksville Bank logo were made in all three colors. This special order commemorated the bank's 80th year.

Plate 201.
Row 1.
1. Tawny butter dish, 7½", $20.00 – 30.00.
2. House 'n Garden shaker, 3", limited production, 1965, $20.00 – 25.00.
3. Flint Continental mug, 6", "3rd Annual American Art Pottery Association
    Convention, Zanesville, Ohio 1982" logo, $30.00 – 40.00.
4. House 'n Garden shaker, 3", limited production, 1965, $20.00 – 25.00.
5. Flint butter dish, 7½", $20.00 – 30.00.
Row 2.
1. Flint handled server, 11½", $40.00 – 60.00.
2. Tawny individual covered casserole, 5", $12.00 – 16.00.
3. Tawny handled server, 11½", $40.00 – 60.00.
Row 3.
1. Tawny Gingerbread Man server, 10", $100.00 – 125.00.
2. Gingerbread Boy coaster/spoon rest, 5", inscribed "Crooksville Bank 80th
    Year, 1982," $25.00 – 35.00.
3. Gingerbread Man server, 10", $60.00 – 80.00.
4. Flint Gingerbread Boy coaster/spoon rest, 5", $25.00 – 35.00.
5. Flint Gingerbread Man server, 10", $100.00 – 125.00.
Row 4.
1. Flint cookie jar, 9", $135.00 – 210.00.
2. Tawny Gingerbread Man cookie jar, 12", $450.00 – 650.00.
3. Flint teapot, 6½", $40.00 – 60.00.

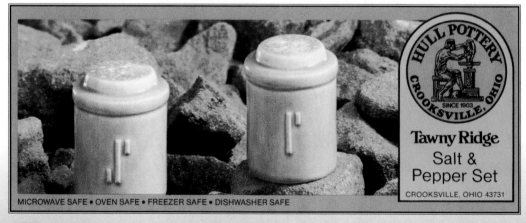

Original company advertisement.

Plate 201.

HEARTLAND

PRODUCTION DATES: 1982 – 1985.

TRADEMARKS: Illustrations 81, 83, 84, and 85, appendix A.
Incised "hull, Ovenproof, USA" and area of origin, "Crooksville, Ohio."

Described in a company advertisement as "handmade by American craftsmen," Heartland was decorated in a "satin creamy glaze with hand applied brown decoration and gold shading on rims." This is a satin ware closely resembling Pfaltzgraff wares, and it's no surprise that it was designed by the same freelance designer, Maury Mountain.

In the early 1980s, Hull Pottery was taking very serious pride in its work. The pottery was genuine in its desire to regain the dinnerware market lost to stagnate designs, continuous labor strikes, and poor management decisions. So intense was this dedication that costly dinnerware lines, newly designed molds and color glazes, and hand decorations such as this country heart stamp were executed.

Plate 202.
1. Fruit bowl, $8.00 – 10.00.
2. Salad plate, 6½", $8.00 – 10.00.
3. Dinner plate, 10¼", $15.00 – 22.00.
4. Mug, 5", $12.00 – 16.00.
5. Saucer, 5½", $4.00 – 6.00.

Plate 203.
1. Pie plate, 11", $35.00 – 45.00.
2. Oval platter, $20.00 – 30.00.
3. Covered sugar, 4¾", $25.00 – 35.00.
4. Creamer, 4¾", $25.00 – 35.00.

Plate 204.
Row 1:
1. Salt shaker, 6", $20.00 – 25.00.
2. Pepper shaker, 6", $20.00 – 25.00.
3. Pie plate, 11'', $35.00 – 45.00.
4. Covered jar, "Chowder," 8", $75.00 – 100.00.
Row 2:
1. Duck covered casserole, 8½", $95.00 – 135.00.
2. Experimental handled server, 11", three-flower stamp, $95.00 – 125.00.
3. Mug, 5", $12.00 – 16.00.
4. Pitcher, 4", $25.00 – 35.00.
Row 3:
1. Mixing bowl, 6", $15.00 – 20.00.
2. Mixing bowl, 8", $25.00 – 30.00.
3. Mixing bowl, 10", $35.00 – 45.00.
4. Experimental pitcher, 9", three-flower stamp, $150.00 – 225.00.
Row 4:
1. Canister, "Flour," 9", $100.00 – 125.00.
2. Canister, "Sugar," 8", $75.00 – 100.00.
3. Canister, "Coffee," 6", $75.00 – 100.00.
4. Canister, "Tea," 6", $75.00 – 100.00.

Plate 202. Original company advertising.

Plate 203. Original company advertising.

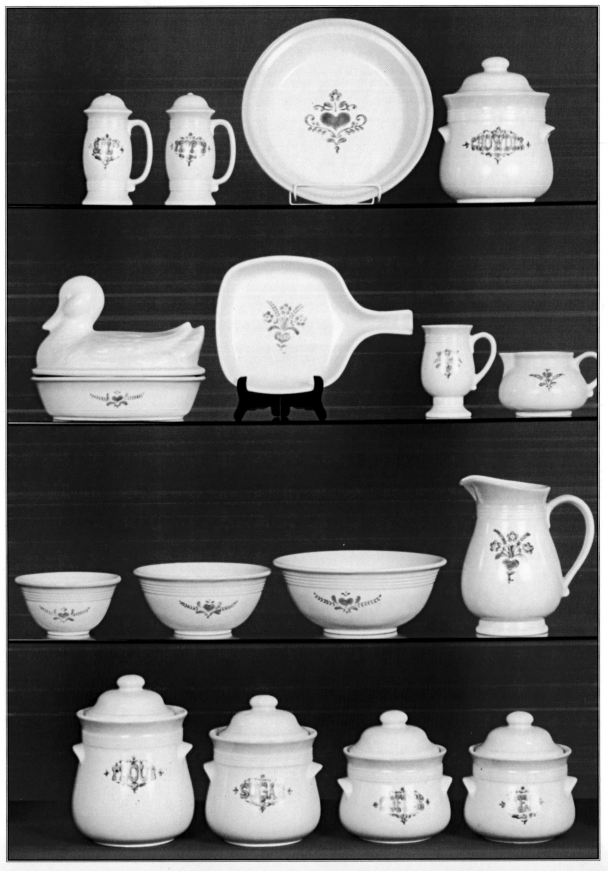

Plate 204.

Heartland

Plate 205.
1. Covered jar, "Baked Beans," 8", $75.00 – 100.00.
2. Cookie jar, 9", $100.00 – 125.00.

Plate 206.
Row 1:
1. Soup/Salad bowl, 8", $15.00 – 20.00.
2. Plate, 7¼", $8.00 – 10.00.
3. Sugar, 4¾", $25.00 – 35.00.
4. Creamer, 4¾", $25.00 – 35.00.
Row 2.
1. Pitcher, 9", $75.00 – 100.00.
2. Covered jar, "Chili," 8", $75.00 – 100.00.
3. Luncheon plate, 8½", $8.00 – 10.00.
Row 3:
1. Almond rectangular baker, no trim, 12", $25.00 – 35.00.
2. Souffle, 8¾", $95.00 – 135.00.
3. Almond divided server, no trim, 11", $45.00 – 75.00.

Plate 205. Original company advertising.

Plate 206.

MIRROR ALMOND

PRODUCTION DATES: 1981 – 1983

TRADEMARKS: Illustrations 83 – 85, appendix A.
   Incised "hull, Ovenproof, USA." Newly molded or remolded items had the incised "Crooksville, Ohio" added to the trademark.

   The kitchenware line illustrated was high-gloss Almond with Caramel trim. It included newly designed items as well as carryovers from the long-lived House 'n Garden Mirror Brown line.
   Items illustrated in allover Almond with no contrasting decoration were those Byron Hull used in his home. Mr. Hull ordered his set without the Caramel trim, as the solid Almond better suited his taste. Many Almond items that did not have benefit of the Caramel trim, such as the cruets, a rectangular baker, and a round divided server, were sold through area pottery outlet stores.

Plate 207.
Row 1:
1. Dinner plate, 10¼", $8.00 – 10.00.
2. Salad plate 6½", $2.00 – 3.00.
3. Mug, 3¼", $3.00 – 4.00.
4. Fruit bowl, 5¼", $3.00 – 4.00.
Row 2:
1. Creamer 4½", $15.00 – 20.00.
2. Covered sugar, $15.00 – 20.00.
3. Oval steak plate, 11¾", $15.00 – 20.00.
4. Oval vegetable bowl, 11", $20.00 – 30.00.
Row 3:
1. Open French-handled casserole, 5½", $12.00 – 18.00.
2. Covered French-handled casserole, 5½", $15.00 – 20.00.
3. Salt shaker, 3¾", $10.00 – 12.00.
4. Pepper shaker, 3¾", $10.00 – 12.00.
Row 4:
1. Stein, 5", $8.00 – 12.00.
2. Divided vegetable bowl, 10¾", $20.00 – 30.00.
3. Oval serving dish, 8¾", $20.00 – 30.00.
4. Ramekin, $20.00 – 25.00.

Plate 208.
Row 1:
1. Vinegar cruet, 5¾", $15.00 – 20.00.
2. Divided bowl, 10¾", $20.00 – 30.00.
3. Jug/Creamer, 4½", $15.00 – 20.00.
Row 2:
1. Mug, 3¼", $3.00 – 4.00.
2. Saucer, 6¾", $2.00 – 3.00.
3. Bowl, 5¼", $3.00 – 4.00.
4. Individual French-handled casserole, 5½", $10.00 – 15.00.
Row 3:
1. Oval steak plate, 11¾", $15.00 – 20.00.
2. Salad plate, 6½", $2.00 – 3.00.
3. Oval steak plate, 12", $15.00 – 20.00.
Row 4:
1. Dinner plate, 10", $8.00 – 10.00.
2. Gingerbread Man server, 10", $65.00 – 95.00.
3. Dinner plate, 10", $8.00 – 10.00.

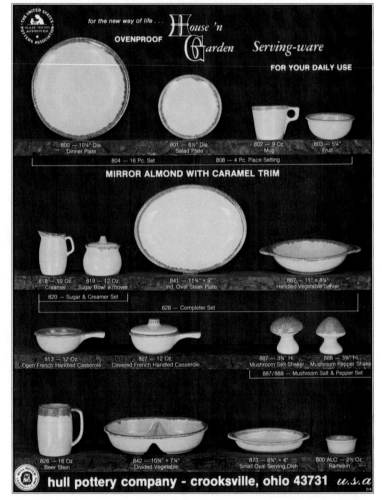

Plate 207. Original company brochure page.

Plate 208.

MIRROR BROWN

PRODUCTION DATES: 1960 – 1985

TRADEMARKS: Illustrations 74, 75, 76, 83, 84, and 85, appendix A.

Incised "hull, Ovenproof, USA" and incised script "Hull, USA." Many later molds (1982 – 1985) carried place of origin and were incised "Crooksville, Ohio." Incised "HP CO" and/or "Ovenproof, USA" were also commonly used trademarks for House 'n Garden dinnerware items. It is not uncommon to find Mirror Brown items marked "Crestone," as molds were shared. Some of the Crestone molds used for Mirror Brown were later reworked to bear the "Hull Ovenproof" mark.

Mirror Brown is characterized by its dark brown high gloss. Dinnerware and accessories with ivory foam became mainstays of the company's business from 1960 through the company's closing in 1985. Popularity remained strong in the United States and Canada for 25 years, and from 1980 to 1984, Hull's Mirror Brown House 'n Garden line was sold in great quantities in Australia at in-home dinnerware parties.

Plate 209.
Row 1:
1. Jug/Creamer, 4¼", $15.00 – 22.00.
2. Salt shaker, 3¾", $8.00 – 12.00.
3. Pepper shaker, 3¾", $8.00 – 12.00.
4. Continental mug, 6", $15.00 – 20.00.
5. Coffee mug, 3½", $4.00 – 6.00.
6. Coffee mug, 3", $4.00 – 6.00.
Row 2:
1. Divided vegetable dish, 10¾", $25.00 – 35.00.
2. Teapot, 6", $25.00 – 35.00.
3. Oval baker, 10", $20.00 – 30.00.
Row 3:
1. Duck covered casserole, 8", 1972 – 1985, $135.00 – 170.00.
2. Imperial vase, lion's heads, unmarked, 6¾", $20.00 – 30.00.
3. Chicken covered casserole, 9½", 1968 – 1985, $135.00 – 165.00.
Row 4:
1. Open baker with Rooster decor, 13½", 1969 – 1972, $135.00 – 180.00.
2. Butter dish, 7½", $20.00 – 25.00.
3. Cylindrical vase, 4", $25.00 – 35.00.
4. Cylindrical vase, 9", $35.00 – 45.00.
5. Cylindrical vase, 6", $25.00 – 35.00.

Plate 209.

DINNERWARE (1960 – 1986)
MIRROR BROWN

    Mirror Brown proved so popular that items in demand went far beyond table accessories. Drawer pulls were produced by way of a contractual agreement between Hull and Amerock Corporation of Rockford, Illinois. The drawer pulls were shipped to the plant from Wisconsin Porcelain in greenware state. Hull was responsible only for the glazing and firing of these drawer pulls, which were then returned to Amerock to be assembled and marketed. These drawer pulls are illustrated in plate 218, on page 281.

Plate 211.
Row 1:
1. Duck planter, "F69," 10", $30.00 – 40.00.
2. Imperial window box, "F10," 12", $35.00 – 45.00.
Row 2:
1. Bowl, marked "Crestone," 6", $4.00 – 5.00.
2. Rectangular salad server, 11", $20.00 – 30.00.
3. Individual French-handled casserole, 5", $12.00 – 16.00.
Row 3:
1. Gingerbread Boy coaster/spoon rest, 5", $20.00 – 30.00.
2. Tab handled baker, 6¾", $15.00 – 20.00.
3. Square baker, 9½", $20.00 – 35.00.
4. Experimental low flower bowl, 9¼", $85.00 – 125.00.
Row 4:
1. Imperial Frog planter, unmarked, 6", $75.00 – 100.00.
2. French-handled casserole, 11¾", $50.00 – 75.00.
3. Pie plate, 9¼", $22.00 – 32.00.
Row 5:
1. Cylindrical vase, 9", $75.00 – 100.00.
2. Bread and butter, 6¾", $3.00 – 4.00.
3. Oval steak plate, 11¾", $20.00 – 25.00.
4. Coffee server, 11" (later redesigned with lock lid), $35.00 – 50.00.

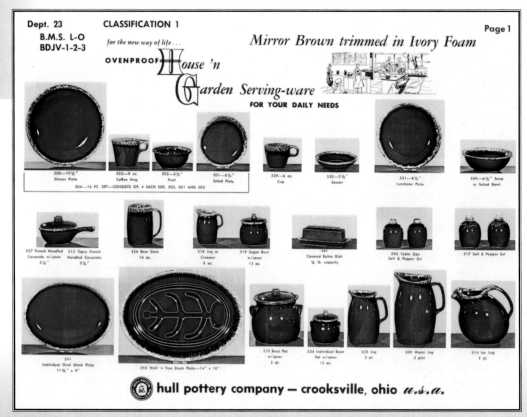

Plate 210. Original company brochure page.

Plate 211.

Dinnerware (1960 – 1986)
Mirror Brown

The dinnerware items shown are from both older and updated molds, but all are dark brown high gloss with ivory foam, a design that became a mainstay of the company's business from 1960 until the company's closing in 1985. Earlier House 'n Garden was characteristically darker and had a deeper, more apparent contrasting foam edge. The experimental glasses in House 'n Garden glazes can double as juice glasses if you are fortunate enough to garner a set. It is desirable to gather a few Imperial vases or planters to include with your table settings.

Plate 212.
Row 1:
1. Experimental glass, solid Mirror Brown, incised "48, 175, 173," 3½", $20.00 – 30.00.
2. Experimental glass, Mirror Brown with drip, incised "9-2, 5-8," 3½", $20.00 – 30.00.
3. Imperial planter, unmarked, 5", $75.00 – 100.00.
4. Soup and sandwich; mug, 5"; tray, 9½"; $20.00 – 25.00.
5. Handled server, 11½", $40.00 – 65.00.
Row 2:
1. Individual French-handled casserole, 5", $16.00 – 20.00.
2. Vinegar cruet, 6½", $30.00 – 40.00.
3. Oil cruet, 6½", $30.00 – 40.00.
4. Bowl, 6½", $4.00 – 6.00.
5. Bowl, 5¾", $4.00 – 5.00.
Row 3:
1. Ice-lip pitcher, 7½", $30.00 – 40.00.
2. Cheese shaker, 6½", $30.00 – 40.00.
3. Plate (Crestone shape without the Crestone mark), 9½", $8.00 – 10.00.
4. Leaf dish, 7½", $15.00 – 20.00.
Row 4:
1. Leaf chip 'n dip, 15", $45.00 – 65.00.
2. Bean pot, 6½", $30.00 – 40.00.
3. Dinner plate, 10½", $8.00 – 10.00.

Original company advertising.

Plate 212.

DINNERWARE (1960 – 1986)

MIRROR BROWN

Plate 213.

Row 1:

1. Chicken covered casserole, Green Agate, 8½", 1968 – 1970, $175.00 – 275.00.

Row 2:

1. Duck covered casserole, Flint, 8", 1984, $175.00 – 250.00.

2. Chicken covered casserole, Mirror Brown, 8½", 1968 – 1985, $85.00 – 125.00.

Row 3:

1. Duck covered casserole, Mirror Brown, 9", 1972 – 1985, $135.00 – 170.00.

2. Chicken covered casserole, Mirror Brown, 11½" x 13½", 1969 – 1972. The baker base has an incised rooster decor. $250.00 – 375.00.

Row 4:

1. Chicken covered casserole, Mirror Brown, 8", 1968 – 1980, $75.00 – 100.00.

2. Covered casserole, Mirror Brown, 7½" x 12", 1968 – 1972, $90.00 – 125.00.

3. Chicken covered casserole, experimental glaze, 8", 1975, $200.00 – 300.00.

Original company advertising.

Original company advertising.

Plate 213.

MIRROR BROWN

Plate 214.

Row 1:

1. Pepper shaker, 3¾", 1978 – 1983, $10.00 – 15.00.

2. Oval salad, incised rooster, 6½", 1968 – 1972, $75.00 – 100.00.

3. Salt shaker, 3¾", 1978 – 1983, $10.00 – 15.00.

Row 2:

1. Individual French-handled casserole in basket,* 5", 1975, $15.00 – 20.00.

2. Jumbo stein, university logo in gold, 1976, $20.00 – 30.00.

3. Spoon rest, 6½", 1978 – 1983, $40.00 – 50.00.

4. Cup and deep-well saucer; cup, 3½", 1963 – 1985; saucer, 5¾", 1963 – 1969; $6.00 – 10.00.

Row 3:

1. Egg plate, 9¼", 1978 – 1983, $75.00 – 100.00.

2. Cookie jar, 9", 1960 – 1985, $50.00 – 85.00.

3. Fish tray, 11", 1978 – 1983, $85.00 – 115.00.

Row 4:

1. Canister, 9", "Flour," 1978 – 1981, $150.00 – 200.00.

2. Canister, 8", "Sugar," 1978 – 1981, $100.00 – 150.00.

3. Canister, 7", "Coffee," 1978 – 1981, $100.00 – 125.00.

4. Canister, 6", "Tea," 1978 – 1981, $100.00 – 125.00.

*A set of six casseroles with lids in wicker basket holders was shipped to Mrs. Richard Watts in Connecticut, but was returned to the company more than once due to incomplete address. This set remains in its original shipping box.

Original company advertising.

Plate 214.

MIRROR BROWN RINGED WARE

PRODUCTION DATES: 1983 – 1985

TRADEMARKS: Illustrations 74, 82, 83, 84, and 85, appendix A.
Incised "hull, Ovenproof, USA" and incised script "Hull, USA." Ridge dinnerware's newly molded or remolded items have the incised "Crooksville, Ohio" added to the trademark.

In 1983, the Hull Collection included Mirror Brown dinnerware molds that had been used since House 'n Garden's inception, e.g., molds for the cylinder cookie jar, ice lip pitcher, four-piece place setting, stein, teapot, and other pieces.
Added to these tried-and-true mainstays, Hull additionally showcased newly molded Ridge dinnerware as well as Mirror Brown dinnerware and accessories that collectors refer to as "Ringed Ware."
In this line, characteristic concentric rings compliment cookie jars, canisters, pitchers, shakers, bowls, and of course, the dinnerware place settings.
The Gingerbread cookie jar, server, coaster, bowl, and mug provided additional interest to the Collection.

Plate 215.
1. Pitcher, 9", $95.00 – 135.00.
2. Bowl, 12", $60.00 – 85.00.

Plate 216.
1. Canister, 8", $100.00 – 150.00.
2. Canister, 9", $100.00 – 150.00.
3. Canister, 6", $100.00 – 135.00.
4. Canister, 6", $100.00 – 135.00.

Plate 217.
Gingerbread Train Canister Set, $1,600.00 – 2,500.00.
1. Caboose, 7½".
2. Kiddie car, 8".
3. Express car, 7".
4. Engine, 9".

Plate 218.
Row 1:
1. Ashtray, "18," 7", $20.00 – 30.00.
2. Shaker, 3¼", discontinued in early 1970, $15.00 – 20.00.
3. Shaker, 3¼", discontinued in early 1970, $15.00 – 20.00.
4. Carafe, 6¾", discontinued by late 1970, $30.00 – 40.00.
5 & 6. Drawer pulls, 1¾" diameter, contractual item, 1981, $10.00 – 15.00 each.
7. Ashtray, unmarked, 8", $20.00 – 25.00.
Row 2:
1. Batter bowl, unmarked, 10½", $35.00 – 45.00.
2. Mixing bowl, unmarked, 9", $20.00 – 30.00.
3. Mixing bowl, unmarked, 8", $20.00 – 25.00.
Row 3:
1. Casserole with warmer, 8" overall, 1963 – 1978, $85.00 – 125.00.
2. Gingerbred Man cookie jar, 12", 1984, $150.00 – 250.00.

Plate 215. Original company advertising.

Plate 216. Original company advertising.

Plate 217.

Plate 218.

Provincial

PRODUCTION DATE: 1961

TRADEMARK: Illustration 74, appendix A.
    Incised "hull, Ovenproof, USA."

Provincial consists of ovenproof House 'n Garden casual serving ware glazed in Mirror Brown with all-white interiors and lids.

Plate 219.
Row 1:
1. Dinner plate, 10¼", $7.00 – 10.00.
2. Salad plate, 6½", $4.00 – 5.00.
3. Fruit bowl, 5¼", $4.00 – 5.00.
4. Mug, 4", $3.00 – 5.00.
5. Coffee server, 11", $50.00 – 75.00.
Row 2:
1. Mixing bowl, 5¼", $10.00 – 15.00.
2. Mixing bowl, 6¾", $15.00 – 20.00.
3. Mixing bowl, 8¼", $26.00 – 36.00.
4. Pitcher, 9", $40.00 – 60.00.
5. Pitcher, 7½", $22.00 – 30.00.
6. Pitcher, 4½", $18.00 – 22.00.
Row 3:
1. Bean pot, 6½", $40.00 – 50.00.
2. Individual bean pot, 3½", $15.00 – 20.00.
3. Covered sugar, 3½", $16.00 – 22.00.
4. Creamer, 4¼", $16.00 – 22.00.
5. Covered casserole, 3 pt., $40.00 – 60.00.
6. Individual French-handled casserole, 5", $25.00 – 30.00.
7. Stein, 6", $10.00 – 15.00.
Row 4:
1. Ice-lip pitcher, 7½", $40.00 – 60.00.
2. Salt shaker, 3¾", $8.00 – 12.00.
3. Pepper shaker, 3¾", $8.00 – 12.00.
4. Chip 'n dip, 15", $30.00 – 40.00.
5. Cookie jar, 9", $50.00 – 85.00.

OVENPROOF
Provincial
SERVING WARE

700 Dinner Plate
10¼" Dia.

701 Salad Plate
6½" Dia.

703 Fruit
5¼"

702 Mug
9 oz.

722 Coffee Pot
w/cover (lock lid)
60 oz.

Four Piece Place Setting

705 Mixing Bowl
5¼"

706 Mixing Bowl
6¾"

707 Mixing Bowl
8¼"

709 Water Jug
5 pint

725 Jug
2 pt.

718 Jug
½ pt.

710 Bean Pot
w/cover
2 qt.

724 Individual Bean
Pot w/cover
12 oz.

719 Sugar Bowl
w/cover
4" Dia.

718 Creamer
8 oz.

711 Bake Dish
3 pt.
712 Casserole
w/cover
3 pt.

713 French Handled
Casserole
5¼"
727 French Handled
Casserole
w/cover

726 Beer Stein
16 oz.

714 Ice Jug
2 qt.

715 Salt Shaker
w/cork
3¾" Hi.

716 Pepper Shaker
w/cork
3¾" Hi.

721 Leaf Shaped
Chip 'n' Dip
15" x 10½"

723 Cookie Jar
w/cover
94 oz.

Hull Pottery Company -- Crooksville, Ohio

Plate 219. Original company brochure page.

Rainbow
Avocado

PRODUCTION DATES: Rainbow, 1961 – 1967; Avocado, 1968 – 1971

TRADEMARK: Illustration 74, appendix A.
   Incised "hull, Ovenproof, USA."

Hull's Rainbow consisted of ovenproof casual serving ware in solid high-gloss colors of Mirror Brown, Tangerine, Green Agate, and Butterscotch, all with contrasting foam edge. This ware was an assortment created to be mixed and matched. The combination of colors was referred to as Rainbow, for what the company advertised as a "rainbow" table setting. Rainbow's Tangerine became a spin-off dinnerware line. Hull also created a Green Agate line, referred to as Country Squire.

Hull intended for Rainbow to be a mix-and-match dinnerware line, so let's not forget to have fun when collecting and putting dinnerware sets together. Hull produced many shapes other than kitchenware that can be used as accessories to its dinnerware lines. Be sure to add an item or two, whether it be a florist vase, an ashtray, a Duck planter, or even a set of experimental glasses for juice, to your dinner table.

Avocado was ovenproof dinnerware in high gloss or satin Avocado color with or without an ivory foam edge. This line was created at the time avocado kitchen appliances emerged on the market and was intended to produce a desire for coordinated dinnerware sets.

Plate 220.
Row 1:
1. Rainbow luncheon plate, 8½", $6.00 – 8.00.
2. Rainbow soup & sandwich; tray, 9¾"; mug, 5"; $20.00 – 25.00.
3. Rainbow luncheon plate, 8½", $6.00 – 8.00.
Row 2:
1. Rainbow dinner plate, 10½", $8.00 – 10.00.
2. Rainbow soup & sandwich; tray, 9¾"; mug, 5"; $20.00 – 25.00.
3. Rainbow dinner plate, 10½", $8.00 – 10.00.
Row 3:
1. Avocado pepper shaker, 3¾", $10.00 – 15.00.
2. Avocado salt shaker, 3¾", $10.00 – 15.00.
3. Avocado mug, 3½", $5.00 – 7.00.
4. Avocado teapot, 6½", $40.00 – 65.00.
5. Avocado butter dish, 7½", $20.00 – 25.00.
Row 4:
1. Rainbow bud vase, "F90," 6½", $15.00 – 20.00.
2. Rainbow pitcher, 9", $40.00 – 60.00.
3. Avocado baker, 10", $15.00 – 22.00.
4. Avocado dinner plate, 10½", $8.00 – 10.00.

Plate 220.

TANGERINE

PRODUCTION DATES: 1961 – 1967

TRADEMARK: Illustration 74, appendix A.
    Incised "hull, Ovenproof, USA" and incised script "Hull, USA."

DESCRIPTION:
    The kitchenware illustrated is a line that evolved from Hull's Rainbow dinnerware. The initial orange line was referred to as Hull's 900 series, Tangerine House 'n Garden. A short time later, Golden Anniversary dinnerware entered the market. Both glazes were one and the same, although different assortments were available. This same glaze was also known as Burnt Orange when offered exclusively by the J.C. Penney Co.
    Tri-State Grocery Company advertised its 50th golden anniversary gala and used Hull's House 'n Garden line in Tangerine (this was the line called Golden Anniversary) as an incentive to buy groceries. With grocery purchases, customers earned dinnerware coupons redeemable for the ware. Fifteen items could be coupon-earned during this event. Hull's Tangerine dinnerware line included at least 40 shapes in this great glaze.

Plate 222.
1. Experimental coffee mug, 3½", $20.00 – 30.00.
2. Toast 'n cereal tray, 9¾", Bowl, 6½", $20.00 – 25.00.
3. Experimental coffee mug, panel design, unmarked, 3½", $20.00 – 30.00.
4. Deep-well saucer , 5¾", $2.00 – 3.00.
5. Coffee mug, 3", $4.00 – 6.00.

Plate 223.
Row 1:
1. Creamer, 4½", $15.00 – 22.00.
2. Salt shaker, 4", $8.00 – 12.00.
3. Pepper shaker, 4", $8.00 – 12.00.
4. Covered sugar, 4", $20.00 – 30.00.
5. Butter dish, 7½", $20.00 – 30.00.
Row 2:
1. Teapot, 6½", $15.00 – 22.00.
2. Ashtray, 8", $25.00 – 35.00.
3. Pitcher, 6½", $35.00 – 50.00.
4. Gravy boat/Syrup, 6", $45.00 – 65.00.
Row 3:
1. Leaf dish, 7", $15.00 – 22.00.
2. Leaf chip 'n dip, 15", $45.00 – 65.00.
3. Luncheon plate, 8½", $6.00 – 8.00.
4. Bud vase, 9", $20.00 – 30.00.
Row 4:
1. Bean pot with warmer, 9", $60.00 – 80.00.
2. Tidbit server, 10", $50.00 – 75.00.
3. Leaf dish, 12", $45.00 – 65.00.

Plate 221. Original company brochure page.

Plate 222.

Plate 223.

Experimentals, Specials, Trials, and Samples

The next several pages illustrate Hull experimentals, trials, special, and sample wares, each an entirely different category. Please make note of the explanation given for each category.

Experimentals

The experimentals in the following pages illustrate items that were not available on the retail market but that did make their way outside the plant. In some cases these items were sold to area pottery shops as seconds or leftover lots, taken from the plant by workers, shelved by the ceramic engineer in his workroom or another section of the Hull plant for reference at a later date, or even thrown in the trash pile by employees during quality control checks. These items have significant historical value and are, in fact, the company's undocumented testimonials of individual craftsmanship.

Experimentals include several levels of variation. The mold itself may have been experimental in nature, a new design or shape; more often than this, the experimentation was in the color or glaze treatment. In some cases the color and glaze were what the company intended for a certain design, and this type of ware usually included an incised code that related to the color and glaze formulation. This incised alphanumeric code was most often a quality-control measure, and many of these items fall into the trial glaze category. However, if the glaze was entirely new or not what was expected, it is considered experimental.

Plate 224.
Row 1:
1 & 2. Baby shoes, 2½", 1925, $75.00 – 100.00 each.
3. Stein, elusive cobalt decor, "492," 6½", 1920, $100.00 – 150.00.
4. Bear figural, 1½", 1925, $100.00 – 125.00.
5. Owl bank, 3¾", 1925, $150.00 – 210.00.
6. Kitten figural, 1½", 1925, $100.00 – 125.00.
7. Frog bank, Rosella clay, 3¾", 1945, $250.00 – 300.00.
8. Kitten figural, 1½", 1925, $100.00 – 125.00.
9 – 12. Rabbit figurals, 2¾", 1925, $80.00 – 100.00 each.
Row 2:
1. Stoneware vase, 7", heavy metallic glaze, 1920, $150.00 – 250.00.
2. Stoneware teapot, inscribed "Mrs. Mary Stewart" at base and initials "M. S." at lid, 6¼", 1925, $150.00 – 200.00.
3. Corky Pig bank, "Frazeysburg Alumni" under glaze, "Hopewell, S. Zanesville, Conesville, Rosecrans, Deaver Town, Union, Glendford," 1960, 5", $175.00 – 250.00.

Plate 224.

In summary, experimentals are characterized by molded wares not in production, or by extreme variation in color and glaze treatment, or a combination of the two. The categories of experimentals included unmarketed molds with unmarketed glaze treatments, unmarketed molds with marketed glaze treatments, and marketed molds with unmarketed glaze treatments. Most wares from experimental molds were unmarked due to the fact that the ware was in an experimental stage and not near enough to inclusion in a marketable line to bear a trademark.

Specials

Experimentals and Specials are two entirely different categories. Specials are wares that have been additionally decorated outside the Hull company. They are not considered experimental. The surrounding pottery villages had many talented craftsmen who purchased bulk lots of pottery, decorated and fired in Hull's usual fashion. These items were then taken to studios or homes with kilns, where not only gold decor was added, but also completely original decorations.

Plate 225.
1. Special Wild Flower no. series vase, "52-6¼"," 1942 – 1943.
2. Special House 'n Garden teapot, luster-decorated and signed by Edna Mae Kettlewell, a local artist for more than 25 years. Kettlewell, taught by Arthur Wagner, was dared to put three lusters to fire; this was the outcome.
3. Special Camellia vase, "123-6½"," 1943 – 1944.
4. Special Water Lily ewer, "L-3-5½"," interior also lined in gold, 1948 – 1949.

Plate 225.

Plate 226. Experimental Little Red Riding Hood covered jar, decorated in matte pink and blue, 9", $750.00 – 1,000.00.

Plate 227. Experimental candleholder, decorated underglaze blue and white stoneware, unmarked, 6½", $250.00 – 300.00.

Trials

Production trials are the wares in marketed molds and marketed colors characteristic of the particular design, with bases being both marked and unmarked, but which most often additionally contain the incised configurations of test glaze formulas. Great are the numbers of trials in Hull's last 25 years of production, because of the magnitude of styles offered in Imperial and House 'n Garden dinnerwares.

Samples

The experimental category may often be confused with label-marked sample wares. Sample items were marked on the ware itself or with a foil or paper label stating "sample," while experimentals were in most cases left unmarked. Sample wares were, in fact, production mold pieces in the color and glaze treatment expected, actually no different than marketed specimens, except for the sample seal.

Plate 229.
Row 1:
1. Experimental Blossom Flite basket, unmarked, 10", 1954, $185.00 – 265.00.
2. Experimental Calla Lily ewer with gorgeous stoneware glaze, "508-10"," 1935, $550.00 – 750.00.
3. Experimental basket, sponged black and white exterior with sponged gold and white interior, "72," 12½", 1952, $150.00 – 225.00.
Row 2:
1. Experimental vase, unmarked, 11", heavy webbing, black and silver Granada Pottery foil label, 1958, $125.00 – 165.00.
2. Experimental Alpine pretzel jar, underglaze decorated by Sylvanus Burdette "Mose" Wilson, 9½", 1925, $450.00 – 650.00.
3. Experimental tidbit server, black and white, edged webbing, 10½", 1960, $125.00 – 200.00.

Plate 230.
1. Experimental vase, embossed star flower, unmarked, 8", $750.00 – 950.00.
2. Experimental Classic vase, matte finished, "T-1-6½," $225.00 – 300.00.
3. Experimental Wild Flower candle holder, unmarked, 3½", $195.00 – 250.00.
4. Experimental Morning Glory ewer, "63," 11", $350.00 – 500.00.

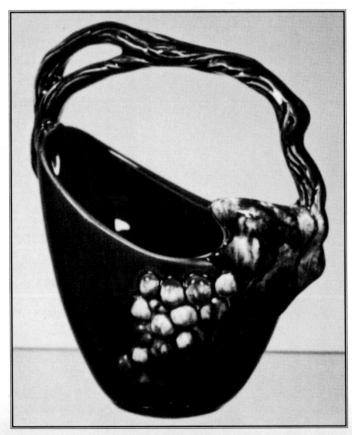

Plate 228. Tokay/Tuscany basket, test glaze, unmarked, 7", $195.00 – 230.00.

Plate 229.

Plate 230.

Plate 231.

Row 1:
1. Experimental candleholder, unmarked, 3½", 1930, $60.00 – 95.00.
2. Experimental console bowl, unmarked, 6½" x 9", 1930, $175.00 – 225.00.
3. Experimental candleholder, unmarked, 3½", 1930, $60.00 – 95.00.

Row 2:
1. Experimental Woodland wall pocket,* "W13-7½"," 1952, $185.00 – 275.00.
2. Experimental Woodland basket,* "W9-8¾"," 1952, $175.00 – 250.00.
3. Experimental Woodland vase,** "W1-5½"," test glaze incised "500-B," 1951, $100.00 – 150.00.
4. Experimental Woodland vase,** "W1-5½"," test glaze incised "500-B," 1951, $100.00 – 150.00.

Row 3:
1. Sample Rosella vase, "R-15-8"," misspelled "Sampel" inscribed into base, 1946, $130.00 – 160.00.
2. Experimental serving dish, unmarked, 13", 1950, $165.00 – 235.00.
3. Special Wild Flower no. series vase, "61-6¼"," 1942 – 1943, $150.00 – 175.00.

Row 4:
1. Special Magnolia vase, "8-10½"," 1946 – 1947, $165.00 – 225.00.
2. Experimental ashtray, made from base of Magnolia vase, "Burt" inscribed into clay, 5½", 1946 – 1947, $165.00 – 225.00.
3. Experimental Magnolia basket, "10-10½"," 1946 – 1947, $400.00 – 550.00.
4. Special Wild Flower no. series vase, "71-12"," 1946 – 1947, $450.00 – 550.00.

* There is great likelihood that this was a separate line produced for a chain store package, since it is most commonly found with the Hull trademark and the color and glaze treatment is consistent.
** The experimental Woodland glazes are consistent with the green with brown flow glaze formula used for Cook 'N' Serve ware during the same production period. However, the Cook 'N' Serve treatment was high gloss, while this is satin finished.

Plate 231.

Plate 232.
Row 1:
1. Trial Tokay/Tuscany basket, inscribed test glaze code "E747A," 7", 1965, $200.00 – 265.00.
2. Experimental Swan, "69," 8", 1954, $175.00 – 250.00.
3. Trial Sun Valley Pastel pedestaled planter, "156," gold veiling, 5", 1956, $100.00 – 125.00.
Row 2:
1. Experimental Woodland wall pocket,* "W13-7½"," 1954, $200.00 – 300.00.
2. Experimental Woodland wall pocket, "W13-7½"," 1953, $225.00 – 275.00.
3. Experimental Woodland wall pocket, "W13-7½"," bisque fired, 1952, $200.00 – 250.00.
4. Experimental Woodland wall pocket, "W13-7½"," 1954, $185.00 – 275.00.
Row 3:
1. Trial vase, inscribed test glaze code "CG 52-B," 9", 1951, $100.00 – 125.00.
2. Experimental leaf dish, unmarked, 12", 1955, $150.00 – 200.00.
3. Trial Fiesta pitcher, "48," 8¾", dark green high gloss, 1956, inscribed with test glaze code,
    $125.00 – 160.00.
Row 4:
1. Trial Woodland ewer, "W24-13½"," inscribed test glaze code "75-A 75-C," 1951, $450.00 – 550.00.
2. Experimental Woodland vase,* "W18-10½," 1954, $200.00 – 300.00.
3. Trial Woodland ewer, "W24-13½"," inscribed test glaze code "77-C, XXG," 1951, $450.00 – 550.00.

*There is great likelihood that pastel satin glazed Woodland blanks composed a separate line produced for chain store sales, since these items are most commonly found with the Hull trademark, and the color and glaze treatment are consistent.

Plate 232.

Gold decorators were plentiful in the Ohio pottery region; some recolored and redecorated the entire pottery item before refiring, while others added gold decor only. Many of these items had specialty foil labels, such as "Hand Painted Fired Ceramic Colors." This label further indicated gold content.

For nearly 50 years, Granville "Grany" Shafer of the Shafer Pottery Company of Zanesville, Ohio, designed and molded his own lines of pottery and, additionally, decorated many local pottery items, including those of Hull, Shawnee, McCoy, and Ungemach, to name a few. Shafer, who was responsible for many of Hull's gold-decorated items, began his decorating business in 1932. With very limited capital, Shafer purchased bulk lots of pottery, which he redecorated and refired in his own kilns. From that meager beginning, Shafer Pottery Company soon had outlets in major cities such as Chicago and Denver for the gold-decorated wares.

Community-minded, Shafer offered his talents to the clay region's annual pottery festivals. A festival announcement of mid-1960 states:

BELIEVE IT OR NOT; THIS YOU WILL HAVE TO SEE!

Zanesville, Ohio, being one of the oldest pottery towns in the U.S.A. now has very few potteries in existence, Next to the oldest pottery now in operation in that city is the G. C. Shafer Pottery Company at 542 Merrick Ave., Zanesville, Ohio. A craftsman in his kind of work. Hand decoration in 23 karat gold, beautiful lusters, over-glaze colors, decal work, and specialties. He has worked in his back yard for the past 32 years! Shafer Pottery ships to florists and gift shops all over the U.S.A.

For the Roseville and Crooksville Pottery Show, he will keep his shop open Friday and Saturday till 9:00 P.M. Sunday — 12:00 Noon till 6:00 P.M.

EXTRA SPECIAL FOR VISITORS! Shafer will have two girls working on four hour shifts starting at 1:00 P.M. Friday, July 16th. The girl you will see is not a hobbiest, but a trained artist decorating beautiful pieces of pottery for a nation. Expect to see many other surprises come out of this small factory.

Other known Ohio gold and specialty decorators who operated between 1930 and 1960 included Bob Young of Roseville, Arthur Wagner of Zanesville's Chic Pottery, Art Richards of the Crooksville China Company, Arthur Pemberton of Roseville, George Earl (known as Pemberton-Earl or P&E Decorators) of Zanesville, and John and Edith Hilaman (known as J&E Decorators) of Zanesville. Additional area artists decorated multitudes of Hull wares, which were sold as souvenirs during the local pottery festivals. Many of the wares were decorated on the spot in cold-color application.

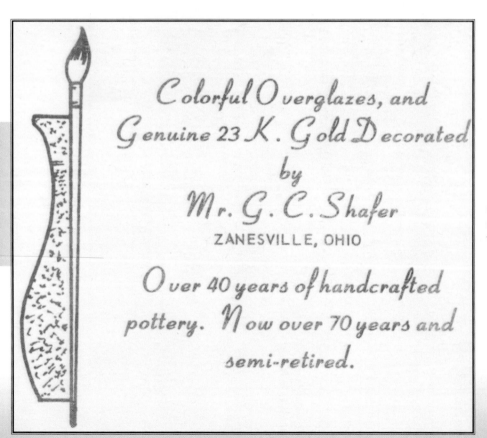

Grany Shafer included this advertising material with many of his decorated wares of the 1960s and 1970s.

Plate 233. Experimental test glaze lids, 3" diameter. Alphanumeric codes relating to ceramic engineer's glaze formulas are on the underside. Hundreds of these lids once hung in the ceramic engineer's workroom at the Hull plant.

Plate 234. Experimental basket, unmarked, 13" x 15", 1950, $500.00 – 750.00.

Plate 235.

Row 1:

1. Experimental Dancing Girl in bright yellow, "955," 7", 1940, $150.00 – 180.00.

2. Experimental Pinecone vase, unmarked, 5", 1936, $350.00 – 400.00.

3. Experimental Wishing Well planter, hand decorated under the glaze, unmarked, 7½". Top area is lacier than the redesigned version that was placed on the market in 1951. $150.00 – 175.00.

Row 2:

1. Experimental Madonna planter, beautifully tooled front and back, unmarked, 10½", 1960, $200.00 – 300.00.

2. Experimental Supreme basket, unmarked, 9", 1960, $150.00 – 225.00.

3. Experimental Lady Head planter, unmarked, company seal "Style F482," 8½" x 8½", 1960, $250.00 – 350.00.

Row 3:

1. Experimental Woodland teapot, gray and bright yellow, "W26," 6½", 1952, $250.00 – 350.00.

2. Experimental vase, unnamed line, unmarked, 8¾", 1940, $900.00 – 1,200.00.

3. Experimental ewer, unmarked, 9½", 1930, $300.00 – 400.00.

4. Experimental Iris vase, blue and bright yellow, unmarked mold, 8¾", 1940, $235.00 – 300.00.

Row 4:

1. Trial Gold-Medal Flowerware Egyptian vase, unglazed base, incised test glaze code "999," 12", 1959, $125.00 – 160.00.

2. Experimental Supreme vase, olive with red, unmarked, 6", 1960, $125.00 – 175.00.

3. Experimental Mardi Gras/Granada vase, matte magenta over high-gloss turquoise, "219-8"," 1940, $125.00 – 175.00.

4. Experimental Supreme vase, satin ebony with white, unmarked, 6", 1960, $125.00 – 175.00.

5. Experimental Pinecone ewer (Butterfly mold with Serenade background color and texture), embossed pine cone and floral design, script "Hull, USA," 13½", 1956, $450.00 – 600.00.

Plate 235.

Experimentals, Specials, Trials, and Samples

There is no set method for determining values of experimentals, trials, specials, and samples, as many, many variables apply. First of all, determine the value of the item as if it were not experimental, and then decide exactly the category or categories in which the item falls. Probably the most important factor is determining the level of experimentation based upon what is normal production for the particular line. Add to this the period and term of production, the item's availability, collector interest, the item's condition, your locale, and of course, your own good judgment. While some lines have surfaced in greater numbers, experimentals were certainly not limited to any particular production years, but were made throughout all eras of Hull manufacture.

Plate 236.
Row 1:
1. Experimental Parchment and Pine cornucopia, "S-2-L," 7¾", wine interior, 1951, $125.00 – 165.00.
Row 2:
1. Experimental Blossom Flite cornucopia, green with tan interior, unmarked, 10½", 1955. Hull later restyled this mold. $175.00 – 245.00.
2. Experimental Blossom Flite jardiniere, "T4," 6", 1955, $175.00 – 245.00.
3. Experimental Blossom Flite cornucopia, pink with yellow and brown, unmarked, 10½", 1955, Hull later restyled this mold. $175.00 – 250.00.
Row 3:
1. Experimental Continental vase/candleholder, incised test glaze "169B," 10½", 1959, $200.00 – 250.00.
2. Experimental Turn-About Cat bank, "198," 11", 1968, $250.00 – 350.00.
3. Experimental Continental vase/candleholder, incised test glaze code "169C," 10½", 1959, $200.00 – 250.00.
Row 4:
1. Experimental Turn-About Cat doorstop, unmarked, 11", 1968, $300.00 – 400.00.
2. Experimental Parchment and Pine ewer, unmarked, gray interior, 14", 1951, $300.00 – 400.00.
3. Experimental Turn-About Cat bank, unmarked, 11", 1968, $250.00 – 300.00.

Plate 236.

Experimentals, Specials, Trials, and Samples

The sculptured designs of Supreme were referred to as "tooled wares" by company personnel. The ware was dipped in glaze, but before firing was run through a series of brushes that scraped the ware to reveal inner layers to which additional color glaze was applied. Some Supreme experimentals never touched those brushes and remained smooth. Although there was a full production run, with brochure pages and advertising ready to follow, the line was never placed on the retail market. Take a close look at the colors and glazes Hull contemplated for this design. The company finally settled on the color combinations of Agate with chartreuse and Ripe Olive with orange. Any piece of Supreme is considered experimental, since it was never placed on the market; however, look for the alternate color combinations. As illustrated, the tooled effect can be from absolute base to top of the ware, with some pieces being additionally decorated with contrasting foam edge. Overall high glosses to semihigh-gloss finishes to satin finishes were available, with color combinations not necessarily limited to two colors. Interiors many times were glazed in contrasting colors.

Plate 237.
Row 1:
1. Experimental Alligator planter, unmarked, 7½", 1951, $350.00 – 450.00.
2. Sample trivet/coaster, satin finished, unmarked, 3", 1951, $75.00 – 100.00.
3. Sample trivet/coaster, satin finished, script "Hull, USA," 3", 1951, $75.00 – 100.00.
4. Sample trivet/coaster, satin finished, script "Hull, USA," 3", 1951, $75.00 – 100.00.
5. Experimental Poodle planter, pink and green, unmarked, 8", 1951, $125.00 – 160.00.
Row 2:
1. Experimental Sun-Glow pitcher, "5½"-90," 1948, $126.00 – 165.00.
2. Experimental Colt figurine, black with pink veiling, unmarked, 5½", 1953, $150.00 – 200.00.
3. Experimental Sun-Glow vase, "6½"-93," 1948, $125.00 – 160.00.
4. Experimental Supreme urn, high-gloss brown with red and yellow, unmarked, 6", 1960, $125.00 – 175.00.
Row 3:
1. Experimental Supreme urn, olive green with blue, incised "7328C," unmarked, 6", 1960, $125.00 – 175.00.
2. Experimental pitcher, embossed orchid decoration, unmarked, 8", 1960, $250.00 – 325.00. (This mold has been reproduced.)
3. Experimental Supreme jardiniere, olive with blue, unmarked, 4¾", 1960, $125.00 – 175.00.
Row 4:
1. Experimental Supreme pedestaled vase, "hull F30 USA," 10", 1960, $110.00 – 145.00.
2. Experimental Supreme vase, unmarked, 12¼", 1960, $150.00 – 225.00.
3. Experimental Supreme jug, unmarked, 9½", 1960, $150.00 – 225.00.
4. Experimental Supreme pedestaled vase, "hull F30, USA," 10", 1960, $110.00 – 145.00.

Plate 237.

Plate 238.
Row 1:
1. Experimental bowl, 5¾", $25.00 – 30.00.
2. Experimental mug, 4", $25.00 – 30.00.
3. Experimental shaker, 3", $30.00 – 35.00.
4. Experimental shaker, 3", $30.00 – 35.00.
Row 2:
1. Experimental creamer, 4", $40.00 – 50.00.
2. Experimental sugar, 3½", $40.00 – 50.00.
3. Experimental stein, 6¼", $40.00 – 45.00.
4. Experimental pitcher, 8", $100.00 – 145.00.
Row 3:
1. Experimental covered casserole, 11", $110.00 – 135.00.
2. Experimental bean pot, 7", $110 – 135.00.
Row 4.
1. Experimental dinner plate, $25.00 – 35.00.
2. Experimental salad plate, $10.00 – 12.00.
3. Experimental mug, 4", $25.00 – 35.00.
4. Experimental bowl, 5¾", $25.00 – 30.00.

Plate 238. Original company brochure page.

Plate 239.
Row 1:
1. Experimental Fantasy planter, unmarked olive with drip, 4½", 1958, $75.00 – 100.00.
2. Experimental Swan, unmarked, 8", heavy greens and blacks, 1953, $150.00 – 200.00.
3. Experimental Supreme bud vase, unmarked, 8", 1960, $125.00 – 160.00.
Row 2:
1. Experimental Supreme jardiniere, unmarked, 4¾", 1960, $115.00 – 140.00.
2. Experimental Supreme candy dish, "F27," 7", 1960, $135.00 – 165.00.
3. Experimental Supreme footed bowl, unmarked, 4¾", 1960, $125.00 – 145.00.
Row 3:
1. Experimental Bicentennial shaker, unmarked, 3", 1976, $30.00 – 35.00.
2. Experimental Bicentennial shaker, unmarked, 3", 1976, $30.00 – 35.00.
3. Experimental baby shoes, unmarked, 3½", 1960, $135.00 – 165.00.
4. Experimental Bicentennial bean pot, unmarked, 7", 1976, $110.00 – 135.00.
5. Experimental Bicentennial covered sugar, unmarked, 3½", 1976, $40.00 – 50.00.
6. Experimental Bicentennial creamer, unmarked, 4", 1976, $40.00 – 50.00.
Row 4:
1. Experimental plate, 10¼", 1967, $30.00 – 50.00.
2. Experimental plate, 10¼", 1965, $75.00 – 100.00.
3. Experimental plate, 10¼", 1967, $30.00 – 50.00.

Plate 239.

Plate 240.

Row 1:

1. Experimental covered casserole, unmarked, 8½", 1945, $75.00 – 100.00.

2. Trial mug, incised test glaze code "6914C," 3", 1968, $15.00 – 20.00.

3. Experimental teapot/jug, incised floral decor, 5", 1968, $100.00 – 140.00.

Row 2:

1. Experimental luncheon plate, cobalt, 8½", 1960. (Note the concentric ring pattern, which is characteristic to reverse sides of many House 'n Garden items.) $20.00 – 30.00.

2. Experimental ice-lip pitcher, cobalt, 7½", 1960, $155.00 – 255.00.

Row 3:

1. Experimental Pineapple teapot, unmarked, 7", 1948, $225.00 – 325.00.

2. Experimental Pineapple cookie jar, unmarked, 11", 1948, $225.00 – 325.00.

3. Experimental Pineapple pitcher, unmarked, 6½", 1948, $200.00 – 300.00.

Row 4:

1. Experimental Cinderella Bouquet plate, unmarked, 9½", 1948, $75.00 – 100.00.

2. Experimental cookie jar, unmarked, 8½", 1945, $125.00 – 145.00.

3. Experimental Cinderella Bouquet divided plate, unmarked, 11", 1948, $125.00 – 150.00.

Plate 240.

Plate 241.

Row 1:

1. Experimental Heritageware bowl, satin-finished copper, "A-1-7½"," 1958, $30.00 – 40.00.
2. Experimental glass, underglazed hand-painted floral, "Jean, 1951" on reverse, $20.00 – 30.00.
3. Experimental coffee server, in trial turquoise, "Hull Ovenproof, USA," 11", 1956, $135.00 – 175.00.
4. Experimental glass, cobalt blue, 1980, $20.00 – 30.00.
5. Experimental Heritageware bowl, unmarked, satin yellow, 8½", 1958, $30.00 – 40.00.

Row 2:

1. Experimental creamer, Cinderella, underglaze hand decorated, "28-4½"," 1948, $30.00 – 40.00.
2. Experimental baker, Cinderella, underglaze hand decorated, "21-8½"," 1948, $125.00 – 150.00.
3. Experimental glass, fired bisque, personally inscribed to this author, "Best of Luck Brenda, Paul Sharkey, 5-31-78." "S" incised on base. $20.00 – 30.00.
4. Experimental Plaidware sugar, yellow with brown banding, unmarked, 3¼". 1950, $50.00 – 70.00.
5. Experimental Plaidware creamer, yellow with brown banding, unmarked, 3", 1950. (The handle was later redesigned on this piece before it was marketed.) 1950, $60.00 – 80.00.

Row 3:

1. Experimental Cinderella Bouquet bowl, script Hull brown ink stamp, 6¾", 1948, $50.00 – 70.00.
2. Trial Cinderella Bouquet creamer, "28-4½"," glaze numbers, 1948, $45.00 – 70.00.
3. Trial Cinderella Bouquet teapot, "26-42 oz.," glaze numbers, 1948, $140.00 – 180.00.
4. Trial Cinderella Bouquet covered Sugar, "27-4½"," glaze numbers, 1948, $45.00 – 70.00.
5. Experimental Cinderella Bouquet bowl, script Hull brown ink stamp, 6¾", 1948, $50.00 – 75.00.

Plate 241.

Experimentals, Specials, Trials, and Samples

The incised grape decor dinnerware was trialed in 1960, at the same time the Hull Pottery Company was producing both the Tokay and the Tuscany artware lines. This experimental dinnerware, glazed in Milk White and Forest Green, was strikingly sophisticated, but was never placed on the retail market.

Plate 242.
Row 1:
1. Experimental plate, incised grape decor, unmarked, 10½", 1960, $40.00 – 60.00.
2. Experimental pitcher, incised grape decor, "Ovenproof, USA," 8½", 1960, $150.00 – 225.00.
Row 2:
1. Experimental coffee mug, incised grape decor, unmarked, 3¼", 1960, $20.00 – 30.00.
2. Experimental bowl, incised grape decor, unmarked, 5¼", 1960, $20.00 – 30.00.
3. Experimental saucer, incised grape decor, unmarked, 6", 1960, $18.00 – 25.00.

Hull House 'n Garden dinner plates were often targets of experimentation. Company employees found it difficult to resist the squiggles they could make with the squeeze bottles of "run down" glazes.

Plate 243.
1. Experimental Tokay/Tuscany pedestaled vase, 10", $95.00 – 140.00.

Plate 244.
1. Experimental plate, 10¼", $75.00 – 100.00.
2. Experimental plate, 10¼", $75.00 – 100.00.

Plate 245.
1. Experimental dinner plate, incised star decoration, unmarked, 10¼", $20.00 – 30.00.
2. Experimental mug; incised flowers, tea kettle, and bean pot; unmarked, 3¼", $20.00 – 25.00.
3. Experimental dinner plate, incised rooster and weather vane decor, "Ovenproof," 10¼", $30.00 – 50.00.

Plate 242.

Plate 243.

Plate 244.

Plate 245.

Plate 246.

Row 1:

1. Experimental square French-handled casserole, unmarked, 7½", 1963. The square casserole was never placed on the retail market. It was molded with a deeply recessed thumbhold for ease in handling. $60.00 – 80.00.
2. Trial bud vase, unmarked, 8¼", 1970. This trialed vase was later retailed in volume. $60.00 – 95.00.
3. Experimental square French-handled casserole, unmarked and unmarketed, 7½", 1963, $75.00 – 100.00.

Row 2:

1. Experimental Bicentennial stein, "hull USA," 6¼", 1976, $30.00 – 40.00.
2. Experimental Bicentennial bowl, unmarked, 5¾", 1976, $25.00 – 30.00.
3. Experimental Bicentennial bean pot, "hull USA," 9½", 1976, $110.00 – 135.00.
4. Experimental Bicentennial mug, unmarked, 4", 1976, $25.00 – 35.00.
5. Experimental Bicentennial pitcher, unmarked, 8", 1976, $100.00 – 145.00.

Row 3:

1. Experimental Teflon-line House 'n Garden French-handled casserole, unmarked, 12", 1962, $100.00 – 150.00.
2. Experimental Teflon-lined House 'n Garden baker, "hull Ovenproof, USA," 9¾", 1962, $100.00 – 150.00.
3. Experimental Teflon-lined House 'n Garden French-handled casserole, unmarked, 12", 1962, $100.00 – 150.00.

Row 4:

1. Experimental Bicentennial stein, unmarked, 6¼", 1976, $40.00 – 45.00.
2. Experimental Bicentennial casserole, unmarked, 11", 1976, $110.00 – 135.00.
3. Experimental Bicentennial pitcher, unmarked, 8", 1976, $100.00 – 145.00.
4. Experimental stein, unmarked, 6¼", 1968, $40.00 – 60.00.

Row 5:

1. Experimental platter, "hull Ovenproof, USA," 12", 1982, $75.00 – 100.00.
2. Experimental Teflon-lined House 'n Garden pie plate, "hull Ovenproof, USA," 9¼", 1962, $80.00 – 100.00.
3. Experimental platter, "hull Ovenproof, USA," 12", 1982, $75.00 – 100.00.

Plate 246.

Experimentals, Specials, Trials, and Samples

With Hull's production of House 'n Garden casual servingware spanning 25 years, there are no doubt several variations as far as experimentals and trials are concerned. Enough variation, at least, to make the search interesting.

The Swirl dinnerware was one of the most attractive dinnerwares produced by Hull. While this grouping proves it was made in a somewhat complete set, little of it was produced, and less has survived. The raised twisted swirl pattern seems to have caught and drizzled the run down glaze quite effectively, and makes this color treatment even more attractive on this ware than on the plain House 'n Garden servingware pieces. The servingware shown was further accented by gold trim decor.

The cobalt blue House 'n Garden dinnerware, produced in 1960 with the use of Continental's Mountain Blue glaze, is quite attractive also. It is not known to what extent this ware was produced; however, there appear to be so few pieces that the ware is classified as experimental.

Provincial House 'n Garden serving ware was manufactured in 1961. The line itself was not experimental, but was in production not more than one year. At least 23 items were available, including a cookie jar. The Provincial experimentals shown on the following page have glaze number designations, and dinner plates have been found glazed in colors other than white.

Plate 247.
Row 1:
1. Trial Corn serving dish, unmarked, 9½". This item is a trial piece that was later marketed in the early 1970s. $75.00 – 100.00.
2. Experimental cobalt saucer, "Ovenproof, USA 5¾"," 1960, $15.00 – 20.00.
3. Experimental cobalt coffee mug, "Ovenproof, USA," 3¼", 1960, $20.00 – 30.00.
4. Experimental cobalt luncheon plate, "Ovenproof, USA," 8½", 1960, $20.00 – 30.00.
5. Experimental covered sugar, unmarked, 3½", 1970, $80.00 – 110.00.
6. Experimental creamer, styled from the coffee mug design, unmarked, 3", 1970, $80.00 – 110.00.
Row 2:
1. Experimental bright Butterscotch coffee mug, "hull Ovenproof," 3½", 1964, $10.00 – 15.00.
2. Experimental bright Butterscotch plate, "hull Ovenproof," 10¼", 1964, $20.00 – 25.00.
3. Experimental bright Butterscotch bowl, "hull Ovenproof," 5½", 1964, $10.00 – 15.00.
4. Experimental Satin Avocado with blue drip coffee mug, "hull Crestone, Ovenproof," 2¾", 1968, $10.00 – 15.00.
5. Experimental Satin Avocado with blue drip plate, "hull Ovenproof," 10¼", 1968, $20.00 – 30.00.
6. Experimental Satin Avocado with blue drip bowl, "hull Ovenproof," 5¾", 1968, $10.00 – 15.00.
7. Trial Provincial plate, hull "Ovenproof," 10¼", glaze numbers, 1961, $15.00 – 18.00.
8. Trial Provincial coffee mug, "Ovenproof USA," 3½", glaze numbers, 1961, $4.00 – 6.00.
9. Trial Provincial saucer, "hull Crestone Ovenproof," 5¾", glaze numbers, 1961, $3.00 – 4.00.
Row 3:
1. Experimental Swirl coffee mug, unmarked, 3½", 1963, $15.00 – 20.00.
2. Experimental Swirl bread and butter, unmarked, 6½", 1963, $8.00 – 10.00.
3. Experimental Swirl bowl, unmarked, 6½", 1963, $20.00 – 30.00.
4. Experimental Swirl bowl, unmarked, 5¼", 1963, $20.00 – 30.00.
5. Experimental Swirl plate, unmarked, 10¼", 1963, $25.00 – 35.00.
6. Experimental Swirl mug, unmarked, 5", 1963, $30.00 – 40.00.
7. Experimental Swirl French-handled casserole, unmarked, 7½", $20.00 – 30.00.

Plate 247.

Plate 248.
1. Experimental Fantasy vase, "72," incised decor on Mirror Black, 8½", 1959, $90.00 – 140.00.
2. Experimental vase, webbed decor, unmarked, 8½", 1960, $130.00 – 165.00.

Plate 250.
Row 1:
1. Experimental ashtray, unmarked; brown, red, and yellow; 10¼", 1960, $75.00 – 115.00.
2. Experimental ashtray, unmarked red textured finish, 10¼", 1960, $100.00 – 145.00.
3. Experimental ashtray, unmarked, Green Agate with turquoise, 10¼", 1960, $75.00 – 115.00.
Row 2:
1. Experimental leaf ashtray, unmarked, olive with red, 12½", 1960, $50.00 – 75.00.
2. Experimental free-form ashtray, unmarked, olive with red, 13", 1960, $50.00 – 75.00.

Plate 248.

Plate 249. Experimental Parchment and Pine teapot, unmarked, 6", 1954, $250.00 – 325.00.

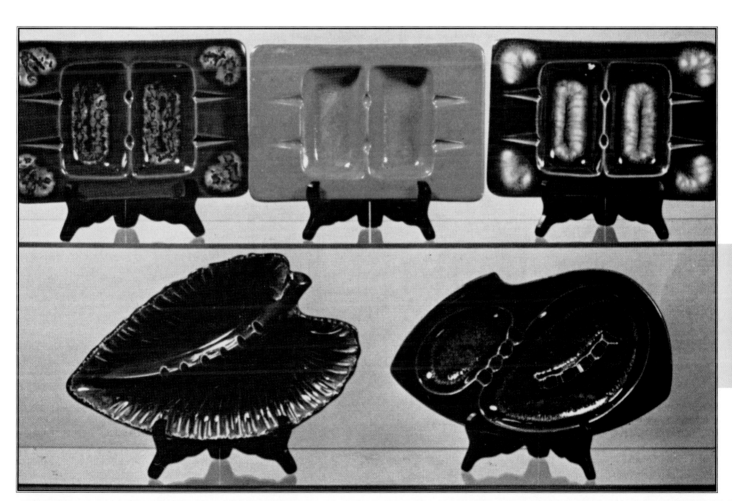

Plate 250.

Plate 251.
Row 1:
1. Experimental ashtray, white-glossed texture, unmarked, 8", 1958, $20.00 – 30.00.
2. Experimental free-form ashtray, unmarked, 10½", 1959, $50.00 – 75.00.
Row 2:
1. Experimental ashtray, unmarked, 8", green and blue, 1960, $75.00 – 100.00.
2. Experimental ashtray, Woodland jardiniere base, "W11," 5¼", 1952, $20.00 – 25.00.
3. Experimental ashtray, incised glaze code "6636A," 8", 1960, $75.00 – 100.00.
Row 3:
1. Experimental ashtray, unmarked, olive with blue and green, 10¼", 1959, $75.00 – 115.00.
2. Experimental ashtray, unmarked, 12", cobalt textured finish, 1958, $85.00 – 120.00.
Row 4:
1. Experimental ashtray, unmarked, 8", 1962, $40.00 – 60.00.
2. Experimental ashtray/server, unmarked, 13", 1960, $70.00 – 100.00.
3. Experimental ashtray, unmarked, 8", 1962, $40.00 – 50.00.

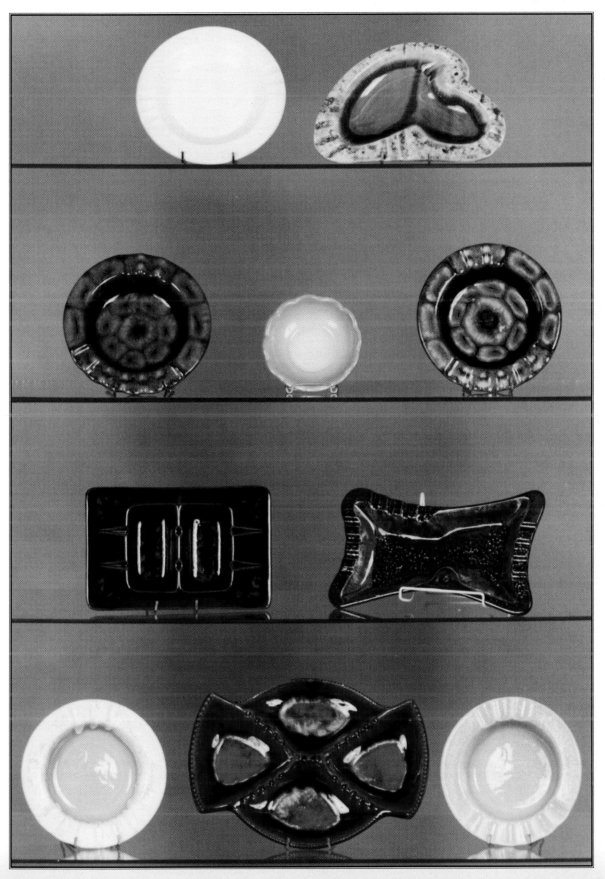

Plate 251.

Appendix A — Trademarks

1. This black ink stamp marked porcelain wares of the Acme Pottery Company (1903 – 1907) of Crooksville, Ohio, purchased by The A. E. Hull Pottery in 1907.

2. The blue ink-stamped wreath with banner, "Hull Pottery, Crooksville, O.," was used circa 1910 to mark utilitarian stoneware jugs and jars. Gallon content was stamped inside the wreath.

3. This black heart ink stamp marked early black-over-white utilitarian stoneware, indicating gallon size within the heart's boundaries. This mark was used around 1912.

4. Most Hull wares remained unmarked until well into the teens. The first trademark incised into the ware appears to be the *H*-in-diamond form. This trademark is found most often on kitchenware and utilitarian wares.

5. By the 1920s, the incised bold capital *H*-in-circle trademark soon followed.

6. The *H*-in-circle trademark soon evolved into this far less bold designation.

7. This mark many times included incised numbers, which indicated mold and size numbers for jugs, diameters for bowls, heights for vases, etc.

8. The *H*-in-circle designation, used well into the 1930s, is found as illustrated in trademarks 5 – 8, as well as in similar variations. This trademark was used on a variety of both kitchenware and artware items.

9. Hull tile was manufactured in both plain and faience styles, with either a flat or cushioned (rounded) surface. Faience tile was marked just that, "HULL FAIENCE." A cushioned tile was further marked "Cushion." The faience cushion trademark is bold and deeply incised, and dates from 1926 to 1931.

10, 11. The "HULL TILE" trademark is found in both raised and embossed form. "Hull Tile" was sometimes embossed in one line, sometimes in two. Size or shape of the tile did not neccessarily affect the positioning of the trademark. "Cushion" was added to tiles with cushioned, or rounded, surfaces. Hull tile was made from 1926 to 1931.

12. Another incised tile trademark, used during tile production 1926 to 1931, included this "Hull Faience Cushion" logo in crisscross fashion.

13. Some early utilitarian items indicated a registered patent assignment in incised form. This particular mark is found on yellow ware batter bowls. This trademark was used as early as mid-1920.

14. This incised trademark incorporated the entire A. E. Hull firm name, and it was used on kitchenware and novelties in the 1930s. It was most often followed by mold and size identification numbers. By the 1930s, nearly all Hull trademarks carried "USA" in some form. In fact, "USA" was marked even when the Hull name was not. Many earlier stoneware, yellow ware, and kitchenware items were marked only with an incised "USA."

15. The incised "Hull Oven-Proof" trademark was used on kitchenware items from the 1930s and into the 1940s. The trademark was usually followed by a mold number and size identification.

16, 17, 18. Throughout the 1930s and 1940s, kitchenware lines were additionally marked by ovenproof foil labels that indicated "heat resisting, cold resisting." These foil labels, which marked many nested bowl and nappy sets, appeared in various colors, including but not limited to red, black, and silver, and were oval, round, rectangular, and bowl-shaped.

19. Plain artwares from the Sueno line, either shaded or overall white, carried no "Hull" mark; however, they were incised with style or mold numbers, which usually included size identification.

20. Illustrated is a variation of the trademark described above. These artware items most often carried the triangular Hull foil label to compensate for being unmarked.

21. Although many novelties from the 1930s and early 1940s carried no "Hull" designation, the incised "HULL MADE" trademark appeared on some of the novelty wares from this era. This trademark was usually followed by the mold number.

22. By 1938, this incised "HULL" mark, followed by "USA" or "U.S.A.," was widely used for matte pastel artwares.

23. Another version of the preceding illustrated trademark shows little difference other than the "USA" designation. Hull soon learned that trademarks were good business, and Hull trademarks soon acted as representatives of a quality product. The advertising aspect was carried a step further with the offer of a complementary A. E. Hull Pottery display plaque with orders totalling more than $20.00.

24. During this same time, it was not uncommon for the Hull trademark to be absent on some very fine artware lines, such as the 500-designation Calla Lily.

25. As with the trademark described above, incised mold numbers and size identifications were almost always apparent, and sometimes followed by "USA." The Hull triangular foil label again compensated for the wares' unmarked state.

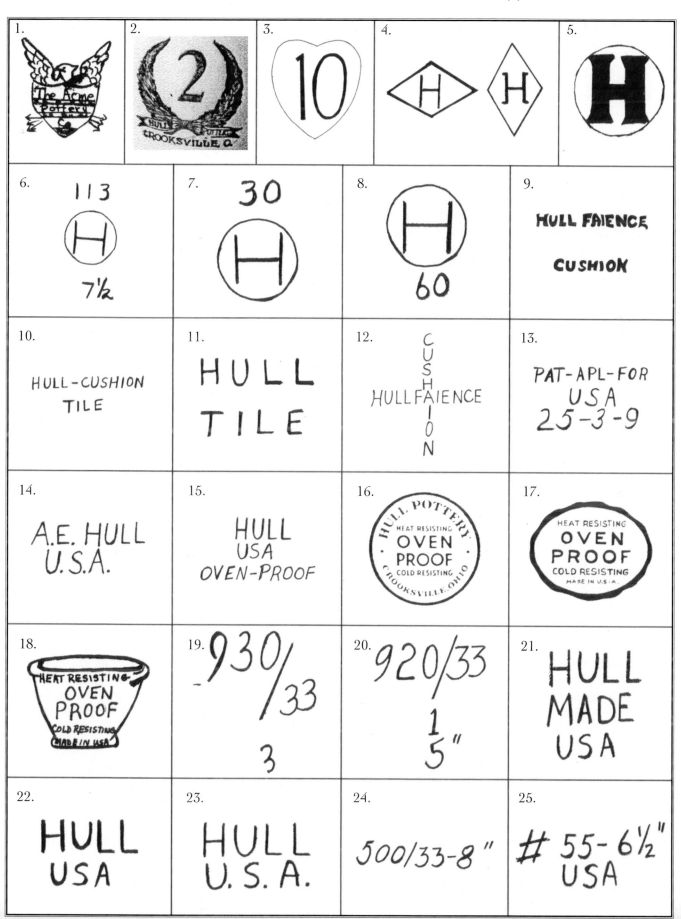

1.
The Acme Pottery Co.

2.
(2) HULL POTTERY CROOKSVILLE O.

3.
10

4.
H   H

5.
H

6.
113
H
7½

7.
30
H

8.
H
60

9.
HULL FAIENCE
CUSHION

10.
HULL-CUSHION
TILE

11.
HULL
TILE

12.
CUSHION
HULL FAIENCE

13.
PAT-APL-FOR
USA
25-3-9

14.
A.E. HULL
U.S.A.

15.
HULL
USA
OVEN-PROOF

16.
HULL POTTERY
HEAT RESISTING
OVEN
PROOF
COLD RESISTING
CROOKSVILLE, OHIO

17.
HEAT RESISTING
OVEN
PROOF
COLD RESISTING
MADE IN U.S.A.

18.
HEAT RESISTING
OVEN
PROOF
COLD RESISTING
MADE IN USA

19.
930/33
3

20.
920/33
1
5"

21.
HULL
MADE
USA

22.
HULL
USA

23.
HULL
U.S.A.

24.
500/33-8"

25.
55-6½"
USA

26. Part of the reasoning behind the trademarks that did not include the Hull name was due to the additional placement of foil labels on the ware. These labels, elongated diamonds or triangular in shape, are either black or maroon with lettering in silver or gold. The foil labels were used consistently to mark a variety of Hull's artware, novelty, and kitchenware lines from the late 1930s to the mid-1940s.

27. Representative, or sample, Hull items were marked with labels such as this paper seal that is green and white. Style number, decoration, and size number were noted directly on the label. The upper half of this seal is green with white lettering, while the lower half of this seal is white with green lettering. Sample seals are also found in black and red. The round sample seal was used prior to 1950, and a rectangular black and white seal was primarily used for post-1950 Hull wares.

28. By early 1940, the Hull trademark, identical to a previously used incised form, was now seen with raised or embossed letters.

29. Only a slightly different version than that described above. The raised versions proved to better meet the needs of manufacturing, since embossed marking was less often obliterated by the remaining glazing processes. Thick glazes often filled the indentations of the incised letters.

30, 31. From 1937 to 1944, product containers manufactured by Hull for Shulton's Old Spice, in the form of shaving lotion and talcum bottles, were marked with these incised trademarks.

32. This incised trademark is found on the figural elephant and pig liquor bottles of the mid-1940s. Patent designation is not always included; it is quite common to find items marked "Leeds, USA" only.

33. Incised "Hull Ware" logos were typical trademarks for 1940s kitchenware nested bowl and nappy sets, as well as cookie jars and Hull Little Red Riding Hood items.

34. Mold numbers, sometimes with size identification, were also included in the above-described trademark, as well as in this variation of "Hull Ware."

35. There is no question as to the identity of items incised "Hull Ware Little Red Riding Hood." This mark is found on many Hull-made wares, although some items were unmarked. This mark was also used without the "Hull Ware" designation. In this instance, it included the patent design number and was used most often for marking Regal-made cookie jars (see trademarks 36, 37). Most all Red Riding Hood items, both Hull and Regal, were accented with gold detailing. It is not uncommon to find items with foil labels stating "Hand Painted Fired Ceramic Colors" and indicating gold content, usually 23K.

36. This incised Little Red Riding Hood trademark was most often used on cookie jars, because they were large enough to accommodate the logo.

37. Many Red Riding Hood items were incised with only patent design number 135889. Red Riding Hood items were produced from 1943 to 1957.

38. This incised script form served as trademark for the Boy Blue cookie jar in 1940.

39. An additional incised script trademark, "Hull, USA," was used for cookie jars and kitchenware in the 1940s.

40, 41. Hull's art designs had gained wide acclaim during the 1940s, with artware sales making up a large portion of the company's retail sales. Provided with this stability, Hull chose to advertise its artwares as such, and designed the incised "Hull Art" trademark for this use.

42. Illustrated is another incised form of the company's "Hull Art" trademark used in the 1940s. This logo is found on the very plain yet stylized art forms that did not have the typical floral embossing of the day.

43. In 1946, Rosella artware not only had its own special clay mixture, it was also accompanied by a specially designed foil label. This rose and banner Rosella label is brown with gold accents.

44. It is interesting to note that the Hull Company used the Potter-at-Wheel logo from the logo's earliest inception through the company's entire history of production. This design, first used on advertising materials and brochure pages, later appeared in foil label form, and it was additionally used on company letterheads after 1950. Many, many of the artware items from the forties were consistently marked with this label. It has a black background with silver, gold, or gray lettering.

45. The "Granada" Potter-at-Wheel foil label graced many chain store art and novelty items. While a specific chain store line was manufactured from 1938 to 1946, the Granada line spanned the years of the mid-1930s through those of the early 1950s. The Granada and Mardi Gras molds were used interchangeably. This label has a black background with gold or silver lettering.

46. The vase-form "Mardi Gras" Potter-at-Wheel foil label is found on assorted art and novelty items. While a specific chain store line was manufactured from 1938 to 1946, the Mardi Gras line spanned the years of the mid-1930s through those of the early 1950s. The Granada and Mardi Gras molds were used interchangeably. This label has a black background with gold or silver lettering. The company reported another foil label in white or silver, which featured a black silhouette of a female flamenco dancer with a mask.

26.	27. SAMPLE THE A.E. HULL POTTERY CO. CROOKSVILLE, OHIO Style No. _____ Decoration _____ Size _____	28. HULL USA	29. HULL U.S.A.
30. EARLY AMERICAN Old Spice MADE IN U.S.A.	31. EARLY-AMERICAN Old Spice SHAVING SOAP USA SHULTON	32. Pat. Appl'd For LEEDS U.S.A.	33. Hull Ware U.S.A.
34. Hull Ware U.S.A.	35. 967 Hull Ware Little Red Riding Hood Patent Applied For U.S.A.	36. Little Red Riding Hood Pat-Des-No- 135889 U.S.A.	37. Pat-Des-No-135889 U.S.A.
38. Hull Ware Boy Blue U.S.A.	39. Hull USA	40. Hull Art U.S.A	41. U.S.A Hull Art
42. U.S.A Hull-Art 750-13½	43. Rosella	44. HULL POTTERY Potter at Wheel CROOKSVILLE, OHIO	45. GRANADA POTTERY
46. MARDI GRAS POTTERY	47. CLASSIC HAND DECORATED OVERGLAZE VASE	48. Hull Art U.S.A	49. U.S.A Hull Art

47. This crown and banner "Classic" foil label used in the early 1940s marked many chain store pottery items. This label has a background of silver or gold and a contrasting green banner with gold and black lettering.

48, 49. Art lines carried the company through the forties, and the "Hull Art" logo prevailed; however, by 1946 it was found in raised form, rather than incised.

50. In 1948, a deeply incised bold "HULL," reminiscent of an earlier day, was the trademark used for Cinderella's Blossom and Bouquet kitchenware designs. Mold numbers and sizes, including ounces, were also incorporated into the trademark.

51. This blue and gold foil label stating "Hand Painted, Oven Proof," was additionally used for promoting Hull's Cinderella kitchenware items, produced in 1948 and 1949.

52. This incised "Ovenproof" trademark with no mention of manufacturer was used for Hull's Modern Plaid kitchenware of 1950.

53. This blue and silver "Hull-Ware" foil label, advertising the "A. E. Hull Pottery Co., Crooksville, Ohio," was used on Cinderella kitchenware, as well as on Hull's Modern Plaid kitchenware line.

54. This embossed, beautifully flowing script "Hull" trademark was presented in 1949, prior to the company's flood and fire, for the Woodland pattern. It was used to mark both matte and gloss Woodland shapes both prior to and after the flood and fire.

55. A very small brown ink stamp was the trademark used for Cinderella kitchenware items made immediately prior to the plant's destruction in 1950, and at the latest, during the time the company operated from a pilot plant in 1951.

56. The incised flowing script "Hull Oven-Proof" trademark was used on Hull's Just Right Floral and Vegetable kitchenwares in 1951. The trademark included mold number and size identification.

57, 58, 59. These lovely flourishing trademarks carried both Hull artwares and kitchenwares successfully through the 1950s. While these trademarks appeared both in raised and incised forms, they varied very little, mainly in the style, size, and intensity of the capital *H*.

60. For identification purposes, the company used this label that indicated style, package, and price. It was used most often for representative or sample items in the 1950s.

61. This is the signature of Granville "Grany" Shafer, who gold trimmed and decorated many Hull items from the 1940s through the 1970s. Many of his gold-decorated wares included a gold hand-stamped block trademark reading "23K Gold Guaranteed, Shafer, USA, Zanesville, Ohio." Sometimes, only "Shafer, USA" was noted.

62. Some of Hull's novelty items of 1950, including the dime piggy banks, were marked with this impressed logo. It was also quite often used (without the "'58" designation) on several House 'n Garden serving ware pieces, from the 1960s through the plant's closing in 1985.

63. The incised Corky Pig trademark was first implemented in 1957, as the mark indicates. This logo continued to be used, with the "1957" designation, through the 1970s.

64. The "H. P. CO." trademark was used in embossed form on ashtrays and novelties from the late 1950s into the 1960s.

65. The incised Tokay trademark was used on the grape-embossed Tokay line. This logo did not appear on Tuscany, a line that shared the Tokay molds. Tuscany was marked with the incised script "Hull."

66. The incised Marcrest logo was used for premium items produced specifically for Marshall Burns, Chicago, in the late 1950s. There were other producers of pottery items for Marshall Burns, one being Western Stoneware, which produced brown Marcrest. Hull's Marcrest dinnerware was usually glazed in solid pastel colors, and while Heritageware molds were used for this production, the line also included molds specifically for Marcrest production.

67. The raised "MARCREST" appeared on a variety of ashtrays, again produced as premium items for Marshall Burns.

68. The raised "SINCLAIR" mark was used for novelty banks made as premium items by Hull in the early 1960s.

69. Regal's majestic incised trademark was used for a variety of chain store vases and novelty assortments. Some earlier pieces from specific lines and assortments sporting different glaze treatments were marked with the Regal logo. The Regal mark was enlisted for wares from both the 1950s and the 1960s.

70, 71. The incised flowing Coronet trademark was used for a variety of chain store vase, novelty, and planter assortments. Many of Coronet's designs were incorporated with brass and wrought iron stands, including a floor model planter and ashtray combination. The Coronet mark was used on wares produced in the 1950s and 1960s.

72. In 1960, the incised classical Pagoda trademark was used for a chain store line of vases and jardinieres of the same name. This chain store assortment had a marked Oriental theme.

50. **HULL** 29-16 OZ U.S.A.	51. HAND PAINTED *Cinderella* HULL POTTERY CROOKSVILLE, OHIO OVEN PROOF	52. 60-5" OVENPROOF U.S.A.	53. A.E. HULL POTTERY CO. **Hull·Ware** CROOKSVILLE, OHIO
54. *Hull* W1-5½" U.S.A.	55. *Hull* USA	56. OVEN-PROOF *Hull* USA No 20-5	57. *Hull* USA
58. SALAD-BOWL *Hull* U.S.A. No 44-10	59. *Hull* T10 USA ©'55	60. HULL POTTERY CO. CROOKSVILLE, O. STYLE $5 PACKAGE 4 Court PRICE	61. SHAFER 23 K. GOLD GUARANTEED *Gravy*
62. USA HP © 58	63. PAT PEND *Corky Pig* © USA 1957 HP Co	64. H.P.©CO. PAT. PEND.	65. *Tokay* U.S.A.
66. MARCREST OVEN PROOF QUALITY MADE IN USA	67. MARCREST	68. SINCLAIR USA	69. REGAL
70. *Coronet* 204 U.S.A.	71. *Coronet* 207 U.S.A.	72. *Pagoda* P3 USA	73. URN-VASE HULL-U.S.A.

73. In 1962, the incised "URN-VASE" trademark was used for a variety of florist ware jardinieres.

74. Most all Hull House 'n Garden casual serving ware was marked by this incised trademark. It was used from 1960 until the plant's closing in 1985, the exception being when a new item was introduced or when it was necessary for an item to be remodeled or retooled. In this instance, a later mold would have incorporated an incised "Crooksville, Ohio" or "Crooksville, O." into the logo.

75. Another House 'n Garden casual serving ware trademark incorporated "H. P. Co." This trademark was used primarily in the 1960s and 1970s.

76. In 1965, this flowing incised "Crestone" trademark was designed specifically for the House 'n Garden casual serving ware in turquoise. This mark appears on Mirror Brown serving ware as well. Brown ware with this Crestone mark is readily available and is not considered experimental.

77. This classical incised Imperial trademark was used from 1960 to 1980 for the massive assortment of florist ware of the same name. In some cases, "hull" additionally adorned the item.

78. This trademark, featuring the incised "hull," was used on both House 'n Garden casual serving ware as well as Imperial florist ware beginning in 1960.

79. This incised trademark was used for a chain store assortment of planters and florist ware items in the 1960s.

80. The rectangular black foil label with gold lettering was used beginning in 1958 to mark novelty and florist ware items. Greatest use of this seal was in the mid-1970s. Collectors beware, as rolls and rolls of these labels were dispersed after the plant's closing and now mark many Hull items claimed to be trials and experimentals. These labels can also be found on items that were not produced by Hull.

81. The serving trays of 1978 soon enlisted this special incised trademark, almost as a warning to keep it off the range top. It was a cooking utensil meant only for microwave and oven use. Earliest serving trays do not bear the "Serving Tray" logo.

82. This incised trademark was used on the Gingerbread Man server introduced in 1978.

83. By 1982, an increased interest in promoting area craftsmen provided the inspiration to include the incised "Crooksville, Ohio" on all new molds and older dinnerware molds that were redesigned or retooled. This new trademark was specifically designed for Hull's 1982 – 1985 dinnerwares, most of which carried the revised trademark automatically. If limited mold space dictated, the origin was abbreviated to read "Crooksville, O."

84, 85. Additional versions of the newly designed incised dinnerware trademark that included the product's origin were used from 1982 to 1985.

74. hull Oven Proof u.S.a.	75. Oven Proof H.P. © Co. u.S.a.	76. hull u.s.a Crestone © OVEN-PROOF	77. Imperial F 71 U.S.A.
78. hull u.S.a. F 14	79. planter, inc.	80. hull u.s.a. crooksville, ohio	81. Serving Tray Oven Proof hull© u.S.a.
82. hull© Gingerbread Man u.S.a.	83. hull © Crooksville, Ohio Oven Proof u.S.a.	84. hull © Crooksville, Ohio Oven Proof u.S.a.	85. Crooksville hull© Oven Proof u.S.a Ohio

Appendix B
Lines and Dates of Manufacture and Plate Index

Although the following listing cannot be considered complete, because new lines will continually be discovered through additional research of the Hull Pottery, it is provided for your easy access to line identification, dates of manufacture, color and glaze treatments, and number of pieces available. Dates entailing several years of production will be noted for categorized items such as cuspidors, combinets, early art, etc.

A

ACME: 1903 – 1907. Porcelain wares produced by the Acme Pottery Company (purchased by the Hull Pottery in 1907). Plate 28.

ADVERTISING SIGNS: At least four advertisements are available for collectors: the 5" x 11" plaque, "The A.E. Hull Co. Pottery"; the 2½" x 5½" plaque, "HULL"; the 6½" x 11½" Regal plaque, "Featuring Little Red Riding Hood, Covered by Pat. Des. No. 135889"; and the 4¼" x 4¼" tile, "TILE BY HULL, INSTALLED BY A. SCHIRMER, CINCINNATI." Plates 5, 51, 69, and 71.

ALPINE: 1915 – 1930. Refers to stoneware tankards, steins, and jars embossed with Alpine scene, highly glazed in golden brown. Plates 37, 38, and 229.

ART POTTERY: 1925 – 1935. All artful semiporcelain and stoneware items, which included vases, jardinieres, pots and saucers, bulb bowls, hanging baskets, etc. Glazes included solid matte Eggshell White, Bermuda Green, Lotus Blue, Oyster White, Autumn Brown, Egyptian Green, Maize Yellow, and others, and a variety of blended glazes in blue, turquoise, maroon, green, Maize Yellow, as well as other combinations.

ATHENA: 1960. Chain store vase and planter assortment, decorated in overall high-gloss colors Lilac or Spring Green trimmed with White Lava, or in allover satin white. Eleven pieces were offered, including an oval picture frame/wall pocket planter. Plate 124 and 128.

AVOCADO: 1968 – 1971. Refers to the House 'n Garden casual servingware offered in Avocado with ivory trim. Satin-finished Avocado was also available during this same period. It most often was not trimmed in ivory. Thirty items were available, including a cylinder-shaped cookie jar. Plates 192, 220, 246, and 247.

B

BAK-SERVE: 1915 – 1935. Also referred to as Banded 100 line. Semiporcelain and stoneware lines that included nested bowls, jugs, bakers, custards, range jars, refrigerator jars, cereal jars, spice jars, pie plates, etc. Semiporcelain items were decorated with green or blue underglaze banding.

Stoneware was glazed in overall high-gloss brown with brown and white underglaze banding. Plates 42 and 45.

BANDED: 1915 – 1940. Any of the varieties of kitchenware items that were decorated by way of overglaze or underglaze color bands. Semiporcelain, stoneware, yellow ware, and Zane Gray bodies were banded. Color bands included, but were not limited to, blue, green, yellow, red, pink, black, brown, and white, as well as gold and luster. Plates 3, 4 , 6, 7, 9, 15, 34, 36, 42, 45, and 47.

BANDED CEREAL WARE: 1915 – 1935. Any of the varieties of cereal ware with either semiporcelain or stoneware bodies, in either round or square shapes, with underglaze or overglaze band decoration in colors including, but not limited to, gold, blue, green, black, and red. Plates 12 and 45.

BANDED ESSENTIALS: 1930 – 1940. Semiporcelain kitchenware line that included nested bowls, jugs, custards, casseroles, etc., decorated with underglaze banding in combinations of pink and blue, blue and peach, and maroon and peach. Other colors were also available. Plates 34 and 47.

BANDED NO. 18 LINE: 1915 – 1935. Semiporcelain kitchenware nested bowls with prominent foot, decorated with underglaze blue bands.

BANDED NO. 20 LINE: 1915 – 1935. Semiporcelain kitchenware nested nappy set with yellow underglaze bands, available with or without gold lines.

BANDED NO. 23 LINE: 1915 – 1935. Semiporcelain kitchenware nested nappy set with blue underglaze banding.

BANDED NO. 25 LINE: 1915 – 1935. Semiporcelain kitchenware nested nappy set with blue underglaze bands, available with or without gold lines.

BANDED NO. 41 LINE: 1915 – 1935. Semiporcelain kitchenware nested nappy set decorated with three underglaze blue lines.

BANDED NO. 50 LINE: 1915 – 1935. Semiporcelain white kitchenware decorated with three underglaze blue lines.

BANDED NO. 100 LINE: 1915 – 1935. Also referred to as Bak-Serve line. Semiporcelain kitchenware line that included nested bowls, jugs, bakers, custards, range jars, refrigerator jars, cereal jars, spice jars, pie plates, etc., decorated with Spring Green or Alice Blue underglaze banding. Plates 36, 42, and 45.

BANDED NO. 100 LINE CEREAL WARE: 1915 – 1935. Refers to round semiporcelain cereal ware jars, spice jars, cruets, and salt boxes that were glazed in transparent high gloss and given underglaze banding in Spring Green or Alice Blue. "Cereal" and "Spices" appear in embossed letters on the fronts of the utility jars. Plate 45.

BANDED NO. 300 LINE: 1915 – 1935. Semiporcelain kitchenware line that included nested bowls, jugs, bakers, custards, ramekins, bean pots, pie plates, etc., decorated in overglaze banding of Pimento Red or Nubian Black, and underglaze banding of Spring Green, Alice Blue, or magenta, with other bandings also available. Marked with a 30-series number. Plates 15 and 47.

BASQUE: 1915 – 1935. Refers to early semiporcelain utility line that included nested bowls, a covered utility jar, a beater jug, and a refrigerator jar.

BEAUTY: 1905 – 1925. Refers to a large embossed open floral decoration used on early stoneware artware and jardinieres. Plate 5.

BICENTENNIAL: 1975 – 1976. Experimental line of ovenproof House 'n Garden casual serving ware glazed in Mirror Brown or Satin Avocado. Items included mugs, steins, low casseroles, bean pots, a creamer and a sugar, and a large pitcher. Plates 238, 239, and 246.

BLACK AND WHITE STONEWARE: 1905 – 1930. Utilitarian wares, used for food storage and preservation, that included meat tubs, churns, shoulder jugs, preserve jugs, milk pans, butters, and more. They had high-fired stoneware bodies glazed black over white.

BLENDED: 1910 – 1940. Refers to semiporcelain and stoneware jugs, jardinieres, cuspidors, vases, bulb bowls, hanging baskets and flower pots, in plain or embossed designs, that were finished in highly glazed or matte blended colors. Plates 15, 18, 19, 21, 29, 31, and 38.

BLOSSOM: 1948 – 1949. Ovenproof kitchenware glazed in allover white with hand-painted six-petal floral, decorated in pink or yellow with green leaves and banding. Fifteen shapes were cataloged, and the line included cookie jars in each color decoration. Plates 63 and 64.

BLOSSOM FLITE: 1955 – 1956. Background combinations of black lattice on overall high-gloss pink, or blue lattice on overall pink with metallic green interior, with additional multicolored embossed floral decoration. It is not uncommon to find heavy gold detailing or overall gold veiling. There were 15 cataloged shapes. Plates 132, 133, 229, and 236.

BLUE AND WHITE STONEWARE: 1905 – 1925. Refers to stoneware bodies whose decoration is characterized by various shadings of light to dark blues. Items were utilitarian, and shapes were both plain and embossed. Items included stoneware dairy jugs, butters, salt boxes, cuspidors, water jugs, water kegs, nested bowls and nappy sets, ewers and basins, and more. Embossed shapes included, but were not limited to, cherries, plums, birds, daisies, wild roses, stags, and cattle. Plates 3, 4, 5, 6, 7, 8, 224, and 227.

BLUE BANDED: 1915 – 1935. White-bodied highly glazed semiporcelain kitchenware items that included bowls, custards, nappies, butters, and jugs, with overglaze or underglaze blue bands.

BLUE BIRD CEREAL WARE: 1915 – 1935. Early cereal ware jars, spice jars, cruets, and salt boxes with blue bird in flight or perched blue bird decal. Fifteen items were included in the complete set. Plate 16.

BLUE FLEMISH: 1915 – 1935. Refers to variety of stoneware and ivory-bodied utility wares, such as butter jars, jugs, etc., decorated with blue tint.

BLUE RIBBON: 1951 – 1954. White highly glazed nested set of five bowls banded in green, with additional green lines on either side. Plate 47.

BOUQUET: 1948 – 1949. Ovenproof kitchenware in overall white highly glazed finish. Decoration included yellow-tinted tops with hand-decorated floral spray in pink, yellow, and blue. Fifteen shapes were available, and these included a cookie jar. An unlisted square serving bowl was also offered. Additional items, which are considered experimental, included square plates, square cereal bowls, and a compartment dish. Plates 64, 240, and 241.

BOW-KNOT: 1949 – 1950. Embossed floral in duotone matte-finished pastel bodies of pink and blue or turquoise and blue combinations. Twenty-nine shapes were cataloged, and an additional square cup and saucer wall pocket were available. Plates 52, 53, and 54.

BOY AND GIRL: 1905 – 1925. Also known as Indian Boy and Girl, or Pilgrims. Refers to an embossed decoration used for blue and white stoneware jugs. This design was also available in blended glazes. Plates 3 and 5.

BROWN AND WHITE LINED WARE: 1905 – 1925. Stoneware utility items that were burned to a very high heat, which vitrified them and caused them to craze less. Items were glazed overall brown with white linings. Plate 4.

BUCKET JARDINIERES: 1959. Bucket- or tub-shaped jardinieres with wire bailed handles. These items were included as part of Gold-Medal Flowerware. Hi-buckets were available in 5", 6", 7", and 9" sizes; Azalea, or tub-buckets, were available in 8" and 10" sizes. Plates 144 and 153.

BUFF GREEN: 1925 – 1935. Refers to a variety of stoneware and ivory-bodied utility ware, dairy jugs, butter jars, etc., which were decorated in green tint. Plates 9 and 15.

BURNT ORANGE: 1963 – 1967. Refers to Tangerine House 'n Garden casual serving ware offered specifically for J.C. Penney. At least forty items were available, including a cookie jar. Plates 220, 221, and 223.

BUTTERFLY: 1956. Raised pastel butterfly and flower motif in a combined gloss and matte finish of white on white, or matte white with turquoise interiors. It is not uncommon to find gold detailing on either glaze treatment. Twenty-five shapes were cataloged. Plates 134, 135, 136, and 137.

BUTTER JARS: 1910 – 1925. Plain, cylinder-shaped open or covered jars in ¼-gallon to 6-gallon sizes, glazed black over white.

BUTTERS: 1910 – 1930. Any of the varieties of open or covered butters, some with wire and wood bailed grips and some embossed "Butters." Included were Zane Grey, ivory- or yellow-bodied ware with blue bands, buff body green tinted, blue Flemish, and others. Also available were plain and embossed shapes in semiporcelain, stoneware, or yellow ware bodies in blended or tinted glazes. These were available in 1- to 5-pound sizes.

BUTTERSCOTCH: 1961 – 1964. Refers to the House 'n Garden/Rainbow casual serving ware produced specifically in Butterscotch-colored glaze. The glaze color later became known as Wild Honey for floristware. Plates 220 and 247.

C

CALLA: 1933. Highly glazed solid or blended stoneware jardinieres and flower pots with embossed pod-shaped floral.

CALLA LILY: 1938 – 1940. Also referred to as Jack-in-the-Pulpit due to embossed floral and arrow-shaped leaves. Various matte tints and duotone colors were available, e.g., solid matte pastels of blue, green, cream, or turquoise, and matte duotone shades of blue to pink, Cinnamon to Dusky Green, Cinnamon to turquoise, rose to Dusty Green, and rose to turquoise. Other color combinations were available. At least 24 items were available, several in graduated sizes. Plates 55, 56, 57, 58, 94, and 229.

CAMELLIA: 1943 – 1944. Also referred to as Open Rose. Hand-decorated embossed florals on shaded pastel backgrounds of matte pink and blue or allover matte white. At least 44 highly diverse shapes were available. Plates 59, 60, 61, 62, 93, and 225.

CAPRI: 1961. Dish garden and figural planter line decorated in Satin Coral with weathered limestone effect or in Seagreen to represent sea-washed rock formations. There were 30 cataloged shapes. Plates 124 and 138.

CASTLE: 1905 – 1925. Refers to an embossed decoration used for early stoneware that was glazed overall brown with white lining. The overall embossed fish scale background has an embossed medallion that encases a castle design. Plate 4.

CATTLE: 1905 – 1925. Refers to an embossed cattle decoration used for early stoneware 5-pint dairy jugs, glazed overall brown with white lining, blue tint, or green tint. Plate 4.

CEREAL WARE, ROUND: 1915 – 1930. Round semiporcelain and stoneware cereal ware sets decorated with gold, yellow, or blue overglaze banding. The set consisted of six cereal jars lettered "rice," "beans," "prunes," "tapioca," "coffee," and "tea," six spice jars lettered "ginger," "allspice," "cloves," "nutmeg," "cinnamon," and "pepper," and a salt box. Plate 12.

CEREAL WARE, SQUARE: 1915 – 1935. Kitchenware sets consisting of canisters, spice jars, salt boxes, and vinegar and oil cruets with underglaze decal decoration. Plain sets in semiporcelain and stoneware bodies were also manufactured in various solid colors. Fifteen items were included in the complete set. Plates 13, 14, and 15.

CHAMBERS: 1910 – 1935. Semiporcelain and stoneware bodies, plain and embossed shapes, with or without lids. Decorations included banding or decals. Plates 3, 8, and 10.

CHECKER: 1920 – 1935. Semiporcelain nested bowls glazed in yellow or green.

CHERRY: 1905 – 1925. Refers to an embossed decoration, used for early stoneware, that was glazed overall brown with white lining or blue tint or green tint. Plate 4.

CHINESE RED CRACQUELLE: 1928. Additional luster line in brilliant red; theme designed outside the Hull plant. At least 15 shapes were offered.

CHURNS: 1920 – 1925. Stoneware open or covered churns in 2- to 6-gallon sizes and glazed in black over white.

CINDERELLA: 1948 – 1949. Overall line name for kitchenware designs of Blossom and Bouquet. Blossom is characterized by an overall white gloss with hand-painted six-petal flowers in pink or yellow and with green leaves and banding. Fifteen shapes are cataloged, including a cookie jar in each of the two designs. Bouquet is characterized by an overall white high-gloss finish. Decoration included yellow-tinted tops with hand-decorated floral spray in pink, yellow, and blue. An unlisted square serving bowl was also offered. Additional Bouquet items, which are considered experimental, included square plates, square cereal bowls, and a compartment dish. Plates 63, 64, 240, and 241.

CLASSIC: 1942 – 1945. Items in overall high-gloss colors of ivory or pink. Raised florals appear on only one side of this ware, which was manufactured in mass for chain store sales. Factory lamps were made from several of the vase shapes offered in Classic. Plates 70, 91, and 230.

CLASSIC, BLUE CEREAL WARE: 1915 – 1935. Early cereal ware jars, spice jars, cruets, and salt boxes decorated with a blue decal. Fifteen items were included in the complete set.

CLASSIC, GOLDEN BROWN CEREAL WARE: 1915 – 1935. Early cereal ware jars, spice jars, cruets, and salt boxes decorated with a blue decal. Fifteen items were included in the complete set.

CLASSIC, GREEN CEREAL WARE: 1915 – 1935. Early cereal ware jars, spice jars, cruets, and salt boxes decorated with a green decal. Fifteen items were included in the complete set.

COLLECTION: 1982 – 1985. Refers to Hull's overall advertising designation for the late lines of dinnerware, e.g., Mirror Brown Ringed, Ridge, Heartland, and Country Belle, and the multitude of dinnerware and accessories glazed in Tawny (tan), Flint (gray), and Walnut (Mirror Brown).

COLORED CEREAL WARE: 1915 – 1930. Semiporcelain and stoneware embossed cereal ware sets in solid high-gloss colors of green, yellow, tan, or blue. Sets included cereal ware jars, spice jars, cruets, and salt box. Fifteen items were included for complete set.

COLORED OVENWARE: 1932 – 1935. Plain undecorated line of kitchenware bake dishes offered in ivory white semiporcelain bodies glazed in transparent Maize Yellow or Lucerne Green.

COLORED TEAPOTS: 1932 – 1935. Teapots offered in dark ivory buff semivitreous bodies. Glazes included, but were not limited to, Opaque, Lucerene Green, and Burgundy Brown.

COMBINETS: 1910 – 1930. Any of the varieties of toilet ware and hotel ware items. Bodies included both semiporcelain and stoneware, and styles were plain or embossed, banded, or decaled. Items were wire bailed, with wooden hand grips, and were offered with or without lids. Plates 3, 8, and 10.

CONTINENTAL: 1959 – 1960. Modern shapes in brilliant high-gloss colors, first offered in Persimmon and Evergreen, and then in Mountain Blue. There were a total of 26 items cataloged. Plates 139, 140, and 167.

CONVENTIONAL ROSE CEREAL WARE: 1915 – 1935. Early cereal ware jars, spice jars, cruets, and salt boxes with a floral decalcomania border design (#132 Pink Double Border). Fifteen items were included in the complete set. Plate 16.

CONVENTIONAL TILE CEREAL WARE: 1915 – 1935. Early cereal ware jars, spice jars, cruets, and salt boxes with a geometric decalcomania border design (#133 Yellow Double Border). Fifteen items were included in the complete set. Plate 14.

CONVENTIONAL VINE CEREAL WARE: 1915 – 1935. Early cereal ware jars, spice jars, cruets, and salt boxes with a decalcomania border design (#131 Blue Double Border). Fifteen items were included in the complete set.

COOK 'N' SERVE: 1952 – 1953. Kitchenware line that included a combination of Cinderella and Just Right Kitchenware shapes. Items were highly glazed and airbrush-decorated in brown and yellow, pink and charcoal, overall mottled green, or overall high-gloss white with black handles and lids. Nineteen items were cataloged exclusively for A. H. Dorman, New York, and included the large and small skillet trays and a cookie jar. Plates 142, 155, and 173.

CORKY PIGS: 1957 – 1985. Although a variety of pig banks were produced by Hull, this item refers to the style of bank that was marked "Corky Pig" and glazed in a variety of color treatments. Although first introduced in 1957, this bank was manufactured through 1985. Plates 130, 131, and 224.

CORONET: 1959. Vases, jardinieres, dish gardens, ashtray and planter combinations in metal stands, etc., produced in mass for chain store sales packages. These were made in solid or tinted high-gloss colors, with or without contrasting foam decoration. While assortments varied per retailer, at least thirteen items were available, including high-styled ashtray and planter combinations with metal accessories. Plates 126, 127, 128, 143, 144, and 200.

COUNTRY BELLE: 1985. One of Hull's Collection dinnerwares, offered in highly glazed winter white background with hand-stamped underglaze decoration of trailing blue florals. A canister set and cookie jar were available with this full line of service ware. Plates 193, 194, and 195.

COUNTRY SQUIRE: 1963 – 1967. Refers to Green Agate with contrasting turquoise foam House 'n Garden casual serving ware. At least 40 items were available, including a cookie jar. Plates 196 and 197.

CRAB APPLE: 1934 – 1935. Semiporcelain and stoneware art pottery vases, hanging baskets, and jardinieres glazed in matte Eggshell White, matte Peacock Blue on white semiporcelain body, hand-painted flowers in rose and leaves in green on stoneware buff body, or bright white on white semiporcelain body. Eighteen shapes were cataloged. Plates 20, 22, 23, 27, 30, 44, and 51.

CRESCENT: 1952 – 1954. Ovenproof line decorated in high-gloss color combinations of chartreuse with dark green trim, or high-gloss Strawberry with maroon trim.

Twelve shapes were available, including a cookie jar. Plates 145 and 146.

CRESTONE: 1965 – 1967. Ovenproof casual serving ware in high-gloss turquoise with white contrasting foam edge. At least 35 items were available. Plates 198, 199, and 200.

CROSS POINT: 1937 – 1940. Also referred to as Diamond Quilt and Evangeline. Part of the ovenproof kitchenware known as Pastel Rainbow/NuLine Bak-Serve. Embossed diamond quilt design in solid high-gloss and matte colors of blue, Seafoam Green, Rose Beige, rose, yellow, cream, and white. At least 22 shapes, including a cookie jar, marked with B-series numbers. Plates 24, 36, and 48.

CUSPIDORS: 1910 – 1935. Hotel (flat based) and parlor (tall, bulbous based) shapes offered in semiporcelain and dark buff bodies, decorated both overglaze and underglaze with decals and/or color bands of blue, green, maroon, brown, yellow, gold, and luster, sometimes combined with matching or contrasting lines. Some cuspidors were additionally banded and/or lined inside interior rims. Plates 3, 4, 5, and 23.

D

DAISY: 1905 – 1925. Refers to an embossed Star/Daisy decoration used for early stoneware. Plate 23.

DAISY AND TRELLIS: 1905 – 1925. Refers to an embossed decoration used for early blue and white stoneware butters. Plate 3.

DEBONAIR: 1952 – 1955. Ovenproof kitchenware line in high-gloss solid chartreuse, combination wine and chartreuse, or high-gloss duotone lavender and pink with black banding. There were 15 items available, including a cookie jar. Plates 146, 147, 148, and 173.

DELFT CEREAL WARE: 1915 – 1935. Early cereal ware jars, spice jars, cruets, and salt boxes decorated with blue ship and harbor scene and/or blue windmill decal. Fifteen items were included for complete set. Plate 13.

DIAMOND QUILT: 1937 – 1940. Also referred to as Crosspoint and Evangeline. Part of the ovenproof kitchenware known as Pastel Rainbow/NuLine Bak-Serve. Embossed diamond quilt design in solid high-gloss and matte colors of blue, Seafoam Green, Rose Beige, rose, yellow, cream, and white. At least 22 shapes, including a cookie jar, and marked with B-series numbers. Plates 24, 36, and 48.

DOGWOOD: 1942 – 1943. Also known as Wild Rose. Hand-decorated embossed florals in shaded colors of turquoise and peach, blue and pink, or allover peach. Twenty-two shapes were available. Plates 65, 66, 93, and 108.

DORIC: 1928. Panelled nested bowl set in glazed white semiporcelain, underglaze banded with three blue lines.

DRAPE AND FESTOON CEREAL WARE: 1915 – 1935. Early cereal ware jars, spice jars, cruets and salt boxes decorated with decalcomania border in rose, blue, green, and black. Fifteen items were included in complete set. Plate 16.

DRAPE AND PANEL: 1937 – 1940. Part of the ovenproof kitchenware known as Trend Pastel/NuLine Bak-Serve. Embossed drape and pastel design in solid and high-gloss colors of blue, Seafoam Green, Rose Beige, rose, yellow, cream, and white. At least 22 shapes, including a cookie jar, marked with D-series numbers. Plate 48.

E

EARLY ART: 1925 – 1938. Miscellaneous semiporcelain and stoneware items that included vases, jardinieres, pots and saucers, bulb bowls, hanging baskets, etc. Glazes included solid matte Eggshell White, Bermuda Green, Lotus Blue, Oyster White, Autumn Brown, Egyptian Green, and Maize Yellow, along with others and a variety of matte and high-gloss blended and solid glazes in pink, blue, turquoise, maroon, green, and Maize Yellow. Plates 15, 17, 18, 19, 20, 21, 22, and 23.

EARLY UTILITY: 1910 – 1938. Refers to the volume of kitchenware and utility items, bowls, nappies, jugs, butters, etc., in semiporcelain, stoneware, Zane Grey, buff, and yellow ware bodies. Items included plain and embossed shapes decorated in solid and blended high-gloss colors with underglaze or overglaze banding decorations, stamped decorations, and decals.

EBB TIDE: 1954 – 1955. Embossed fish and seashell motifs, highly glazed in Seaweed (chartreuse) and wine or Shrimp and turquoise. Gold detailing is not uncommon; this line was available in 16 shapes. Plates 149, 150, 151, and 152.

EMBOSSED: 1934. Semiporcelain embossed nested bowl set highly glazed in solid green.

EVANGELINE: 1937 – 1940. Referred to by a number of marketed names. NuLine Bak-Serve is an overall category of like molds glazed in solid high-gloss and matte colors of blue, Seafoam Green, Rose Beige, rose, yellow, cream, and white. Evangeline, an embossed crisscross design, was marketed primarily as Pastel Rainbow and was also known as Cross point and Diamond Quilt. It was marked with B-series numbers. Molded kitchenware, marked with C-series numbers, had a fish scale design and was also marketed as Pastel Rainbow. A line marked with D-series numbers had an embossed drape and panel design and was marketed as Trend Pastel. Plates 24, 36, and 38.

EWERS AND BASINS: 1905 – 1935. Refers to ewers and basins from toilet ware sets, offered in Hull (smaller) or Rex (fancier, larger) shapes. Bodies were of both semiporcelain and stoneware. Semiporcelain sets, in plain or embossed shapes, were decorated in blended or tinted glazes, or allover highly glazed white. Stoneware sets, in plain or embossed shapes, were decorated in tinted, banded, or allover glaze treatments. Plate 8.

F

FANTASY: 1957 – 1958. Chain store novelties and vases highly glazed in various colors, such as pink, blue, or black, with or without contrasting foam decoration; other colors are possible. Assortments varied with retailer. One assortment included at least 16 shapes. Plates 120 and 153.

FIESTA: 1957 – 1958. Chain store novelty assortment that included plain decorations on embossed fruits and florals on jardinieres and flower pots with metal accessories. Glaze treatments included both solid and tinted high-gloss treatments. Assortments varied with retailer. One such assortment included 14 shapes. Plates 114, 115, 116, 144, 156, 157, and 232.

FISH SCALE: 1937 – 1940. Part of the ovenproof kitchenware line known as Pastel Rainbow/NuLine Bak-Serve. Embossed fish scale design in solid high-gloss and matte colors of blue, Seafoam Green, Rose Beige, rose, yellow, cream, and white. At least 22 shapes, including a cookie jar, and marked with C-series numbers. Plate 48.

FISHSCALE AND WILD ROSES: 1905 – 1925. Refers to an embossed decoration used for early blue and white stoneware ewers and basins. The overall embossed fish scale pattern was further decorated by raised pleated bowl edges and a wild rose floral enclosed in medallions on the fronts of the ewers. Plate 8.

FIVE BANDED: 1915 – 1935. Semiporcelain kitchenware line that included a variety of nested bowls and nappy sets, at least three coffee servers and teapots, graduated pitchers and jugs, bean pots, casseroles, cookie and utility jars, pie plates, etc., in overall highly glazed transparent white with an overglaze banded decoration of five lines encircling the wares' midlines or top edges. The lowest band on each ware was the thinnest; bands widened with each step of elevation in this over-the-glaze decor of Pimento Red or Nubian Black. This kitchenware with highly refined lines had desirable shapes, high-standing handles on servers, and dubbed handles on casseroles, bean pots, and cookie and utility jars. This line was the ultimate in class and style for a semiporcelain kitchenware line. Solid color kitchenware items in glazes including yellow, turquoise, blue, mauve, peach, and others were also available with or without cold-color decorations of fruits and florals. Plate 44.

FLEMISH: 1928. Embossed stoneware butter jars with tinted blue glaze treatments, 2- to 5-pound sizes.

FLINT: 1982 – 1984. A specific glaze coloration rather than a specific line. Flint (gray) was used for the Ridge collection, and in this instance, known as Flint Ridge. Flint itself is the term used for any number of dinnerware and accessory items glazed in gray with white foam trim. Plates 200, 201, and 213.

FLINT RIDGE: 1982 – 1984. Refers to the destinctive molded shapes of the Ridge dinnerware line, which are glazed in overall Flint (gray) and trimmed in white foam. Deeply recessed rims are characteristic of this line.

FLORAL: 1951 – 1964. White high-gloss kitchenware with raised yellow airbrushed daisies, yellow air-brushed lids, and brown banding. Florals appear on one side only. Fifteen items, including a cookie jar, were available. Plates 154 and 155.

FLOR-DES-LIS: 1905 – 1925. Refers to an embossed decoration used for early blended stoneware jugs. Embossed bandings on the jugs enclose a spiral or swirled pattern. Plate 5.

FLORIST WARE: 1928. Early listing offered specifically for floral arrangements; green jardinieres and vases ranging from 6" to 15" in height. At least 13 items were available.

FLOWER CLUB: 1963 – 1965. Chain store florist line in both satin and high-gloss finishes of Wild Honey, Jade Green with or without contrasting foam decoration, or Satin White. Fourteen shapes, which included three swans and one Madonna, were cataloged.

FLOWERWARE: 1957 – 1958. Chain store assortment of vases, planters, and jardinieres and ashtrays in metal stands. Highly glazed solid black and pastel colors were used, as well as Satin White. Assortments varied per retailer; one such assortment included nine items.

FLYING BIRDS: 1905 – 1925. Refers to an embossed decoration used for early stoneware tankards and jugs tinted in blue and white.

FOOTED: 1920 – 1930. Refers to the varieties of early Hull kitchenware, in both semiporcelain and stoneware bodies, that have an extended foot, or base.

FRENCH POTS: 1910 – 1925. Refers to highly glazed stoneware utility pots with wide shoulders. These were made in ½-gallon and 1-gallon sizes.

G

GARDEN DISHES: 1963. A packaged Imperial line for the florist trade. Glaze treatments included high-gloss Moss Green, lilac, Spring Green, Carnation Pink, or Satin White. Thirteen items were cataloged.

GINGERBREAD MAN: 1978 – 1985. Animated character shaped into useful kitchenware items. Server was first introduced in 1978, and in 1982 the idea was expanded to include a cookie jar, a bowl, and a mug. A train canister set was being trialed when the factory closed. A train station and candy jar were created, but were never put into production. Most items are high-gloss Mirror Brown, but Ridge colors Tawny (tan) and Flint (gray) were also used for Gingerbread items. Plates 200, 201, 208, and 211.

GOLDEN ANNIVERSARY: 1963 – 1967. Refers to Tangerine House 'n Garden casual serving ware made specifically as premium items for Tri-State Grocers, when it was celebrating its 50th anniversary. At least 40 items were available, including the cookie jar. Plates 200, 221, and 223.

GOLDEN MIST: 1967. Glaze color/treatment of specific items of Hull's Imperial line. This matte glaze is deep coral embedded with textured/mottled crystals. Plate 138.

GOLD-MEDAL FLOWERWARE: 1959. Chain store line that included vases, bucket planters, Chinese Sage Mask wall pockets, and jardinieres with metal accessories. Glaze treatments included both plain and stippled finishes, and overglaze gold banding was included as part of the package. Assortments varied per retailer. One retailer listed as many as 21 items. Plates 124, 144, 153, 160, 161, and 235.

GRANADA: 1938 – 1946. Matte and high-gloss art lines that spanned several years of novelty chain store assortments. Plain and embossed decorations in satin and gloss white and pastels, and matte-shaded pastels of pink and cream or pink and blue. Plates 34, 35, 51, 82, 83, and 235.

GRECIAN, BLUE CEREAL WARE: 1915 – 1935. Cereal ware jars, spice jars, cruets, and salt boxes with decalcomania border design (#119 blue). Fifteen items were included in the complete set. Plate 16.

GRECIAN, GOLD CEREAL WARE: 1915 – 1935. Cereal ware jars, spice jars, cruets, and salt boxes with decalcomania border design (#121 gold). Fifteen items were included in the complete set. Plate 16.

GREEN AGATE: 1961 – 1967. Refers to the House 'n Garden Rainbow/Country Squire serving ware produced specifically in dark green glaze. Plates 196 and 197.

GREEN AND WHITE STONEWARE: 1905 – 1925. Refers to stoneware bodies whose decoration is characterized by various shadings of tinted greens. Items were utilitarian; shapes were both plain and embossed. Items included stoneware dairy jugs, butters, salt boxes, cuspidors, water jugs, water kegs, nested bowl and nappy sets, ewers and basins, and more. Embossed shapes included, but were not limited to, cherries, plums, birds, daisies, wild roses, stags, and cattle. Plates 3, 4, 5, 6, 7, and 8.

GREEN BUFF: 1933. Embossed stoneware cuspidors, butters, and nested bowl sets decorated in glazed green tinted style.

GREEN TINT: 1933. Buff-bodied fluted bowls and nested bowl sets, butters, and 2- to 5-pint dairy jugs and cuspidors, glazed and tinted green.

H

HARP: 1905 – 1925. Refers to an embossed decoration used for early stoneware artware and jardinieres that were decorated in rich blended glazes. Plates 5 and 36.

HEARTLAND: 1982 – 1985. One of Hull's "Collection" dinnerwares, which was offered in shaded satin cream with a hand-applied brown heart and flower stamp. A bulbous canister set and a cookie jar were available. Plates 202, 203, 204, 205, and 206.

HEARTS AND ARROWS: 1905 – 1925. Refers to an embossed decoration of hearts and arrows that decorated early stoneware blended jardinieres. Plate 5.

HERITAGEWARE: 1959. Ovenproof kitchenware in high-gloss Mint Green or Azure Blue with foam edge, and a textured finish in the same body colors with contrasting white handles and lids. Thirteen items were available, including a cookie jar. Plates 158 and 241.

HOTEL WARE: 1910 – 1935. Semiporcelain plain and embossed chambers, cuspidors, combinets, and jugs, some of which were decorated over the glaze by decals, color bands, and stamps, or were transparent white with no decor. Plates 8 and 10.

HOUSE 'n GARDEN WARE: Refers to any of the color-glazed casual serving ware produced from 1960 to 1985, e.g., Mirror Brown, Provincial, Tangerine, Country Squire, Avocado, Almond, and others.

HULL SHAPE TOILET WARE: 1908 – 1915. White glazed on tinted and decorated semiporcelain, or blue and white decorated stoneware toilet set consisting of a ewer and basin, a covered chamber, a covered combinet, a brush vase, a covered soap dish, and a mug. Plainer, more cylindrical shape than Rex Toilet Ware.

I

IMPERIAL: 1955 – 1985. Began as F1 lists; the name refers to the massive florist line produced by Hull from late 1950 through 1985. Colors included both satin and gloss black, Carnation Pink, Willow Green, lilac, Moss Green, Wild Honey, Bittersweet, Coral, turquoise, and mahogany, as well as others.

IRIS: 1940 – 1942. Hand-decorated embossed floral on tinted backgrounds of blue and rose, rose and peach, or allover peach. There are 14 cataloged shapes, some in graduated sizes. Plates 67, 68, 69, and 235.

IVORY: 1928. Ivory-bodied butters, bowls, custards, casseroles, and jugs with red and blue banding.

J

JARDINIERES: 1920 – 1930. Highly glazed 5" – 10" stoneware jardinieres offered with 16" – 18" pedestal bases.

JARS: 1910 – 1925. Stoneware utility and preserving jars offered as "tall" or "low," glazed in black over white. Low jars were available in 10-, 15-, and 25-gallon sizes. Tall jars were available in ½- to 50-gallon sizes.

JUBILEE: 1957. Chain store assortment of novelty planters and dish gardens, with a selection of jardinieres and ashtray and planter combinations with metal accessories. Glaze treatments varied from high-gloss to satin finishes in a variety of colors. Combinations varied with distributors. At least one retailer offered 17 shapes. Plates 113, 119, 124, 125, 127, 141, and 161.

JUGS: 1905 – 1925. Refers to the varieties of stoneware dairy jugs with embossed decorations such as cattle, castles, cherries, birds, etc. Decorated in solid, blended, or tinted glazes. Plates 3, 4, and 5.

JUST RIGHT KITCHENWARE: 1951 – 1954. Overall kitchenware designation for Floral and Vegetable embossed designs. Floral, manufactured from 1951 to 1954, was decorated in white high gloss with raised yellow airbrushed florals, yellow airbrushed lids, and brown banding. Florals appeared on one side only. Fifteen items were available, including a cookie jar. Vegetable was ovenproof kitchenware manufactured in 1951, with relief vegetable decoration (one side only) in solid high-gloss glazes of Coral, yellow, and green. Fifteen shapes were available, including a cookie jar. Plates 154, 155, 173, and 174.

L

LEEDS: 1940 – 1944. Novelty elephant and pig bottles manufactured for liquor, in high-gloss blue or pink, with underglaze hand detailing. Plate 131.

LITTLE RED RIDING HOOD: 1943 – 1957. Includes the varieties of kitchen and novelty items produced in the Red Riding Hood character form. Most items are referred to as Hull, even though most wares were manufactured by Regal China Corp. Items included teapots, cookie jars, shakers, canister jars, spice jars, etc. Plates 71, 72, 73, 74, 75, and 226.

LOVE BIRDS: 1905 – 1925. Refers to an embossed decoration used for early stoneware tankards tinted in blue and white or glazed overall in brown with white lining. Embossed

Love Birds appeared on these jardinieres and jugs with blended glazes. Plates 3, 4, and 23.

LUSTER: 1925 – 1930. Kitchenware line of bowls and tankard jugs in white semiporcelain bodies with luster banded decorations. Banding included a wide red band with small blue stripes, a wide ivory and brown band with small blue stripes, and a wide green band with small black stripes.

LUSTERWARE: 1927 – 1930. Semiporcelain art and florist line in overall very brilliant and iridescent luster glazes of lavender, slate, orange, Shammy, Golden Glow, light blue, iridescent dark blue, and emerald. At least 35 items were available. Plates 28, 29, 49, 50, and 51.

M

MAGNOLIA, MATTE: 1946 – 1947. Hand-decorated embossed florals on shaded matte pastels of pink and blue or dusty rose and yellow. There were 27 cataloged items, with vase 21-12½" available with either open or tab rope handles, and the 10-10½" basket available with either closed or laced handle. Plates 77, 78, and 231.

MAGNOLIA, NEW GLOSS: 1947 – 1948. Hand-painted, embossed floral decoration of blue or pink on allover transparent pink highly glazed background. Many items were detailed in gold, quite common for this line. Twenty-four shapes were cataloged, with Basket H14 - 10½" available with either closed or laced handle. Plates 76, 80, and 81.

MARCREST: 1958. Kitchenware line made specifically for Marshall Burns as promotional items. Decorations included high gloss solid pastel colors of Azure Blue, Mint Green, Shrimp, and yellow. Although not all molds from Heritageware were used, Marcrest shared molds with Heritageware. Marcrest ashtrays are found in both high-gloss and satin finishes in a variety of colors. Plate 158.

MARDI GRAS: 1940. Semiporcelain line manufactured exclusively for F. W. Woolworth Company that Spanish pots, Italian pots, flower vases, jardinieres, and mixing bowls. Spanish pots were plain, while other items had raised concentric rings. Decorated in solid matte or high-gloss colors of mauve, cobalt, turquoise, yellow, and others. Plates 23, 24, 35, and 36.

MARDI GRAS: 1938 – 1946. Matte art lines that spanned several years of novelty chain store assortments. Plain and embossed decorations in satin and gloss white or pastels, and matte shaded pastels of pink and cream or blue and pink. Plates 34, 35, 51, 82, and 235.

MAYFAIR: 1958 – 1959. Chain novelty and florist assortment in solid high-gloss pastels and black, all with white foam trim. Assortment numbers varied with retailers; however, at least one retailer offered 16 shapes. Plates 120, 124, 128, 144, and 153.

MEAT TUBS: 1910 – 1925. Stoneware utility jars in sizes ranging from 15 to 30 gallons, decorated with black over white glaze. Heart-shaped stamp on front of jar indicated gallon size.

MEDLEY: 1962. Novel chain store assortment of swirled urn vases, a Swan, a Dolphin, a Teddy Bear planter, a Cat vase, and items with metal accessories. Decorated in Satin White, Green Agate with turquoise trim, or Persimmon with yellow trim. There were 25 items available. Plates 120 and 162.

MEXICAN: 1930 – 1940. Early semiporcelain kitchenware items that were cold-color decorated with a Mexican motif, e.g., the 300-series gallon-sized cookie jar and the 850-series 2-quart jug. A smoking Mexican in a sombrerro, seated under a black cactus, is painted in colors of red, ivory, and yellow. Plate 24.

MILK PANS: 1910 – 1925. Stoneware, flat or round bottomed, wide shouldered pans decorated in black or white, in ½- to 2-gallon sizes.

MIRROR ALMOND: 1981 – 1983. House 'n Garden casual serving ware line glazed in overall Almond with Caramel trim. At least 30 items were available, including a cookie jar. Plates 206, 207, and 208.

MIRROR BLACK: 1955 – 1957. Refers to any of the various wares glazed in overall high-gloss black. Fantasy, Fiesta, and a variety of kitchenware items and jardinieres with metal accessories were included. Plates 161 and 165.

MIRROR BROWN: 1960 – 1985. Refers to the wide variety of House 'n Garden dinnerware offered in high-gloss Mirror Brown with ivory foam trim. Over one hundred items were available during the 25-year manufacturing period.

MIRROR COBALT: 1960. Refers to experimental House 'n Garden serving ware produced specifically in cobalt with white flow or run-down glaze. Plates 167, 240, and 247.

MIST: 1955 – 1957. Also referred to as Royal. Various mold blanks such as Ebb Tide, Butterfly, Woodland, and Imperial lavabo sets, jardinieres, novelties, and ashtray planters in metal stands. Used for various chain store assortments decorated in overall highly glazed backgrounds of pink or turquoise with charcoal gray trim, sometimes having contrasting interiors: outer turquoise with pink interior and outer pink with turquoise interior. Assortment numbers varied with retailers; however, one particular chain store assortment contained 27 different shapes. Plates 125, 175, 176, 177, and 178.

MODERN: 1950. Overall line name for Plaid kitchenware manufactured just prior to the company's being destroyed by flood and fire. The company most likely intended to use this overall name for lines that followed, lines that were interrupted by the company's tragedy. It does not appear that the company went back to this line after the fire, although the molds were used for other kitchen lines, e.g., Floral, Vegetable, Cook 'n' Serve. Plates 172, 173, and 241.

MORNING GLORY: 1940. Embossed design featured trumpet-shaped florals in allover matte white or tinted matte blue to pink. This appears to be a part of the MardiGras/Granada line, rather than an experimental line. Even as part of Mardi Gras/Granada, Morning Glory decorated in matte pastels is considered experimental. Plates 82, 93, and 230.

MOTTLED: 1905 – 1925. Refers to glazing and color decoration treatment used on early stoneware such as butters and cuspidors. This was a sponging, or mottling of the glaze, usually in blue and with or without additional banding. Plates 3 and 8.

N

NULINE BAK-SERVE: 1937 – 1940. Also known as Pastel Rainbow and Pastel Trend, this is ovenproof kitchenware in solid high-gloss and matte colors of blue, Seafoam Green, Rose Beige, rose, yellow, cream, and white. Three embossed patterns of like wares that included B, Cross Point, also referred to as Diamond Quilt and Evangeline; C, a fish scale design; and D, a drape and panel design. Patterns B and C were primarily marketed as Pastel Rainbow, while D was marketed as Trend Pastel. At least 22 shapes were available, including a cookie jar. Plates 24, 36, and 48.

NURSERY: 1920 – 1932. Refers to semiporcelain or ivory-bodied deep baby plates embossed with animals, referred to as old style and new style, and cups, saucers, mugs, and bread and milk sets.

O

ORANGE TREE: 1918 – 1930. Refers to the embossed orange tree decoration on semiporcelain and stoneware utility and artware items. Items were decorated in both solid and blended high-gloss and matte finishes. Plates 15, 19, 21, 23, 31, and 36.

ORCHID: 1939 – 1941. Hand-decorated embossed florals on tinted matte backgrounds of blue and rose, rose and cream, or allover blue. There were 15 cataloged shapes, many in graduated sizes. Plates 84, 85, and 93.

OVERLAP NO. 75: 1915 – 1935. Refers to yellow or green semiporcelain kitchenware line that included nested bowls, bake dishes, jugs, a teapot, casseroles, range and refrigerator jars, bean pots, and a covered sugar.

P

PAGODA: 1960. Plain jardinieres, flower bowls, and vases with a distinct Oriental flair, offered in three high-gloss, solid glazes:

Persimmon or green with black trim, and white with gray trim. Twelve items were cataloged. Plates 124, 166, and 167.

PANDORA: 1915 – 1935. Also referred to as 150 line. Semiporcelain kitchenware assortment that included utility jars, steins, and salt boxes highly glazed in yellow or green.

PANELLED BLUE BAND: 1915 – 1935. Octagon-design semiporcelain kitchenware of nested bowl and nappy sets with panelled design and raised underglaze blue bands.

PARCHMENT AND PINE: 1951 – 1954. High-gloss art-ware with embossed pine sprays, decorated in pine greens and browns, with either brown or black interiors. There are 15 cataloged shapes, with later entries of the S14 center bowl and S15 instant coffee server. All shapes were offered through 1954, with the exception of the S14 center bowl, which was discontinued January 1, 1954. Plates 168, 169, 170, 171, 236, and 249.

PARROT CEREAL WARE: 1915 – 1935. Early cereal ware jars, spice jars, cruets, and salt boxes decorated with a decal of a dark blue parrot in a yellow panel. Fifteen items were included for complete set.

PASTEL RAINBOW: 1937 – 1940. Also known as Nuline Bak-Serve. Ovenproof kitchenware in most often high gloss but also matte, and offered in blue, Seafoam Green, Rose Beige, rose, yellow, cream, and white. Three embossed patterns included B Crosspoint, also referred to as Diamond Quilt and Evangeline; C, a fish scale design; and D, a drape and panel design. D was also marketed as Trend Pastel. At least 22 shapes were available, including a cookie jar. Plates 24, 36, and 48.

PERSIAN: 1928. Additional luster line, which originated by theme outside the company. At least 15 shapes of vases and jardinieres were available.

PIG BANKS: 1935 – 1985. Hull manufactured several different styles of piggy banks, ranging from dime banks to foot-long banks. Corky Pig was a popular and long-tenured bank design that was first made in 1957, and was manufactured until the plant's closing. Corky pigs were decorated in a variety of solid and airbrush-blended glazes. Dime banks had both plain and incised bodies, and foot-long banks had both plain and floral-embossed bodies. Glazes and decorations were most often underglaze high gloss. However, some of the foot-long banks were decorated overglaze with cold-color treatment. Plates 130, 131, and 224.

PINECONE: 1938. Simplistic raised pinecone spray on solid matte pastel backgrounds of blue, pink, or turquoise. One vase shape known. Plate 83.

PLAIDWARE: 1950. One of Hull's Modern kitchenware lines, this ovenproof kitchenware was decorated with a green or red crisscross plaid design on highly glazed yellow-over-white, horizontally swirled backgrounds. Eleven items, including a cookie jar, were available in each decoration. Plates 172, 173, and 241.

PLAIN CEREAL WARE: 1915 – 1935. Refers to semiporcelain cereal ware jars, spice jars, cruets, and salt boxes that were glazed in transparent high gloss and devoid of any further decoration. Fifteen items were included in the complete set. Plate 16.

PLAIN WHITE: 1933. High-gloss white semiporcelain kitchenware devoid of decoration. Included hotel ware, restaurant ware, and toilet ware lines. Plates 10 and 16.

PLEATED WARE: 1920 – 1930. Refers to stoneware kitchen line of utilitarian items, e.g., nested bowls, covered casseroles, jugs, etc. Solid high-gloss colors were used on this ware, characterized by its pleating, or overlapping pattern of decoration. Plate 30.

PLUM: 1905 – 1925. Refers to an embossed decoration used for early blue and white stoneware dairy jugs. Plate 3.

POPPY: 1942 – 1943. Hand-decorated embossed florals on tinted backgrounds of blue to pink, pink to cream, or allover cream, and in at least 12 shapes, several in graduated sizes. Plates 86 and 108.

PRESERVE JARS: 1910 – 1925. Covered stoneware cylinder-shaped jars, glazed black over white, and in ½- to 3-gallon sizes.

PRIMROSE: 1937 – 1940. Semiporcelain embossed floral kitchenware in high-gloss solid colors of maroon, green, white, yellow, and blue. Incised with a 400-series number, and sold exclusively by Sears Roebuck and Company. Includes gallon cookie jar. Plates 35 and 36.

PROVINCIAL: 1961. Ovenproof House 'n Garden casual serving ware glazed in Mirror Brown, with white interiors and lids. At least 23 shapes were available, including a cookie jar. Plates 219 and 247.

R

RAINBOW: 1928. Kitchenware line of white semiporcelain with red and yellow, brown, or red and blue underglaze banding.

RAINBOW: 1961 – 1967. Ovenproof House 'n Garden casual serving ware in solid high-gloss colors of Mirror Brown, Butterscotch, Tangerine, and Green Agate, with contrasting foam edge. When mixed, the shades formed a rainbow table setting. At least 40 items were offered, including cookie jars in each of the four colors. Plates 200 and 220.

REGAL: 1952 – 1960. Novelty assortments, for chain store sales, that included florist ware, novelty planters, and vases in a variety of high-gloss colors. Items produced in 1952 were glazed in colors of chartreuse and dark green or wine and dark green. Figural vases such as the Unicorn, the Twin Deer, the Flying Duck, the Flamingo, and the Parrot planter were decorated in green and white combinations trimmed in brown. Plates 116 and 128.

RESTAURANT WARE: 1910 – 1935. High-gloss white semiporcelain kitchenware devoid of decoration and also referred to as Plain White, which consisted of chili, oyster, and St. Dennis bowls, and mugs, tumblers, a water jug, and other pieces.

REX TOILET WARE: 1908 – 1915. White-glazed or tinted and decorated semiporcelain toilet ware consisting of a ewer and basin, covered chamber, a covered combinet, a brush vase, a covered soap dish, and a mug.

RIDGE: 1982 – 1984. Overall line name of dinnerware that is characterized by deeply recessed rims. This dinnerware line was marketed in three colors: Tawny (tan), Flint (gray), and Walnut (Mirror Brown). Plate 261.

RINGED WARE: 1983 – 1985. The Mirror Brown dinnerware line, marketed as part of the Hull Collection and characterized by a band of concentric rings as stylized trim on plates, canisters, bowls, etc. Plates 215 and 216.

ROSELLA: 1946. Embossed wild rose decor, hand tinted under the glaze on either a Coral or an ivory body. While 16 shapes were cataloged, there was also an additional pitcher, a teapot, three lamps, a dimpled vase, and a window box. Plates 70, 87, 88, and 231.

ROYAL: 1955 – 1957. Also referred to as Mist. Various mold blanks such as Ebb Tide, Butterfly, Woodland, and Imperial lavabo sets, jardinieres, novelties, and ashtray planters in metal stands. Used for various chain store assortments and decorated in overall highly glazed backgrounds of pink or turquoise with charcoal gray trim, sometimes having contrasting interiors: outer turquoise with pink interior and outer pink with turquoise interior. One particular chain store assortment contained 27 different shapes. Plates 125, 175, 176, 177, and 178.

ROYAL BLUE: 1908 – 1920. Tinted underglaze blue utilitarian stoneware consisting of nested bowls and nappies, Hall Boy jugs, bean pots, and toilet ware.

ROYAL BUTTERFLY: 1955 – 1957. Also referred to as Mist Butterfly. Butterfly pattern mold blanks (devoid of embossing) decorated in overall high-gloss pink or turquoise with mottled white crystals. Trim was charcoal gray. Sold as a chain store assortment. Plates 175 and 176.

ROYAL EBB TIDE: 1955 – 1957. Also referred to as Mist Ebb Tide, this was Ebb Tide redirected as a chain store

assortment and glazed in overall high-gloss pink or turquoise with mottled white crystals. Trimmed in charcoal gray. Plates 176, 177, and 178.

ROYAL IMPERIAL: 1955 – 1957. Also referred to as Mist Imperial, this was Imperial redirected as chain store items. Overall high-gloss colors included pink or turquoise with mottled white crystals, trimmed in charcoal gray. Royal Imperial included several jardiniers marketed in metal floor stands. Contrasting glazed interiors were not unusual. Plates 125, 175, 177, and 178.

ROYAL WOODLAND: 1955 – 1957. Also referred to as Mist Woodland, Royal Woodland used Woodland mold blanks (devoid of original pattern embossing). It was decorated in overall high-gloss pink or turquoise with mottled white crystals. Trim was charcoal gray. Sold in chain store assortments. Plates 176, 177, and 178.

S

SALT BOXES: 1915 – 1935. Refers to a variety of salt boxes offered in Hull's early years. Bodies ranged from stoneware to semiporcelain, Zane Gray, and yellow ware, and encompassed both plain and embossed shapes. Glaze treatments included overglaze banding, decals, stamped decorations, and mottled glazes. Salt boxes were available in round, square, rectangular, paneled, or octagonal shapes. Lids, both pottery and wooden, were original to the boxes. Plates 13, 14, 16, 36, 40, and 45.

SANITARY WARE: 1910 – 1935. White, high-fired semiporcelain in plain, banded, stamped, or decaled decorations, which included kitchenware and cooking ware items, along with restaurant ware, toilet ware, and hotel ware. Plates 10, 11, 12, and 16.

SCROLL CEREAL WARE: 1915 – 1935. Early cereal jars, spice jars, cruets, and salt boxes decorated with a terra-cotta double border decal. Fifteen items were included for complete set.

SERENADE: 1957. Textured exteriors of matte Regency Blue with Sunlight Yellow gloss interior, matte Shell Pink with Pearl Gray gloss interior, or matte Jonquil Yellow with Willow Green gloss interior were backgrounds for embossed bough and chickadee decor. Twenty-four items were available. Plates 179, 180, and 181.

SHAFER GOLD: 1960 – 1979. Refers to specific items decorated with gold by Granville Shafer, in the studio of the G. C. Shafer Pottery Company of Zanesville, Ohio. These items will be stamped "Shafer, USA." Plates 82, 116, and 160.

SHAFER LUSTER: 1968 – 1979. Refers to specific luster treatments by Granville Shafer, G. C. Shafer Pottery Company, Zanesville, Ohio. Items will be stamped "Shafer, USA." Plate 160.

SHAMROCK: 1925 – 1935. Yellow ware nested bowl and nappy sets, referred to as "fancy shaped" and having underglaze brown bands.

SHOULDER JUGS: 1910 – 1925. Stoneware jugs glazed black over white, in ½- to 5-gallon sizes.

SHULTON: 1937 – 1944. Cosmetic containers for shaving soap, aftershave lotion, and talcum for men, manufactured by Hull under contractual agreement for Shulton's Old Spice men's products. Items produced had white highly glazed bodies with blue fired-on illustrations of sailing vessels the Friendship, the Mount Vernon, the Recovery, and the Grand Turk. Plate 32.

SPIRAL: 1960. Florist line jardiniere bowls and vases with a raised spiral design. Glazes included Satin White and high-gloss mahogany or Moss with contrasting white foam edge. Plate 160.

SQUARE CEREAL WARE SETS: 1915 – 1935. Semiporcelain canisters, salt boxes, spice jars, and cruets, glazed plain white and decorated with decalcomania decorations. Fifteen items were included in the complete set. Plates 13, 14, and 16.

SQUARE FOOTED: 1935. Dark ivory buff semivitreous square-footed kitchenware with transparent Popcorn Yellow glaze and wide Colonial Blue stripe with one Shell Bloom Pink pinstripe on each side. Also offered in solid high-gloss colors of yellow or turquoise with or without hand-painted florals. A square-footed 1-gallon cookie jar was available in the various color treatments. Plate 24.

SQUARE RIM: 1920 – 1930. Any of the varieties of utility lines characteristic of having a deep rim for ease in handling. Bodies ranged from dark ivory semivitreous buff to yellow ware to ivory, with assorted banded colors, solid high-gloss colors, or blended colors.

STAG: 1905 – 1925. Refers to the embossed decoration used for early blue and white stoneware sanitary water kegs with spigots, in 3-, 4-, 5-, and 6-gallon sizes. Plate 3.

STAR AND LATTICE, BLUE CEREAL WARE: 1915 – 1935. Early cereal ware jars, spice jars, cruets, and salt boxes decorated at the top with a blue openwork lattice decal. Fifteen items were included in the complete set. Plate 16.

STAR AND LATTICE, GOLD CEREAL WARE: 1915 – 1935. Early cereal ware jars, spice jars, cruets, and salt boxes decorated at the top with a gold openwork lattice decal. Fifteen items were included in the complete set.

STREAMLINE ARTWARE: 1930 – 1940. Chain store assortment of semiporcelain vases, jardinieres, flower pots with saucers, round jardinieres, and hanging baskets. A draped effect streamlined the embossed design vertically on all pieces except round jardinieres, and added dimension to these rather plain shapes. Items were glazed in high-gloss pastel colors of yellow, turquoise, Rose Beige, and matte white. Plates 23, 24, and 35.

SUENO: 1938. Refers to overall chain store line name for Tulip, Calla Lily, Thistle, and Pinecone designs.

SUN-GLOW: 1948 – 1949. Combination kitchenware and artware line that included nested bowls, pitchers, wall pockets, etc., decorated in backgrounds of solid high-gloss pink or yellow with an embossed floral and butterfly motif. Molds were later shared with the Bow-Knot line, and these items may be found with Bow-Knot's glaze treatments of pink and blue or blue and turquoise. Twenty-nine shapes were available, including four wall pockets and two styles of tea bells. Plates 89, 90, 91, 92, and 113.

SUN VALLEY PASTELS: 1956 – 1957. A 17-piece chain store assortment in which 11 items were offered in satin-finished pink with high-gloss gray interior, or satin-finished turquoise with high-gloss yellow interiors. An additional seven items were offered in satin exterior finishes of pink, Willow Green, and white. Retailers selected assortments that suited their own needs, sometimes mixing pieces with items from other chain store assortments. Plates 157 and 158.

SUPREME: 1960. Experimental ware, never placed on the market, for which some Imperial molds were used. A series of wire brushes scraped the surface after glazing and prior to firing. Company workmen referred to this as tooled ware. Nine shapes were offered in combinations of Agate and chartreuse or Ripe Olive and orange. Plates 235, 237, and 239.

SWING BAND: 1938 – 1940. Figurines of members of a 5-piece band, averaging 6" in height, in ivory matte and finished with gold trim and hand-painted features. Included were a band leader, an accordionist, a clarinet player, a drummer, and a tuba player. Plates 24 and 33.

SWIRL: 1965. An experimental line of ovenproof House 'n Garden casual serving ware with swirled design. Plates, cups, saucers, two sizes of bowls, a stein, and a trench-handled casserole were made. Plate 247.

T

TANGERINE, 900 SERIES: 1963 – 1967. Refers to the House 'n Garden casual serving ware line produced specifically in Tangerine. At least 40 items were available. Also referred to as Burnt Orange and Golden Anniversary, originally this color was taken from the Rainbow line. Plates 220, 221, and 223.

TAWNY: 1982 – 1984. A specific glaze coloration rather than a specific line. Tawny (tan) was used for the Ridge Collection, and in this instance, known as Tawny Ridge. Tawny itself is the term used for any dinnerware or accessory item glazed in tan with white foam trim. Plates 200 and 201.

TAWNY RIDGE: 1982 – 1984. Refers to the distinctive molded shapes of the Ridge dinnerware line that are glazed in overall Tawny (tan) and have white foam trim. Deeply recessed rims are characteristic of this line. Plates 200 and 201.

TEAPOTS: 1935. Semivitreous dark ivory buff body in opaque Lucerne Green or Burgundy Brown glaze, or with high-gloss yellow or green semiporcelain bodies, and devoid of further decoration.

TEFLON-LINED DINNERWARE: 1962. Experimental House 'n Garden Mirror Brown dinnerware having no white flow or run-down and lined in colored teflon of white, blue, or brown. Plate 246.

THISTLE: 1938 – 1941. Embossed realistic thistle motif on solid matte backgrounds of pink, blue, or turquoise. There are four known shapes. Plate 58.

TILE: 1926 – 1931. Hull manufactured plain and faience floor, wall, and ornamental tiles with matching accessories such as towel bars, soap dishes, etc., with special orders accepted, in a variety of solid, blended, and stippled colors. Both high-gloss and matte glazes were offered. Plate 51.

TOILET WARE: 1910 – 1935. Plain and embossed toilet ware items for the home or hotel, of semiporcelain or stoneware. Items were decorated by decalcomania, banding, stamping, and tinting, while others remained glazed transparent white with no decoration. Plates 8 and 10.

TOKAY: 1958 – 1960. Relief grape and leaf decor in color glazes of light green and Sweet Pink or Milk White and Forest Green. Both glazes were available during 1958. After 1958, only the white and green combination was available. There were originally 18 cataloged items, but a 14" caladium leaf, a 15½" pedestaled vase, and a 14" ewer followed. Plates 124, 182, 183, 228, 232, and 243.

TREND PASTEL: 1937 – 1940. Also referred to as NuLine Bak-Serve. Ovenproof kitchenware in solid colors, most often high gloss, but also matte. Offered in blue, Seafoam Green, Rose Beige, rose, yellow, cream, and white. Three embossed patterns of like wares included B, or Cross Point, also referred to as Diamond Quilt and Evangeline; C, a fish scale design; and D, a drape and panel design. Patterns B and C were primarily marketed as Pastel Rainbow, while D was marketed as Pastel Trend. At least 22 shapes were available, including a cookie jar. Plates 24, 36, and 48.

TROPICANA: 1959. Decorated Caribbean characters depict the tropics in this line, which was glazed in an allover white background and edged in Tropic Green. The line included seven shapes. Plates 184 and 185.

TULIP: 1925 – 1935. Tulip-embossed stoneware jardinieres, pedestals, and vases, some with overglaze cold-color detail to florals. Items were overall glazed in backgrounds of deep brown, with or without white interiors. 7½" jardinieres and 7½" matching pedestals each wholesaled for $21.60 per gross. Plate 4.

TULIP: 1928. Graduated semiporcelain line of tankard jugs in backgrounds of overall transparent white, decorated with overglaze tulip decal.

TULIP: 1938 – 1941. Hand-decorated embossed tulip motif on shaded combinations of blue and pink or blue and cream, or on an allover blue. There were 15 cataloged shapes, many in graduated sizes. Plates 58, 93, and 94.

TUSCANY: 1958 – 1960. Relief grape and leaf decor in color glazes of Sweet Pink and Gray Green, or Milk White and Forest Green. Both glazes were available during 1958. After 1958, only the white and green combination was available. There were originally 18 cataloged items, with a 14" caladium leaf, a 15½" pedestaled vase, and a 14" ewer that followed. Plates 124, 182, 183, 228, 232, and 243.

U

URN VASES: 1962. Imperial florist line of jardinieres, many in graduated sizes, that were first offered in Satin White or high-gloss Moss Green. Additional colors followed.

UTILITY JARS: 1910 – 1935. Refers to 2- to 4-gallon plain-shaped covered jars of both semiporcelain and stoneware bodies, with plain or embossed shapes. Some were decorated with various color banding treatments. Available with or without lettering: "Cakes," "Bread," "Flour," etc. Plate 11.

V

VEGETABLE: 1951. Ovenproof kitchenware with relief vegetable decoration in solid high-gloss glazes of Coral, yellow, or green. Fifteen shapes were available, including a cookie jar. Plates 173 and 174.

VEILED WARES: 1955 – 1957. Refers to a free-form line decoration, or "spider-webbed" treatment, on overall solid high-gloss or matte colors for kitchenware, artware, and florist ware. Area decorators also used veiled treatments. Plates 121, 125, 127, 164, 165, 175, and 232.

VICTORIAN: 1974. Imperial line of heavily embossed dish gardens and florist ware in overall solid gloss glazes of olive with Willow Green and green with turquoise. Also offered in Satin White. Plate 160.

W

WALNUT RIDGE: 1982 – 1984. Refers to the distinctive molded shapes of the Ridge Collection dinnerware line that are glazed in Walnut (Mirror Brown) and have white foam trim. Deeply recessed rims are characteristic of this line.

WATER JUGS: 1910 – 1935. Refers to 2- to 6-gallon covered water jars with metal spigots. Bodies were both semiporcelain and stoneware, with plain or embossed shapes, one being a stag. Decorations included decals, banding, or color tints.

WATER LILY: 1948 – 1949. Hand-decorated embossed Water Lily floral on matte shaded backgrounds of Walnut and Apricot or turquoise and Sweet Pink. Gold decoration is not unusual on this line. There were 28 shapes available. Plates 95, 96, 97, 98, and 225.

WATER LILY, NEW GLOSS: 1949 – 1950. Hand decorated embossed Water Lily on high-gloss backgrounds of white or cream. There were 28 shapes available in gloss Water Lily. Plates 70 and 111.

WEBBED: 1955. Refers to decoration treatment of a heavy glaze with ingredients added that built up in the glaze, giving the glaze a rough, or "coconut," texture. Some items decorated with webbing were lined with a high-gloss contrasting color. Webbing was used for both kitchenware items and artware items. Plates 121, 229, and 248.

WHEAT: 1915 – 1935. Refers to canister jars, spice jars, cruets, and a salt box with an embossed wheat design, produced in both semiporcelain and stoneware and glazed green, yellow, blue, or tan. Plate 40.

WILD FLOWER NO. SERIES: 1942 – 1943. Artware line with embossed hand-decorated florals on matte duotone tinted backgrounds of blue and pink or russet and pink, or on an allover cream. Several of the items have an embossed butterfly motif included in the lid, handle, or within the body of the embossed decoration. There were 29 cataloged items available. Plates 103, 104, 105, 106, 107, 108, 225, 230, and 231.

WILDFLOWER W SERIES: 1946 – 1947. Hand decorated embossed motif of trillium, mission, and bluebell on shaded backgrounds of pink and blue or yellow and dusty rose. There were 22 cataloged shapes. Plates 99, 100, 101, and 102.

WOODLAND: 1949 – 1950. Matte-finished backgrounds of Dawn Rose or Harvest Yellow, with hand-decorated embossed florals. There were 30 cataloged shapes of pre-1950 Woodland. Plates 109 and 110.

WOODLAND, HI-GLOSS: 1952 – 1954. High-gloss tinted backgrounds of blue-gray and Forest Green, chartreuse and pink, pink and Shrimp, chartreuse with or without dark green interiors and trim, or allover high-gloss glazes of white, cream, or pink. The hand-decorated embossed floral appears on only one side of this ware. Allover glazes with contrasting interiors were first called Two-Tone and later placed in the category of Hi-Gloss. Heavy gold detailing is not uncommon on the lighter glazes. Twenty-one shapes were available in Hi-Gloss Woodland. Plates 186, 187, and 191.

WOODLAND, NEW GLOSS: 1949 – 1950. High-gloss backgrounds of white, cream, or pink with hand-decorated embossed floral. Heavy gold detailing is not uncommon. There were 30 cataloged shapes of pre-1950 New Gloss Woodland. Plates 187, 188, 189, 190, and 191.

WOODLAND, NEW MATTE: 1950. Matte-finished artware on backgrounds of Dawn Rose or Harvest Yellow, with hand-decorated embossed floral on one side only. Twenty-one shapes were available in post-1950 matte Woodland. Plate 187.

WOODLAND, TWO-TONE: 1952 – 1954. High-gloss solid chartreuse backgrounds with contrasting dark green interiors and trim. Twenty-one shapes were available in Two-Tone Woodland. Plate 190.

Y

YELLOW WARE: 1910 – 1925. Any of the varieties of utility ware that included jugs, bowls, butters, casseroles, custards, etc., with yellow ware bodies. These were manufactured in durable bright glazes, and were plain, embossed, or banded. Plates 8, 9, 15, 24, 36, 41, and 42.

YELLOW WARE BANDED NO. 100 LINE: 1915 – 1928. Yellow ware utility line of jugs, nested bowls, bakers, custards, etc., decorated with underglaze brown line with narrow white lines on either side. Plate 42.

YELLOW WARE BANDED NO. 400 LINE: 1915 – 1935. Yellow ware line that included nested bowls, jugs, bakers, custards, range jars, cereal jars, spice jars, pie plates, etc., decorated with underglaze brown line with white lines on either side, or with blue bands. Plate 15.

Z

ZANE GREY: 1928. Stoneware body with durable high-quality Bristol glaze with underglaze blue banding. The same basic shapes as those for blue-banded semiporcelain wares were used, in order to provide a more economical product for the trade. Items offered included jugs, jars, bowls, nappies, custards, butters, and 1- to 6-gallon food containers. Plates 6 and 7.

Appendix C
Glossary of Related Terms

ARTIST MARK: Specific mark (number or initials), incised into the base of a pottery item, that represents the individual(s) responsible for finishing and/or decorating the item.

ARTIST SIGNATURE: Incised signature of the individual responsible for creating or decorating a particular piece of pottery.

BEEHIVE KILN: A conical, or beehive-shaped, brick furnace used for firing ceramic wares.

BISCUIT FIRED: Fired unglazed earthenware or pottery.

BLUE AND WHITE STONEWARE: Dense stoneware body defined by its glaze coloration; usually utilitarian.

BODY: Term referring to the specific type and content of the material used to form a pottery item.

BUFF: A clay body distinguished by the color of buff, a light yellow shading toward pink, gray, or brown.

CASTING: The process in which liquid clay, or slip, is poured into plaster molds to form desired wares.

CATALOG NUMBER: Number assigned to a pottery item for retail purposes and listed in company catalogs or brochures pages. Many items never carried the numbers as part of their ware trademarks.

CERAMICS: Term that pertains to a variety of fired clay products.

COLD COLOR: A method of decorating pottery over the glaze. If left unfired, the decoration will not be permanent.

CRAZING: A network of fine cracks in the surface of the glaze produced by expansion or contraction between the body and the glaze.

CUSHIONED TILE: Tile distinguished by a rounded, rather than flat, surface.

DECALCOMANIA: A prepared decal or design that is transferred to an item in the decorating process.

DECORATOR: The person who applies color or provides embellishment or adornment of an ornamental nature.

DESIGNER/MODELER: The person who develops and creates a proposed item for trial or manufacture.

DIE: A device used for forming a block containing holes through which clay, soup, or other tactile material is extracted or drawn to make molds. Refers to any of the various tools or devices for imparting a desired shape, form, or finish to a material or for impressing an object or material.

EMBOSSING: A bas-relief or raised design created by molding or jiggering pottery in a mold.

EXPERIMENTAL: Ware produced as a basis of experimentation or trial and that undergoes a series of changes or tests, usually for final product examination.

FAIENCE: Ware or tile distinguished by a thick, coarse, porous body covered by heavy, opaque glaze.

FETTERS: Protective kiln furniture made of fire clay and in which ceramic articles are set or stacked. Fetters protect pieces during the firing process.

FETTLERS: Persons responsible for finishing processes. Synonomous with finishers/trimmers.

FINISHERS: Persons responsible for sponging and smoothing out defects in unfired ware, as well as for attaching any appendages.

FINISHER NUMBER: Number, usually incised into the clay during the manufacturing process, that represents the individual responsible for finishing and/or decorating. In mass production, used primarily for quality control measures.

FIRING: A rapid, persistent chemical change that releases heat and light and is accompanied by flame. To bake in a kiln is to fire.

GLAZE: A coating of colored, opaque, or transparent material applied to ceramics before firing.

GREENWARE: Molded ceramic wares not yet decorated or fired.

GRIDIRON: A flat framework of parallel wooden or metal bars used in the process of tile production for marking, embossing, or dividing.

GRILLE: A barrier, mold, or grating used in the process of tile production to mark, emboss, or divide.

GROG: A mixture of dust made by pounding and sifting broken pieces of biscuit-fired or unglazed pottery.

JIGGER (also referred to as a Jolly): Manufacturing wherein a paddle or stick is lowered into the mold and used to press the clay into the sides of the mold as it spins on a wheel.

KILN: A furnace or large oven used for firing ceramic wares.

KILN FURNITURE: Any of the protective casings or risers that are used to stack unfired wares for kiln processing.

LUSTER: A glaze with the brilliance, radiance, and patina of metals, produced through the use of metallic oxides.

MATTE: A dull decorative glaze that lacks luster or gloss and is free from shine or reflection.

MOLD NUMBER: A number assigned for identification purposes by the company, specific to a pattern and item. Mold numbers may be either incised or raised. A measurement that follows the mold number represents height on vertical items or length on horizontal items.

MOLDS: Sectional forms that are used to manufacture pottery. Liquid clay, or slip, is poured into the mold and allowed to stand until a desired thickness builds up on the wall of the mold. Molds are used for both casting and jiggering.

MUFFLE KILN: A kiln in which pottery can be fired without being exposed to direct flame as the heat radiates through the walls of the kiln.

PORCELAIN/SEMIPORCELAIN: A hard, fine-grained, non-porous body produced by firing a purer state of clay that has a high content of silica.

OPAQUE: A dense glaze treatment having no luster and not reflective of light.

POTTERY: A clay body mixture that contains less silica than porcelain and that when fired remains opaque, as the body is dense and will not readily absorb the glaze.

RAM PRESS: A machine used for the compression of moist clay into molds, usually for flat or holloware items.

SAGGARS (also referred to as setters): Protective ceramic casings or risers in which delicate ceramic articles are set or stacked for firing. Also refers to the clay bodies used to make these ceramic casings.

SAMPLES: First-quality, marketed production ware, with foil or paper label stating "sample."

SLIP: Liquified clay, also called soup, used for casting in molds or attaching handles, knobs, spouts, or other appendages.

STILTS: Protective kiln furniture made of fire clay and in which ceramic articles are set or stacked for the firing process.

STONEWARE: A heavy, dense clay body that is high fired, usually used for utilitarian wares.

TINTERS (also referred to as spray gun operators): Persons responsible for applying and blending background colors on wares in their unfired state as part of the final finishing process.

TRIALS: Wares in marketed molds and marketed colors characteristic of the particular design, with bases being both marked and unmarked, and most often containing the incised configurations of the test glaze formulas.

TRIMMERS: Persons responsible for the process of removing and smoothing excess clay from unfired, or greenware, items prior to firing.

TUNNEL KILN: A lateral kiln in which cars filled with ware entered and exited.

UNDERGLAZE: A method of decorating under the glaze, which caused the decoration to become permanent after firing.

UPDRAFT KILN: A brick kiln that was designed to allow flames to pass up through holes in the floor and through and around the stacks of wares being fired.

UTILITARIAN: Any of the pottery wares designed specifically for home or kitchen utility use for preserving, storing, cooking, or serving.

YELLOW WARE: Earthenware, of various densities of stoneware, primarily defined by clay body color and usually used for utilitarian wares.

BIBLIOGRAPHY

"A. E. Hull Cereal Sets." *Pottery, Glass, and Brass Salesman,* May 31, 1917.

Bell Telephone Company Directory for Zanesville, Ohio, 1922.

Ceramic Industry. June 1956.

China and Pottery, catalog of the Blackwell Wielandy Company, 1940. Reprinted 1968.

Crooks, Guy E. *Brief History of the Pottery Industry of Crooksville 1868 – 1932*, booklet in the *Crooksville Messenger.* Crooksville, Ohio.

"Crooksville Battered By Flash Flood: Woman Drowns, Fire Levels Pottery." *Columbus Evening Dispatch*, June 17, 1950.

"Crooksville Bicentennial Community." Official souvenir program of the Crooksville-Roseville Area Pottery Festival, Crooksville, Ohio: Advance Printing Co., 1975.

"Damage Hits Millions in Wake of Cloudburst." *Columbus Evening Dispatch*, June 16, 1950.

Dougherty, John Wolfe. *Pottery Made Easy.* New York, New York: The Bruce Publishing Company, 1939.

"Early American Toiletries, Old Spice" listings in Shulton company catalogs from 1938, 1939, 1940, and 1942.

Filkins, C. C. *The China Painters, A B C.* Buffalo, New York: The Courier Company, 1915.

Hammer, Michael L. "History of The Hull Pottery Company." Second annual souvenir program of the Crooksville-Roseville Pottery Festival, July 1967.

Hommel, O. Company correspondence regarding crystaline glazes, directed to W. K. McClellan. Pittsburgh, Pennsylvania: April 21, 1927.

_____. Company correspondence regarding overglazes, directed to W. K. McClellan. Pittsburgh, Pennsylvania: March 29, 1934.

Hull advertisements. *Better Homes and Gardens*: February, May, October, November, and December 1946; February, April, May, August, October, and November 1947; April, June, October, November, and December 1948; April, June, August, and October 1949; and April 1950. *Encore Magazine*: Ridge Collection advertisement, 1982. *House and Garden*: May 1950 and May 1957. *House Beautiful*: April and May 1947, May 1948, October and December 1949, and September 1955. *McCall's*: Hull Shulton Old Spice advertisement, December 1942.

Hull Pottery Company. Seniority lists dated 1968; August 10, 1977; and 1985; and seniority lists that are undated.

Huxford, Sharon and Bob. *The Collector's Encyclopedia of Roseville Pottery.* Paducah, Kentucky: Collector Books, 1976.

_____. *The Collector's Encyclopedia of Weller Pottery.* Paducah, Kentucky: Collector Books, 1979.

"J. Brannon Hull Scholarship Fund." *Crooksville Exempted Village Schools*, January 1987.

Knittle, Rhea Mansfield. "Antiques, Ohio Pottery Jars and Jugs." The Ohio Historical Society, vol. 24, no. 1, July 1933.

Krause, George H. "The Growth of Our Pottery and Tile Industry." *Zanesville Sesquicentennial, 1797 – 1947*, 21 – 25, Zanesville, Ohio: Zanesville Chamber of Commerce, 1947.

Lehner, Lois. *Complete Book of American Kitchen and Dinner Wares.* Des Moines, Iowa: Wallace-Homestead, 1980.

Lewis, Thomas W. *A History of Southeastern Ohio and the Muskingum Valley*, vol. 3. Chicago, Illinois: S. J. Clarke Publishers, 1928.

_____. *Zanesville and Muskingum County Ohio History*, vols. 1 and 2. Chicago, Illinois: S. J. Clarke Publishers.

_____. *Zanesville — For the Manufacturer, Merchant, and Home Seeker.* Zanesville, Ohio: Zanesville Chamber of Commerce, 1923.

Martzolff, Clement L. *History of Perry County Ohio.* New Lexington, Ohio: Ward and Weiland, 1902.

"Morale Mounting in Flooded Areas." *Zanesville Times Recorder*, June 20, 1965.

Muskingum County directories for 1936, 1937, and 1938. Springfield, Ohio: Southwestern Ohio Publishing Company.

Ohio Historical Society. *Echoes*, vol. 1, no. 11, November, 1962.

Peaslee-Gaulbert Co. General Catalog. Louisville, Kentucky: C. T. Dearing Printing Co., 1927.

"Perry County Towns Flooded." *Zanesville Times Recorder*, June 17, 1950.

Phillips, David R. "Finding Treasures in Your Attic." *Lady's Circle*, September 1981.

Rickett, Beth. "A. E. Hull Started Pottery in 1907." *The Times Recorder*, February 9, 1991.

Roberts, Brenda. *The Collector's Encyclopedia of Hull Pottery.* Paducah, Kentucky: Collector Books, 1980.

_____. *Roberts' Ultimate Encyclopedia of Hull Pottery.* Marceline, Missouri: Walsworth Publishing Co., 1992.

_____. *The Companion Guide to Roberts' Ultimate Encyclopedia of Hull Pottery.* Marceline, Missouri: Walsworth Publishing Co., 1992.

_____. "Family Tradition Ends...Hull Pottery Closes." *American Clay Exchange*, August 30, 1986.

_____. "Hull Art Pottery: Rosella." *The Collector*, March, 1981.

_____. "Hull Headlines: Banking Your Investment." *The Glaze*, May and June 1980.

_____. "Hull Headlines: House 'n Garden." *The Glaze*, July 1980.

_____. "Hull Headlines: Jarring Update." *The Glaze*, October 1980.

_____. "Hull Headlines: Nuline Bak-Serve." *The Glaze*, December 1980.

_____. "Hull Headlines: Old Spice Product Containers." *The Glaze*, August 1980.

_____. "Hull Headlines: Rainbow and Crestone Dinnerwares." *The Glaze*, November 1980.

_____. "Hull Headlines: Rosella." *The Glaze*, September 1980.

_____. "Hull Pottery: Behind the Lines." *The Antique Trader Weekly*, March 4, 1981.

_____. "Hull Pottery Closes." *The Antique Trader Weekly*, August 1986.

_____. "Hull Pottery Closes, an End to a Family Tradition." *The Collector*, September 1986.

_____. "Hull Pottery: Closing Doused Family Tradition." *Antique Week*, September 22, 1986.

_____. "Hull Pottery: Cookie Collecting." *American Clay Exchange*, March 1981.

_____. "Hull Pottery Old Spice Product Containers." *The Collector*, December 1980.

_____. Personal collection of Hull Pottery Company brochures, price lists, original company correspondence, and photographs of employees and plant operations.

_____. Personal collection of notebooks encompassing glaze and body formulas of ceramic engineers William K. McClellen and Edgar McClellan.

_____. Personal interviews and/or correspondence with J. B. Hull, Robert W. Hull, Byron Hull, Louise Bauer, William Callihan, Larry Taylor, Marlin King, Jack Frame, Harold Showers, Douglas Young, Gene Whitlatch, Edgar McClellan, Granville Shafer, Daine Neff, Esta Marshall, Gladys Showers, Helen Aichele, Marie Bradshaw, Hattie Sturgill, Bernice Walpole, Lois Lee, Russell Lee, Elsie Robinson, Isabella Dusenberry, Gene Dusenberry, and Paul Sharkey.

Schneider, Norris F. "Clay Industry." *Zanesville Times Signal*, November 3, 1957.

_____. "Decorative Tile." *Zanesville Times Recorder*, May 21, 1972.

_____. "Hull Pottery." *Zanesville Times Recorder*, April 25, 1965.

_____. "Potter's Alley." *Zanesville Times Signal*, November 16, 1958.

_____. "Roseville Grew Rapidly During 1890 Boom." *Sunday Times Signal*, August 2, 1959.

_____. "Shawnee Pottery." *Zanesville Times Recorder*, October 16, 1960.

_____. *Zanesville Art Pottery*. Zanesville, Ohio: Published by author, 1963.

Shawnee Pottery Company Prospectus. Zanesville, Ohio: Shawnee Pottery Company, 1937.

"Ship Pottery from Crooksville." *Zanesville Times Recorder*, June 23, 1950.

"Shulton's Old Spice." *Modern Packaging Magazine*, September 1953.

Smith, Marvin E. *Cue Sheet, National Association of Variety Stores Inc.* Chicago, Illinois: April, 1972.

"The Stoneware Story." *The Crooksville Advance*, 1902.

"Stricken Villages Clean Up Flood Debris." *Zanesville Times Recorder*, June 19, 1950.

Supnick, Mark E. *Collecting Hull Pottery's Little Red Riding Hood*. Gas City, Indiana: L-W Book Sales, 1989.

Taylor, Robert Hull. *Hulls in 1850, a Directory of Persons Surnamed Hull in the U.S. in 1850*. Baltimore, Maryland: Gateway Press, Inc., 1983.

United States Patent and Trademark Office. "Little Red Riding Hood." Washington, D.C., 1943.

"Youngest Potter to Start in Roseville." Official souvenir program of the Crooksville-Roseville Area Pottery Festival, 10, Crooksvile, Ohio: Advance Printing Co., 1971.

Index

Scrapbook

A typical 100-degree August day inside an unairconditioned plant for Esta Marshall. Esta began employment for Hull in 1920 as a hand-decorator, retiring in 1979. Shown with author.

Lois and Russell "Peanut" Lee at their home in Crooksville, Ohio. Lois began working at Hull in 1937 at 26¢ per hour. Lois worked as a finsher, trimmer, tinter, and decorator. Peanut worked as a caster and jiggerman, beginning at 21¢ per hour.

Hattie Sturgill at her home in Crooksville, Ohio. Hatte was a decorator of much of the ware displayed. Hatte began working at Hull in 1945.

Granville "Grany" Shafer at his pottery shop in Zanesville, Ohio. Grany was responsible for many of the gold-decorated items available on today's market. He began his decorating business in 1932. The Shafer Pottery Company also produced many original molds designed by Shafer.

Hull employees Esta Marshall and Bernice Hicks Walpole take a break to chat with author Brenda Roberts about the pottery process.

This author with Bernice Hicks Walpole. Bernice began her work with Hull as a decorator in 1938.

This author with Douglas Young, assistant superintendent of Hull at the time this photo was taken. Doug, grandson of Hull Company founder Jeptha Darby Young, had worked in all phases of the pottery, beginning in 1925.

This author with "Tacky" Stephenson, a night supervisor at the Hull plant.

Esta Marshall at her home in Crooksville, Ohio, with one of her favorite Hull pieces.

Helen Aichele at her home in Crooksville, Ohio. Helen began work at the Hull Company in 1929. Helen is holding a favorite wall pocket.

COLLECTOR BOOKS
informing today's collector

www.collectorbooks.com

For over two decades we have been keeping collectors informed on trends and values in all fields of antiques and collectibles.

DOLLS, FIGURES & TEDDY BEARS

6315	**American Character Dolls**, Izen	$24.95
6317	**Arranbee Dolls**, The Dolls that Sell on Sight, DeMillar/Brevik	$24.95
2079	**Barbie Doll** Fashion, Volume I, Eames	$24.95
4846	**Barbie Doll** Fashion, Volume II, Eames	$24.95
6546	Collector's Ency. of **Barbie** Doll Exclusives & More, 3rd Ed., Augustyniak	$29.95
6451	Collector's Encyclopedia of **Composition Dolls**, Volume II, Mertz	$29.95
5904	Collector's Guide to **Celebrity Dolls**, Spurgeon	$24.95
5599	Collector's Guide to **Dolls of the 1960s and 1970s**, Sabulis	$24.95
6030	Collector's Guide to **Horsman Dolls**, Jensen	$29.95
6455	**Doll Values**, Antique to Modern, 8th Edition, DeFeo/Stover	$14.95
5689	**Nippon Dolls** & Playthings, Van Patten/Lau	$29.95
5365	**Peanuts Collectibles**, Podley/Bang	$24.95
6336	Official **Precious Moments** Collector's Guide to Company **Dolls**, Bomm	$19.95
6026	**Small Dolls of the 40s & 50s**, Stover	$29.95
5253	Story of **Barbie**, 2nd Ed., Westenhouser	$24.95
5277	**Talking Toys** of the 20th Century, Lewis	$15.95
2084	**Teddy Bears**, Annalee's & Steiff Animals, 3rd Series, Mandel	$19.95
4880	World of **Raggedy Ann** Collectibles, Avery	$24.95

TOYS & MARBLES

2333	Antique & Collectible **Marbles**, 3rd Edition, Grist	$9.95
6649	Big Book of **Toy Airplanes**, Miller	$24.95
5150	**Cartoon Toys & Collectibles**, Longest	$19.95
5900	Collector's Guide to **Battery Toys**, 2nd Edition, Hultzman	$24.95
6471	Collector's Guide to **Tootsietoys**, 3rd Edition, Richter	$24.95
5169	Collector's Guide to **TV Toys** & Memorabilia, 2nd Ed., Davis/Morgan	$24.95
3970	Grist's Machine-Made & Contemporary **Marbles**, 2nd Edition	$9.95
6633	**Hot Wheels**, The Ultimate Redline Guide, 2nd Ed., Clark/Wicker	$29.95
6466	**Matchbox Toys**, 1947 to 2003, 4th Edition, Johnson	$24.95
5830	**McDonald's** Collectibles, 2nd Edition, Henriques/DuVall	$24.95
6840	**Schroeder's Collectible Toys**, Antique to Modern Price Guide, 10th Ed.	$17.95
6638	The Other **Matchbox Toys**, 1947 to 2004, Johnson	$19.95
6650	**Toy Car** Collector's Guide, 2nd Edition, Johnson	$24.95

FURNITURE

3716	American **Oak** Furniture, Book II, McNerney	$12.95
1118	Antique **Oak** Furniture, Hill	$7.95
6474	Collector's Guide to **Wallace Nutting** Furniture, Ivankovich	$19.95
5359	Early **American** Furniture, Obbard	$12.95
3906	**Heywood-Wakefield** Modern Furniture, Rouland	$18.95
6338	**Roycroft** Furniture & Collectibles, Koon	$24.95
6343	**Stickley Brothers** Furniture, Koon	$24.95
1885	**Victorian** Furniture, Our American Heritage, McNerney	$9.95

JEWELRY, HATPINS, WATCHES & PURSES

4704	Antique & Collectible **Buttons**, Wisniewski	$19.95
6323	**Christmas Pins**, Past & Present, 2nd Edition, Gallina	$19.95
4850	Collectible **Costume Jewelry**, Simonds	$24.95
5675	Collectible **Silver Jewelry**, Rezazadeh	$24.95
6468	Collector's Ency. of Pocket & Pendant **Watches**, 1500 – 1950, Bell	$24.95
6453	**Costume Jewelry** 101, Carroll	$24.95

4940	**Costume Jewelry**, A Practical Handbook & Value Guide, Rezazadeh	$24.95
5812	Fifty Years of Collectible **Fashion Jewelry**, 1925 – 1975, Baker	$24.95
6330	**Handkerchiefs**: A Collector's Guide, Guarnaccia/Guggenheim	$24.95
5695	**Ladies' Vintage Accessories**, Johnson	$24.95
1181	100 Years of Collectible **Jewelry**, 1850 – 1950, Baker	$9.95
6645	100 Years of **Purses**, 1880s to 1980s, Aikins	$24.95
6337	**Purse Masterpieces**, Schwartz	$29.95
4729	**Sewing Tools** & Trinkets, Thompson	$24.95
6038	**Sewing Tools** & Trinkets, Volume 2, Thompson	$24.95
6039	Signed Beauties of **Costume Jewelry**, Brown	$24.95
6341	Signed Beauties of **Costume Jewelry**, Volume II, Brown	$24.95
6555	20th Century **Costume Jewelry**, Aikins	$24.95
5620	Unsigned Beauties of **Costume Jewelry**, Brown	$24.95
4878	Vintage & Contemporary **Purse Accessories**, Gerson	$24.95
5923	**Vintage Jewelry** for Investment & Casual Wear, Edeen	$24.95

ARTIFACTS, GUNS, KNIVES, TOOLS, PRIMITIVES

6021	**Arrowheads** of the Central Great Plains, Fox	$19.95
1868	Antique **Tools**, Our American Heritage, McNerney	$9.95
6469	Big Book of **Pocket Knives**, 2nd Edition, Stewart/Ritchie	$24.95
4943	Field Gde. to Flint **Arrowheads & Knives** of the N. American Indian, Tully	$9.95
3885	**Indian Artifacts** of the Midwest, Book II, Hothem	$16.95
4870	**Indian Artifacts** of the Midwest, Book III, Hothem	$18.95
5685	**Indian Artifacts** of the Midwest, Book IV, Hothem	$19.95
6565	**Modern Guns**, Identification & Values, 15th Ed., Quertermous	$16.95
2164	**Primitives**, Our American Heritage, McNerney	$9.95
6031	Standard **Knife** Collector's Guide, 4th Ed., Ritchie & Stewart	$14.95

PAPER COLLECTIBLES & BOOKS

5902	**Boys' & Girls' Book** Series, Jones	$19.95
5153	Collector's Guide to **Children's Books**, 1850 to 1950, Volume II, Jones	$19.95
6553	Collector's Guide to **Cookbooks**, Daniels	$24.95
1441	Collector's Guide to **Post Cards**, Wood	$9.95
6627	Early 20th Century **Hand-Painted Photography**, Ivankovich	$24.95
2081	Guide to Collecting **Cookbooks**, Allen	$14.95
3973	**Sheet Music** Reference & Price Guide, 2nd Ed., Pafik/Guiheen	$19.95

GLASSWARE

5602	Anchor Hocking's **Fire-King** & More, 2nd Ed., Florence	$24.95
6321	**Carnival Glass**, The Best of the Best, Edwards/Carwile	$29.95
5823	Collectible **Glass Shoes**, 2nd Edition, Wheatley	$24.95
6821	Coll. **Glassware** from the 40s, 50s & 60s, 8th Edition, Florence	$19.95
6626	Collector's Companion to **Carnival Glass**, 2nd Ed., Edwards/Carwile	$14.95
1810	Collector's Encyclopedia of **American Art Glass**, Shuman	$29.95
6830	Collector's Encyclopedia of **Depression Glass**, 17th Ed., Florence	$19.95
1961	Collector's Encyclopedia of **Fry Glassware**, Fry Glass Society	$24.95
1664	Collector's Encyclopedia of **Heisey Glass**, 1925 – 1938, Bredehoft	$24.95
3905	Collector's Encyclopedia of **Milk Glass**, Newbound	$24.95
5820	Collector's Guide to **Glass Banks**, Reynolds	$24.95
6454	**Crackle Glass** From Around the World, Weitman	$24.95
6559	**Elegant Glassware** of the Depression Era, 11th Edition, Florence	$24.95
6334	Encyclopedia of **Paden City Glass**, Domitz	$24.95

3981	Evers' Standard **Cut Glass** Value Guide	$12.95	5918	Florences' Big Book of **Salt & Pepper Shakers**	$24.95
6628	**Fenton Glass** Made for Other Companies, Domitz	$29.95	6320	Gaston's **Blue Willow**, 3rd Edition	$19.95
6462	Florences' **Glass Kitchen Shakers**, 1930 – 1950s	$19.95	6630	Gaston's **Flow Blue China**, The Comprehensive Guide	$29.95
5042	Florences' **Glassware Pattern Identification** Guide, Vol. I	$18.95	2379	Lehner's Ency. of **U.S. Marks** on Pottery, Porcelain & China	$24.95
5615	Florences' **Glassware Pattern Identification** Guide, Vol. II	$19.95	4722	**McCoy Pottery**, Collector's Reference & Value Guide, Hanson/Nissen	$19.95
6142	Florences' **Glassware Pattern Identification** Guide, Vol. III	$19.95	5913	**McCoy Pottery**, Volume III, Hanson & Nissen	$24.95
6643	Florences' **Glassware Pattern Identification** Guide, Vol. IV	$19.95	6333	**McCoy Pottery Wall Pockets** & Decorations, Nissen	$24.95
6641	Florences' **Ovenware** from the 1920s to the Present	$24.95	6135	**North Carolina Art Pottery**, 1900 – 1960, James/Leftwich	$24.95
6226	**Fostoria** Value Guide, Long/Seate	$19.95	6335	Pictorial Guide to **Pottery & Porcelain Marks**, Lage	$29.95
5899	**Glass & Ceramic Baskets**, White	$19.95	5691	**Post86 Fiesta**, Identification & Value Guide, Racheter	$19.95
6460	**Glass Animals**, 2nd Edition, Spencer	$24.95	1440	**Red Wing Stoneware**, DePasquale/Peck/Peterson	$9.95
6127	The **Glass Candlestick** Book, Volume 1, Akro Agate to Fenton, Felt/Stoer	$24.95	6037	**Rookwood Pottery**, Nicholson/Thomas	$24.95
6228	The **Glass Candlestick** Book, Volume 2, Fostoria to Jefferson, Felt/Stoer	$24.95	3443	**Salt & Pepper Shakers** IV, Guarnaccia	$18.95
6461	The **Glass Candlestick** Book, Volume 3, Kanawha to Wright, Felt/Stoer	$29.95	3738	**Shawnee Pottery**, Mangus	$24.95
6648	Glass **Toothpick Holders**, 2nd Edition, Bredehoft/Sanford	$29.95	6828	The Ultimate Collector's Encyclopedia of **Cookie Jars**, Roerig	$29.95
6329	**Glass Tumblers**, 1860s to 1920s, Bredehoft	$29.95	6640	Van Patten's ABC's of Collecting **Nippon Porcelain**	$29.95
5827	**Kitchen Glassware** of the Depression Years, 6th Edition, Florence	$24.95	5924	**Zanesville Stoneware** Company, Rans/Ralston/Russell	$24.95
6133	**Mt. Washington Art Glass**, Sisk	$49.95			

6556	Pocket Guide to **Depression Glass** & More, 14th Edition, Florence	$12.95
6448	Standard Encyclopedia of **Carnival Glass**, 9th Ed., Edwards/Carwile	$29.95
6449	Standard **Carnival Glass** Price Guide, 14th Ed., Edwards/Carwile	$9.95
6035	Standard Encyclopedia of **Opalescent Glass**, 4th Ed., Edwards/Carwile	$24.95
6644	Standard Encyclopedia of **Pressed Glass**, 4th Ed., Edwards/Carwile	$29.95
6241	Treasures of **Very Rare Depression Glass**, Florence	$39.95
6476	**Westmoreland Glass**, The Popular Years, 1940 – 1985, Kovar	$29.95

POTTERY

4929	**American Art Pottery**, Sigafoose	$24.95
4851	Collectible **Cups & Saucers**, Harran	$18.95
6326	Collectible **Cups & Saucers**, Book III, Harran	$24.95
6344	Collectible **Vernon Kilns**, 2nd Edition, Nelson	$29.95
6331	Collecting **Head Vases**, Barron	$24.95
6621	Collector's Encyclopedia of **American Dinnerware**, 2nd Ed., Cunningham	$29.95
4931	Collector's Encyclopedia of **Bauer Pottery**, Chipman	$24.95
5034	Collector's Encyclopedia of **California Pottery**, 2nd Ed., Chipman	$24.95
6629	Collector's Encyclopedia of **Fiesta**, 10th Ed., Huxford	$24.95
3431	Collector's Encyclopedia of **Homer Laughlin China**, Jasper	$24.95
1276	Collector's Encyclopedia of **Hull Pottery**, Roberts	$19.95
5609	Collector's Encyclopedia of **Limoges Porcelain**, 3rd Ed., Gaston	$29.95
6637	Collector's Encyclopedia of **Made in Japan** Ceramics, First Ed., White	$24.95
2334	Collector's Encyclopedia of **Majolica Pottery**, Katz-Marks	$19.95
5677	Collector's Encyclopedia of **Niloak**, 2nd Edition, Gifford	$29.95
5679	Collector's Encyclopedia of **Red Wing Art Pottery**, Dollen	$24.95
5618	Collector's Encyclopedia of **Rosemeade Pottery**, Dommel	$24.95
5841	Collector's Encyclopedia of **Roseville Pottery**, Vol. 1, Huxford/Nickel	$24.95
5842	Collector's Encyclopedia of **Roseville Pottery**, Vol. 2, Huxford/Nickel	$24.95
5917	Collector's Encyclopedia of **Russel Wright**, 3rd Edition, Kerr	$29.95
6646	Collector's Ency. of **Stangl Artware**, Lamps, and Birds, 2nd Ed., Runge	$29.95
3314	Collector's Encyclopedia of **Van Briggle Art Pottery**, Sasicki	$24.95
5680	Collector's Guide to **Feather Edge Ware**, McAllister	$19.95
6124	Collector's Guide to **Made in Japan Ceramics**, Book IV, White	$24.95
6634	Collector's Ultimate Ency. of **Hull Pottery**, Volume 1, Roberts	$29.95
6829	The Complete Guide to **Corning Ware & Visions Cookware**, Coroneos	$19.95
1425	**Cookie Jars**, Westfall	$9.95
6316	Decorative **American Pottery & Whiteware**, Wilby	$29.95
5909	**Dresden Porcelain** Studios, Harran	$29.95

OTHER COLLECTIBLES

5838	Advertising **Thermometers**, Merritt	$16.95
5898	Antique & Contemporary **Advertising Memorabilia**, Summers	$24.95
5814	Antique **Brass & Copper** Collectibles, Gaston	$24.95
1880	Antique **Iron**, McNerney	$9.95
6622	The Art of American **Game Calls**, Lewis	$24.95
1128	**Bottle** Pricing Guide, 3rd Ed., Cleveland	$7.95
6345	**Business & Tax Guide** for Antiques & Collectibles, Kelly	$14.95
3718	Collectible **Aluminum**, Grist	$16.95
6342	Collectible **Soda Pop** Memorabilia, Summers	$24.95
5060	Collectible **Souvenir Spoons**, Bednersh	$19.95
5676	Collectible **Souvenir Spoons**, Book II, Bednersh	$29.95
5666	Collector's Encyclopedia of **Granite Ware**, Book 2, Greguire	$29.95
5836	Collector's Guide to **Antique Radios**, 5th Edition, Bunis	$19.95
3966	Collector's Guide to **Inkwells**, Identification & Values, Badders	$18.95
4947	Collector's Guide to **Inkwells**, Book II, Badders	$19.95
5681	Collector's Guide to **Lunchboxes**, White	$19.95
6558	The Encyclopedia of Early American **Sewing Machines**, 2nd Ed., Bays	$29.95
6561	Field Guide to **Fishing Lures**, Lewis	$16.95
5683	**Fishing Lure** Collectibles, Volume 1, Murphy/Edmisten	$29.95
6328	**Flea Market Trader**, 14th Edition, Huxford	$12.95
6458	**Fountain Pens**, Past & Present, 2nd Edition, Erano	$24.95
6631	**Garage Sale** & Flea Market Annual, 13th Edition, Huxford	$19.95
4945	**G-Men and FBI Toys** and Collectibles, Whitworth	$18.95
2216	**Kitchen Antiques**, 1790–1940, McNerney	$14.95
6639	**McDonald's Drinkware**, Kelly	$24.95
6028	Modern **Fishing Lure** Collectibles, Volume 1, Lewis	$24.95
6131	Modern **Fishing Lure** Collectibles, Volume 2, Lewis	$24.95
6322	Pictorial Guide to **Christmas Ornaments** & Collectibles, Johnson	$29.95
6839	**Schroeder's Antiques** Price Guide, 24th Edition	$14.95
5007	**Silverplated Flatware**, Revised 4th Edition, Hagan	$18.95
6647	**Star Wars** Super Collector's Wish Book, 3rd Edition, Carlton	$29.95
6139	Summers' Guide to **Coca-Cola**, 4th Edition	$24.95
6827	Summers' Pocket Guide to **Coca-Cola**, 5th Edition	$12.95
4935	The W.F. Cody **Buffalo Bill** Collector's Guide, Wojtowicz	$24.95
6632	Value Guide to **Gas Station Memorabilia**, 2nd Ed., Summers & Priddy	$29.95
6841	Vintage **Fabrics**, Gridley/Kiplinger/McClure	$19.95
6036	Vintage **Quilts**, Aug/Newman/Roy	$24.95

This is only a partial listing of the books on antiques that are available from Collector Books. All books are well illustrated and contain current values. Most of these books are available from your local bookseller, antique dealer, or public library. If you are unable to locate certain titles in your area, you may order by mail from **COLLECTOR BOOKS**, P.O. Box 3009, Paducah, KY 42002-3009. Customers with Visa, Master Card, or Discover may phone in orders from 7:00a.m. to 5:00 p.m. CT, Monday – Friday, toll free **1-800-626-5420**, or online at **www.collectorbooks.com**. Add $4.00 for postage for the first book ordered and 50¢ for each additional book. Include item number, title, and price when ordering. Allow 14 to 21 days for delivery.

1-800-626-5420   Fax: 1-270-898-8890

www.collectorbooks.com

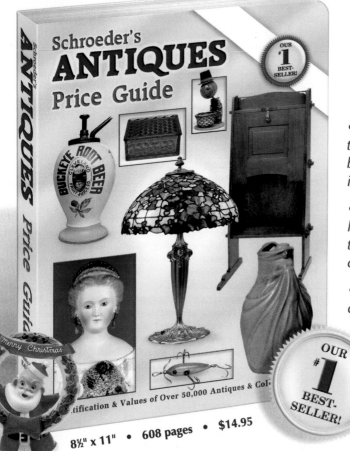